The American Critical Tradition

M. Thomas Inge
General Editor

Theodore Dreiser: The Critical Reception
Edited by Jack Salzman
Long Island University

Thomas Wolfe: The Critical Reception
Edited by Paschal Reeves
University of Georgia

Ernest Hemingway: The Critical Reception
Edited by Robert O. Stephens
University of North Carolina

William Faulkner: The Critical Reception
Edited by M. Thomas Inge
Virginia Commonwealth University

Thomas Wolfe:
The Critical Reception

Thomas Wolfe

The Critical Reception

Edited with an Introduction by
Paschal Reeves

David Lewis New York 1974

For
Richard S. Kennedy

General Editor's Preface

When we speak of a writer's reputation in critical terms, we should recognize that he actually has two: the response of book reviewers and critics during his own lifetime to each of his works as it was published, and the retrospective evaluation of his achievement by literary historians and academic critics in the decades after his career is concluded. The primary concern of modern scholarship has been the latter, on the assumption that the passage of time is essential before a writer's achievement can be objectively viewed and assessed. The purpose of the volumes in the American Critical Tradition series, however, is to provide overviews of the critical reputations earned by major American authors in their own times. Such overviews are necessary before the full impact of a writer's influence can be properly evaluated and an understanding of how he related to his contemporary cultural milieu achieved.

The few efforts hitherto made in summarizing a writer's contemporary critical standing have usually been based on a reading of sample reviews or vague impressions retained by veterans of the era. Seldom have literary historians gone back to locate and read all or most of the comment elicited by a career in progress. In the present volumes, the editors have sought to unearth every known review of each book in the contemporary newspapers, journals, and periodicals, and to demonstrate the critical response chronologically through reprint, excerpt, or summary. Selective checklists of reviews not included in the text are appended to each chapter, and the editor has provided an introduction summarizing the major trends observable in the criticism. The results not only elucidate the writer's career, but they reveal as well intellectual patterns in book reviewing and the reception of serious writing by the American reading public. Each volume is, therefore, a combined literary chronicle and reference work of a type previously unavailable.

M. Thomas Inge
General Editor

Contents

Acknowledgements

The editor wishes to thank the following newspapers, journals, individuals, and publishers for permission to reprint reviews: *Accent* for "Wolfe's Farewells." *American Literature* for review of *The Letters of Thomas Wolfe*. *American Mercury* for "The Long Dream of Thomas Wolfe," "Wolfe, Farrell and Hemingway." *American Review* for "The Noble Savage as Novelist." *American Spectator* for "Wolfe, Wolfe!" *Archive* [Duke University] for "Rare Wine Mixed With Stiff Corn." *Arts and Decoration* for review of *Look Homeward, Angel*. *Asheville Citizen* for "Stirring First Novel By Local Man Making Big Hit in Literary World." *Asheville Times* for "Amazing New Novel Is Realistic Story Of Asheville People." *Atlanta Constitution* for "Last Work of a Genius." *Atlanta Journal* for review of *The Web and the Rock*, review of *Thomas Wolfe's Letters to his Mother*, "Buds of Wolfe's Genius Found in 'Mannerhouse,'" "Wolfe's Notebooks." *Atlantic Monthly* for "The Man of the Month: Thomas Wolfe." *Baltimore Sun* for "A Novel By Thomas Wolfe." *Best Sellers* for review of *The Short Novels of Thomas Wolfe*. *Book-of-the-Month Club News* for review of *The Web and the Rock*, review of *You Can't Go Home Again*, review of *A Stone, A Leaf, A Door: Poems by Thomas Wolfe*. *Booklist* for review of *Look Homeward, Angel*, review of *Of Time and the River*, review of *The Web and the Rock*, review of *You Can't Go Home Again*, review of *The Letters of Thomas Wolfe*. *Boston Evening Transcript* for "A Modern Epic of the Life of a Pennsylvania Youth." *Boston Herald* for "Awareness of Life, Love and Cruelty." *Boston Transcript* for "'Lycidas Is Dead.'" *Boston Traveler* for "Wolfe Play Dwarfs Work of Moderns." *Buffalo Evening News* for "Wolfe Adds Fresh Fuel To His Fire: Posthumous Novel Continues Story of Search for Understanding." *Catholic World* for review of *You Can't Go Home Again*. *Charleston* (S.C.) *News and Courier* for "Wolfe's Last Work Collected." *Charlotte News* for "Wolfe Pictures Men And Carolina Scenes." *Chicago Sun* for "Thomas Wolfe's Letters." *Chicago Sunday Tribune* for "A Gargantuan Primer to Novels of Thomas Wolfe." *Chicago Tribune* for "Thomas Wolfe Attains Heights of True Genius." *Christian Register* for review of *Look Homeward, Angel*. *Columbia, S.C. State* for "Wolfe Bit Off More Than He Could Chew." *Commentary* for "An American Writer," Reprinted from *Commentary*, by permission; Copyright (c) 1956 by the American Jewish Committee. *Common Sense* for review of *Of Time and the River*. *Commonweal* for "Thomas Wolfe's Posthumous Book," and review of *You Can't Go Home Again*. *Current History* for obituary of Thomas Wolfe. *Dallas Times Herald* for "Thomas Wolfe's

Mother Compiles Book of Letters." *Detroit News* for "A New View of Wolfe." *El Paso Times* for "The Notebooks of Thomas Wolfe." *Fort Wayne News-Sentinel* for "Stories Show Wolfe at His Best." *Forum* for review of *Of Time and the River. Hartford Courant* for "Romantic 'Closet Dramas.'" *Houston Post* for "Tom Wolfe's Drama: Filling A Gap in the Over-All Picture." Huntington, West Virginia *Herald-Advertiser* for "Thomas Wolfe Shows Genius and Prolixity." *Kansas City Star* for "Wolfe's Last Look Homeward." *Library Journal* for review of *You Can't Go Home Again. Literary Digest* for review of *Of Time and the River. Los Angeles Herald-Examiner* for "The Intimate Notebooks of Thomas Wolfe." *Los Angeles Times Calendar* for "Thomas Wolfe 'Caught Hot and Instant,'" Copyright 1970, *Los Angeles Times.* Reprinted by permission. *Los Angeles Times* for review of *You Can't Go Home Again* and review of *A Stone, A Leaf, A Door: Poems by Thomas Wolfe. Louisville Courier-Journal* for "A Southern House And Its Downfall," "Thomas Wolfe Unbosoms Himself to Mother." *Mazomanie* (Wisconsin) *Sickle* for "Book of the Week." *Miami News* for "Gather Ye Cliches While Ye May." *Milwaukee Journal* for "Turning Prose of Thomas Wolfe Into Fine Poetry." *Modern Monthly* for "Thomas Wolfe and the Great American Novel." *Modern Quarterly* for "Thomas Wolfe." *MS: A Magazine for Students of Creative Writing* for review of *Look Homeward, Angel. Nashville Banner* for "Unposed Self-Portrait of Wolfe," "Lost Modern Who Found Himself." *Nashville Tennessean* for "Farewell— and Hail!", "Voluminous 'Jottings' Illuminate Writings." *Nation* for review of *Look Homeward Angel,* "The Name

is Sound and Smoke," obituary of Thomas Wolfe, "Thomas Wolfe, Autobiographer," "Look Homeward," "Mother and Son." (New Iberia, La.) *Sunday Iberian* for review of *The Notebooks of Thomas Wolfe.* New Orleans *Times-Picayune* for "Wolfe's Letters Reveal A Background of Genius." *New Outlook* for review of *Of Time and the River,* "Books." *New Republic* for review of *Look Homeward, Angel,* "Mountain View," "Tom Wolfe," "Thomas Wolfe: A Summing Up." *New York Evening Post* for "A First Novel of Vast Scope: 'Look Homeward, Angel' an American Saga in Southern Setting." *New York Herald Tribune* for "The American Family," "Turns With a Bookworm," "Books and Things," "The Ecstasy, Fury, Pain and Beauty of Life: Thomas Wolfe Sings and Shouts in His Gargantuan New Novel," "Thomas Wolfe, Six-Foot-Six," "Self-Portrait of an Artist as a Young Man," "Thomas Wolfe," "Violently, Desperately, Hungeringly Alive," "The Vision of Thomas Wolfe." *New York Mirror* for review of *You Can't Go Home Again. New York Post* for "Books on Our Table," "Thomas Wolfe's Superb Farewell." Reprinted by Permission of *New York Post. New York Star* for "Wolfe Looks Homeward in His Only Play." *New York Sun* for "A Book in Which a Man Reveals His Soul and Writes With His Soul," "Wolfe Dividend." *New York Times* for "A Novel of Provincial American Life," Sinclair Lewis: Press Conference on Winning the Nobel Prize, "Mr. Wolfe's Pilgrim Progresses," "Speaking of Books," "Thomas Wolfe's Last Book," "Faithfully Yours, Thomas Wolfe." (c) 1929, 30, 35, 40, 41, 56 by The New York Times Company. Reprinted by permission. *New York World* for "The Conning Tower," "Ah, Life! Life!" *New York World-Telegram* for "Thomas Wolfe's Posthumous Work, *The Web and the Rock*, Recalls His *Of Time and The River.*" *New Yorker* for "Literary Estate." *Newark News* for "Flowering Talent." *North American Review* for "A Promise and a Legend," review of *Of Time and the River. North Georgia Review* for review of *The Web and the Rock. Oakland* (Calif.) *Tribune* for "Wolfe Collection Is a Revelation," "Literary Genius." *Outlook and Independent* for review of *Look Homeward, Angel. Philadelphia Inquirer* for "Tom Wolfe: A Requiem For a Giant," "Echo of Thomas Wolfe." *Pittsburg Press* for "Wolfe Still A Master." *Providence Journal* for "Thomas Wolfe as He Revealed Himself in Letters to Mother." *Pseudopodia* [*North Georgia Review*] for "Thomas Wolfe: The Story of a Marvel." *Publishers Weekly* for "American First Editions," Reprinted from the August 15, 1931, issue of *Publishers Weekly,* published by R. R. Bowker Company, a Xerox company. Copyright 1931 by R. R. Bowker Company. "Thomas Wolfe: A Writer's Problems," Reprinted from the December 24, 1938, issue of *Publishers Weekly,* published by R. R. Bowker Company, a Xerox company. Copyright 1938 by R. R. Bowker Company. "Forecasts," Reprinted from November 17, 1969, issue of *Publishers Weekly,* published by R. R. Bowker Company, a Xerox company. Copyright 1969 by Xerox Corporation. Jonathan Daniels for "Wolfe's First Is Novel of Revolt: Former Asheville Writer Turns In Fury Upon N. C. And The South." *The Man from Main Street: A Sinclair Lewis Reader;* Selected Essays and Other Writings, 1904-1950, ed. Harry E. Maule and Melville Cane, assisted by

Philip Allan Friedman. Random House, N.Y., 1953. *Review of Reviews* for "Man's Hunger." *Richmond Times-Dispatch* for "Last Is One of Wolfe's Best." *Roanoke Times* for "Hungry Gullivers' Itch To Tell It All." *St. Louis Post-Dispatch* for "Letters of Thomas Wolfe: A Portrait of His Mother," "The Best of Wolfe." *San Francisco Chronicle* for "The Last Work of Thomas Wolfe, Significant Artist of His Time," "Thomas Wolfe's Last Book Proves He Was a Genius." *Saturday Review* for "C'est Maitre Francois," Copyright 1929 The Saturday Review Company, Inc.; renewed 1957 Saturday Review, Inc. "The River of Youth," Copyright 1935 The Saturday Review Company, Inc.; renewed 1962 Saturday Review, Inc. Edward Tatnall Canby. "Thomas Wolfe's Short Stories," Copyright 1935 The Saturday Review Company, Inc.; renewed 1963 Saturday Review, Inc. Howard Mumford Jones. "Genius Is Not Enough," Copyright 1936 The Saturday Review Company, Inc.; renewed 1963 Saturday Review, Inc. "Always Looking Homeward," Copyright 1936 The Saturday Review Company, Inc.; renewed 1966 Saturday Review, Inc. George Stevens. "Thomas Wolfe's Torrent of Recollection," Copyright 1940 The Saturday Review Company, Inc.; renewed 1967 Saturday Review, Inc., Estate of Stephen Vincent Benet. "Thomas Wolfe Looks Homeward," Copyright 1943 The Saturday Review Associates, Inc.; renewed 1970 Saturday Review, Inc. by permission of estate of Thomas Sugrue. "Thomas Wolfe, Poet," Copyright 1945 The Saturday Review Associates, Inc. "Pick of the Paperbacks," Copyright 1965 Saturday Review, Inc. "Motes in the Eye of a Mountainous Man," Copyright 1970 Saturday Review, Inc. Harry T.

Moore. *Savannah News* for review of *Mannerhouse*. *Sewanee Review* and Robert E. Spiller. for "Wolfe Is Still at the Door." *South Atlantic Quarterly* for review of *The Notebooks of Thomas Wolfe*. *Southern Literary Journal* for "An 'Interior Biography' of Thomas Wolfe." *Southern Review* for "Prodigal," "Notes on the Novel." *Southwest Review* for review of *You Can't Go Home Again*. *Springfield Republican* for "Unselective Bulk." *Survey Graphic* for "The Storm and Stress Period." *Theatre Arts Monthly* for "A Young Man of Promise." *Trend* for "Here We Go Again." *Virginia Quarterly Review* for "The Dandridges and the Gants," "Social Notes on the South," "A Mine of Literary Origins." *Washington Sunday Star* for "Writer and Hero Merge In 'Discovery of Life.'" *Wings* [*Literary Guild*] for review of *Look Homeward, Angel*. *Wisconsin Library Bulletin* for review of *Of Time and the River*. *Writer's Digest* for "Thomas Wolfe—In Memoriam." *Yale Review* for review of *Of Time and the River*, "Thomas Wolfe," Copyright Yale University. Review of *The Letters of Thomas Wolfe*, Copyright Yale University Press. Louis Untermeyer for "New Books in Review."

Introduction

When Thomas Wolfe burst upon the American literary scene in 1929, he soon became controversial and has remained a controversial figure ever since. Although he has long since become established as one of our major American writers, dispute still swirls about his merit as an artist, and critical confusion persists over his books. Actually, Wolfe's work put unwary critics to the severest test of any American writer since Whitman. His autobiographical fiction defied any attempt to categorize it with conventional critical terminology, and he fitted into none of the accepted molds. Like Poe and Whitman, he became a legend in his own lifetime, and the exaggeration and distortion of legend have tended not only to shape the popular image of Wolfe but also to perpetuate the controversy about his work. In spite of the changing winds of critical taste that have blown both hot and cold on his work, it has remained as a solid literary achievement that has elicted the highest praise from his chief contemporary, William Faulkner. When Faulkner was once asked to rank his fellow novelists, he replied: "Among his and my contemporaries, I rated Wolfe first because we had all failed but Wolfe had made the best failure because he had tried hardest to say the most."

Wolfe's career as a writer is unique in several ways. Originally his burning aspiration was to be a playwright. A charter member of the Carolina Playmakers, he studied under Professor Frederick H. Koch, and his first creations were one-act plays. After graduating from the University of North Carolina in 1920, Wolfe spent three years studying playwriting with George Pierce Baker at Harvard and the next three years writing plays and trying to gain Broadway production. He came very close to achieving this goal when the Theatre Guild seriously considered *Welcome to Our City*, but eventually declined to produce it. Finally, as a frustrated playwright, Wolfe turned to fiction in 1926 and continued until his death in 1938.

The twelve years that he devoted to fiction writing is the shortest career of any of the major novelists of his time. Wolfe's writing span was only half as long as Fitzgerald's and but a third of Faulkner's or Hemingway's. Yet the intensity with which he pursued his purpose was very great. Driving himself mercilessly, he wrote furiously and voluminously as if he were engaged in a hectic race with time. It is no wonder that Faulkner declared Wolfe "had tried hardest to say the most."

A more unusual aspect of his fiction is that, of his total corpus, half of it was not published until after his death, and then from unfinished manuscripts. The fact that the author did not live to see half of his work through the press, and the uncertainty at the time of the role of the editor in shaping the material, continued to fuel the controversy and to becloud the record.

Another aspect of Wolfe's writing was his practice of drawing upon his own experience for his fictive material. While his creative method was the distillation of experience, that experience had to be his own. He felt that in order to write about anything he must first make it a part of himself. Therefore, like Stephen Crane and Ernest Hemingway, he expended himself in quest of experience to provide the grist for his mill. Possessing an encyclopedic memory and the power of almost total recall, Wolfe became his own Boswell and his work is freighted with what he once called "the enormous cargo of my memory." The result of his method led to the charge that his books were not properly novels, an accusation that reminds one of G. K. Chesterton's description of Charles Dickens's works. In 1906, long after Dickens's death, Chesterton wrote:

> Dickens's work is not to be reckoned in novels at all. Dickens's work is to be reckoned always by characters, sometimes by groups, oftener by episodes, but never by novels. You cannot discuss whether "Nicholas Nickleby" is a good novel, or whether "Our Mutual Friend" is a bad novel. Strictly, there is no such novel as "Nicholas Nickleby." There is no such novel as "Our Mutual Friend." They are simply lengths cut from the flowing and mixed substance called Dickens—a substance of which any given length will be certain to contain a given proportion of brilliant and bad stuff.

Today, there are those who in retrospect see Wolfe's books as "lengths cut from the flowing and mixed substance" called Thomas Wolfe. But to the reviewers who dealt with each work as it appeared, no such perspective was possible. Their response to each work as it was published adds a chapter to the growth and development of Wolfe's reputation and to our understanding of America's critical heritage as well.

LOOK HOMEWARD, ANGEL

After vain attempts to market his plays, *Welcome to Our City* and *Mannerhouse*, in the spring of 1926, Wolfe began writing a novel the following summer in England using an accounting ledger to write in. Working from an autobiographical background, he continued steadily at his task until the novel, then entitled *O Lost*, was completed in March 1928, seventeen ledgers later. Rejected by several publishers, it was finally accepted by Charles Scribner's Sons and was published on October 18, 1929, as *Look Homeward, Angel: A Story of the Buried Life*, priced at $2.50.

That was hardly a propitious time for an ambitious literary work to appear. Eleven days later on "Black Tuesday" the stock market crashed and plunged the nation into the worst economic depression it has ever known. In spite of the gathering storm of financial collapse, the book continued to make its way. Three weeks after publication a second printing was ordered, and the novel continued its slow but steady sales that have lasted to the present. *Look Homeward, Angel* was never a best seller in America, though it did become one in both England and Germany.

The response to *Look Homeward, Angel* covered the entire spectrum from admiration to revulsion. Wolfe's writing has always evoked strong emotional response in his readers and his first book was no exception. As a first novel by an unknown writer, it was not widely reviewed by newspapers, but since it was issued by a prestigious house, it did receive attention from some of the more significant book-reviewing media on the national scene, as well as the heated reviews it provoked in his native state of North Carolina.

Although the reviewer for the Boston *Evening Transcript* thought Eugene Gant was "plucked from a small Pennsylvania town," and the *Nation* considered the Gants "a mad clan of Georgians," North Carolina readers never doubted for an instant that the setting was indeed Asheville. Walter S. Adams, reviewing the book for *The Asheville Times*, set the keynote for Asheville's reaction when he declared "the book is written about Asheville and Asheville people in the plainest of plain language" and that it was a story "told with bitterness and without compassion." Jonathan Daniels, in the Raleigh *News and Observer*, expanded the focus by claiming that "North Carolina and the South are spat upon." Lola M. Love, in the Asheville *Citizen*, gave the book a more sympathetic review than did her fellowtownsman Adams, preferring to dwell on its artistic merit and overlooking the local angle except to give a brief biography of the author. But local astonishment soon gave way to anger, and the furor swept from street corner to parlour to pulpit, where Wolfe was denounced on every hand. Six months later May Johnson Avery, writing in the Charlotte *Observer*, recounted Asheville's agony in the shock of recognition, and she felt the tide was beginning to turn toward one of revaluation of the novel. But the intensity of his hometown's outraged protest startled the young writer. Many years later in a speech at Purdue University, Wolfe said, "Their outrage and anger, although mistaken were unmistakable: there is no doubt that from the moment of the book's publication, I became an exile from my native town. I could not come back at that time, and it was seven years, in fact, before I wanted to come back and did return."

Elsewhere reviewers were not concerned with the native heath and while some were not too favorable and treated the book lightly, others found substance and promise. The first important review in a New York newspaper was Harry Hansen's in the *World*. Entitled "Ah, Life! Life!" he admitted the book gave "an impression of strength and promise" but he took occasion to twit Wolfe for his "Meredithian prose" and "musings over destiny, fate, love." However, the two most important newspapers, the New York *Times* and the *Herald Tribune*, both gave the novel serious, thoughtful reviews which contributed to its early success. Margaret Wallace in the New York *Times* recognized the originality and power of the novel and prophetically concluded that "the final decision upon it, in all probability, rests with another generation than ours." Margery Latimer in the *Herald Tribune* also found the novel meritorious, and these two reviews helped to set *Look Homeward, Angel* on its way.

Magazine reviews tended, by and large, to reinforce the position taken by the leading newspapers. Geoffrey Hellman in the *New Republic* stated flatly that "Unheralded, *Look Homeward, Angel* will hardly remain unsung," and his prediction proved accurate. Except for an occasional strident dissent, like Edwin Fairley's in the Unitarian *Christian Register*, most reviewers found Wolfe's novel praiseworthy. Even though a number had some reservations, they praised the present achievement and expressed anticipation of his future work. John Chamberlain in *The Bookman* deplored some of Wolfe's rhetoric but declared that "No more sensuous novel has been written in the United States." Robert Raynolds in *Scribner's Magazine* compared Wolfe with Melville and Whitman, and Carl Van Doren in *Wings* lauded his characterization. Representative of this combination of qualification and enthusiasm is Basil Davenport's review in the *Saturday Review of Literature*, which found in the book, despite its "faults of luxuriousness," a kinship with Rabelais "in a rare combination of fineness and largeness." Especially illuminating is the review by Stringfellow Barr in the *Virginia Quarterly Review* that compares Wolfe's novel with one by an established Southern writer also published by Scribner's, Stark Young's now-forgotten *River House*.

Barr sided with the newcomer and hailed *Look Homeward, Angel* as a contribution to world literature.

Since American literary opinion of this era was still quite responsive to English reaction, it is worth noting that when Heinemann published *Look Homeward, Angel* in London on July 14, 1930, it was greeted by British reviews that, much like their American counterparts, covered the entire spectrum. Richard Aldington was eulogistic in the *Sunday Referee*, but Frank Swinnerton took an opposite position in the *Evening News*. Gerald Gould, as if trying to outdo Swinnerton, stated in the *Observer* that he could "see no reason why anybody should read" the novel. A more balanced review appeared in the influential *Times Literary Supplement*, and the opinion voiced by its anonymous reviewer is more typical of the reaction of the English to *Look Homeward, Angel*.

In addition to formal reviews there was a stream of readers who volunteered their praise of *Look Homeward, Angel* by letter to Wolfe or in public statement. A visiting English man of letters, Hugh Walpole, was quoted in a newspaper interview as saying: "His novel is as nearly perfect as a novel can be. I feel it a duty as a literary man to say something in his favor." But the most dramatic endorsement the book received was from the chief American novelist of the time. Sinclair Lewis wrote Wolfe on October 23, 1930:

> I wish there hadn't been quite so many brisk blurb-writers these past twenty years, using up every respectable phrase of literary criticism, so that I might have some fresh phrase with which to express my profound delight in *Look Homeward, Angel!* There is, you needn't be told, authentic greatness in it. It and *Farewell to Arms* seem to me to have more spacious power in them than any books for years, American OR foreign. . . . God, your book is good!

Two weeks later Lewis became the first American to win the Nobel Prize in Literature. At his New York press conference, after the announcement was made, he gave his highest praise to Wolfe, and it was lavish indeed, saying not only that he may become the greatest American writer but even "one of the greatest world writers." Lewis repeated his admiration for *Look Homeward, Angel* in his formal acceptance speech in Stockholm, and his ringing tribute from this prestigious forum not only brought international attention to the book, but enhanced its standing at home.

On the eve of the publication of *Look Homeward, Angel* the apprehensive young author asked his editor, Maxwell Perkins, what the verdict on his first novel would be. Perkins's reply was both reassuring and prophetic: "The book will find its way." It certainly has. Never out of print, it has maintained popular appeal and endured the buffeting of changing winds of critical taste, from Marxist to formalist, for more than four decades.

No account of *Look Homeward, Angel* would be complete without pointing out one of the great ironies of the theatre. In spite of Wolfe's frustration as a playwright, his first novel did make Broadway as a play. Adapted by Ketti Frings, twenty years after Wolfe's death, *Look Homeward, Angel* had a long and successful run. More recently, *Playhouse 90* presented an adaptation of the Frings' play on nationwide television during prime time on the evening of February 25, 1972. This dramatic version may well have reached more viewers than all the readers of the novel combined, and its favorable reception attests to the durability of *Look Homeward, Angel.*

OF TIME AND THE RIVER

The five and a half years that elapsed between *Look Homeward, Angel* and the publication of *Of Time and the River* were a time of struggle, trial, and despair for Wolfe, during which he made a number of false starts. His ambition was fired by the reception of his first novel, and he set his sights high. His work throbbed to the epic impulse as he sought no less than to capture the essence of the American character and the American experience in fiction. To achieve these lofty aims, he formulated numerous plans and tested various themes. Winning a coveted Guggenheim Fellowship enabled him to spend a year in Europe. The Guggenheim year was the second great creative period in Wolfe's life, and he returned to America with much written but with no finished novel. Settling in Brooklyn he worked away for four years and the long anticipated second novel was published on March 8, 1935.

The huge novel (912 pages of close print) was greeted with mixed reactions. Its lack of adherence to novelistic tradition and its experimental nature found critics as ill prepared to deal with it as an earlier generation had been to confront Whitman. Some were simply stunned; some were quick to attack Wolfe's violation of cherished critical tenets; and still others hailed it as the fulfillment of the promise of greatness given by *Look Homeward, Angel.* Popularly it was well received and became the only one of Wolfe's books to make the best seller lists in America. The publication of *Of Time and the River* swept Wolfe into a position of importance on the national literary scene, but it also provoked controversy that would profoundly affect his career, and it set off debates on critical questions that are still unsettled.

While the initial reception given *Look Homeward, Angel* was relatively modest, *Of Time and the River* was greeted with such widespread attention that it became the literary event of 1935. Both the New York *Times* and the *Herald Tribune* gave it enthusiastic front page reviews and it was prominently featured in all leading media. Reviewers everywhere were impressed by the magnitude of Wolfe's effort but by no means were unanimous in their appraisal of the result. Even those who found fault with the book also included high praise. Clifton Fadiman in the *New Yorker* said, "Just watching Mr. Wolfe release his magnificent, inexhaustible energy leaves one flushed and punch drunk. It will be some time before the literary bookkeepers have cast up their accounts and told us just how good a novel he has written." Fadiman admitted Wolfe had "a kind of genius" but he also had some reservations: "It is open to debate whether he is a master of language or language a master of him; but for decades we have not had eloquence like his in American writing." Malcolm Cowley in the *New Republic* thought that the book cut into half would be twice as good, but he stated that "Thomas Wolfe at his best is the only contemporary American writer who can be mentioned in the same breath with Dickens and Dostoevsky." Robert Penn Warren in his widely reprinted review, "A Note on the Hamlet of Thomas Wolfe," summed up the critical objection to Wolfe's structure:

> What, thus far, he has produced are fine fragments, several brilliant pieces of portraiture, and many sharp observations on men and nature: in other words, these books are really voluminous notes from which a fine novel, or several fine novels might be written.

Warren concluded with one of the most famous barbs ever cast at Wolfe: "And meanwhile it may be well to recollect that Shakespeare merely wrote *Hamlet;* he was *not* Hamlet."

But these dissenting notes were almost lost in the welling chorus of praise that greeted the book, and attacks were often modified by admiration for Wolfe's talents. Terms like genius, Great American Novel, and comparison with the great authors dominated many of the reviews. *Time* magazine's reviewer spoke for many when he declared, "In form it is variously a narrative, an epic, a diatribe, a chronicle, a psalm, but in essence it is a U.S. voice." Though the book's faults had not gone undetected, its power had projected Wolfe into a major literary figure and the subject of continuing debate.

FROM DEATH TO MORNING

Scribner's followed up the success of *Of Time and the River* by bringing out in November a collection of Wolfe's short pieces entitled *From Death to Morning*. These fourteen magazine stories, whose arrangement from the negativism of "No Door" to the affirmation of "The Web of Earth" expresses the progression implied in the title, range widely but demonstrate Wolfe's ability to work within restricted compass and to achieve the intense personal world of his novels. This very fact seemed to perplex the reviewers. Accustomed now to his huge books they reacted uneasily to sprawling manner and rich detail in a compact form. Fellow writer Hamilton Basso declared, "Only in the broadest sense of the word are most of them short stories." Edith Weigle in the *Chicago Tribune* spoke for many when she wrote, "Mr. Wolfe takes the form of the short story and twists it and shapes it to his own ends." Most reviewers responded warmly to certain selections, and considered the whole rather uneven.

The book proved to be a commercial disappointment in that it is the only one of Wolfe's books that did not sell out in its first edition. Of the 7,500 copies printed, about a thousand were remaindered in 1940 (though since then both hard and soft cover reprints have appeared). Although it is true that most selections are enhanced by a reader's familiarity with Wolfe's total work, the miscellaneous nature of *From Death to Morning* proved difficult to reviewers and has caused the book, in fact, never to receive the attention it merits.

THE STORY OF A NOVEL

The last book Wolfe published during his lifetime was the smallest of all, only ninety-three pages, but it was an extremely important one in shaping the remainder of his career and work. Invited to lecture at the University of Colorado Writers' Conference, Wolfe joined Robert Frost, Robert Penn Warren, and other prominent authors in Boulder in July, 1935. He delivered an hour-and-forty-minute lecture on "The Making of a Book," a frank and disarming account of his own experience in writing *Of Time and the River* that proved to be the highlight of the conference. An abridged version of the lecture appeared in the *Saturday Review of Literature* in December, and Scribner's published the full lecture in April, 1936, as *The Story of a Novel*. His complete candor and honesty in acknowledging the help of his editor, Maxwell Perkins, won many new friends, but his frankness also made him vulnerable to attack by hostile critics, and the attack came swiftly. Four days after publication of the book Bernard DeVoto in a vicious review led the onslaught. DeVoto, at his satiric best, berated the author, condemned his work, and declared Wolfe's books were actually products of an assembly line at Scribner's. Though other reviewers were more objective and understanding, DeVoto's review served to fuel anew the controversy. Wolfe felt that his integrity as a writer had been questioned. Beset by other problems—legal, professional, and personal—Wolfe entered a troubled period of his life.

The publication of *The Story of a Novel* set in motion a train of complex circumstances that led Wolfe eventually to declare his independence of Scribner's and to seek another publisher.

OBITUARY

On September 15, 1938, two weeks before his thirty-eighth birthday, Thomas Wolfe died. News of his death was widely disseminated, and was viewed by most literary commentators as a tragic loss to American literature. Many considered it Keatsian and premature to have occurred at the height of his powers. The collective comment at the time of his death assesses his reputation based on his then published work.

Perhaps the general feeling toward Wolfe's death was best summarized in a letter Edgar Lee Masters wrote to Wolfe's sister, Mabel:

We can lament that Tom did not have time to say all that was in him, but neither did Keats or Shelley. Something fashions the story and whether it be the finished or the unfinished picture, at last it takes its place as the picture and seems not unfitting. . . . And in spite of everything you have the consolation . . . that he, in his brief years, went ahead with the swiftness that marks men of genius, and left a name for you and America to treasure.

THE WEB AND THE ROCK

Death, however, did not mean *finis* to Wolfe's literary contribution. The next three years witnessed the publication of three books of fiction, and important non-fiction (letters and notebooks) was to appear over the next three decades. In total bulk, Wolfe's posthumous work exceeds that published during his lifetime.

The fall of 1936 was the third great creative period of Wolfe's career. It also marked a change in his method of writing, as he began dictating to a secretary. Prior to this time he had done all his writing in longhand. In addition to changing his method of writing, he also modified his plans as he worked on new books. He gradually abandoned the series of which *Of Time and the River* was to be the second of six in the Gant saga, and developed a new protagonist, George Webber. Finally severing his connection with Scribner's, he signed with Harper and Brothers as his new publisher in December, 1937, and received a $10,000 advance on his next book. He spent the winter of 1937 and spring of 1938 getting together a publishable manuscript for his new editor, Edward C. Aswell. Yielding to an inner compulsion to incorporate all the material he had written for several projected books, Wolfe pulled it all together into an ever-growing autobiographical narrative, and he prepared a long outline and synopsis for Aswell.

Wolfe had accepted an invitation to speak at Purdue University on May 19, 1938. He realized he was far from being through with his mammoth manuscript, and was uncertain whether to let Aswell see it in its unfinished state. Heeding the advice of his agent and friend, Elizabeth Nowell, he did leave the huge package with Aswell before his departure so that Aswell might become familiar with the material in his absence. Wolfe anticipated a long period of revision, cutting, and reweaving on his return. But his death precluded all those plans. His unfinished manuscript lay on the desk of his new editor.

Aswell had only been associated with Wolfe for six months and the task confronting him was a formidable one indeed. He worked assiduously at the job with enthusiasm, and where he felt unsure of Wolfe's intentions he drew on the generous advice of Maxwell Perkins—who was Wolfe's literary executor as well as former editor—and Elizabeth Nowell. From this massive typescript Aswell edited the three posthumous books of fiction: *The Web and the Rock* (1939), *You Can't Go Home Again* (1940), and *The Hills Beyond* (1941). While these books would undoubtedly be different if Wolfe had lived to see them through the press, and Aswell's editorial work on them was greater than Perkins's part in *Of Time and the River*, they do constitute half of the six books of fiction upon which his reputation rests, and were, of course, evaluated by the reviewers in the form they appeared.

The Web and the Rock was published on June 22, 1939, with no indication of the editorial labors of Aswell, and was greeted by a divided critical response. Wolfe's admirers, who were legion, were elated at the prospect of another book by him. May Cameron in the New York *Post* advised her readers, "Run, do not walk, to your nearest bookstore." Many did, and with a first edition which ran to 31,126 copies Harper's had a publishing success. While the general reader was devouring the novel, critics and reviewers found cause for both praise and blame.

Malcolm Cowley in the *New Republic* raised many of the old charges of excess, and maintaining that Wolfe's novels were a mixture of "the nearly sublime and the silly," contended that Wolfe "was actually at his best in episodes and novellas." Howard Mumford Jones writing in the Boston *Transcript* said that some of the episodes are "more billiantly written, more powerfully 'seen' than can be found in the work of any other recent American novelist." But he added: "There are also passages which contain as much bad writing as can anywhere be found."

The "Author's Note" at the beginning of the novel unfortunately caused a great deal of critical confusion. Early in 1938, Wolfe wrote out "A Statement of Purpose" which describes a book much like *You Can't Go Home Again*, on which he was then working. Aswell took portions of the "Statement" about Wolfe's fictional aims and inappropriately placed them at the beginning of *The Web and the Rock*. This "Author's Note," which was dated May 1938, led critics to maintain that Wolfe's declared intentions were not successfully carried out in the book. Clifton Fadiman, writing in the *New Yorker*, quotes part of the "Author's Note" and laments, "How keenly one wishes the novel itself confirmed his brave words!" The reviewer for *Time* magazine entitled his review "Bitter Mystery" and complained that "Exhausted readers, dazed and deafened from their long buffeting, may seek in vain for Wolfe's 'objectivity,' for an identity in Monk's demented passions with their own." J. Donald Adams in a front page review for the New York *Times Book Review* stated it a little more kindly and perceptively when he observed, "If Wolfe believed what he wrote [in the "Note"], and there is no reason to think that he did not, he deceived himself, though not completely." John Chamberlain in *Harper's* conceded, "Presumably the words were meant also to apply to the second of the two posthumous works, the novel which will eventually be published under the title of *You Can't Go Home Again*. But whatever the intention of the foreword, it probably represents more of a hope than a reality." There the matter seemed to rest, and many would agree with George Stephens that "*The Web and the Rock* contains and magnifies all Wolfe's faults and all his virtues."

YOU CAN'T GO HOME AGAIN

Wolfe's stated intentions are more successfully accomplished in *You Can't Go Home Again*, which was published on the second anniversary of his death—again without any indication of Aswell's labors on the manuscript. Astute critics were quick to note the difference. For example, Claude Simpson in the *Southwest Review* declared, "The seemingly ill-advised preface to *The Web and the Rock*, if applied to the entire sweep of the two novels, is not so wide off the mark." Many others tended to agree with him. In spite of its episodic nature, and the leaner style, the book was generally well received. Its social criticism, coming at the end of the depression decade and the beginning of World War II, made a powerful appeal. Joseph Henry Jackson seemed to speak for the majority when he wrote in the San Francisco *Chronicle:* "Thomas Wolfe, in spite of his faults, was a genius." Kimball Flaccus in the *Catholic World* saw "the tragedy of Wolfe" as "during his lifetime he was judged by the standards of conventional fiction; only after his untimely death is he beginning to be recognized as the great poet he undoubtedly was."

The critical debate about Wolfe continued. So much so, that Carlos Baker felt constrained to write in the *Nassau Lit:* "But let none of Wolfe's detractors tell you that he didn't learn to write great novels." And Baker goes on to state that *You Can't Go Home Again* "is far and away the best novel he ever wrote—mature, controlled, logical, wise." Not all of Wolfe's admirers would agree with that opinion, but the general concensus of critics was that he had made a major advance, and despite his admitted flaws, the writers with whom he was most frequently compared were Whitman and Melville. Perhaps a more accurate keynote of the critical reception was sounded by Dayton Kohler in the *Southern Literary Messenger:* "He is the least perfect of novelists, but he remains the most challenging figure of his literary generation." The eventual position of Wolfe in American literature seemed likely to be considerably more substantial than Isabel Patterson predicted in *Mademoiselle:* "His talent was completely undisciplined, and getting no better fast. All the same, it was an authentic and original talent, and will have at least a foot-note in American literature."

THE HILLS BEYOND

The third posthumous book appeared in October, 1941, and differed considerably from the previous two. Aswell brought together the incomplete story of the Joyners, the maternal forebears of George Webber, as ten chapters of an unfinished novel which gave title to the volume. He also collected ten of Wolfe's fugitive stories and sketches that include two of his best short stories, "The Lost Boy" and "Chickamauga." Finally, he added to the end of the volume "A Note on Thomas Wolfe" which revealed for the first time his editorial part in the posthumous volumes.

As might be expected, the reception was mixed. Wolfe's admirers were delighted by more material from his gifted hand, no matter how fragmentary, and his detractors remained still unconvinced. Clayton Hoagland entitled his review in the New York *Sun*, "Wolfe Dividend" and thought, "This short novel may come to be known as his most mature work." Clifton Fadiman called his review in the *New Yorker* simply "More Posthumous Wolfe" and maintained that "People have made up their minds about Wolfe, and this volume will not cause them to alter their opinions." Most reviewers saw the volume as more proof of unfulfilled promise. W. A. S. Dollard declared in the New York *Herald Tribune Books* that "If the book had been completed it might have been the great realistic Southern picture of Reconstruction days." Others saw his change in style as yet another sign of maturity. The reviewer for *Time* declared, "Somewhere past midstream in his transition from wild lyric romanticism to humanism, this prose here lost in effusive splendor, but gained in wit, firmness and control." The debate on Wolfe would continue, but with the publication of *The Hills Beyond,* the posthumous books were rounded out and his canon almost complete.

THOMAS WOLFE'S LETTERS TO HIS MOTHER

Wolfe's autobiographical fiction elicted such a deep and widespread interest in the personality of the author himself that every scrap of information available was sought out. The result was often rumor, anecdote, and a growing but distorted legend. In his "Note on Thomas Wolfe" at the end of *The Hills Beyond,* Aswell had quoted at length from a letter Wolfe had written his mother from Harvard when he was only twenty-two. This letter attracted much attention and sparked a demand for more of Wolfe's letters. Accordingly, Scribner's published Wolfe's letters to his mother in 1943. The letters were edited by John Skally Terry who provided an introduction that included reminiscences of Mrs. Wolfe about her famous son.

To say this volume was enthusiastically received is to put it mildly. John T. Fredrick began his review in the *Chicago Sun* by claiming, "This book will hold interest and value for American readers a century from now, two centuries from now," because the letters "throw indispensable light on his life and work." This response was echoed in varying degrees by other reviewers, with John Selby stating in the New Orleans *Times-Picayune* that he was more affected by the letters than "by anything else Wolfe ever wrote." Not that this attitude was unanimous by any means, but it was a preponderant one despite the demurrers that also greeted this widely-reviewed volume. The Dallas *Times Herald* accurately summed up the response: "Thomas Wolfe usually is either greatly admired or thoroughly detested by the literary world. For those millions who form the first group, the letters will be a treasured possession." Even John Chamberlain admitted in the New York *Times* that the letters "are a brilliant, warm record of the odyssey of a valiant spirit."

The reception of the volume of letters to his mother reflect the enormous fascination with the personality of Wolfe and the desire to know "what he was really like." (The volume remained the principal biographical source for students of Wolfe for more than a decade and was not superceded until 1968 when C. Hugh Holman and Sue Fields Ross brought out a more carefully edited edition of the original documents.)

A STONE, A LEAF, A DOOR: POEMS BY THOMAS WOLFE

The lyrical quality of Wolfe's prose written in his early style was often recognized, and the word "poetic" was not infrequently applied to his work. In fact, in 1939 Scribner's published a selection entitled, *The Face of a Nation: Poetical Passages from the Writings of Thomas Wolfe*. The passages were selected by John Hall Wheelock, himself a well known poet, who was a friend of Wolfe's and a Scribner's editor. In the introduction Wheelock asserts, "The essential Thomas Wolfe is here, and he is a poet." The volume, printed in the original prose format, enjoyed a modest success but was overshadowed by the posthumous books and the forthcoming absorption of the nation in World War II.

In 1945 Scribner's published *A Stone, A Leaf, A Door: Poems by Thomas Wolfe*. This time the passages were selected by John S. Barnes and were arranged in verse form, and Barnes included selections from the posthumous works. In a brief introduction, Louis Untermeyer declared to the post-war readers, "Those who are not intimately acquainted with the novelist will discover a new American poet." Other critics echoed this idea. William Rose Benét agreed in the *Book-of-the-Month Club News* that "He was first of all a poet." Robert Hillyer declared in the New York *Times Book Review* that while the book may not introduce a new poet, "it makes us more conscious of the poetic essence we always felt in Wolfe, but had not the patience to distill for ourselves." Though Wolfe occasionally attempted formal composition of poetry, as his pocket notebooks show, his poetic qualities best expressed themselves in lyrical prose. The result of Mr. Barnes' book was to emphasize afresh the poetic quality of Wolfe's work, even in his late style, and to demonstrate the continuity of the underlying poet who frequently burst to the surface in all of Wolfe's prose.

MANNERHOUSE

The attempt to show Wolfe in the role of poet was followed three years later by presenting him in yet another role—that of playwright—when Harper's brought out *Mannerhouse* in 1948. Wolfe's long struggle to become a playwright is well known, so that this role is indeed a bona fide one, though it harkened back to a youthful author and antedates all his prose fiction. Wolfe had completed *Mannerhouse* in 1925, but it remained unproduced and unpublished during his lifetime. Its appearance in print a decade after his death created a minor flurry of excitement because Wolfe himself had discussed the play in the guise of fiction, but under its own title, in *Of Time and the River* (pages 544-549). Now readers had an opportunity to compare the play with the author's assessment of it, and to see how well the sprawling novelist had succeeded within the more restrictive confines of drama.

The predictable mixed chorus arose. George White Graice in *Theatre Arts* declared "Much ado is being made of this play," but felt that it was "a very young and smallish bird on the back of its author's maturer eagle." Other reviewers encountered much the same difficulty as that expressed by John Woodburn in the *New Republic:* "Peering at this play across the massive novels which followed, it is difficult to evaluate in terms of itself, to bring it out from under the long shadows of Eugene Gant and of Thomas Wolfe, who has already, after ten years, taken to himself of the color of the myth which so held and concerned him." And Thomas Quinn Curtiss in the New York *Times Book Review,* attempting to focus on the play as drama, found that "in it—as in his other works—we see again the anguish of his struggle, the desperate struggle of an enormous talent endeavoring to become a genius." The general view was that the play was more important for its full array of Wolfe's talents than as dramatic achievement. Some doubted that it was stageworthy. *Mannerhouse* has, in fact, never won popularity in the United States, but it was later to enjoy great success in productions in Germany.

THE LETTERS OF THOMAS WOLFE

A long expressed desire for more biographical information on Wolfe
was met in 1956 when Scribner's published a collection of his letters.
Collected and carefully edited by his faithful agent and friend, Elizabeth
Nowell, the volume was of Wolfean proportions itself. It was almost
800 pages of small type and included over 700 of Wolfe's letters written
from 1908 to his famous last letter, to Maxwell Perkins, from the hospital
in Seattle. Here, at last, was Wolfe expressing himself, without the guise
of fiction, on a plethora of subjects. Though the volume, like a Wolfe
novel, was somewhat overwhelming, the response was generally enthusiastic, though many reviewers used the occasion for a reappraisal of
Wolfe, and some found in the letters new evidence for their previous
opinions. Maxwell Geisman's prediction in the New York *Times Book
Review* that "The first value of the present collection of Wolfe's letters
will be to dispel the myths and legends which sprang up around his
large-size frame and talent, and to clarify his true literary position,"
proved to be only partially fulfilled. A similar hope was expressed by
the *Yale Review:* "This collection ought to stimulate new talk about
Wolfe of the kind to which his achievement entitles him."

Milton Hindus admitted in *Commentary* that "these letters have
changed my opinion of Wolfe somewhat." Horace Reynolds in the
Christian Science Monitor broadened their scope in concluding "that
these letters are a significant American document." But the *New Yorker*
spoke for the anti-Wolfeans when it labeled the volume "Still another
autobiographical roar from one of the noisiest egoists who ever lived."

Perhaps the main result was best summarized by *Time:* "it is impossible
to read the *Letters* without wanting to go hungrily back to the novels
that . . . go deeply into the mighty American spirit." The volume
unquestionably renewed interest in Wolfe, promoted a renewed—or
original—reading of his novels, and also tightened the lines of debate
about his position in American letters.

THE SHORT NOVELS OF THOMAS WOLFE

When *The Short Novels of Thomas Wolfe* appeared in 1961, many
a critic was startled and had his stereotyped image of Wolfe shaken.
As Dennis Powers confessed in the Oakland *Tribune:*

We think of him (if we think of him at all) as a disheveled genius who wrote magnificent prose but whose endless novels are marred by his immoderation and his shocking disregard for form and discipline.

It was to correct this type of misconception that C. Hugh Holman published the five best of Wolfe's short novels as Wolfe had constructed them and had published them in magazines in the early thirties. The result was a somewhat surprised concensus that Wolfe possessed an additional artistic dimension that had been largely lost sight of. As Robert E. Spiller admonished in the *Sewanee Review:*

> The student who now turns to the documents as collected by Mr. Holman may further explore the evidence and make up his own mind on larger issues. In doing so he may learn something about the varities of literary experience and the dangers of too rigid critical formulae.

THE NOTEBOOKS OF THOMAS WOLFE

In 1970, when the University of North Carolina Press brought out *The Notebooks of Thomas Wolfe,* the most important unpublished documents for evaluating Wolfe's life and work were at last made available. As Richard Walser observed in the *Virginia Quarterly Review,* "Among the primary documents of Thomas Wolfe long witheld from publication, the appearance of none has been more anticipated than that of his Notebooks." The reception of the notebooks was generally enthusiastic. The New York *Times Book Review* devoted its front page to a review by Richard Gorham Davis who declared, "Nostalgic, terrifying, the notebooks in their naked immediacy show this [the author as archetype] even more than the published letters and the fiction." And Davis went on to observe that "Wolfe did mature, though in irregular, undependable, and costly ways." Harry T. Moore, in the lead essay in the *Saturday Review,* generally praised the work as adding greatly to the understanding of Wolfe and his work. In *Newsweek* Albert H. Norman was even more enthusiastic: "Every line breathes with the clean, flushed face of youth." But Dorothy L. Parker in the *Christian Science Monitor* referred to the notebooks as "that gigantic dustbin into which he hurled the refuse of his life" and felt that they "confirm again what has long been apparent—that he didn't know what to put in or when to stop." The richly informative notebooks have stimulated a renewed and continuing reassessment of Wolfe and his work, but they have also served to stimulate the controversy of Wolfe the artist and his proper place in American letters.

Time was a peculiar obsession of Wolfe's. He grappled with its philosophical concept and wrestled with its artistic rendition. In his effort to wreak his vision in fiction he engaged in a race with time, the hectic nature of which he was keenly aware. But time was not only a challenge and a symbol, it was also an adversary, as he articulated in his plaintive cry that time is the enemy. Wolfe was the loser in his physical struggle with time, but there is strong indication that in the ensuing contest, time's inexorable winnowing, he is gradually besting his ancient adversary.

❁ ❁ ❁ ❁ ❁

This collection is intended to reflect the development of Thomas Wolfe's literary reputation in his native land. Thus, the reviews reprinted and, for the most part, those listed in the checklists are ones which appeared in American newspapers and journals. However, because of their considerable influence at the time, certain British reviews are listed. The purpose has been to provide a representative sampling from various media across the nation of the response to Wolfe's work as it appeared. To avoid repetition, plot summaries, biographical material, and extraneous information have been deleted. These deletions are noted by ellipses.

In the preparation of this volume I have received assistance from many people, whom I wish to thank for their kind help. The list is too long to enumerate, but I wish to express my appreciation especially to Mr. Burroughs Mitchell for allowing me access to the Scribner's files, and to Mr. M. S. Wyeth, Jr. for permitting me to examine the files at Harper and Row. I am grateful to Mr. James Meehan, Curator of the North Carolina Room at the Pack Memorial Library in Asheville for his assistance, to Mr. Syed Obeidullah Stalin, who served as my research assistant on much of this project, and to Mrs. Dawn Tolbert who prepared the manuscript. To M. Thomas Inge and Stanley Lewis I am grateful for their patience.

Paschal Reeves

Look Homeward, Angel

A Story of the Buried Life

BY

THOMAS WOLFE

*"At one time the earth was probably a white-
hot sphere like the sun."*
　　　　　—TARR AND MCMURRY

CHARLES SCRIBNER'S SONS

NEW YORK

1929

Look Homeward, Angel

Walter S. Adams. "Amazing New Novel Is Realistic Story Of Asheville People." Asheville *Times,* October 20, 1929, p. 1.

An amazing new novel is just off the press which is of great and unique interest to Asheville. This community in fact, is going to be astounded by it. Some few well known residents may be shocked into chills. Others will probably be severely annoyed. Many others will snicker and laugh.

The reason is that the book is written about Asheville and Asheville people in the plainest of plain language. It is the autobiography of an Asheville boy. The story of the first twenty years of his life is bared with a frankness and detail rarely ever seen in print. The author paints himself and his home circle, as well as neighbors, friends and acquaintances with bold, daring lines, sparing nothing and shielding nothing.

Thomas Wolfe son of Mrs. Julia E. Wolfe, of 48 Spruce Street, wrote the book, the title of which is "Look Homeward Angel." The novel is just off the press of Scribners. The scene of the work is laid in Asheville with only momentary shifts to Chapel Hill and other cities. The major part of the action takes place in Asheville while virtually all the characters are residents of this city.

Young Wolfe now 29 years old and a teacher in New York University, covers the first twenty years of his life in this novel. It is the utter frank story of himself, his home, neighbors and people about town. It is quite apparent from the book that the author was not happy. His life here, as he boldly sketches it, was crowded with pain, bitterness and ugliness.

While the characters in the book are undoubtedly painted true to life, according to the author's idea of it, the names are changed and juggled around. However, any resident of Asheville who knew this city and its people during the period 1900 to 1920, will not have the slightest trouble in filling in the names of the real persons whom Wolfe made characters in his book. Asheville in this novel goes by the name of Altamount.

. . .

The sub-title of the novel terms it "A Story of the Buried Life." The character and quality of this unusual book is indicated with considerable clearness by an excerpt from a letter by the author which accompanied the

1

manuscript when it was submitted to the publishers:

"The book covers the life of a large family (The Gants of Altamount) for a period of twenty years. It tries to describe not only the visible outer lives of all these people, but even more their buried lives."

To the outlander, "Look Homeward, Angel" is an outstanding novel possessed of unquestioned literary merit. The portraiture is vivid, the style is incisive, the narrative flows with a freedom that sweeps along the most resisting reader.

In the preface, Wolfe raises the question whether the work is really autobiographical and then hastens to beg the question with clever twists of phrases. The net result is that the reader is left to make his own decision and the verdict of the Asheville readers will be unmistakably decisive. The intrinsic proof is overwhelming that Wolfe is relating the story of his own life and of those other lives which interlaced with his own.

This young man who is called Eugene Gant (in reality, Thomas Wolfe, the author) is of a highly sensitive nature. He suffers much from misunderstanding at home, at school and in his relations with other boys. This misunderstanding which seems to be his unvarying lot gives to his life all the aspects of a tragedy which culminates in the death of his brother.

Most of the Asheville people who appear in the novel wear their most unpleasant guises. If there attaches to them any scandal which has enjoyed only a subterranean circulation, it is dragged forth into the light. If they have any weaknesses which more tolerant friends are considerate enough to overlook, these defects are faithfully described. In describing them, the author must often convey the impression to the unknowing that these weaknesses were the distinguishing characteristics of the persons.

The novel will be acclaimed to literary critics as a work of real distinction. But the suspicion is strong that Asheville people will read it not because of its literary worth but rather in spite of any artistic merit which it may possess. They will read it because it is the story, told with bitterness and without compassion, of many Asheville people.

. . .

Jonathan Daniels. "Wolfe's First Is Novel of Revolt: Former Asheville Writer Turns In Fury Upon N.C. And The South." Raleigh *News and Observer*, Editorial Section, October 20, 1929, p. 2.

More than a novel, Thomas Wolfe's first book, "Look Homeward, Angel," is the record of the revolt of a young spirit. Tom Wolfe, once of Asheville, has gone the way of rebels and in a sense this first novel of his is the reign of terror of his talent. Against the Victorian morality and the Bourbon aristocracy of the South, he has turned in all his fury and the result is not a book that will please the South in general and North Carolina in particular. Here is a young man, hurt by something that he loved, turning in his sensitive fury and spittin [*sic*] on that thing. In "Look Homeward, Angel," North Carolina, and the South are spat upon.

In this novel which is admittedly autobiographical in some part, the author Wolfe says of his hero who is easily identifiable with Wolfe:

"His feeling for the South was not so much historic as it was of the core and dark romanticism. . . . Finally, it occurred to him that these people had given him nothing, that neither their love nor their hatred could injure him, that he owed them nothing, and he determined that he would say so, and repay their insolence with a curse. And he did."

"Look Homeward, Angel" is that curse. And in just so far as the curse has entered into the creation, his work has been injured but it is a novel fine enough to show that once Mr. Wolfe has got this little score paid off to his own country he should be able to move on in greater serenity of spirit.

And there may be injustice in calling this book that curse. It is not impossible that he merely chose for artistic reasons the device of writing about North Carolina and North Carolina people through the Gant family, of Altamont (Asheville). Seeing any section through the Gant family would be like looking upon that section through the barred windows of a madhouse. In such a case the hysteria of the madhouse is apt to color the whole country outside. So it is here.

It is a book written in a poetic realism, the poetry of dissolution and decay, of life rotting from the womb, of death full of lush fecundity. The book is sensuous rather than cerebral. It picture[s] a life without dignity—cruel and ugly and touched only by a half-mad beauty. It moves slowly but at almost hysterical tension through twenty years of the life of the lower middle class Gant family, a life stirred only by the raw lusts for food and drink and sex and property. And this picture of the Gants is a cruel picture, drawn not in sympathy but in bitterness. Only one character in the whole book, the perpetually doomed Benfi [*sic*] is drawn with tenderness and feeling.

In photographic detail the Gants are presented through 626 pages of quarrelling life. W. O. Gant, the father, is a wanderer, tombstonemaker, a selfish and self-pitying, bombastic drunkard. The mother, Eliza Pentland Gant, is a stingy, petty woman, avaricious member of the acquisitive mountain Pentlands. There are the children: Daisy, who is an unimportant figure of a girl; Helen, like her father but wiser and kinder; Steve, who is a hopeless degenerate; Luke, the buffoon; Grove, who dies in childhood; Ben, the doomed one, a night worker hungry for beauty and dignity; and Eugene, the hero, a strange figure of sensitiveness, aspiration and inferiority. And beside them are innumerable minor characters, prostitutes, white and black; loose women, Negroes and dope-fiends, drunken doctors, tuberculars, newsboys and teachers.

The book moves slowly with a somewhat too diffused point of view. There is hardly any growth in character but only growing details and passing time. The novel, with its central scene set in Asheville, moves in the South from Maryland to New Orleans and west to St. Louis. There are Negroes in it and cavaliers and all the other figures of Southern legend but the sense of reality is not in them. They are all figments of the Gant madness.

3

It is a book which shines too steadily with the brilliance of lurid details of blood and sex and cruelty. There is beauty in it but it is not a beautiful book. Mr. Wolfe writes with a splendid vividness but there is a heavy quality of sameness in so much stark color. The whole book seems somehow the work of a man who is staring rather than seeing.

In many places Mr. Wolfe has taken no pains adequately to disguise the autobiographic material set down as fiction. His very disguises seem made to point at the true facts. Asheville people will undoubtedly recognize factual material which escapes other readers, and no one who attended the University of North Carolina contemporaneously with Wolfe can miss the almost pure reporting which he presents in the story of his life there.

. . .

Lola M. Love. "Stirring First Novel By Local Man Making Big Hit In Literary World." Asheville *Citizen,* October 20, 1929, p. 8C.

This first novel by Thomas Wolfe, of Asheville, is, according to those who have been already privileged to read it, destined to be the sensation of the fall literary season. This young man, born in Asheville and educated at the State University, has taken the world of publishers by storm with the rugged and colorful sincerity with which he presents his characters. His publishers, Charles Scribner's Sons, asked him to start a second book even before "Look Homeward, Angel" had come from the press. It is also predicted that, before many weeks, the book will be asked for in some of the leading European countries. The book has been eagerly awaited by literary circles in New York and it is expected that it will be one of the most discussed novels of the fall.

"Look Homeward, Angel" was begun while the author was staying in England and the news that his manuscript would be published reached Mr. Wolfe three years later in Vienna. At present he is teaching in New York University and living at the Harvard Club in New York City.

The book is a genius' combination of reality, which will not shrink from even the most sordid details of everyday life, and of a child-like expression of the most delightful fantasy. Both realism and thought are clothed in a vibrant language which pulses with the joy which life's ordinary happenings bring to the author. There is delight in reading words which have been used by Mr. Wolfe to cram the book with meaning and with living people.

Many books of today have, like "Look Homeward, Angel," revealed the life of the small American city. But they have shown it as dull and drab. Mr. Wolfe's book shows that, under conditions imposed by ethics and "culture" life burns with the deep colors of human emotions and richly marked characters.

The characterizations in the book are excellent—made so by the way in which the author has brought to them the little charms which accompany the day-by-day knowledge of a person's habits and entirely human thoughts. The hero in real life does not speak in impassioned periods always, nor does he always act after prayerful premeditation. He is like Mr. Wolfe's characters, who snore and swear, eat and drink, and have their earthy desires as do the best of living men.

In effect, "Look Homeward, Angel" covers the life "of a large family (the Gants of Altamont) for a period of 20 years. It tries to describe not only the visible outer lives of all these people, but even more their buried lives." But essentially the story is that of the life of Eugene Gant, youngest son of this family. It is his vision and his absorbed attention to the rich detail of life which bring the others of the family into being. After all, each man is his own story in real life, and other people exist only as they seem to him.

They were an intensely alive family—these Gants. They loved, hated, and took each other's part with all the vigor they possessed. And it was this vigor—translated to the dreamer and visionary of the family—which made the pattern of life, in all its tragic and meaningful beauty, a thing of wonder.

According to Mr. Wolfe, "This book was written in simpleness and nakedness of soul. When I began to write the book 20 months ago (this from the time when the manuscript was submitted) I got back something of a child's innocency and wonder. It has in it much that to me is painful and ugly, but, without sentimentality or dishonesty, it seems to me that pain has an inevitable fruition in beauty. And the book has in it sin and terror and darkness—ugly dry lusts, cruelty—the dark, the evil, the forbidden. But I believe it has many other things as well, and I wrote it with strong joy.—"

. . .

Thomas Wolfe, born in Asheville in 1900, is the youngest son of Mrs. Julie E. Wolfe, of 48 Spruce Street, Asheville, and of the late W. O. Wolfe, who died in 1922. For 35 years the W. O. Wolfe Monument Works stood on the south side of the Square here, on the site of the present Jackson building, which was the first "skyscraper" in the growing town. It was on the porch of this old building that a marble angel stood—"poised on one pathistic foot"—to watch the weaving destinies of Eugene Gant.

According to Mrs. Wolfe, proudly telling of this youngest child of hers who has made such a brilliant mark for himself in the world of literature, "Tom" (the name by which he is known to family and friends) seemed to be destined for the life of a student from the beginning of his life. When he was less than two years old, his happiest moments were when his father or his mother would read stories to him. After the story had been repeated two or three times he would take the book, and, using the pictures as a guide, would repeat the whole tale, even with pauses for punctuation at the right moment! It was this uncanny precision which made many people think that he was really reading the stories. At the same time he could speak very plainly.

When he was little more than five years old, a neighbor lad, who was six, started to school and nothing would do but that Tom should go, too. His mother says that she can still recall how eagerly he ran home to her with his little list of books he needed. In his work, he easily kept up with those who were several years his senior. School was his whole life from that time on, and he was ready to enter the University of North Carolina when he was little

5

more than 15 years old.

His rapid progress through the grammar grades can be traced, in no little measure, to his mother, who used to take him with her on many trips through various parts of the country. All the other children were so many years older than he, that his mother found he would carry on with her during their travels. The school books always went with them on these trips and Mrs. Wolfe heard lessons each day just as though Tom would go to school the next morning. In this way, he kept up with his classes and even got ahead of them, for Mrs. Wolfe had a way of hearing much longer lessons than did the teachers.

Perhaps it was the constant association with older people which gave the author of "Look Homeward, Angel" such an insight into the mental life of people of every age, as is manifest in his book.

In 1920, Thomas Wolfe graduated from the University of North Carolina and three years later received his Master of Arts degree from Harvard University, where he worked with George Pierce Baker in the '47 Workshop, following up dramatic experience as a member of the Carolina Playmakers.

He is over six feet five,—this young author whose eagerness and childlike faith in life have taken him so far. He does not like tailors or large social gatherings. So he wears a suit of warmest brown homespun which came from somewhere on the continent and has seen much service, and he sleeps in the morning, coming out to revel in the busy world which works at night when most people are asleep. He will listen for hours to the conversation of queer characters gathered together in some "Greasy Spoon." And the roar and bustle of a newspaper plant will give him pleasure all through a night, while his eager mind feeds on a wealth of color and character.

"Look Homeward, Angel" came from the press Friday, October 18, and the eager readers of this bright pageant, so essentially youthful, will doubtless be numbered in the tens of thousands.

Harry Hansen. "Ah, Life! Life!" New York *World,* October 26, 1929, p. 15.

Among the first novels that give me an impression of strength and promise is "Look Homeward, Angel," by Thomas Wolfe, an instructor in New York University. It is a big, fat novel in the Thackeray manner about a commonplace American family in a drab American town. There is rich emotion in it, there is understanding sympathy in it, and there is in it the presence of an author who is aware of himself and his theme, who is more than a recorder.

Many new novels reject everything that this author includes. The young men and women who are making a record of life as it is, whether of actions or mental attitudes (Gertrude Diamant, John Riordan, Josephine Herbst, for example), are not interested in taking the roofs off houses and looking in, or in taking the tops off skulls and watching the convolutions of the brain. They report, for the most part, objectively; they eliminate non-essentials; they take for granted that ages of novel-writing have put the reader in the possession of aspects, points of view, atti-

6

tudes that we take for granted. Not so Thomas Wolfe.

When I opened "Look Homeward, Angel," and read the author's apology for using real people out of the old home town—transmuted, of course, for his novel—I knew that he would have his say. He used a whole page to announce what most authors put into a sentence: "Many of these characters are reminders of actual people, but although all are reminiscent, none is an actual portrait." Even that has been simplified by many authors to a line that protects them from libel suits: "The characters in this book are entirely imaginary."

But Mr. Wolfe is determined to do a full portrait. He has behind him, as internal evidence shows, the range of English literature. He knows Thackeray's manner (in his worst writing) of jumping into the text. He knows George Meredith's musings over destiny, fate, love, ah me! ah me! He is able to sprinkle phrases out of English authors into his pages without quotation marks, without references to footnotes, and thereby paying his reader the compliment of intelligence. He observes behavior, but to him behavior is not enough.

So "Look Homeward, Angel," becomes a rather formidable book, loaded down with details about the family of the Gants—about Gant, the father, who made tombstones in the provincial town of Altamont; and Eliza, the mother, who, after a protracted period of childbearing, opened a boarding house; and Eugene, the son. All egotists in their own way, all going forward to what? "Look Homeward, Angel," is a negation of any plan in life. This family sprawls, uses up its best talents without direction, finds its vitality

spent in frustrated efforts, gets nowhere. On the wife's side were the Pentlands—"that strange, rich clan, with its fantastic mixture of success and impracticality, its hard moneyed sense, its visionary fanaticism." To this end the elder Gant, who had drowned in liquor his protest at the imprisonment of the spirit, did not belong. His son Eugene felt its irony and futility in greater measure, as neither of his two adolescent ambitions—to be loved and to be famous—proved the origin of lasting happiness.

All those varied forces that make for the success and the failure of American life are here brought to bear on the fortunes of a single family, and on one man, Eugene, the lad whose romantic appraisal of life was gradually worn down by defeat. We follow him in his Odyssey, half of the mind, half of the body, and watch him beating on the great door that imprisons life. What message has life to give him? The best of his discovery comes with the words of his dead brother, who appears to him to say that there is no happy land, no end to hunger. "You are your world," says Ben. The only lesson Eliza gains from life comes also at the end when she parts with Eugene: "We must try to love one another." In his Meredithian prose Wolfe continues: "The terrible and beautiful sentence, the last, the final wisdom that the earth can give, is remembered at the end, is spoken too late, wearily. It stands there, awful and untraduced, above the dusty racket of our lives. No forgetting, no forgiving, no denying, no explaining, no hating. O mortal and perishing love, born with this flesh and dying with this brain, your memory will haunt the earth forever."

Moralizing such as this has been

absent from novels these thirty years. In the days of James Lane Allen it became a bit cloying. To-day it is something of a surprise. Mr. Wolfe's commendable strength makes criticism seem captious. He has glaring defects, chief of which seems to be a lack of clearness at the beginning. He treats Oliver Gant so sympathetically that we have difficulty believing his excesses when they occur. But apparently his aim is to portray life without directing the feelings of the reader against any one character. Toward the whole he has the forgiveness that comes with understanding. His second novel will tell us whether he has staying power as a novelist, whether he will be more than a one-book man.

Margaret Wallace. "A Novel of Provincial American Life." New York *Times Book Review,* October 27, 1929, p. 7.

Here is a novel of the sort one is too seldom privileged to welcome. It is a book of great drive and vigor, of profound originality, of rich and variant color. Its material is the material of every-day life, its scene is a small provincial Southern city, its characters are the ordinary persons who come and go in our daily lives. Yet the color of the book is not borrowed; it is native and essential. Mr. Wolfe has a very great gift—the ability to find in simple events and in humble, unpromising lives the whole meaning and poetry of human existence. He reveals to us facets of observation and depths of reality hitherto unsuspected, but he does so without outraging our notions of truth and order. His revelations do not startle. We come upon them, instead, with an almost electric sense of recognition.

The plot, if the book can be said to have a plot at all, is at once too simple and too elaborate to relate in synopsis. "Look Homeward, Angel" is a chronicle of a large family, the Gants of Altamont, over a period of twenty years. In particular, it is the chronicle of Eugene Gant, the youngest son, who entered the world in 1900. W. O. Gant was a stonecutter, a strong, turbulent, sentimental fellow, given to explosions of violent and lavish drunkenness, and to alternating fits of whining hypochondria. Eliza Gant, his second wife and the mother of his family, was an executive woman with a passion for pinching pennies and investing shrewdly in real estate. The Gants grew in age and prosperity with the growth of the sprawling mountain town of Altamont.

By 1900 the Gants were firmly and prosperously established in Altamont—although under the shadow of the father's whining dread of the tax collector, they continued to live as if poverty and destitution lay just around the corner. They kept a cheap, garish boarding house called Dixieland, living their daily lives on the fringe of a world of paying guests whose necessities had to be considered first. Eugene Gant grew from childhood into an awkward and rather withdrawn adolescence, hedged about by the turbulent lives of his family and singularly lonely in the midst of them. Indeed, each of the Gants was lonely in a separate fashion. Mr. Wolfe, in searching among them for the key to their hidden lives, comes upon no unifying fact save that of isolation.

Through the book like the theme of a symphony runs the note of loneliness and of a groping, defeated search for an answer to the riddle of eternal solitude.

> Naked and alone we come into exile. In her dark womb we did not know our mother's face; from the prison of her flesh have we come into the unspeakable and incommunicable prison of this earth. Which of us has known his brother? Which of us has looked into his father's heart? Which of us has not remained forever prison-pent? Which of us is not forever a stranger and alone?

Eugene grew into life hating its loneliness and desolation, its lack of meaning, its weariness and stupidity, the ugliness and cruelty of its lust. For the rawness and evil of life was early apparent to him—hanging about the depressing miscellaneous denizens of Dixieland, delivering his papers in Niggertown, growing up in the streets and alleys of Altamont. He found a poignant beauty in it, too—the simple beauty of things seen in youth, the more elusive beauty to be found in books, and later, after his years at college and the death of his brother Ben, the terrible beauty flowering from pain and ugliness. But always there remained in him that loneliness, and an obscure and passionate hunger which seemed to him a part of the giant rhythm of the earth.

"Look Homeward, Angel" is as interesting and powerful a book as has ever been made out of the drab circumstances of provincial American life. It is at once enormously sensuous, full of the joy and gusto of life, and shrinkingly sensitive, torn with revulsion and disgust. Mr. Wolfe's style is sprawling,

fecund, subtly rhythmic and amazingly vital. He twists language masterfully to his own uses, heeding neither the decency of a word nor its licensed existence, so long as he secures his sought for and instantaneous effect. Assuredly, this is a book to be savored slowly and reread, and the final decision upon it, in all probability, rests with another generation than ours.

Margery Latimer. "The American Family." New York *Herald Tribune Books,* November 3, 1929, p. 20

Sometimes an intense shock or a pain that has to be endured will give you a monstrous delight in life, as if the cautious habitual self in you had had its death blow and you were thrown out of yourself into the universe. This book is like that. There is such mammoth appreciation of experience and of living that the intention of the novel cannot be articulated. It comes through to you like fumes or like one supreme mood of courage that you can never forget, and with it all the awe, the defilement and grandeur of actual life. Mr. Wolfe makes you experience a family through twenty years of its existence. He gives the disharmony, the joy, the hideous wastefulness and the needless suffering, and yet not once do you dare shrink from life and not once are you plastered with resentment and loathing for reality and experience. The author has stated in his introduction that he wrote this book with strong joy, not counting the costs, and I believe it. He also has said he tried to compre-

9

hend his people not by telling what they did but what they should have done.

This "should-have-done" is the lyrical, subtle part of the book that comes to you in moments of peril. Ben, the elder brother, finally dies. He has never been educated because of his mother's iron determination to own all the real estate in Altamont and his father's riotous capacity for enjoyment. His whole being has been at the mercy of his parent's whims and the working out of their characters. As he dies the terrible vanity of the family rises above the calamity, their desire to vindicate themselves shuts him out of the world and finally, as they reveal themselves, you reach the rock bottom of their characters—innocence. Compared to some rational, ideal pattern of living they are mad, insane, as innocent as animals who kill each other for food and cannot do otherwise.

"Then, over the ugly clamor of their dissension, over the rasp and snarl of their nerves, they heard the low mutter of Ben's expiring breath. The light had been reshaded; he lay like his own shadow, in all his fierce gray lonely beauty. And as they looked and saw his bright eyes already blurred with death, and saw the feeble beating flutter of his poor thin breast, the strange wonder, the dark rich miracle of his life surged over them its enormous loveliness. They grew quiet and calm, they plunged below all the splintered wreckage of their lives, they drew together in a superb communion of love and valiance, beyond horror and confusion, beyond death!"

Eugene, the youngest son, suddenly understands and possesses his family for a moment. As he looks at his brother he thinks, "That was not all! That really was not all!" And you think, reading, "O lost! that part of people that cannot be understood or possessed or expressed, O lost world of people—each one mysterious." But every act of these people is inevitable, so are their clothes, so are their words. Stevie, for example, "J. T. Collins, that's who! He's only worth about two hundred thousand. 'Steve,' he said, just like that, 'if I had your brains'—he would continue in this way with moody self-satisfaction, painting a picture of future success when all who scorned him now would flock to his standard." And Eliza at the very beginning does not need to be described when she says, "If I'd been there, you can bet your bottom dollar there'd been no loss. Or, it'd be on the other side." And then Gant, who part of the time is "picked foul and witless from the cobbles" and the rest of the time is making his house roar with fires and rich talk, making the outside of his house rich with vines and carving angels on grave stones. Or he is bringing into the warm kitchen great bundles of meat.

In them all, like the vast crude breathing of the earth, is their will to live. Mr. Wolfe describes with monstrous torrential joy the sensual delights of eating. He isn't content to describe a meal in a sentence, but he uses a page, bringing the food before you until it is so tangible it is intolerable, until it is so rich and abundant that it pierces you with awe of life. All the time you are eating that food as if it were actual. He describes the monstrous pleasures of the body in the same way until there is a gigantic picture of living flesh enjoying the universe. But like a Greek chorus or an angelic whisper from the center of this excess are the words, "O lost!"

10

The story is always present. There is always the tremendous excitement of the life of this family, of what they will do and say and feel. Eugene, who in the author's mind is the central character of the book, is interesting only in connection with his family. The story is really the family with its distorted relationships shadowed by their angelic possibilities. Each person is a distinct reality but they are bound together, and when they are sundered the life of the book dwindles. Eugene at college is not as interesting or as real as Eugene the paper boy trying to collect from the prostitutes in Niggertown. But Eugene's life away from his family is only one hundred pages or so, and the fact that Ben's death marks the highest point in feeling and interest does not diminish the value of the book as a whole. The author proudly and naively says "It sometimes seems to me that this book presents a picture of American life that I have never seen elsewhere." I agree with him, and if I could create now one magic word that would make everyone want to read the book I would write it down and be utterly satisfied.

W.E.H. "A Modern Epic of the Life of a Pennsylvania Youth." Boston *Evening Transcript*, November 9, 1929, p. 2.

A first novel that attains six hundred pages is something of a novelty. Indeed, it is more than that, for one must recollect the faith and sporting instinct of a publisher willing to embark in partnership with an author on such a venture. Mr. Wolfe, a Southerner and a graduate of the famous 47 Workshop, when the latter still remained a Harvard institution, has written a Gargantuanlike pseudo-epic of the life of a strange, weird lad named Eugene. In so many words, he informs the reader that the youth lived an early life very similar to his own.

With something of the sweep and color, but none of the selective genius of Balzac, the author of this novel has sought to record the ideas and emotions of his sensitive hero, whom he has plucked from a small Pennsylvania town and an existence close to the soil. He tells the story in the loosest possible fashion. As Dr. Johnson once remarked, and Mr. Wolfe vaguely reminds us from another point of view, story is sometimes nothing. And, indeed, that is true of "Look Homeward, Angel." For if one does not find interest in the wealth of imaginative detail, in the color and emotional portrayal of small town life in the United States, he will never live to finish Mr. Wolfe's opus.

The author says that he is writing without bitterness or rancor, of experiences now long past. We do not feel, however, that he is correct, when he says he has digested them. Admit that the wealth of vivid scenes, momentary flashes of character in this great, oversized volume is tremendous. The reader nevertheless feels the closeness of the simile of the over-stuffed divan. Mr. Wolfe's remarkable gift for writing, a style of prose at times nearly akin to poetry, does not unify his pageant of scenes, people, emotions save as they may all be said to be properly related to the Gant family, and to the idea of waste and futility in life. "And as they sat there," the author writes on one occasion, "more quietly now, swarming pity rose in them—not for themselves, but for each other, and for the waste, the confusion, the groping accident of life." That is his theme; the trouble, however, seems to be that Mr. Wolfe has engaged an even larger symphony orchestra than the proudly advertised one on display at Roxie's, to sound his music. And the composition itself is too vast for ordinary minds, pre-occupied with their own humdrum affairs, to take in or properly evaluate the multiplicity of detail, the elaborate network of ideas.

Yet there is another weakness. The work in its present form is greatly in need of cutting. Mr. Wolfe has a torrential flow of words. The thing that saves him is the fact that his ideas pour forth in equal abundance. Nearly all the scenes and the moments of narrative have a value of some kind, but in many cases these have not been tied up to the main thread with the stern sense of self-discipline which marks even the greatest of writers. One feels that Mr. Wolfe has simply turned on the spigot and allowed himself free range. Were he to consider himself extravagant for even a single moment, he would no doubt find much to leave by the way-side; interesting though it might seem to be. This novel is essentially a sentimental one, but not in any ordinary manner. Mr. Wolfe does not sentimentalize over his characters, but rather—and this is the unusual quality—over his ideas.

Kenneth Fearing. "A First Novel of Vast Scope: 'Look Homeward, Angel' an American Saga in Southern Setting." New York *Evening Post,* November 16, 1929.

For any variation in the few elementary patterns from which the majority of contemporary novels are out, there is apt to be stirred in the reader, depending upon his conviction in such things, a feeling of either gratitude or annoyance. And because even a little variation is felt as extraordinary, the gratitude or annoyance will perhaps be exaggerated beyond a point merited by the performance in itself.

"Look Homeward, Angel" is such a performance, an unusual novel, almost an eccentric one. The author, Thomas Wolfe, is an amateur, partly in the sense that "the artist is always an amateur," and partly in the sense that he has written a thing innocent of structural perfection. He has attempted to give life to a vast, illusive American experience, using whatever language or form he was able to devise to meet the moment's need, rather than adhering throughout to a simpler, neater, but less ambitious formula. And this is not to say that "Look Homeward, Angel" is wholly an original. The book is closely related to a familiar genre, the family saga, and in its writing, shows influences that are well known, notably those of James Joyce and Sherwood Anderson.

The story is of the Gant family, Oliver

and Eliza, and of their seven children, Eugene Gant in particular. Back of them is the story of the town of Altamont, in North Carolina. And in back of Altamont, the story is of the whole South from the latter part of the nineteenth century until the present. Oliver Gant, the Wanderer, driven by savage appetites and by dreams only half-understood, settled at last in Altamont and married the stolid, property-loving, patient, half-shrewd Eliza Pentland, and there began a life-long battle between them. "Eliza came stolidly through to victory. As she marched down these enormous years of love and loss, stained with the rich dyes of pain and pride and death, and with the great wild flare of his alien and passionate life, her limbs faltered in the grip of ruin, but she came on, through sickness and emaciation, to victorious strength."

But her victorious strength, if it sustained Oliver and herself and the children, at the same time blighted them all. Eliza's blindness to everything save the need for property and money drove the children into harsh, incessant contacts with the world at early ages, and in the home the struggle between Eliza and Oliver, assuming insane proportions, dulled or humiliated or embittered all feeling of the family relationship.

Of them all, Eugene Gant is the only one of the children to escape in the end, partially at any rate, the Gantian struggle and seeming spiritual self-destruction. Here the novel becomes two novels. With the adolescence of Eugene, "Look Homeward, Angel" gradually ceases to be a family saga, and becomes slowly the semi-autobiographical story of a sensitive youth. This, too, is closely related to a familiar type, but the author is still extraordinarily lavish, in the fullness with which he portrays Eugene's life, in the scope of the background and in his own interjections, taking the form of ironic, romantic or realistic comments that sum up the given situation, and suggest some Gantian relationship with the universe as a whole. "Naked and alone we came into exile. In her dark womb we did not know our mother's face; from the prison of her flesh have we come into the unspeakable and incommunicable prison of this earth. Which of us has known his brother? Which of us has looked into his father's heart? Which of us has not remained forever prison-pent? . . . O waste of loss, in the hot mazes, lost, among bright stars on this most weary unbright cinder, lost! . . ." Such writing may come uncomfortably close becoming merely fine writing, but it is sincere, and suggests the author's ambitious attempt, sustained in the book as a whole by the far reach of the actual story.

Horace Coon. *MS.: A Magazine for Students of Creative Writing,* December, 1929.

Into our pale and flaccid world of dull and tasteless writers there comes a giant from the hills; and now, because we have no brighter name, we must fall back on stupid labels and call this dark and brooding spirit genius. There is no technic [sic] about such writing as he gives us: this is simply and greatly the out-pouring of a generous talent, fresh from profound and poetic springs, which falls into no critical category; and because he has poured so much of his energy into this book it has taken its own shape, commanded by the deeper laws of artistic creation. By a furious upheaval Thomas Wolfe has delivered an autobiography such as never before has been tossed on the insect heap of American literature.

Mr. Wolfe is more a poet than a novelist; but he is more than that: he is a Bard in the sacred sense of one who sings of the experience of the race, who dares to tell us of the dreams which for some are whispers of a forgotten time and who then spills upon the trembling page a drama of drunken, mad, filthy, lecherous, magnificent people who are the selves we fear to face. His sentences have a flowing rhythm learned from myths of Greece and Rome; his chapters smell of earth and people; they are drawn from a tradition rooted in Smollett, Defoe and Fielding; but his poetic cries are the screams of a soul possessed and tortured by the life that you and I must suffer every day.

This is a book which may be easily dismissed by the academic tipsters of the contemporary literary steeplechase as a raving autobiography, or it may get fawning acclamation from the band wagon hacks and the speakeasy publishers. That does not matter. What does matter is that here at last is a man by whom the magazine pygmies may be measured; here is writing that will forever place in its true perspective the sophomoric, sexless, pale pink, anemic dribble anointed by reviews, book clubs, and guilds. Here is prose by which your own may find a measure,— but only if you have the frenzy of the gods.

The story is simple and is suggested by a first sentence which long after you have read it will ring in your ears: "A destiny that leads the English to the Dutch is strange enough; but one that leads from Epsom into Pennsylvania, and thence into the hills that shut in Altamont over the proud coral cry of the cock, and the soft stone smile of an angel, is touched by that dark miracle of chance which makes new magic in a dusty world." And out of that dusty world Mr. Wolfe has brought the magic of a story of the Gants, their sprawling family, their life in Asheville, and particularly of Eugene Gant, who grew up in the haunted hills of North Carolina, but who has in his eyes the longing for far quests and the nostalgia for worlds yet unvisited by man. Never since *Moby Dick* has such energy, fire, intensity, gone into a piece of American writing. There is swift and merciless character drawing, there are scenes so strong in their unbearable vividness that they will strike you like a physical blow; there are glimpses of the late War for Hyprocrisy, and of the Chapel Hill campus which glow with irony and glamour.

Mr. Wolfe may never write another book—everything he has must have gone into this—but *Look Homeward, Angel* may be compared with only one other: *The Portrait of the Artist as a Young Man;* and if he is permitted to develop he may contribute as much to our times as has James Joyce. If you think that is negligible, then this book is not for you.

14

Richard L. Young. "Wolfe Pictures Men And Carolina Scenes." Charlotte *News,* December 15, 1929, p. 5B.

North Carolinians should be proud of Thomas Wolfe, for soon the nation will doubtless hail him as one of our greatest contemporary writers. "Look Homeward, Angel," his first novel, stamps him as a true interpreter of life and an accurate delineator of human emotions and passions.

In fine literary style, which frequently swings into the most appealing sort of writing, the book sets forth the deep seated emotions that disturb the heart and soul of a restless youth and portrays the tragedy, the sorrow, the pathos of just an ordinary family in a small town. Contrary to most similar attempts Tom Wolfe records these every day happenings with a sympathetic understanding and reveals that humdrum living in such locations is not all sham and Babbittism but is full of strong human emotions. The dark, dry lust, the mean and the ugly are treated as the beautiful, the appealing and the gentle are.

The story centers about the Gants of Altamont, a large family, and extends over a period of 20 years. To Tar Heels, Altamont can readily be recognized as Asheville, the birthplace of the author. Carolinians will be particularly interested in the book because of its picturesque Carolina atmosphere and the reader with knowledge of the State will be intrigued in spotting real places and characters, in his fiction. Chapel Hill is designated in the book as Pulpit

Hill and his description of the place and the life there is enthralling to those who know that charming center of the State's culture and enlightening to those who do not.

University students will easily recognize the sympathetic Greek professor of Freshman Gant. He is none other than the well-known and beloved "Bully" Bernard.

Knowing Tom Wolfe as a student at Chapel Hill and coming in daily intimate contact with him in the same fraternity chapter house, we are constrained to believe that in some elements, Eugene Gant is none other than Wolfe himself. The author will doubtless deny this. Yet the restless, moving, idealistic Gant appears a counterpart of Wolfe, the young student, fresh from the mountains. The groping for the beautiful, the soulful, the big and great of life was Wolfe's as well as Gant's.

Chapel Hill and to hundreds of University graduates he is well known. He was prominent in the Carolina Playmakers and some eight or nine years ago appeared here at the old auditorium in "The Return of Buck Gavin," which he wrote.

. . .

Geoffrey T. Hellman. *New Republic,* 61 (December 18, 1929), 122.

Unheralded, "Look Homeward, Angel" will hardly remain unsung. Stamped with the approval of no book-of-the-moment club, lacking even the customary blurb-writer's accolade, it is an extraordinarily fine novel, not to be mentioned in the same breath with all the forgotten blue-ribbon winners of the past few years. In it Mr. Wolfe tells the story of the Gant family of Altamont, North Carolina. Oliver Gant, a dead wife behind him, comes to Altamont and marries Eliza Pentland, his opposite in every way. Gant is a dreamer, unconventional, poetic, but at the same time full of a very earthy vigor, to put it mildly; Eliza is dull, insensitive, strong, above all, practical. Imbued with a Forsyte-like mania for money and property, she knows what every lot in town is worth, foresees land developments, saves every penny to be used in buying up real estate, turns her own home into a boarding house, forcing her family into smaller and smaller quarters to make room for the increasing number of lodgers.

Thus she saves her husband and children (there are seven) from the poverty which Gant's shiftlessness would otherwise have reduced them to, but at the same time deadens their spiritual and intellectual development. Eugene is the exception; his unusual mind, which even his mother cannot disregard, wins him the privilege of continuing his education at an age when his brothers and sisters are struggling to earn a living. As the book continues, he supplants his father as central character, and "Look Homeward, Angel" becomes less a family chronicle revolving about the rebellious Gant and more a character study of his equally rebellious but more complex son. Mr. Wolfe takes Eugene from birth through early manhood; in passages that range from what is generally known as "rare lyric beauty" to the most downright realism imaginable, he shows him in every conceivable mood.

"Look Homeward, Angel" has been criticized for its style and its lack of structural form. Whenever Mr. Wolfe feels like it, which is fairly often, he launches into episodes, descriptions and proclamations of his own that could be cut out without impairing the architectural unity of his book. Such deletions, however, would rob it of its gusto, and anyone in favor of making them is the sort of person who thinks that "Moby Dick" would be a good book if it weren't for Mr. Melville's digressions. Totally unnecessary characters and events inspire magnificent passages in "Look Homeward, Angel." Mr. Wolfe lavishes his enthusiasm upon people who enter on one page and make their final exit on the next.

. . .

Mr. Wolfe has a quality that is rare enough in itself and is practically never found (as it is here) combined with literary ability, taste, and a scholarly background: relish. He has, in addition, an ironic wit and a sincerity that should prevent his emotional passages from seeming affected to even the most violent prose-poetry haters.

Frances Lamont Robbins. *Outlook and Independent*, 153 (December 25, 1929), 669.

. . .This reviewer finds Thomas Wolfe the most important newcomer among American novelists. His book, *Look Homeward, Angel,* is a typical American story, the story of the turbulent, frustrated Gants, their beginnings, rise and disintegration, and it portrays a typical American character in which gusto quarrels with wondering loneliness, and sensuality with fastidiousness, in which bravado masks a tragic sensitivity. It is chaotic, weighty, over-emotional, exhausting, often hard to follow, sometimes revolting, but always robust, always impassioned. It is full of faults, but they are not inglorious ones, and it is probable that the poise which recognition should give, and the discipline which his own intellect and character may administer, will shape Mr. Wolfe's next novel into a work as powerful and passionate as his first and stronger for being perfectly co-ordinated.

. . .

Basil Davenport. "C'est Maitre François." *Saturday Review of Literature,* 6 (December 21, 1929), 584.

If it were customary to head reviews with a motto, like a chapter of Walter Scott, a review of "Look Homeward, Angel" might well take a phrase from Mr. Arthur Machen's "The Street Glory": *"C'est Maître François! Maître François en très mauvais humeur peut-être, mais Maître François tout de même!"* The analogy must not be pushed too far; there are of course many important differences, notably a violent emotional intensity in Mr. Wolfe that is entirely lacking in Rabelais, but they have the same fundamental and most unusual quality, a robust sensitiveness.

Extraordinary keenness of perception usually makes a character like Roderick Usher or Des Esseintes, or, in real life, Proust, one who is forced to shut himself away from bright lights, loud sounds, and strong feelings, and occupies himself with infinitely cautious and delicate experiments upon himself. But Mr. Wolfe, like Rabelais, though plainly odors and colors and all stimuli affect him more intensely than most people, is happily able to devour sensations with an enormous vigor; his perceptions have a rare combination of fineness and largeness.

In manner, Mr. Wolfe is most akin to James Joyce, somewhere between the ascetic beauty of the "Portrait of the Artist as a Young Man" and the unpruned fecundity of "Ulysses"; but he resembles many other people by turns. His hero, Eugene Gant, amuses himself by registering at country hotels as John Milton or William Blake, or by asking for a cup of cold water and blessing the giver in his Father's name; so Mr. Wolfe amuses himself by writing here in the manner of one author and there of another. He will suddenly fall into a dada fantasia, such as often appears in *transition,* as:

> A woman sobbed and collapsed in a faint. She was immediately carried out by two Boy Scouts . . . who administered first aid to her in the rest-room, one of them hastily kindling a crackling fire of pine boughs by striking two flints together, while the other made a tourniquet, and tied several knots in his handkerchief,—

and so on, and half a dozen pages later he will enumerate, in the painfully unimaginative manner of "An American Tragedy," the real holdings of Mrs. Gant:

"There were, besides, three good

building-lots on Merrion Avenue valued at $2,000 apiece, or at $5,500 for all three; the house on Woodson Street valued at $5,000," and so on for a page and a half. That is, it seems to be the great gift of Mr. Wolfe that everything is interesting, valuable, and significant to him. It must be confessed that he has just missed the greatest of gifts, that of being able to convey his interest to the ordinary reader.

Upon what was his vitality nourished? Rabelais fed on all the fulness of the French Renaissance, a dawn in which it was bliss to be alive; what would he have been like if he had been a poor boy in a small southern town, with a drunken father, a shrewish mother, and a family of quarreling brothers and sisters? Mr. Wolfe's answer seems to be that, in his childhood at least, he would have done unexpectedly well. Eugene, in pitifully cramped surroundings, somehow has a greater fulness of life than most boys have. From his father, especially, he draws some sense of Dionysian madness, of Falstaffian greatness. The teaching he has is very bad, but he gets somewhere, from it or from himself, a real feeling for Latin and Greek. His first money is earned on a paper route that takes him through the negro quarter, his first knowledge of women comes from a negress who is in arrears to his company, yet he is never without a sense of the wonder and pain of desire and hunger. Years ago Mr. Tarkington said: "There's just as many kinds of people in Kokomo as there is in Pekin," but he carried little conviction, for his melodrama was too obviously arranged. It is Mr. Wolfe's contribution that he has drawn an unsparing picture of character and emotion. For those who can see it, there is everywhere a wealth of vitality that is almost enough.

But it is the little less, after all, and his town grows more insufficient as Eugene grows older. There is one chapter, in manner probably inspired by "The Waste Land," describing an afternoon in the square, with a running comment of quotations.

"Give me a dope, too."
"I don't want anything," said Pudge Carr. Such drinks as made them nobly wild, not mad . . .
Mrs. Thelma Jarvis, the milliner, drew, in one swizzling guzzle, the last beaded chain of linked sweetness long drawn out from the bottom of her glass. Drink to me only with thine eyes. . . . She writhed carefully among the crowded tables, with a low rich murmur of contrition. Her voice was ever soft, gentle, and low—an excellent thing in a woman. The high light chatter of the tables dropped as she went by. For God's sake, hold your tongue and let me love!

It is good enough, the town and the soda-water, but it should be so much better! A great company of poets are called on to set the beauties of the world against their pitiful analogues in Altamont. Mr. Wolfe's criticism of the narrowness of his hero's surroundings is the more bitter because he has done it such abundant justice.

The bitterness grows when Eugene goes to the state university. Here Eugene, developing rapidly, becomes more difficult to understand, more difficult perhaps for his author to picture. It is often observable in books that begin with the birth of a boy that they grow confused as he approaches the age of the author. Here too the goat-foot that always belongs to the followers of Joyce is shown. Eugene becomes morbidly conscious of his physique, and yet unnaturally neglectful of it. He does not have his teeth filled or his hair cut; he does not bathe. He is naturally not popular, and he resents his want of popularity, in a way that is not far short of megalomania; he revolts against American sanitation and cleanliness, declaring that health is for fools, and great men have always shown signs in their lined faces of the disease of genius. Now this is hardly comprehensible, and hence hardly credible, even when the first two thirds of the book has given one the will to be as sympathetic as possible. There are possible reasons for Eugene's cult of dirt, ranging from a subconscious fear of impotence and a confused desire to be like the Horatian he-goat, *elentis mariti* (there is something like that in Mr. D. H. Lawrence), to a rankling sense of social inferiority, perverted by a fierce pride into a resolve to emulate the Fraternity Row aristocracy in nothing, not even in cleanliness (there is something like that in Mr. Wilbur Daniel Steele's "Meat"), through a dozen others. But Eugene here is not clear, as if Mr. Wolfe did not understand him, or understood him too well to think him worth explaining.

In the end Eugene is left wondering, with the same sense of the loneliness and greatness of the soul that informs the book from the beginning. "Look Homeward, Angel" though it has the faults of luxuriousness, has the great virtue that it always has the vision of something half-comprehensible behind the humdrum life, and that in the reading it carries conviction with it.

Edwin Fairley. *Christian Register,* 109 (January 9, 1930), 31.

We gather from the jacket that the publishers kept this book three years before they published it. In our judgment, they ought to have burned it. It is the small-town life of a small-town family of futilitarians. But why write of them? They could swear, and visit brothels, and quarrel no end; but what of it? Even the similes in this foul book are vile. Why? To mirror life? We could stand a little low life if there was some high ideals; but this book has none. We confess a supreme distaste for such sentences as "Came a day," and the man's vocabulary is beyond us. Here are some words culled at random: "alexin," "octopal," "funky," "convolved," "conspirate," "gabular," "adyts," "bigged," "calvered"; but why go on? One disgusting situation follows another until we are nauseated. Why did a reputable house put out such a book?

Burton Rascoe. *Arts and Decoration,* 32 (February 1930), 106.

One of the best of the recent novels is *Look Homeward, Angel,* by Thomas Wolfe. It is the story of a Southern family during a period of twenty years, with particular reference in the last part to a sensitive youth, son of a wastrel father, who through poverty, degrading experience and disillusions follows always a vision of beauty. It is powerful and dramatic, throbbing with life, dealing with drab and ugly events but with beautiful and joyous events also. Toward the end, Mr. Wolfe has disconcerted me somewhat by suddenly switching from realistic narrative to pure fantasy and I have no doubt that he will disconcert many other readers; the only reason I can advance for his having done this is that he knew no other way to end his novel. But, except for this reservation, the novel is one of power and distinction, written with a nervous intensity and with an urgent desire to present life truthfully.

Carl Van Doren. *Wings* [Literary Guild], February 1930, p. 17.

What particularly characterizes this remarkable first novel is a kind of magnificence in its manner. The magnificence is not always quite suited to the matter momentarily in hand, and it sometimes happens that this or that passage of the book will not stand the close scrutiny which looks to see whether splendid rhetoric is really supported by a sufficient substance of thought or emotion. But on the whole the magnificence of the manner is matched by the substance behind it. Mr. Wolfe has undertaken to tell the story of a Southern family through many vicissitudes, and he tells it with a fresh and moving power. No doubt the same family might have been told about in a dry, cynical, contemptuous tone, and still have been represented with a good deal of truthfulness. Mr. Wolfe, however, is a novelist of a different stamp. He sees with passion, he writes with passion. It is not enough for him, as it would probably be

impossible for him, to chronicle the Gant family in their native dustiness. He has breathed upon them till they all burn with a fierce vitality. He knows, what is often forgotten, that the heroic qualities of characters of fiction do not come altogether from the originals of the characters themselves. Small novelists can make small characters out of heroes. When characters, themselves not unmistakably great, are made heroic, it is because there was something heroic in the novelist. As it happens, American novelists have for some time seldom allowed themselves to be heroic, even if they actually were. They have preferred to be satiric or idyllic or else to repeat traditional heroic attitudes—which are never heroic at all. Mr. Wolfe, with much that is heroic in his constitution, has had the courage of his heroism. He has dared to lift his characters up above the average meanness of mankind, to let them live by their profounder impulses, and to tell about them the things which smooth, urbane novelists insist on leaving untold about men and women. Mr. Wolfe with his first novel has made himself a novelist who must be taken into account, whether he ever writes another novel or not. But he writes like a man who will write other novels, and better ones.

Franklin P. Adams. Column, "The Conning Tower." New York *World*, February 6, 1930.

There were many things in "Look Homeward, Angel" that we considered fine stuff. There was a remarkable bit of memory—or observation—in the account of Eugene's years at the State University. To us, vague about the South, it sounded like the University of Georgia or North Carolina or Alabama. There was a good piece about Eugene's work in Latin—how he always, in order to have a smooth recitation, wrote out the translations. Now this is excellent training, not only in Latin, but also in English, for it reduces the number of inaccuracies that a student may make. Besides, if you write it all out, you have to do the whole assigned lesson, and not slide over something that may not be clear in a . . . "pony." His translations in class always were smooth and good. The professor—who must have been a dull and unperceiving fellow—told him one day that he oughtn't to use a translation. Eugene, embarrassed, tried to explain, but the prof wouldn't have it. So Eugene got a pony, counterfeited hesitation over translating when he was called on, and earned the teacher's commendation for having worked harder.

There are remarkable pages of description, of persons and places, in the book. It seems—probably everybody knows it, though it was news to us— that Altamont, the scene of the book, is Asheville, N.C. Ever since the book was published the townspeople, according to a present townsperson, are raucous in their condemnation of the book and its author. "I gather," says our informant, "that the book is photographic to the last detail, and absolute autobiography—so absolute, in fact, that no one in these parts can consider it upon any basis except the emotional. You cannot get a disinterested view either of the novel or of Mr. Wolfe.

Many of the older inhabitants can name every character mentioned, and there is a great deal of sniggering and jest until the story hits too close to home to be thought funny. The surgeon who could not operate unless he were totally drunk, and the 'lung specialist' who, in his car, would chase Jews up onto the sidewalk if he could not run them down on the street, are both well known. In some instances the author does not bother even to make the name unrecognizable. Thus College Street is 'Academy Street,' Raleigh is 'Sidney,' Chapel Hill is 'Pulpit Hill,' and so forth. Street car conductors will point out every block and every turn on the way from the railroad station up past the Square, out College Street to Woodfin (Woodson), all of which was described in such detail when Gant returned from six weeks in California.

"I do not know what the Chamber of Commerce thinks of the novel (probably not much), but ministers denounce it from the pulpits, and a Mother Superior at a big Catholic hospital told the proprietor of a small pay-by-the-day library that she would confiscate and burn every copy of 'Angel, Look Downward' that came to that institution. It is not allowed on the shelves of the local Public Library.

"Having read the book and having listened to local comment, I cannot say whether I think the book literature or not. One characteristic of art, in my opinion, is that there is a power of discrimination, a blotting out of unessentials and a concentrating upon important points, whereas a photograph must needs show every detail caught by the lens when the shutter snaps, and so lacks a unified tone, as many unimportant details stand out with equal prominence. I shall be interested in a

21

novel by Mr. Wolfe on a subject not so closely related to his own emotional life."

Which is offered in spite of the fact that our informant misquoted the title of the book, spelled Mr. Wolfe's name "Wolf" throughout the copy, and spelled other words carelessly. Also, we distrust the critical judgment of a person who wants a novel "not so closely related to his own emotional life." All good novels—and most poor ones—the psychos tell us, are closely related to the author's emotional life.

Donald Davidson. "Farewell—and Hail!" Nashville *Tennessean,* February 16, 1930.

Odious and unjust as comparisons may be, one must perforce reflect now and then on the singular conjunction of events. It so happens that James Branch Cabell says farewell to the novel at the time when Thomas Wolfe makes his first appearance as a novelist. And although "The Way of Ecben" and "Look Homeward, Angel" are not of a like order, it is not stretching the truth to say that they come from the same condition of mind. It is not exactly a lamentable condition, for the by-products and incidental features are such as give delight to many persons; but it gives no firm assurance to those who may look for the shadow of a great rock in a weary land.

Mr. Cabell, already a veteran of a distinction that we must all respect, tells one of his old stories over again, or a variation of his perpetual theme that "the dream is better," that beauty

is elusive and not to be held for more than a moment, and that, nevertheless, men do well to prefer to spend their lives seeking it rashly, in spite of the certainty of defeat. . . .

. . . Here Mr. Cabell delivers his personal confidence about his generation, his own writing, and his firm determination to bring the biography of Manuel and associated projects to an end with this book. Some of his statements have already had great publicity—notably his opinion that novelists ought to cease writing at the age of 50. But not so much has been said of this comment on his own generation.

. . .

As to the perpetuity of Mr. Cabell's generation and of certain of his own works, I think we can easily give solid reassurances. But in acknowledging the refusal of himself and others to "offer a panacea," he has come very near the truth. Yet "panacea," which is spoken, I fear, out of secret and mistaken pride, is the wrong term. Mr. Cabell's generation, after subjecting us to a series of drastic purgatives, now can neither heal us nor feed us; in fact, it has rendered us practically incapable of taking nourishment at all. What Mr. Cabell should have said is that his generation has offered no convictions alive enough to straighten the disordered pattern of our lives, no sure direction that we can take with comfort, no centrality and no doctrine. For literature, this is a barren legacy, equivalent almost to a curse. To the generation of rising younger novelists, Mr. Cabell and his fellows bequeath fine words and a bucket of ashes.

In Mr. Wolfe's fine novel, I believe, one may discover more than a trace of this inheritance. One gives "Look Homeward, Angel" much the same sort of disturbed admiration as to Ernest Hemingway's works. The performance is superb; it is already enough to captivate an entire chorus of New York reviewers into warm twitterings of praise and prophecy. Yet surely virtuosity of performance is not enough. I feel the lack in Mr. Wolfe's novel of what must be called, for want of a better term, "point of view," or conviction, or purposiveness. Or to put it differently, there is evidently no real harmony between this artist and the materials he deals with; and the result is inevitably a kind of inner confusion, which, though it does not destroy the incidental merits of the book, does hurt its total effect.

The materials here are the materials of Southern life. Specifically, the story is of a large Southern family, begotten and reared in some mountain town (let us say Asheville, North Carolina). The progenitor is a stonecutter named Gant, of English-American extraction, who strays into the country, carpet-bagger-wise, in the wake of the Civil War, marries Eliza Pentland, one of an old and numerous clan, and settles down. The incurable romanticism of Gant, which vents itself all through his long life in rhetorical maundering and wild bursts of energy, is thus wedded to the stable, property-loving nature of Eliza. And this dual nature, a combination of the vulgar, and the sensitive is exhibited in their various progeny, whose history the novelist chronicles in detail. Incidentally, the chronicle of the Gant family is also the chronicle of the mountain town as "progress" and a modicum of wealth, acquired by hotel-keeping and investments, impose a veneer of change.

So far, so good. The reader is prepared to consider this to be something like an American Forsyte Saga, all in one immense volume. But the book is not a Forsyte Saga; it has, with all its detail and involved stratification, none of the solidity of Galsworthy. As it gradually develops the book is about Eugene Gant, the youngest son, and the most sensitive and poetic creature of the lot. It is almost sufficient to say of Eugene that he is both tortured by his environment and drawn to it. In the end, after a long riot of sensitivity and seeking, which often expresses itself in impulsive outbursts, much like those of the elder Gant, he simply runs away to Yankee-dom forever.

This account seems to give the book more coherence than it actually has. Eugene goes through the years of his life in alternate puzzlement and disgust, with only occasional spasm of delight. His confusion and hurt are, I am convinced, identical with the confusion and hurt of the author. The book must be considered, in a very real spiritual sense, autobiographical. Indeed, the author practically tells us in so many words that Eugene (who is evidently himself) entertains a certain hatred and loathing for the South, perhaps all the more because he recognizes it as a part of himself, which he has now honestly put on record. Therefore we must deduce that the real subject of the novel, so far as it has a single subject is some mixed and not very clear thesis, which might be stated thus; "Why Young Men Leave the South."

Is this not a tragic condition of mind for an ambitious and able novelist, at the very outset of his career? With all the equipment for his craft that could be wished—power of observation, insight into character, robustness and largeness of manner, an extensive vocabulary, and a supple style whose range includes the armchair coziness of a good Victorian method as readily as the wilder methods of Joyce and Proust (perhaps too readily)—with all this, the novelist must yet assume a negative attitude and must betray the disorder of his mind in a general desultoriness. The detail of the book is everywhere good. Take it piecemeal, and you have remarkable pictures and incidents of family and individual life, of newspaper offices in drear mornings, of the slinky, blowzy atmosphere of resort hotels, of the furtive harlotries of small towns, of youth in a Southern university (the University of North Carolina, perhaps?), of the tumult and fever of love. And perhaps few novelists of our time have created, at a single stroke, such an interesting gallery of individuals—for they are individuals, rather than types.

But brilliant and powerful as it is— even magnificent, at times—"Look Homeward, Angel" has a sickness in its marrow, a sickness of divided aims and of dislikes that are everywhere stronger than likes. "Eugene," says the author, "was quite content with any system which would give him comfort, security, enough money to do as he liked, and freedom to think, eat, drink, love, read and write what he chose. And he did not care under what form of government he lived—Republican, Democrat, Tory, Socialist or Bolshevist—if it could assure him those things." Maybe Eugene could be indifferent to "systems" without harm, but I do not think that Mr. Wolfe can be. The separation of art from life can only be injurious and confusing. Let us hope it will not be a permanent separation, for Thomas Wolfe is too fine a writer to succumb to the defeatism which might be called Cabellian.

Unsigned. *Nation*, 130 (February 19, 1930), 225.

Between the apostrophes, soliloquies, and philippics, through the torment, the despair, and the rapture of this prodigious first novel run the story of a mad clan of Georgians and the social history of that lost class which manages to escape the lot of Negroes and poor whites without becoming the eminent minority. Here is a fragment of the American scene unfamiliar to our social novels; here is "naked life" described with scope and fervor. As in the best tradition of naturalism, nothing has been omitted—nothing except that unobtrusive artifice which bestows upon a great novel the aesthetic quality, the impression of something other than life. There is novelty in the book's intensive compound of romantic fancy and irony, and there is great vitality in the episodes, but the vigor never becomes strength because it is dissipated by incoherence and the lack of a steady emphasis. Like life it is incomplete and unfinished—it might go on forever. The author gives no structural reason for it to stop.

Thomas J. Shaw, Jr. "Rare Wine Mixed With Stiff Corn." *Archive* [Duke University], 42 (March 1930), 23-24.

First published in the late autumn of last year, Mr. Wolfe's *Look Homeward, Angel,* has been uncommonly well received by both the journalistic and the serious critics of the American scene. As a work of art coming out of the confused and chaotic currents of our literature, this novel has every right to command the attention of discerning readers. Around the experiences and character of the young "boy-into-man," Eugene Gant, Mr. Wolfe weaves a poetic and ruthless but damning picture of frustrated revolt from the poverty and materialism of the world.

In slow but sure fashion the author builds up the background of the family into which the boy Eugene is born. There is the stern, hard drinking and lustfulliving father, W. O. Gant, impractical but beauty-seeking by nature. There is, in contrast, the penny-wise, and land hungry, misdirected mother, Eliza, who strives in vain to weld her heterogeneous brood into the pattern of life that is her own. Also, there are Eugene's brothers and sisters equally like himself through their common inability to drink the wine of life without draining it to the dregs of dispairing disillusionment. There are, in addition, a host of minor characters, his mother's boarders and roomers, his school ieachers, his school and university companions, his girls, and the people of his professional contacts, who by their coming and going help to fill out the canvas of the book and to explain by indirection the complex characters of the house of Gant.

Look Homeward, Angel, has within it the strong emotions and the vital reactions to life as Mr. Wolfe sees it lived by those in the lower middle class of American society. Struggle and toil and trouble, lightened by wild moments of joyous but drunken abandonment, leave little time for the cultivation of that life of artistic beauty and quiet so much needed by the sensitive Eugene. There are interludes when the boy, under the wise influence of Margaret Leonard, his teacher, and the hard but kindly control of his brother Ben, has given to him a glimpse of that social ease and peace for which his soul is questing. At the end of the chronicle, after his no less bitter university episodes, now grown to a hard but unbowed manhood, Eugene Gant stands with his face to the world. Forever behind him, but unforgotten, is the shadow of his environment.

With all that can be said in favor of *Look Homeward, Angel* as a record of human aspiration and failure, and too much cannot be said, as a novel it has obvious defects. As a book it is by far too long. Mr. Wolfe is confronted with a jumbled pile of memories and emotions. Afraid to cast off even one stone from that pile lest he omit a part of the truth, he ends by giving the whole *enmasse.* His style is at places poetically beautiful, as in the description of the death of Ben; at other times it is a mere confusion of words. Professional teachers of English would delight in using their blue pencil without mercy. They might, and probably would end, by crushing the heart out of the book.

One other weakness that *Look Home-*

ward, Angel has, comes through no fault of the author. Rather it comes, perhaps, as a logical result of his environment. Mr. Wolfe views life consistently through the eyes of a man born into the lower level of society. For the purposes of his book, at least, he looks with suspicion and distrust upon the smug life of culture and ease (and incidentally wealth) led by those very people who possess by virtue of their position in the world the freedom and refinement that is denied to Eugene. For local readers this defect in his perspective will have more than a personal interest. He is a native of Asheville and a graduate of the University of North Carolina. His none too flattering thumb-nail sketches of Raleigh, Durham, Chapel Hill, and his native town (all thinly veiled under substitute names) can hardly contribute to the local vanity of the inhabitants thereof. Indeed, his treatment of personalities is often more caustic than deserved. Such reactions come merely because of drawn blood, however, and are not to be considered in the final evaluation of the novel. Since *Look Homeward, Angel* is so largely autobiographical in its source material it would be unwise to predict what will be the result when Mr. Wolfe writes a second novel. Undigested as it is, his present venture carries with it the power of truth, and even if his future writing be but half as good he need feel no cause for shame.

Stringfellow Barr. "The Dandridges and the Gants." *Virginia Quarterly Review,* 6 (Spring 1930), 310–313.

Stark Young's "River House" and Thomas Wolfe's "Look Homeward, Angel" are both novels about the South written by Southerners. But a foreigner would not readily discover in the two books reflections of the same civilization. "River House" is a backward glance at a dying culture submerged and overwhelmed not merely by America but by its own Americanized youth. "Look Homeward, Angel" is the saga of a human soul, the soul of a boy who happened to grow up in North Carolina.

. . .

I should call "Look Homeward, Angel" the work of a genius, but that the word is somewhat overworn of late. In any case I believe it is the South's first contribution to world literature. I am aware that "Uncle Remus" is read wherever English is spoken and that in our own generation writers like DuBose Heyward and Julia Peterkin have created real literature. But it seems to me extremely significant that generally speaking the Southern writer has had to turn to the negro when he wanted to paint life as it is. The life of the white Southerner has been for political and traditional reasons so compact of legal fictions and dying social shibboleths that it has been difficult to do anything with it unless one sentimentalized. Even "River House" had to be composed in a minor key, perhaps the only key available to a defeated culture. Thomas Wolfe, on the other hand, has constructed a really tremendous novel out of the mean and sordid life of a North Carolina town. A lesser artist looking on that scene, would have become excitedly denunciatory or triumphantly analytical and would have discovered in it no more than another Zenith City or another Winesburg, Ohio. What Mr. Wolfe beheld was the travail of the human spirit, blind to its own stupidities, its cowardice, its lusts. His novel is of epic proportions, physically and spiritually.

His hero's father "reeled down across the continent" from Pennsylvania to North Carolina and spawned a family of children as terrifyingly different from each other as most brothers and sisters really are: Helen, with her tempestuous affections and antagonisms and her inherited bibulous tendencies; Luke, with his genius for acquaintance and his incapacity for real feeling; Steve, whining, boasting, and stinking of nicotine; Eugene, about whom this epic really centers; Ben, with his fierce spiritual isolation, perpetually murmuring over his shoulder to his particular angel: "God! Listen to that, won't you!" Above them all the father, W. O. Gant, towers like the elder Karamazov, screaming profanity and obscenity at his wife and children, reciting eternally from Shakespeare and a dozen other bards, roaring for every one's pity, drinking himself into cancer, and being hauled out of brothels by his eldest son.

Which of Thomas Wolfe's particular skills has contributed most to this book's making? Over and over again his prose slips into sheer poetry. Over and over again one ironic sentence creates a character. But above all his loving pity for all of lost humanity gives his work that religious quality one gets in Dostoevsky.

Does Mr. Wolfe add anything to our comprehension of the South? It is a difficult question to answer. His book is not about the South of Major Dandridge at all. Indeed, that Old South is not very obvious to anybody who ever saw "Altamont," which is the name Mr. Wolfe gives his native Asheville. The Gants are certainly not typical of the Southern upper class, though neither are they quite what that upper class means by "common." They are socially unclassifiable. "Look Homeward, Angel" is not concerned with the problem of a surviving Southern culture. When its author mentions the South it is chiefly to speak of "the exquisite summer of the South," the "opulent South," or the "fabulous South." The natural beauty of the land lies deep in his blood but the politico-social problems of its people touch him scarcely at all.

I do not believe that Mr. Wolfe's novel has invalidated one iota the significance of whatever the Old South produced of human beauty; and I am certain that Mr. Wolfe himself would feel soiled at being thought of as a "debunker." But I do think that he is the first novelist of the new dispensation in the Southern States, the first to grow up sufficiently outside of River House to look with a child's eyes at the life about him. Whenever, as in Poland or Italy or Ireland, the sense of a culture distorted by outside pressure has directed the artist's eyes to programs like national resurgence, the highest art has been the chief sufferer. The South has labored precisely under that handicap; unable to recapture a social synthesis that Reconstruction had destroyed, it had not the heart, or the stomach either, to adopt frankly the American solution of life. Nor has Mr. Wolfe adopted it, but his conflict is no longer the political conflict of the South and the North but the artistic conflict of his own spirit with the souls about him. With "Look Homeward, Angel" the South has contributed to the literature of the world a novel, strongly provincial in its flavor, universal in its terrible tragedy.

Unsigned. *Booklist,* 26 (May 1930), 315.

Nothing is omitted in this long realistic first novel about the large tempestuous Gant family in a small southern town. The first twenty years of the youngest son's life, filled with rapture, hatred, shyness, romanticism, are covered in great detail. The story is chaotic, sordid, often incoherent, but it has flashes of vigorous and ironic writing which indicate real ability.

Sinclair Lewis. Press Conference on Winning the Nobel Prize. New York *Times,* November 6, 1930, p. 27.

. . .

Sinclair Lewis will not reject the Nobel Prize, as he did the Pulitzer Prize in 1926. This he made clear yesterday afternoon in an interview with representatives of the press of his country and Europe at the offices of his publishers, Harcourt, Brace & Co. He will accept the award, he said, because it is "an international prize with no strings tied."

. . .

"The Pulitzer Prize, on the other hand, is cramped by the provision of Mr. Pulitzer's will that the prize shall be given 'for the American novel published during the year which shall best present the wholesome atmosphere of American life and the highest standard of American manners and manhood.' This suggests not actual literary merit but an obedience to whatever code of good form may chance to be popular at the moment.

"As a result of this the Pulitzer Prize has been given to some merely mediocre novels along with other admirable novels. It is sufficient criticism of the prize to say that in the last few years it has not been awarded to Cabell's 'Jurgen,' Dreiser's 'An American Tragedy,' Hemingway's 'A Farewell to Arms,' Wolfe's 'Look Homeward, Angel,' or Cather's 'A Lost Lady.' "

Mr. Lewis said that he would go to Stockholm with Mrs. Lewis to receive the prize, which he understood would be presented on Dec. 10.

The American writer to whom he paid the highest tribute was Thomas Wolfe, a young author who has written only one novel, "Look Homeward, Angel." If Mr. Wolfe keeps up the standard which he has set in this work he "may have a chance to be the greatest American writer," Mr. Lewis asserted.

"In fact, I don't see why he should not be one of the greatest world writers.

His first book is so deep and spacious that it deals with the whole of life."

. . .

Sinclair Lewis. "The American Fear of Literature," address on receiving the Nobel Prize in Literature, December 12, 1930. *The Man From Main Street: Selected Essays and Other Writings 1904–1950,* ed. Harry E. Maule and Melville H. Cane. New York: 1953, p. 17.

". . . there is Thomas Wolfe, a child of, I believe, thirty or younger, whose one and only novel, *Look Homeward, Angel,* is worthy to be compared with the best in our literary production, a Gargantuan creature with great gusto of life. . . ."

Merle Johnson. "American First Editions." *Publishers' Weekly,* 120 (August 15, 1931), 615.

America seems to be searching for new literary formulas such as the Old World has acclaimed in James Joyce.

Submitted here are two modern au-

thors whose work may be precursors of the new era. Sufficiently inclusive from the practical viewpoint of this column, the following books in first editions of both authors are today at a premium.

WILLIAM FAULKNER 1897-

. . .

THOMAS (CLAYTON) WOLFE 1900-

Compiled by Capt. Louis Henry Cohn "Look Homeward, Angel." *New York,* 1929.

The first edition carried a dustjacket which had printed on it a picture of the author and a brief autobiography. The English edition, *London* (1930), carried a dustjacket on the reverse of which was printed the author's foreword to the novel. The first printing of the English edition so stated on the copyright page.

"Carolina Folk Plays," (Second Series) *New York,* 1924.

Compiled and with an introduction by Frederick H. Koch. Contains: "The Return of Buck Gavin, the Tragedy of a Mountain Outlaw," by Wolfe.

Mr. Wolfe is at present engaged on another work which is to be published next spring. The tentative title had been "October Fair" but since this title may apply to a projected series of novels in all probability the forthcoming book will bear another name.

Checklist of Additional Reviews

Weekly [Chapel Hill], October 18, 1929.

Tar Heel [University of North Caro-

29

lina], October 24, 1929.

"Alumni Write Books." *University of North Carolina Alumni Review*, 18 (November 1929), 45.

John Chamberlain. *Bookman*, 70 (December 1929), 449-50.

Robert Raynolds. "Gargantuan First Novel." *Scribner's Magazine*, 86 (December 1929), "Literary Sign-Posts," 34, 38.

John Mebane. "Laughter and Tears." *University of North Carolina Magazine*, 59 (February 2, 1930), 4.

May Johnston Avery. "Asheville People Smart Under Lash of Genius." Charlotte *Observer*, March 30, 1930.

Richard Aldington. "American Novelists." London *Sunday Referee*, July 6, 1930, p. 6.

"Look Homeward, Angel." London *Times Literary Supplement*, No. 1486 (July 24, 1930), p. 608. Reprinted No. 2746 (September 17, 1954), p. lxxxviii.

Frank Swinnerton. "Where Are the Story-tellers?" London *Evening News and Evening Mail*, August 8, 1930, p. 8.

Gerald Gould. London *Observer*, August 17, 1930, p. 5.

Felix Walter. "Thomas Wolfe." *Canadian Forum*, 11 (October 1930), 25-26.

Notes

OF TIME AND THE RIVER

A LEGEND OF MAN'S HUNGER

IN HIS YOUTH

By

Thomas Wolfe

*"Who knoweth the spirit of man that goeth upward, and
the spirit of the beast that goeth downward to the earth?"*

CHARLES SCRIBNER'S SONS

· NEW YORK

1935

Of Time and the River

Richard Sheridan Ames. "Wolfe, Wolfe!" *American Spectator*, 3 (January 1935), 5-6.

The American reader, fooled so often by his critical Cassandras, is himself loathe to acclaim an incipient fine talent which appears quietly without incriminating *kudos*.

Nevertheless, "Look Homeward, Angel" has gone through six large editions since its publication in 1929 and Thomas Wolfe's more casual prose has practically subsidized *Scribner's Magazine* during lean years. His major germination, "Of Time and the River," an immense novel of 450,000 words, is at last in the hands of the printer and the earlier work, recently canonized as a popular reprint Giant, may at length introduce our only young writer of any considerable stature to a wider public.

Wolfe, whose powerful, often ungainly prose placed him at once among the generic novelists of tradition, has not lacked individual praise. Speaking before the Nobel Olympians at Stockholm in 1930 Sinclair Lewis said: "Thomas Wolfe, a child . . . whose one and only novel, 'Look Homeward, Angel,' is worthy to be compared with the best in our literary production, a Gargantuan creature with great gusto of life." And Percy Mackaye termed Wolfe's shorter work "quintessential poetry."

But there has been no organized cry of "Wolfe, Wolfe!", no publisher's pyrotechnics. Though it seems almost too good to be true, a young American writer has emerged in the fulness of his initial power without being swaddled in ruinous comparisons or suffocated by that contemporaneity surcharged with doom which gives him his blatant hour of photographs, autographs and literary teas—and certain extinction.

To my knowledge no one has yet written that Thomas Wolfe "writes like an angel." He has not run afoul of the law, the book clubs, the Pulitzer prize, or the literary lobbyists who inflate reputations and are effectively laxative in purging the reader's consciousness of all taste while confecting their best-sellers.

Wolfe is, almost literally, a Scribner virgin.

He is that *rara avis,* a modern author who writes, who writes diligently and enormously from a kind of inner solitude. Gertrude Stein didn't hatch him. He is indigenous to America and lives—of all prosaic places—in Brooklyn. His prenuptial liaison with letters was placid, for he did not learn about life from the insides of a shark or the small talk of Pamplona *aficionados.* He has been mercifully reticent about himself, and if his first novel grazed in the pastures of autobiography it did not come to a full stop beside a narcissist pool nor was its general objectivity blemished.

Wolfe's defects and faults of artistic discipline can be judged in time by the proper criteria of competent critics. The general public is permitted to read him for what he is worth and has not been forced to speculate as to whether he is a love-child or a hermaphrodite, a Marxian or post-Humanist throwback. His is the name above the printed work, that alone, and properly. The fortunate iconoclasm of such a position is attested to by the dislocated launchings of the apostolic Paul Engle, Paul Horgan, William Saroyan, Tess Schlesinger, *et al.* One does not need to get Van Wyck Brooks from the shelf to fathom the plight of the writer in America. Exploitation is the first frost that nips the careers of the youngsters. It seems to sell mouth-washes, but it is fallible in building up authors' reputations.

Some new writers possess creditable competence and it is no easy matter for them to get a hearing. No Upton Sinclair has arisen with an EPIC plan for the economics of literature. As things stand, the unendowed author who creates even passably worth-while stuff has no right to expect that his work will support him. If he is versatile and predatory he may wrangle handouts from the radio, the cinema, or the newspaper syndicates. But the reasonable dividends from his own profession, practised conscientiously, won't supply him with a change of galluses annually or any personal real estate more impressive than a lean-to. Unless he subsists on the government pay-

rolls, a young writer must construe self-expression as something of a luxury—of no value economically and of scant interest to other beleaguered citizens outside his own kind.

Only the ablest can hope to survive indifference and the lack of cash. A literary tyro who expects a villa at Cannes or some private Vallambrosa in Beverly Hills as the result of one hastily spewed volume will, in the vernacular, get stung very badly. The youth with something important to say may experience the devil of a time while he says it, but his progress will be normal. His middle years of mature craftsmanship should provide reasonable security and stimulation sufficient for enviable accomplishment. Such writers may have to wait a decade before their names will mean anything in public libraries, but once there they will stick. They will be read because they have conceived something memorable, not merely a temporary gland stimulator.

One magazine has referred to the "incomparable richness" of Thomas Wolfe's work. Even his poorest pieces have vitality and his best, like "No Door," were conceived by a prodigous, untrammelled imagination and executed with such robust energy that one is forced to ponder again the source and resources of genius—an uncommon procedure in these days when we have flung at us the most provocative examples of what genius certainly is not.

The fate of a writer whose honesty and power prevent him from becoming a morbid fashion, whose creative sources are artesian rather than lightly sub-surface, who lacks critical coddling and the notoriety furnished by fraternal Peeping Toms, is currently a matter for

34

intense speculation. Contemporary literary trends are as hard to chart as the ecstatic explorations of the New Deal. It is already a toss-up whether the work of the ascendant proletarian school or the intermittent swan songs of the writers who decorated the dreary post-war decade will be forgotten first. While the critics are sorting out the infant Whitmans and dolling up Iowa's Engle to be America's Rupert Brooke, Thomas Wolfe has the field of the traditional novel almost to himself. He projects no new formula and invents no dewy patois. He seems content to portray character, a love of earth and sky, and the troubled souls of men, all built into an impressive edifice by a poet's integration.

Can he be the real thing, at last?

Isabel M. Paterson. Column, "Turns With a Bookworm." New York *Herald Tribune Books,* February 24, 1935, p. 18.

. . .

Thomas Wolfe is dishing them up liberally in his new book, "Of Time and the River." . . .

It looks like a best seller—not a record-breaker, but a handsome sale. . . . Harry Scherman wrote us amicably (in reference to "Salah and His American"), that he still doesn't know what makes a book sell. . . . We have gone into that several times, but don't mind repeating—it is excess. . . . There are various elements of popularity: action, sentimentality, striking character, comedy, timeliness. . . . Whatever it is,

the best seller gives you more of it for your money. . . . Sheer literary quality comes last in immediate sales value, but lasts longest. . . . Mr. Wolfe is a lavish writer. . . . He steps up the scale of everything—all his principal characters are highly exaggerated. . . . They are seven feet tall, with megaphone voices. . . . We don't mind; he does manage to keep up the excitement. . . . But it might be an interesting experiment to take one of his chapters and eliminate all the superlatives, the adjectives indicating altitude, volume, and violence. . . . Step it down again to life size, and see what would remain. . . . Let the characters say what they have to say, instead of roaring, whining, stuttering or gasping. . . . The remainder, we feel sure, would still be interesting, but would it impress the genteel critics so much? . . .

Exaggeration, of course, is quite valid in the arts. . . . Life-size in sculpture is somehow unsatisfactory—the heroic scale is about one-seventh larger than life. . . . It is selection by emphasis, and there must be selection. . . . Mr. Wolfe has relied on it too exclusively, but that's how he sees things. . . . He automatically doubles all measures. . . . We could pick out one amusing instance in the book from personal knowledge, but it is not necessary. . . . When little Willie reported excitedly that there were a hundred cats in the barn, and a count showed only "our old cat and another," the phrase nevertheless justified itself. . . . We like human beings a little better than these towering monsters, but we prefer the latter to the nullities of "behavioristic" fiction. . . .

. . .

[Editors Note: Only the two ellipses

in the center of the page are editorial deletions. All other ellipses occur in the original article.]

Lewis Gannett. Column, "Books and Things." New York *Herald Tribune,* March 8, 1935, p. 17.

Thomas Wolfe writes like a mighty, furious Paul Bunyan, with the passionate love of America of a Walt Whitman and the enraged adolescent idealism of a Shelley also pulsing in his veins. The 912 pages of the long-awaited sequel to "Look Homeward, Angel"—"Of Time and the River"—tumble, pour, roar, sing with the savage joy and fury of a man who must be almost the wildest and most copious of contemporary writers.

It is an autobiographical novel—the story of that same Eugene Gant who, in "Look Homeward, Angel," grew up in the state of Catawba (North Carolina) and stormed through the state university. Here he takes graduate work in dramatic art at Harvard under "Professor Hatcher" (G. P. Baker); he teaches fools and a few wise Jews at New York University; he invades Oxford and discards England; he souses a drunken path through France, and there discovers the fleeting quality of time and the passionate Americanness of his own soul.

All the time he writes: "The words were wrung out of him in a kind of bloody sweat, they poured out of his finger tips, spat out of his snarling throat like writhing snakes; he wrote them with his heart, his brain, his sweat, his guts; he wrote them with his blood, his spirit; they were wrenched out of the last secret source and substance of his life. And in those words was packed the whole image of his bitter homelessness. . . ."

This man thinks, writes, reads, eats, talks—I almost added "loves," but he hardly loves at all—gigantically. "Within a period of ten years he read at least 20,000 volumes—deliberately the number is set low—and opened the pages and looked through many times that number." When he quotes from his diary, the words are "picked at random from the ferment of ten thousand pages and a million words . . . a picture of a man's soul and heart—the image of his infuriate desire—caught hot and instant, drawn flaming from the forge of his soul's agony"—and you believe him as you scan his tempestuous pages.

Walt Whitman heard America singing and lovingly catalogued its names:

Okonee, Koosa, Ottawa, Monongahela, Sauk, Natchez, Chattahoochee, Kaqueta, Oronoco, Wabash, Miami, Saginaw, Chippewa, Oshkosh, Walla-Walla.

I doubt if any one since Whitman has taken such sensuous delight in American names; though "Of Time and the River" is cast in prose and catalogued as fiction, you could extract from it poems such as the pale philosophers and ecstatic rhymesters of today seldom approach:

"In the red-oak thickets at the break of day, long hunters lay for bear—the rattle of arrows in laurel leaves, the war-cries found the painted buttes, and the majestical names of the Indian nations—.
. . ."

Or that song of rivers (the book is full of the imagery of rivers) with its quick, deft scorn for the oft-sung, petty rivers of the Old World:

"By the waters of life: the names of great mouths, great maws, the vast, wet, coiling, never-glutted and unending snakes that drink the continent. Where, sons of men, and in what other land will you find others like them, and where can you match the mighty music of their names? . . ."

This turbulent and enormous "novel" is full of singing passages about the power, beauty, magic, fury, hunger, savagery of this land. Wolfe is obsessed with the importance of living every second of life to the full, and with a dark realization that life is slipping fast. Death does not disturb him. "It is not the death of the dying that is terrible," he makes his family doctor say. "It is the death of the living." He has a savage hate of fear, and of gray, thwarted people who live in fear of life. Sometimes, in his exuberance he tumbles almost into absurdity.

The man is young; his very regrets of youth have a touch of persistent adolescence about them. "All youth is bound to be misspent," he proclaims sententiously. "Youth is something which only young men have, and which only old men know how to use." "Immortal drunkenness"; he sings, "What tribute can we ever pay, what song can we ever sing, what swelling praise can ever be sufficient to express the joy, the gratefulness and the love which we, who have known youth and hunger in America, have owed to alcohol? . . . We were young, and drunk, and twenty, and the power of mighty poetry was within us, and the glory of the great earth lay before us—because we were young and drunk and twenty, and could never die!"

But this is not the book of Eugene Gant, of Thomas Wolfe, alone. It is the story of a pilgrimage through life, crowded with the sharply sketched portraits of the myriad people whom Wolfe—Gant—met in his wanderings. Here are the pitiful family in Catawba; the thwarted Boston Irish and equally thwarted Boston Puritans; the esthetes of Baker's class—that story alone is enough to excuse President Lowell for letting Baker go to Yale; here is an unforgettable scene at the death of Eugene's husky father, when the boy learns that mechanics, not bank officers, were his father's real friends; here are an East Side Jewish family and the dead respectables at the University Place hotel; the moonlit empty beauty of the life of the Hudson River aristocracy; the scared, lonely Rhodes scholars vainly trying to become English aristocrats; a memorable, hopeless British middle-class family; and equally unforgettable, scheming but frugally kind French countess; the drunken party in France—hundreds, thousands, Wolfe himself would say millions, of individual characters.

The story ends in the air, with a vision of a girl's face, a story to be continued in the next mighty volume. It gets nowhere; but it is an enlivening experience to read it. I emerged, after reading steadily for two days, not overwhelmed but refreshed.

Herschel Brickell. Column, "Books on Our Table." New York *Post*, March 8, 1935, p. 7.

If you see crowds gathered in the neighborhood of bookstores today the reason will be that Thomas Wolfe's second novel, "Of Time and the River," is at last available after many postponements. It is five years since the publication of Mr. Wolfe's "Look Homeward, Angel."

If the bookstores are empty for the next couple of months the reason will be that the people who bought Mr. Wolfe's second novel are spending their time at home reading it.

For it is, as you may know by this time, a work of some 450,000 words, or 912 pages, and written in a variety of styles, none of which makes for rapid reading.

It may be as well to try to answer the most important question that can be asked about any book first, before going into the details. This is, of course, does the Wolfe novel seem worth the time it will take to read it?

My answer is an emphatic yes. I felt when I finally finished it after what seemed to me weeks in its company that I had been associating with an active volcano, a cyclone and a couple of comets; in other words, a bit dizzy, but very well aware that I had had an experience. I can still hear Mr. Wolfe's "demented winds" roaring and screaming in my ears, can still feel the lift and surge of his rhapsodic passages on America, gloriously Whitmanesque.

"Of Time and the River" is a direct sequel to "Look Homeward, Angel," the novel which made Mr. Wolfe one of the most discussed of living writers, therefore autobiographical, and when you are with Mr. Wolfe you are in the presence of a personality that is like nothing so much as a force of nature.

You can't, if you are of ordinary stature and vitality, believe completely in his gigantic world of shadow shapes, where everything is magnified and in-

tensified, but you will be fascinated just the same, swept along on the tides of his passions, carried away with the gargantuan appetite of a man who wishes to swallow life whole when most of us are content to chew a tiny fragment in our frightened and dyspeptic way.

There is an additional reason why "Of Time and the River" is without any question the event of the publishing season.

This is because it carries the title of a vast autobiographical novel of which "Look Homeward, Angel" was the beginning. The first four books, says the publishers' announcement, have already been written and the third, "October Fair," follows directly upon the present book in point of time.

. . .

An ambitious project in which an American of our own day relates the symbolical search for his father, which is the theme of the Wolfe books, an autobiographical novel that will reach a total of around 3,000,000 words if it is completed, thus making Marcel Proust's "Remembrance of Things Past" look like a novelette.

Mr. Wolfe writes with an inhuman, a "possessed," energy; he has produced 2,000,000 words in the five years that have elapsed since the publication of "Look Homeward, Angel," so there is no reason to doubt that "Of Time and the River" will finally stand complete upon the library shelves.

The realization that the present book, then, is merely a section of a tremendous screen upon which Mr. Wolfe expects to project the account of his wanderings in time and space makes it a reviewer's duty, I think, to talk more about what there is in the present volume than to try to write a critical essay on the place of the author in world literature.

. . .

His novel is the saga of a lusty youth burning with a love of life and suffering from an insatiable hunger for sensations of the mind and body. Here is an example, which a daily book reviewer read with an inevitable feeling of envy, Mr. Wolfe's description of Gant's reading:

> Now he would prowl the stacks of the library at night, pulling books out of a thousand shelves and reading them like a madman . . . Within a period of ten years he read at least 20,000 volumes—deliberately the number is set low—and opened the pages and looked through many times that number. Dryden said this about Ben Jonson: "Other men read books but he read libraries"—and so now it was with this boy.

This is just a suggestion of the gusty and tempestuous quality of Mr. Wolfe's young man in search of a father, whose relation to the world is what the book is about.

But if it be necessary to await the completion of Mr. Wolfe's whole task before we can get the full effect of what he is trying to say to us about Man and the Universe, and, more especially, about us, for his book is profoundly American in spite of his occasional confusion of himself with his country and all its inhabitants, there are many things in it to be enjoyed as it stands.

Things, for example, such as pages relating to Bascom Hawke, who appeared in Scribner's Magazine some months ago, or relating to Professor Hatcher and his students, or what Gant found out about the English, or of his amusing experiences in France with a broken-down Countess, or some of the rhapsodic passages already mentioned.

A multitude, a confusion of heaped-up riches, given form of a sort, a mass of ore, some of it clean-minted, some of it not, which is rather baffling to the assayer who has to work against time as do those of us who write about books every day.

There is much more I should like to say about Mr. Wolfe's book; some things I should like to quote from it, for example. Also there is comment to be made upon the way he has woven his tapestry, in which the pattern is often worked out with great cunning. And particularly the curious depth of feeling about America and the passionate understanding of it throughout the book, a feeling that transcends sectional boundaries and embraces a continent.

I hesitate to use superlatives, particularly when I am still under the spell of a book that is as moving as "Of Time and the River," but is it out of place to suggest that perhaps there is a chance at least that Mr. Wolfe's big book will be the Great American Novel so long talked about, that his incredible vitality will enable him to do something many of us have thought would never be done?

A nice question for the future . . . In the meantime, any one who reads "Of Time and the River" is in for a rare and memorable experience. Maybe it's genius; anyway, it's something strange and overpowering we stand in the presence of in this book.

Henry Seidel Canby.
"The River of Youth."
*Saturday Review of
Literature*, 11 (March 9,
1935), 529–530.

There was much laughter when years ago D. H. Lawrence in his "Studies in Classical American Literature" described an Old Indian Devil who was always plaguing the great Americans with sudden flushes of paganism, great resurgences of sex, and obstinate maladjustments between their European souls and their unfenced continent. It is not so funny now, for some devil, Indian, Marxian, or psycho-analytic, has surely been torturing the best American writers of our era. They squirm, they lash, they spit out filth and imprecations, they whine, they defy. They are not at ease in this Zion of our ancestors.

For Thomas Wolfe in his new novel, "Of Time and the River," the curse is impotence. There is for him a brooding loneliness in the American landscape which drives the man-mass into a nervous activity of hurrying on trains, motors, subways, airplanes, a restlessness which drives the sensitive writer into an agony of frustration because the towns, the cities, the countryside oppress him with unrealized and inexpressible energy. It is a country that grips the imagination and lets the heart go, a country in which humanity mixed and at the boiling point—black Negro flesh, amber Jewish flesh, dark, light, sanguine—is incited by fierce energies toward no end but movement and frustration, a country where life has sacrificed its mass for its force, and

the observer can neither hold on or let go of a rush of experience that always seems to have, yet never quite achieves, a meaning.

The impotence of America is an impotence of expression. When in Wolfe's novel Gene Gant's train shrieks through the night on his first journey northward, he feels the enormous push of continental energy and can rise to it only by drunken hysteria. When in the last chapter he takes the ocean liner from France for home, he sees that vast organization of speed and change floating above his tender, and knows that it is America again, clutching at his sensitive spirit. In three hundred years the American soul has not made itself a home.

And hence the strange impulse toward autobiography which has carried so many Americans to the verge of incoherence!—Melville in "Moby Dick" wrestling with transcendental interpretations of his restlessness, or Whitman in the "Song of Myself" blatantly proclaiming his identity with the expansiveness of a continent. They cannot write novels, these rebel Americans, there is nothing stable to write of. They can only proclaim their egoes, in defiance of the inhumanity of a continent which the energy of their race has exploited but to which they are not yet assimilated. Hence an impotence which prevents complete expression, and books which are, as the eighteenth century would have said, far more nature than art.

"Of Time and the River," time being the time of youth, the river that mysterious current of life which flows under the perplexing surface of America, is the epitome, after so many books, of the troublous and disintegrating years of the twenties when Mr. Wolfe was young. And those who wish to get in fullest and most impassioned form the spiritual record of those years, or who would see as in a news-reel the typical scenes of that period as youth saw them, will find, if they are persistent, what they want in this book, which is neither fiction nor autobiography, but both.

For although the scene of Mr. Wolfe's long expected narrative changes from North Carolina to the biting realities and warped romance of New England, from New England to the aloofness of Oxford, from Oxford to the loneliness of an American's France, yet it is a wholly American book, one of the most American books of our time. It is in the direct tradition of those earlier anguished spirits and great seekers on our soil, Thoreau, Melville, Whitman. It is in the tradition, but with a momentous difference for which the break-up of the twenties and Mr. Wolfe's own idiosyncrasies are responsible. Yet if I should wish to know what these twenties meant to an American youth still asking the questions asked by his spiritual ancestors, "Why are we here?", "What does this continent mean to us?", "What are we becoming?" I should go to this book. If I fail to give a clear account of Mr. Wolfe's thousand-page story of how a passion-driven youth tried to tear all knowledge from the Harvard library, all experience from America, all wisdom from Europe, and to pluck out, in his twenties, the secret of the loneliness and the fascination of America, forgive me. Have you ever tried to review the Encyclopedia Britannica?

Mr. Wolfe's odd thousand pages are condensed but not adequately described in the paragraphs above. He calls them fiction, and fiction they are of the kind that he put into "Look Homeward, Angel," but better organized, more poetical where poetical, more sharply realistic when realistic; and they are to be followed by a million words more or less in which the ego which is the raison d'etre of them all is to conclude the story. But fiction in the strict sense they are not, nor story, nor drama, but rather spiritual autobiography in which the thousand incidents, many of them trivial, and the dozens of characters, many of them extraordinary, have as their excuse for being that a youth met them on his way. Plot there is none. Structure in the ordinary narrative sense, there is none. It is a picaresque novel with the distraught mind of a poet of the twenties as *picaro,* and the incidents adventures in seeking a spiritual home.

To be more precise, this book is a study of American dualism and it is this which gives it poignancy. Leaf through it and you will see as in a moving picture successive moments of prose and poetry. Here are the fleshy people of an intensely actual Carolina, of a literal Boston, and of a photographic France. No reporter could have done them more vividly as news, and indeed Wolfe is a great reporter. No one of them is usual, indeed for such a passionate student of humanity no man or woman could be merely usual; most of them are eccentrics, half mad from pain, or love, or greed, or vanity, or frustration; or wholly lost in what is really fantasy, like Starwick the homosexual, or the pathetic collegiate Weaver, or the gross sensualist Flood who is like some mushroom sprung from, yet alien to, the good earth. And between these flashes of intimate, literal humanity from the man-swarm, the novel leaves the literal entirely and in a poetic prose that owes much to Whitman and a little to Joyce, but has become Wolfe's own, rises into a chorus of anguish, perplexity, and delight, which chants the loneliness and the impotence and the beauty of this America, and struggles to break through to some solution which will satisfy the seeker, who is the youth Gant, the hero, and the excuse for all this profusion of words.

And linking the two worlds is the decaying but still mighty figure of the Father, the old stone cutter who was the center of "Look Homeward, Angel." Dying (and his death scene is Mr. Wolfe at his best), he still dominates the imagination of the youth, for he in his vast energy and incredible vitality is the old America where man almost became worthy of his continent; and in his cancerous decline, in his frustrated career, and in the immense confusion of his brain, he symbolizes what has happened in a twentieth century in which there seems to be no graspable relation between the prose and the poetry of a continent.

So much for the purpose of this novel. Its achievement is less. With all its richness of detail, its passion, its poetry, and its intense realism of contemporary life, there is an impotence in this book like the impotence Wolfe ascribes to his America.

In America it is an impotence of wandering men at home wherever wheels carry them yet never strong enough to grip the continent and make it serve their happiness. In this America, "so casual and rich and limitless and free," they become arid or lonely or broken, or have got the "new look" of the machine-ridden masses. With Mr. Wolfe the impotence is exactly equivalent. His imagination has provided him with a great theme and his accurate memory flashes infinite exact detail of the life of which he intends to make his book. But he cannot control the theme or reduce his substance to a medium. He will write neither poetry nor prose, but both. He will not be content with the literal autobiographic description of men and events which his journalistic sense supplies so readily but must intersperse with passages of sheer fantasy or poetical uplift. He will stick neither to fiction nor to fact. Hence the reader never enters into that created world of the real novelist which has its own laws, its own atmosphere, its own people, but goes from here to there in Mr. Wolfe's own life, seeing real people as he saw them, and often recognizing them (as with George Pierce Baker in Professor Hatcher, and many others) not as created characters but as literal transcripts from the life. So that the effect is always of being in two worlds at once, fiction and fact, until curiosity takes the place of that ready acceptance of a homogeneous life in the imagination which a fine novel invariably permits. You are forced to read this book as an autobiography with a poetic accompaniment, and for the first five or six hundred pages the personality of the narrator, this passion-driven youth, is too vague, too unimportant to hold suspense, so that it is for the objective realistic incidents that one reads and these change and succeed one another without relation or real consequence, except that one ego experiences them all. Hence a book that is verbose, and which seems much more verbose, much more repetitive than it is. Not until well past its vast middle is the reader caught up and carried on. Before that he reads either a passage of extravagant but vital poetry (drunken poetry in this quotation)—

42

Casey Jones! Open the throttle, boy, and let her rip! Boys, I'm a belly-busting bastard from the State of old Catawba.

. . .

Or he reads a complete realistic episode in which the Pentlands snigger "k, k, k, k, k," pull at their cleft chins, smoulder with their hidden fires. Or an aggressive Jew boy pulls out the stopper of young Gant's wrath, and makes a friend for life. Or an attempted seduction. Or a satire on silly young Harvard intellectuals poohing and pahing and saying "Ace" for "Yes." Immense power, immense variety, little control, less continuity, and an almost complete failure to make this true epic of longing youth in a lonely, disintegrated America either drama, fiction, poetry, satire, any *one* thing, *one* medium of expression, into which the imagination of the reader can enter and stay, for more than twenty pages, at home.

I think that this novel, like many other fiery and ambitious American books—like Melville's "Pierre," like many of Whitman's poems, like the now forgotten romantic-philosophic extravaganzas so common in the magazines of a century ago—is an artistic failure. And Mr. Wolfe's books, as wholes, will continue to be artistic failures until he finds and controls a medium in which the ego is sublimated into an imagination less involved in the immediate circumstances of his life. Yet it is an important book, and Mr. Wolfe is an important writer. He has more material, more vitality, more originality, more gusto than any two contemporary British novelists put together, even though they may be real novelists and he is not. He stands to them as Whitman stood to the wearied "Idylls of the King." And he entirely escapes the sordid, whining defeatism of so many of his American contemporaries. I am not fool enough to try to teach him how to write. No one can do that. He can write like his own angel now, he can make speech that is a new speech in fiction and yet unmistakably authentic, he can strike off flashing pictures.

. . .

But he has not yet made his book. He has poured out his heart into a mould, over a mould, spilling through a thousand pages. He has tried to be philosopher, poet, journalist-observer, satirist, story teller, historian, and dreamer, not all at once which is quite possible, but one after the other, which cannot be done in a book, which, like a man, no matter how complex, should be integrated, harmonious, homogeneous, and unmistakably not many but one.

Burton Rascoe. "The Ecstasy, Fury, Pain and Beauty of Life: Thomas Wolfe Sings and Shouts in His Gargantuan New Novel." New York *Herald Tribune Books*, March 10, 1935, pp. 1, 2.

Thomas Wolfe has chaos in him and he is giving birth to a whirling nebula. Sometimes he writes like an intoxicated Gargantua bestriding the world and bellowing of pain and beauty. Again he is like a normal, virile and elephan-

43

tine Proust roaring his minute remembrances of things past in the sententious and stentorian manner of the Victor Hugo of "la Légende des Siècles" and "Postscriptum de ma vie," the Hugo who cracked hickory nuts with his molars in his seventies and identified himself with Aeschylus, Isaiah and Dante.

Thomas Wolfe has a magnificent malady: it may be called gigantism of the soul. All the conditions of his life have determined this malady and, because he is also lyrically and vociferously articulate, we have a voice in this novel which sounds as if it were from demons, gods and seraphim—in chorus—and, strangely, a voice speaking of intimate and common things—of a boy's leaving his family in a boom town in the South and going away to college, of his studying there and of what he read and saw and thought and heard, of his awed introduction to the metropolis of New York, and of his seeking a key to the mystery of life in a memory-haunted, nostalgic, fevered and insatiate search in London, in Paris, in Provence and, finally, of the lonely, wild, tempestuous, independent youth's return to America, and his capitulation to love. . . .

While reading Thomas Wolfe it is requisite or advisable to suspend one's ordinary critical faculties, trained, sharpened and selective as they may be by familiarity with the hard, clear image, the deft concision, the precise pattern of much of our modern writing; for Wolfe is lush and exuberant, word-drunk like an Elizabethan, with utterable and unutterable music pounding in his brain. To the calm, the phlegmatic, the insensitive, the sophisticated, the disillusioned or the imperturbable reader much of Thomas Wolfe's first

and second novels (the novel under review is the second of a planned six) may appear like the rough draft of multitudinous notes from which a novel, in the more ordinary sense of the term, might be selected, edited, polished and builded. But, like the novels of Rabelais, Sterne and Fielding these are not novels by any prosaic or academic definition. They are a deluge of intensity.

Thomas Wolfe makes a frenzied and beautiful effort to arrest time and to catch in words not only beauty but the very evanescence of beauty. Every instant, every moment in life, however trivial appearing, is pregnantly important to him. He cries in anguish and agitation at our obtuseness. "Nothing is trivial. What you said and did today, the glance you gave a stranger, your purchase of an evening paper at a subway kiosk, your brief momentary thought of your grandfather and of the kind of man he was, that caught glimpse of two lovers quarrelling—all that is important, all that is gone, it is a part of time, it will never happen again. See all the splendor and grandeur of it, the momentous pain and beauty of it, the essence and the whole of it. Here, open your eyes and ears and let me show it to you. . . ."

One can almost hear the admonitory Thomas Wolfe saying after that recital, "See? There is more to it than a ship lying out there and your going back on it. There is more to it than your fretting about whether all your baggage will be put aboard or not, but even that fretting has significance and importance in Time. There is more to it than just a sea of faces of other passengers eager to get aboard the ship. There is all that I just told you."

People, like small happenings,

achieve a stature, heft and consequence in Thomas Wolfe's novels quite abnormal in comparison with the stature, heft and consequence of characters in most novels. He will take a little trait and reiterate it, insist upon it, drive it in upon you with force and repetition until that trait seems almost to become the character instead of the trait's being a feature of the character's personality. The sister of Gene Gant never speaks without sniggering "hoarsely" or "derisively" until she becomes in the reader's mind not a woman but an obscene, inanimate, derisive snigger. Starwick, a student-instructor in the playwriting class at Harvard, becomes by a repetitious use of adjectives not a man but the abstract, luminous concept of all disabused, aristocratic, cultivated taste and gentility. And by contrast Uncle Bascom becomes the embodiment of all pushing, pious and pompous, insensate vulgarity. I have not counted them but Mr. Wolfe must use the word "lovely" twenty thousand times in this 450,000-word novel; and it is a very curious thing about this repetition of this usually banal, noncommital and inexplicit word: Wolfe uses it so often that you begin to think about what the word really means; and finally you perceive with some astonishment that the word can be used appropriately and with point, like a woman's "because." He employs the symbol of the watch and the river so often that before you reach the end of the 450,000-word novel you begin to catch on that Time is fleeting, death is inevitable and we have but a brief time here on earth to reflect upon the fact that we have but a brief time here on earth.

Nearly all of his men are "enormously proportioned, six feet, two or three inches tall and weighing about 300 pounds." His women are either "lovely" (and I mean lovely) or masculine or parchment-skinned or sluttish; they are not nouns but modifiers in negligee or dresses. When Gant gets drunk he gets drunk in the grand manner, in a manner never equaled outside of Stephen's drunk in "Ulysses." Even Wolfe's erudition is like Ben Jonson on a bat. When Wolfe describes a speculative mania in a town, a college class, a binge in Paris or a walk in the woods, he heightens the effect so extravagantly as to tight-rope walk along the abyss of burlesque. He keeps his balance, however. He has no evident sense of humor; nor any true sense of comedy. Even when he attempts to be playful or funny the effect is the disconcerting and uncomfortable one of a rictus, an attack of giggles, or the fantastic laugh of "l'homme qui rit."

In her first great lyrical outburst, "Renascence," Edna St. Vincent Millay said poetically that she could not love, she could not hug the world enough. In a long novel Mr. Wolfe has said pretty much the same thing, lyrically, ecstatically, with detailed testimony, in words that race, tumble, fumble and sing.

If you look for a plot, a story in the usual sense in "Of Time and the River" you will not find it; but you will find a hundred stories and five years of life, richly experienced, deeply felt, minutely and lyrically recorded. The diaries containing Gene's opinion of Shaw are here reproduced as well as the minutiae of his dialogues in love, his impressions of London and the Louvre, his sentiments when he sees a first-night audience at a Broadway musical comedy. Here is the intellectual, emotional and spiritual record of five years of a young man's life. And it is a strange life. You will note that even as a young man Gene Gant never read a book for pleasure, for entertainment, for a glimpse into an imagined world but always for a purpose, for an open sesame to life, for a knowledge of what people and life are like. This novel is a reflection of such a curiosity-consumed and hungry quest.

In these days when some of our best writers are tired or short of breath it is thrilling to contemplate and to read the teeming novels of Thomas Wolfe. They furnish also another satisfaction; they so effectively give the lie to such solemn, half-persuasive essays as those of Burke, Wilson et al., which allege that literature is running down in bulk, beam, vitality and gusto because civilization itself is running down. Wolfe writes as though the Spanish Armada had not very long ago been sunk by Drake and the expansion of the North American continent had just begun, for all that he is Southern born, a Harvard graduate and a Brooklyn resident intent upon leaving vivid and candid testimony of his experience on this earth.

Peter Monro Jack. "Mr. Wolfe's Pilgrim Progresses." New York *Times Book Review,* March 10, 1935, pp. 1, 14.

The superabundance that Thomas Wolfe shares with the great writers, who have rarely practised a niggardly economy—the surplusage, in Pater's disparaging phrase—is in the very nature of this richest of young American writers. Where other men write a sentence he writes a paragraph; where they write books he writes libraries. There must be all of 400,000 words in this second novel of his, and it covers no more than five years of the stream of time down which Mr. Wolfe is careering . . . the years from 1920 to 1925. This is not to be dismissed as a writing-mania. It is an essential belief in the richness and variety of living, to which only a "huge chronicle of the billion forms, the million names (of) the huge, single, and incomparable substance of America" can do justice. For this ambitious program Mr. Wolfe has been born lucky.

A backward glance at "Look Homeward, Angel" reminds us at once that the driving power lay in the astonishing Gants and Pentlands of North Carolina from whom Eugene sprang. In them was a living force that exhausted the extremes of comedy and tragedy. The emotional richness of their life, solidly and stubbornly maintained; their gross and mountainous sensuality, their ever-rising fury, the oaths and the violence, the terror and the sudden pity; above all, the unappeasable hunger for sensation—all this is an overflowing spring of life, as ungovernable as it is enriching. Mr. Wolfe's characteristic material is continuous and dynamic where so much in contemporary fiction is static; it expands where so much else contracts into a poverty of spirit. The Gants and the Pentlands of North Carolina who descend on Boston and New York and London and Paris in the person of Eugene are in the great tradition that life is most fully lived when it is most fully alive. The symbolic sign posts, somewhat pretentiously used to orient the book, are from such sources of potency from Homer,

Euripides, Marlowe, Telemachus and Jason, Orestes, Faustus. It is not surprising that Mr. Wolfe should write so much. It is surprising that a portion of this illimitable material should find itself within the manageable covers of a book.

Where the life of North Carolina is dominant the novel is at its best. There is nothing comparable to the figure of Eliza throwing out her hand in a loose and powerful gesture, "her powerful, hopeful, brooding, octopal and web-like character, with all its meditative procrastination, never coming to a decisive point, but weaving, reweaving, pursing her lips, meditating constantly and with a kind of hope, even though in her deepest heart she really had no serious belief that he (Eugene) could succeed in doing the thing he wanted to do." Or to Helen with her undercurrent of lewd passion, or Luke with his excited babble of pure good-heartedness, or old Mr. Gant wetting his thumb preparatory to an ecstasy of oratory. A new one turns up in Boston while Eugene is at Harvard, the tremendous crazy figure of Uncle Bascom (a Pentland), whom one will never forget ushering his visitor to the door "howling farewells into the terrible desolation of those savage skies," while his little old wife snuffles and cackles and whoops into her pots and pans in the kitchen.

Beside these figures, which we may haphazardly describe as Dickensian extravagance done over with the realism of Joyce, the newcomers are thin and shadowy. Harvard is treated with a contemptuous brevity, or, when characters are singled out, like Professor Hatcher of the play-writing class, and Starwick his assistant, and Miss Potter, the Cambridge hostess, they are written

up in a brutal caricature. The "pavement lives" of New York seem to him horribly undeveloped: "these raucous voices, the pitiable sterility of these feeble jests, that meager and constricted speech consisting almost wholly of a few harsh cries and raucous imprecations that recurred intolerably, incredibly through all the repercussions of an idiot monotony—all of the rootless, fearful, and horrible desolation of these young pavement lives. . . ." His Jewish students at Washington Square college are dismissed with a merciless scorn; and yet, in an attempt to be fair, Eugene follows one of them, Abe Jones, into his home life—but little enough comes of this. It should be remarked, either as a necessary difficulty of the plan of the book (which is to run into six novels) or as a fault in the rewriting, that there are many loose ends: characters appear and disappear with alarming suddenness, characterization and speech seem sometimes to be moments of sheer virtuosity, not part of a fictional scheme; and too often one feels the weakness of all autobiographical fiction—that something is put in because "it happened so."

The rich and powerful sense of life inherited from the Gants and Pentlands is thus a burden as well as a blessing to Eugene. He looks for its counterpart and can match it nowhere in his travels. As he wanders further away from it, to England and France, the book loses some of its zest in action and character, while it grows in the poignancy of its longing for a lost integrity. Eugene's character has ugly moments, displayed in the murderous fury toward Starwick because he turns out to be abnormal, and in the horrible dinner with Ann where he excites himself sexually by heaping dirty names on a Boston spin-

47

ster. Indeed, much of the French material, though no doubt a necessary part of the plan, is aimless, and so a little wearying. But by himself again, in the train journey to Orleans (Wolfe has a genius for trains: there is not a dull train journey in the book), with the fantastic countess in the Orleans hotel, and at Tours, the book mounts to its old height. It is coming nearer to terms with itself. Eugene is learning not to be disappointed with people for not being what he is. He no longer expects places and people automatically to educate him and help him find himself. The supercilious or brutal treatment of Harvard, Oxford and his friends in Paris will probably not occur again, not because he has changed his belief in himself but because he has deepened it; he expects less from outside and is not upset when he gets nothing. He returns to Ben's wisdom in the remarkable last chapter of "Look Homeward, Angel": "Where, Ben? Where is the world?" "Nowhere," Ben said. "*You* are your world."

It is the journey back to self and back to America. The consciousness of America is a deep undercurrent in the book. Wolfe broods over it constantly: surely in no other country could a young man wake every morning so astonished at belonging to his nation. Yet this is necessary to his soaring spirit, to attach himself to the whole meaning of America, to be its living counterpart.

It will be seen that this book is only one movement in an enormous machine for recapturing Wolfe's past and his present idealism. It has infinite possibilities for moving backward or forward. It has a continuing pattern of time that never comes to an end, and so it has that sense of being constantly living, constantly working itself out in the present tense. This sense of immediacy is on every page. Mr. Wolfe's sensuous perceptions are, as he describes Helen's, "literal, physical, chemical, astoundingly acute." He thinks with his blood and feels with his head. The reality of what he sees possesses him in every part of his body and there is no peace until every part of it, every least and peculiar aspect, is caught up in a welter of evocative words. No American novelist is so vigilant in the perception of character or so urgent in its expression. Nor is any one, except perhaps Dreiser, so unafraid of the immensity of life. This tremendous capacity for living and writing lifts "Of Time and the River" into the class of great books. It is a triumphant demonstration that Thomas Wolfe has the stamina to produce a magnificent epic of American life.

A. J. Cronin. "A Book in Which a Man Reveals His Soul and Writes With His Soul." New York *Sun*, March 11, 1935.

In "Of Time and the River" Thomas Wolfe has written a great long novel, but the novel might have been greater still had it been less long. This is no general indictment of long novels but merely a feeble protest against the waste tissue which in books makes for bulk rather than bone. Mr. Wolfe is, of course, naturally voluminous in style. One adjective is never enough. There must be three and often four. Here is no Stevensonian admission of

48

le mot just, but a gush of verbiage, a Niagara, a very Etna of savage emotion which stuns, bewilders, browbeats and . . . yes, it must be added . . . overwhelmingly convinces.

Mr. Wolfe has attempted the inevitable theme of all young writers, that is, the life story of the young writer himself. At least we strongly suspect this novel to be autobiographical. In England lately we have been bored to tears by scores of pallid novel-autobiographies, petunia-tinted, wilted and poetically sad. How refreshing to turn to Mr. Wolfe's (by way of contrast) autobiography which bears the colors of storm and sea and sky, the rude virility of the earth, the electricity of the lightning flash itself!

. . . Hundreds of characters throng the pages of this lengthy chronicle, all clearly drawn, all carefully observed. You will not readily forget Bascomb Pentland, Eugene's uncle, who preached himself through the pulpits of every denomination into a final fever of agnosticism. Nor Bascomb's wife with her pre-radio gramaphone complex; nor Eliza Gant, dark and bitter to the end; nor Helen, Eugene's neurotic sister, who clutched at the joys of life and found always ashes in her hands.

These characters live, but beyond Mr. Wolfe's undoubted power to create real men and women is his strikingly effective and individual sense of place. He has the rare gift of etching a scene so sensuously, so vividly that the words fade, the page recedes and there exists only that Jewish home in the Bronx, or that house upon the Hudson, or that chateau stuck in the very center of France.

Since Mr. Wolfe loves his native soil with an almost passionate intensity his splendid descriptive talent emerges most noticeably in his rich realization of the American landscape. Where could be found two finer passages than these? . . .

You see, this man Wolfe is not afraid, in the ecstasy of composition, to reveal himself. He may pretend in less inspired moments, after the hard-boiled fashion of the moderns, that he writes "with his guts." I prefer to believe that he writes with his soul. For those who yield themselves to this book will find therein a true spiritual experience, agonized at times, perhaps bitter and hopeless in many places, but on the whole surging with the aspiration of a man who lives, who lives with courage and fears not the darkness which must finally ensue.

There must be a sequel to this novel and I, for one, shall not miss it. But is it too much to ask Mr. Wolfe to remember that the finest books, like the finest blooms, thrive upon the pruning knife!

Unsigned. *Literary Digest,* 119 (March 16, 1935), 30.

Thomas Wolfe already is a legendary figure in American literature. "Look Homeward, Angel," published five years ago, made his fame. That book was a frankly autobiographical novel, telling the story of *Eugene Gant* in the State of *Catawba,* obviously the North Carolina where Wolfe grew up and went to college.

The book attracted scant attention when published; but its fame grew steadily—Sinclair Lewis, in his Nobel Prize address, recognized Wolfe as perhaps the most promising "new" writer in America.

For years his next book has been promised. Stories have been told of his appearing at the Scribner office with manuscripts totaling half, or three quarters of, or a million words, of his being asked to cut it in half, of his anguish in deleting passages, and of his final return with thousands of words scratched out, but more added than he had omitted. . . .

"Of Time and the River" is the story of five years (1920-'25) in Wolfe's own life, but it also is an epic of American youth, the story of quest for the essential America, which begins in North Carolina, is pursued in Boston and New York, followed in exile in England and France, and concludes with the return of the writer to his home.

Thomas Wolfe writes with a frenzy unparalleled among modern writers. He writes with fury and ecstasy, with a rare frankness of turbulent emotion, with a sense of the importance of every second of life which stands in passionate contrast to the futilitarianism of so much modern writing.

His book is a patchwork of a hundred short stories linked with prose poems to North Carolina, to New England, to Manhattan, to the rivers and forests of America, written in fever-heat, in the knowledge that despite the swift cataract of his words, the intangible can not be touched, and before he can get it down on paper "the imperial and magnificent minute is gone forever which, with all its promises, its million intuitions, he wishes to clothe with the living substance of beauty."

If there is a certain lack of restraint, of decorum, of selectivity in his furious prose, there still is an aliveness which is peculiarly American. The young hero (himself) plunges eagerly into life. He wants to read all the books that have ever been written, to know all the people, see all the places.

What he hates most of all is weary acquiescence in defeat. It may be "young," Wolfe seems to be shouting, to retain the proud and foolish hopes and dreams of youth, but it is all that makes life worth living, and America is unique in the world in that it retains that hope and youth.

He had read of England, but the rivers of England turned out to be so small, the people so hidebound, the food so tasteless. The boy concludes that the writers of England had written so magnificently of good because they so seldom had it, had been the greatest poets because the love and substance of great poetry were so rare among them.

So the youth returns to the land where his fathers had felled trees, fought Indians, and been buried, still questing, still undaunted. The book ends with the passengers climbing aboard one of those huge transatlantic liners which, tho built in Europe, without America have no meaning.

"Of Time and the River" is a book almost as big as "Anthony Adverse," as full of life and adventure and of faith in man's destiny, but contemporaneously alive and unblushing as Walt Whitman in its proclamation of the poetry of America.

50

Florence Codman. "The Name is Sound and Smoke." *Nation,* 140 (March 27, 1935), 365–66.

Thomas Wolfe is what may best be described as a great natural, a man in whom the compulsion to write is so diversely conditioned and magnified that few of the usual criteria seem adequate or necessary for his measure. The profusion of his talent is obvious; he has a magic treasure of language; the size of his narrative load could break the pens of several lesser men; the force of his emotions and the strength of his conviction of the importance of his story arrest attention by their magnitude and urgency alone. Since he is a giant not much is gained by pointing out that so far—this is the second book in a series of six—his material is solely autobiographical; that there is so much of it there is no room for improvisation, no need to make things up; and that its weight is so pressing that there is no leisure for storing, sorting, and labeling. What he writes occurs in no sequence of his planning but as he remembers it. For he is, he tells us, "suspended in a spell of time and memory." The ordinary concerns of style do not affect him, for he uses not one style but many. He gives a cock-of-the-wilderness shout, or chants a dirge to his father, or raises an anthem to America, and begins his book with as flat and factual a sentence as ever Cooper used. Whether he is rhetorical or lyrical, rhapsodical or cheaply journalistic, depends on the way he feels, and it is his feelings, the reflections of the author's tempera-ment, that link the sequences together and fuse the styles into a whole. How great this naturalism is depends ultimately on how convincing and significant Mr. Wolfe can make these feelings which shape and govern it.

In "Look Homeward, Angel" a sentiment of grandeur turned Altamont into a dwelling of superhuman creatures. Old Gant was no ordinary stone-cutter with a love for the bottle and oratory. His carousals were bacchanalian, and Eliza's land grabbings were an Olympian obsession. Ben died a hero, and there was no incongruity that people so violently human in their character and deeds should tread like gods, because Mr. Wolfe's wonder of life made a logical inflation. In this book Gene, their youngest son, is beset by a truly Gantian madness, a fury—Mr. Wolfe uses the figure of Orestes—that drives him from home to Harvard, New York, and Europe for five years of wandering in a search for all knowledge, an effort to read all the books ever printed, to encompass life wholly within himself. He must watch his father's slow, tortured death from cancer, scorn Harvard's famed class in dramatic writing, take the measure of the Jewish students in New York and of the wealthy Hudson River families, follow the expected pattern of an American student in Europe, all the time his inner fury driving him relentlessly. He is "caught in the Faustian web," "haunted by the dream of time." All the while he is conducting vast cosmic explorations. A sense of mystery clouds the universe; time becomes an irreducible "magic of now and forever;" vast indefinable emotions surge through him. Only the earth remains certain, only America, "that is the sound and silencer of forever," seems constant.

Just once after Gant dies and Gene leaves Eliza for good does he meet a figure of Altamont proportions. Bascom is Eliza's brother and receives Mr. Wolfe's relish for the originals of the older generation. The eccentric old man stalks like a gorgeous grotesque. Except for the clear, gentle glimpse of the French peasant in the railroad carriage, no character escapes satiric treatment. Mr. Wolfe's attitude toward his characters has changed. These people contain none of the remembered glamor of Mr. Flood and Dr. McGuire, who are parts of the fabric of his mind and body; they are only milestones, something to experience and go beyond on this frenzied search for "certitude and love." They are not whole characters but cartoons outlined by the threads of the web in which Mr. Wolfe becomes lost.

He is lost in a murky film, in a tangled gossamer of his own emotions. His feelings have got the better of him. Time and again they destroy the truth of his vision. American earth in October can be "a cry, a space, an ecstasy," but not even the magic of Mr. Wolfe's language can transform a World Series ball game into anything as "single, strange, and beautiful as all life, all living, and man's destiny." The exciting animism he believes in at sight of the South Station in Boston, a skyscraper, a de luxe ocean liner is unacceptably exaggerated. His sense of the repeated mystery of every pretty woman he sees, of the deep secrecy included in hospitals and battlefields is puerile. When the darkness of time never loses it allure, when sentiments—too frequent to count—flood over him, leave him engulfed, wordless, overwhelmed but always highly satisfied with them, the suspicion is confirmed. He is mired in the Faustian fallacy. "Feeling is all in all," Faust exclaims, "the name is smoke and fury." The balance of the intellect is outcast. Yet this same balance is Mr. Wolfe's greatest need. It is needed to cut the unnecessary volume of his words, to define and so assure for himself and his reader the why and wherefore of his feelings.

Grounded in this confusion is an admirable and sympathetic talent. Mr. Wolfe is a poet and a realist, supersensitive, receptive, generous, passionate. His scope is enormous and he does possess a faculty to temper the simple, inevitable course of his father's dying, mixing humor, horror, and love into tragedy. He can unobtrusively intimate the scrap of wisdom behind Miss Potter's farce as well as he can convey the torment of Gene's efforts to find himself, the faith of youth in its own high destiny. No more vitalizing talent has appeared in America this century. It still sprawls under the impact of its bulk and fresh immediacy, but there is as yet no reason to suppose that it does not contain its own corrective.

H. R. Pinckard. "Thomas Wolfe Shows Genius and Prolixity." Huntington, West Virginia *Herald-Advertiser*, Sunday supplement, March 31, 1935, "Today's Books," p. 1.

This is one of the important books of the year. In size alone it dominates the field, and the project of which it is a part towers above all else—in sheer bulk at least—on the contemporary literary horizon.

It was five years ago that "Look Homeward, Angel" made its appearance, calling forth applause so tumultuous and so prolonged that young Thomas Wolfe has not been forgotten, even momentarily, during the hiatus between that novel and this. Both fit into the series of six books which the author expects eventually to see published under the collective name "Of Time And The River."

. . .

Thus briefly told, the plot seems amazingly simple; and so it is. Dramatic climaxes are few, yet the element of suspense is rarely lacking. Obviously it is the kind of suspense which makes each individual's affairs his own most important concern—which is another way of saying that Eugene Gant's life is described in such a way as to capture the reader's sympathy and interest with hardly an important lapse. At times this interest mounts to heights of breathless tension. Sometimes movement is painfully slow, but this physical sluggishness of plot is largely offset by mental pyrotechnics the brilliance of which is not altogether visual. To explain (if I may be permitted to follow out the metaphor) one reads passages of this novel with the feeling that he is suffering along with Thomas Wolfe under the goad of a restless urge to know, to feel, to see—as though, in order to enjoy the blinding beauty of a fireworks display, one had to sit where the sparks fell in scorching profusion and the smoke swirled down in overpowering clouds. This for example,

as Eugene swings across Virginia on the way to Harvard.

. . .

Time and again, through the medium of Eugene Gant's disturbed thoughts, Wolfe returns to that theme—voices again his desperate cry for understanding, for light, for a roof, a door, a wall. Here is a line which may mean everything and may mean nothing, but which at any rate, I have not been able to forget:

> We are so lost, so lonely, so forsaken in America: immense and savage skies bend over us, and we have no door.

No door for what? It doesn't matter. I'm not at all positive I know what he is talking about, but I assure you the doubt disturbs me to an inconsequential degree. Fundamentally, of course, and down deep beneath the words that sometimes reveal and sometimes disguise his emotions, Wolfe is asking the answer to the riddle of life. But I think you will be too enraptured or too bored to question every such passage, or to quibble over the varied phrasing of his favorite theme.

Decidedly this book is capable of boring you. With all its power, its fire, its human drama, its superb and virtually endless panorama of characters, it is still a heavy and sometimes labored document. Much could have been eliminated with distinct gain in readibility, [sic] but at some sacrifice in earnestness; because life for all of us is often labored, often tedious, often distressingly obscure.

I cannot understand why Wolfe and the tremendous literary task he has undertaken have not been compared with Vardis Fisher and his tetralogy,

53

now nearing completion. There is such striking similarity of theme and principal character, if not of style, that the resemblance is inescapable. In the present space I can no more than mention it, but if Wolfe and Fisher between them do not achieve the Great American Novel it will not be written by this generation. "Of Time And The River," then, is a novel you must read and one I think you will be proud to have on your shelf of worthwhile books.

Unsigned. "Unselective Bulk." Springfield *Republican*, March 31, 1935.

The reader of Thomas Wolfe's "Of Time and the River: A Legend of Man's Hunger in His Youth" may modify his opinion of the judgment of the chorus girl who discouraged the selection of a book as a present for her friend, on the ground that the friend already had a book. If the friend's book ran close to 912 pages of 400 words each—close to 360,000 words, and like those good old Encyclopedias of Universal Knowledge—

> "Up from Earth's center through the Seventh gate
> Arose, and on the Throne of Saturn sate
> And many a Knot unraveled by the road,
> But not the master-knot of human Fate"

—if the friend's book were a book like that, the chorus girl may have been right in thinking that to present her with another book might prove an act of supererogation.

He may decide that a volume of 360,000 words in the course of which the substance takes all shapes from Man

to Mahi, is, if not too copious and amplitudinous, certainly too formless to impress the mind, except with an awe-full amazement that the world is so full of a number of things capable of being associated mentally with the life and experience of an individual person; also that any writer should attempt to assemble them all in a single book representing the "Pilgrim's Progress of Youth" and offer the result as artistic achievement in the field of fiction.

Mr. Wolfe's devotion to his purpose is so stern that he occasionally labors his attempt—can be heard hammering out some piece of metalwork or knocking together his scaffolding. The amount of material he works up would be sufficient for four or five novels of common length to which his one volume is equivalent and which, with application of Herbert Spencer's all-but-forgotten principle of "economy of means and of effect" would together surpass "Of Time and the River" in both appeal and artistic quality.

The author's technic [*sic*] is excellent in spots, but in the volume as a whole it is unequal to a complete fusing of so huge an amount of heterogeneous material. It does not discriminate and select; it is, in fact, omnivorous—it tends too often to substitute ideas and emotions as the active agents of narrative development for the human actor concretely exemplifying the idea and the emotion.

There is some internal evidence which supports the impression created otherwise by the work itself, that the volume is an autobiography, that its inmost and essential framework is a skeleton of fact and chronology corresponding with some closeness to the outline of actual personal history. The size of the book thus springs from dilatation and accretion, is the result of overlaying this framework with a huge amount of material arrived at through attempts to rerealize the events themselves of personal history and at the same time to discover and, as it were, psycho-analyze their mental and emotional penumbra in extreme detail.

The internal evidence is the lapsing of the narration in a few places into outright first-person phrasing—"my aunt bent . . . her eyes glaring madly at us." That such lapses represent unconscious dropping into the phrasing consistent with the actual point of view of the writer, which elsewhere he has conceded behind the veil of third-person form, seems more likely than that in an earlier draft he had employed the first person, merely for its presentational effect, and later, in changing to the third person, overlooked a few places where the form should have been changed. Is the reader to be blamed for regarding "Of Time and the River" as another of the many, many stories that have failed to attain their full potential of artistic achievement through the error of attempting to employ "true experience" directly as the immediate basis of fiction, instead of indirectly and mediately, as the source rather of greater creative understanding?

So far as "Of Time and the River" comes short of achieving all that could be desired from the author's indisputable seriousness of purpose and the amount of effort evident in the work, Mr. Wolfe is perhaps the victim of contemporary influences outside himself. Both its realistic attitude toward material and its mood of unsatisfied seeking for it does not know just what are characteristically contemporary—

not necessarily either ill or good in and of themselves. But the mood of seeking is in the spirit of straying disillusionment that was so dominant in the "younger generation" of the century's second decade and persists today, at least as a survival. The time is out of joint. Oh! cursed spite that I was ever born to set it right when I myself am lost in it and can only rebel desperately against life, face life fearfully behind a cynic mask, or flee from life to some hermit cave or anchorite cell!

Like much contemporary work, Mr. Wolfe's volume is an essay toward segregating and analyzing the ultimate entity, the spirit of America, and why, under what conditions, and particularly how the reactions of his "American" environment upon the young American may affect, mold, dwarf, misshape, stultify, frustrate him in his intellectual and idealist existence.

Robert Cantwell. *New Outlook,* 165 (April 1935), 10.

Few recent novels have received reviews as enthusiastic as those devoted to Thomas Wolfe's "Of Time and the River," and yet few have been reviewed so ambiguously. It is a fine book, the reviewers say; it is perhaps a great book, and it certainly suggests the emergence of a great talent; it has power, life, beauty, ecstasy, "grand, wild, humor"—but it is also repetitious, overwritten, confused, chaotic, and downright bad.

As you read the novel, however, and check back over the reviews, a good deal of light is thrown on the character of American reviewing by the very response of all these critics. And, incidentally, a good deal of light on the condition of contemporary American fiction. For what is there about the novel that makes it stand out above the other contemporary productions of its kind? Obviously, its vitality, or exhuberance, or intensity—the sense it gives of a rich and inexhaustible creative power in its author. Each reviewer calls attention to this. In fact, it is most cleverly said by Burton Rascoe: "In these days when some of our best writers are tired and short of breath, it is thrilling to contemplate and to read the teeming novels of Thomas Wolfe. . . . They so effectively give the lie to such solemn, half-persuasive essays . . . which allege that literature is running down in bulk, beam, vitality and gusto because civilization itself is running down."

But do they? In the mere quantitative sense of production, the writing of works of a relatively high level, compare Wolfe's efforts with those of Melville, the writer whose name is so frequently linked to his. Between 1849 and 1852 Melville wrote *five* novels almost as long as "Of Time and the River," and including "Moby Dick." In the matter of imaginative effort, each of these books, even "Redburne," which was as autobiographical as "Of Time and the River," was based upon some sweeping imaginative concept that lifted it above the plane of literal reporting. Each showed an inventive resourcefulness beside which the repetitions of Wolfe's prose-poems seem confessions of imaginative bankruptcy. Nor is it enough to point out, as Chamberlain does, that Melville was also guilty of mystical routings and uncontrolled verbal spasms. We know that Melville was acutely and bitterly conscious of these shortcomings in his work, that his creative heart was literally broken because he did not have the opportunity to revise and finish his books—"Moby Dick" was put into type page by page, as Melville wrote it.

The second characteristic that all the reviewers have hailed is Wolfe's ostentatious Americanism. Page after page of this second novel is filled with incoherent rhapsodies on America—or, more exactly, on the South and East. Although he stems from Whitman, and imitates Whitman's catalogues of American and Indian place-names, he seems to think of America as that stretch lying between Asheville, North Carolina, and Boston, beside the railroad tracks. His vision of America is indeed that of a man who looks out upon it from a Pullman window, and lets his imagination race, ungoverned by its realities; "Of Time and the River" is laid in Asheville (Altmont in the book), in Cambridge, in New York, in Paris and in Oxford. True, the European trip serves to convince Eugene Gant, the hero of the volume, that his place is in America, and he vigorously defends America, the America of picturesque and honest placenames, of overpowering restlessness and excitement, against the slurs of some elegantly infantile ex-patriots. But again the "Americanism" of the book stands out only in comparison with the novels of the people who have spent most of their lives abroad, or who are rooted in some special section, Tennessee or New Mexico or New England, which they identify with the country as a whole.

This is not to say that there are not some extremely suggestive and inspiring passages in "Of Time and the River." Parts of it are rich and lyric, and when Wolfe writes of his own people, of his own family and community, his talent is firmly under control; the literal accuracy of his observation is impressive. Moreover he understands that a high standard of accuracy is not incompatible with a lyric statement, and so avoids the weakness of Dreiser and others who wrote as if a "dull" life could only be written about in dull and uninspired language.

Wolfe is obviously at home with the "common people"—insofar as the common people mean the lower middle class Southerners, the salesmen, the landlords, the real estate agents—and he delights in their picturesqueness, their queer turns of speech, their repetitions, their homely philosophy; he is acutely conscious of the gap between their culture, the culture of baseball games, politics, local gossip, and the self-conscious "culture" of the isolated, cultivated, intellectuals. "Of Time and the River," like "Look Homeward, Angel!" is a dramatization of this theme; the basic pattern of the two books is determined by the conflict between the real culture of the people and the pretensions of the recognized carriers of "culture." As such it is of great value, though its value would be greater if Wolfe had selected, for his representatives of "culture," not the spineless and brainless frauds, but the most gifted and eloquent and best-informed figures to play off against the vital Gants. "Of Time and the River" is one of those novels that are highly and properly praised, but in most cases for the wrong reason, or in an undiscriminating fashion that, if generally applied, would make all our critical distinctions meaningless.

Mary M. Colum.
Forum, 93 (April 1935), 218-19.

By a long way the two most significant books in this spring's catalogue are Thomas Wolfe's *Of Time and the River* and Francis Hackett's *Francis the First*. The first-mentioned is a book that by a stretch might be called a novel but which actually belongs to all literary forms. . . . Both Wolfe's book and Hackett's have behind them minds of magnificent abundance and imaginations that stake a great deal on the value of a warm, rich vocabulary. There, naturally, resemblance ends, though both writers may be said to have brought a new life into their respective genres.

Excessive enthusiasm for current literature is not a usual characteristic of these pages of THE FORUM, so perhaps my readers will be more likely to put faith in the opinion now expressed here that Thomas Wolfe's *Of Time and the River* is one of the best books ever produced in America, one of the three or four most original books produced in the last decade or so, and the most successful attempt since Joyce and Proust to instill new blood and life into that withered literary form, the novel. The term novel is here used only for convenience and because the book is so classified in the spring lists, but it is practically a new form, made up of a combination of many older literary forms—poetry, oratory, biography, autobiography, criticism, the story, and the essay—all woven together, all kneaded together, into one grand pattern to give this writer's revelation of life. Like everything truly original that is produced in any art, it is by one learned in his own art, who loves it and all the masters of it to the marrow of their bones.

There is a passage, in the portion of the book called "Proteus," where the hero contemplates on a rich man's bookshelves the great work of all the dead, lying there unread, from Aeschylus to Poe, where he imagines the mightly dead speaking to him who is bursting with dreams of giving tongue to America. . . . And then they ask him, if he does give tongue to America, what does he hope to gain from the anguish, the hunger, and the effort. I draw attention to this passage not because it is one of the best in the book—there are very many much better—or because it brings back into literature the lost art of oratory, which it does, but I mention it for the reason that this particular page or two shows an artist attaining that stage of consciousness. It is part of the illumination that came to all the great artists, as if some one in the watches of the night came to give them a revelation about seed sown in them by some mysterious paraclete, seed which they alone could bring to fruit.

Of Time and the River has as subtitle "A Legend of Man's Hunger in His Youth," and each chapter is titled by the name of some great figure out of the past of literature—Orestes or Faustus or Proteus—and is an account of the progress of a young man during those years when he passes through all the great experiences of spirit, mind, and body which have been symbolically chronicled in all the great tales: he is young Faust in search of all knowledge, young Telemachus in search of his father, Jason on his quest, Antaeus renewing his strength. This highly intellectual and imaginative conception gives the book an epic framework, and what might at first appear formlessness, to readers accustomed to the neatly arranged novels of realistic writers, becomes a massive shapeliness as the book proceeds—a shapeliness given by one who has had to forge for himself a tool for the ordering of chaos. Without underestimating one whit the sensuality and grossness that is in the life he shares, there is nothing of that empty realism and that craze for recording stereotyped physical facts which, in their overplayed realism, did so much to demote the novel. One can declare that this book has a spiritual conception—there is no flight of the mind or the spirit that the author fails to understand. In that one short passage on page 267 describing the death of old Gant, the hero's father, there is an emotional power, an imaginative radiance that we sometimes feared might never come into American literature. This radiance occurs over and over again in a book with which I lament having so little space to deal, though indeed an analysis of it or of the personages in it could give little of the character of the whole. The best I can do is to advise my readers to read it. It is one of those books that open new windows to the mind.

Naturally after this I pass over, among the spring books, those long, dull, realistic novels about farms and families in the West and all those photographic representations of a life where the spirit never seems to enter, where the author can get down to nothing but what his eyes see and his ears hear and where he knows no land except where his feet walk . . . *Kennst du das Land, wo die Zitronen blubn* . . . so this remarkable book opens.

58

Unsigned. *Booklist,* 31 (April 1935), 268.

The second of a projected series of six novels, continuing the life of a character of *Look Homeward Angel.* Written with great turbulence, it omits nothing, whether beautiful, sordid, painful, or merely trivial, in the history of the five years of Eugene Gant's youth in which he seeks, distraught and bewildered, to find a meaning in life and a solution of his emotional problems. The introspection, the lack of plot, and the chaotic profusion of words make it difficult reading and limit its appeal.

Eleanor Clarke. *Common Sense,* 4 (May 1935), 27.

We are all looking for America: in its poets, migrations, labor problems, in Scandinavian or Italian or Mayflower faces passed silently in the street or seen in the far corner of a Chinese restaurant. Needing to make our future or be broken by it we are all involved in the struggle to discover ourselves and our own country. This is by way of remarking that Thomas Wolfe's latest book is as timely as it is unconcerned with the political battles that we have learned to expect in any great literature of this time. And "timely" is picayune praise for a book which lifts out of the bog of formula in which we love to dump them, the pride and love and nostalgia of millions of Americans. These are a part of us, we need perception of them, they must be reckoned with like a factory or a wheat field but

they reveal themselves more jealously. Only a few writers in our history have sensed accurately more than a small part of the substance which is America. Thomas Wolfe is one of these.

We must begin by partly discounting the autobiographical hero of this book. He is valuable for his gigantic energy and humor and because his wanderings are the only strand of continuity in the book. But he is often maudlin, though on a grand scale; his character engulfs situations which would be more pointed if left to carry their own implications, and his groping for intangibles is projected riotously into other characters not suited to it, such as old Gant and a woman glimpsed on a ship. His hunger for knowledge and experience is in itself exciting, but serves the author as an excuse for many overeloquent passages that were better left unsaid, attempts to define the vastness and loneliness of America and the flight of time, mostly ending with "and this place, this life, this time, were stranger than a dream" or an equivalent letdown, phrases so often repeated that they amount to a sort of cosmic ridicule of the hero and his vocabulary. Eugene was more moving and less rhetorical in Mr. Wolfe's first book, "Look Homeward Angel." His exploits here are often gawky and his Paris diary conveys less the growing-pains of a genius than of an over-blown Cicero. After being rebuffed by a girl Eugene is "stabbed again by wild, rending pity, sick with horror at her devastating terror." The same attempt to insist, by means of superlatives, on the validity of a scene or emotion weakens many other passages in the book. A sketch of two French waiters in a cafe is blurred by the author's summary of the scene as "brief, pleasant, and somehow poignantly unforgettable." It was, until labelled so, or until lost in the violent swirl of Mr. Wolfe's own personality.

But the sprawling of this book is that of America, and Eugene's hunger includes the longing of Americans to bring some unity out of the generosity and cruelty of this country. The torrent of awareness in which Eugene flounders is precise and clear in portraits of Uncle Bascom, of Starwick, of Eugene's mother, irrational and enduring, of a bum in "the million-footed city," of aggressive not-quite literati from Iowa, in the society cat-chat of a Hudson estate. There is greatness of feeling in these places, as undisciplined as the forests of a new continent but alive and right, and always at the core of it we remember the great hands of the stone-carver, Eugene's father, symbol of strength and solidity in men. For all its extravagance this is a book, like "Ulysses," to feed and grow on, to be taken into the blood and made a part of one's living.

Robert Cantwell. "Books." *New Outlook,* 165 (May 1935), 10.

In the past few years the nearest approach to a literary school in American creative life—with the exception of the proletarian writers whose purpose is frankly political—has been the emergence of the Southern novelists.

In one respect, the fiction of the Southern novelists has dominated the spring book season, just as Freeman's life of Lee has been outstanding among the biographies. Thomas Wolfe's *"Of Time and the River"* stands out, despite its weakness and occasional tiresome

bombast, as the most original of the new novels, and the one most likely to influence contemporary American fiction. Hamilton Basso's *"In Their Own Image,"* dealing with the free-for-all smart-set doings of Aiken, North Carolina, although it has received little of the enthusiastic comment devoted to Wolfe's book, reveals the quiet and sure progress of a writer who is perhaps more familiar with the South as a whole than any of his contemporaries and rivals. Barry Fleming's *"Siesta"*— though not nearly so impressive as the other two novels, deals with a typical Southern village, and gives to it a unity that could scarcely be detected in any comparable Northern town.

The other Southerners deal with little local islands—Stark Young writes of Mississippi, and occasionally of Texas and Louisiana; Tate and Caroline Gordon of Tennessee; while Wolfe gives the impression of being thoroughly lost and miserable as soon as he gets beyond the city limits of Asheville, North Carolina. . . .

S. L. "Man's Hunger." *Review of Reviews,* 91 (May 1935), 4.

These columns are usually given over to books which are concerned with realities rather than romance. But it is difficult sometimes to decide where fact leaves off and fiction begins. It is a commonplace that the novel often is truer to life than the thesis. *Of Time and the River* by Thomas Wolfe is one of those novels which come along at rare intervals. Then the reviewer puts his routine reading aside and says plainly to the reader: here is a man who really has something to say. Wolfe takes nine hundred pages to say it, and sometimes the reader yearns for a blue pencil, but one puts the book down with the feeling that here is a man whose thinking is not circumscribed.

Of Time and the River is the second of a projected six volume series dealing with the life and experiences of a young American. The first volume, *Look Homeward Angel*, brought the autobiographical hero from the South to the metropolis. This second volume takes him to Oxford, to Paris and other places and back again to America where he knows he "belongs." Wolfe sees America with new eyes, as a young and growing country "with all its clamor, naked struggle, blind and brutal strife, with all its violence, ignorance and cruelty, and with its terror, joy and mystery, its undying hope, its everlasting life."

Wolfe has been described as Whitmanesque, and the phrase is apt. He writes of America with enthusiasm, with richness and breadth. Unlike many of our contemporaries he does not think that exactness of detail makes great writing. His hero, Eugene Gant, is not content to look inside his own mind. He has a great awareness of people, places, feelings, gestures, ideas, sensations, passions, character.

. . . This reviewer knew Wolfe casually while teaching in the English Department of N.Y.U. Wolfe is of large stature and walks much like he talks; at a rapid, bowling rate. Wolfe promised his publishers that this present work would be completed in 1931 but no one will consider the intervening time badly spent. Nobody hurries him, and thus he differs from a hundred million other Americans. Sinclair Lewis has said of him that "he may

have a chance to be the greatest American writer." . . . It is not a book which can be read in one sitting, or five, but a volume which should go on your *must* list for the coming summer.

Edward Hooker Dewey. "The Storm and Stress Period." *Survey Graphic*, 24 (May 1935), 255.

Of Time and the River is the second in a series of six books which, when completed, will deal with the life and times of Eugene Gant (alias Thomas Wolfe.) The theme of the first book, Look Homeward Angel, was the eternal bewilderment of youth with its cry "Oh lost, lost!" In the present book this theme gives way to one of frenzied perpetual motion. In a roaring odyssey of man in his youthful hunger Mr. Wolfe traces the course of his hero from his career as a graduate student of drama at Harvard, through abortive years as teacher, Oxford parasite, and dilettante in Paris, to his homecoming. Eugene's Faustian *Sehnsucht* and his unquenchable zest for living bring him into many and varied companies. The effeminate Starwick of the Harvard graduate school days, the bitter, honest Abraham Jones, Eugene's only friend among his East Side Jewish students, soft-voiced, big-bodied Ann from Boston, the extraordinary tribe of Gants themselves are only a few of the scores of richly rounded characters. Mr. Wolfe has recorded this human adventure in a style at once so opulent, so varied, and so full of movement that the reader is swept through 900 closely printed pages unconscious of the passing of time. Mr. Wolfe writes best when he is aroused to ecstasy or bitterness, although bitterness, as exemplified in the Harvard episode, does not lend him the clean knife-edge of a Sinclair Lewis, but rather glows with a sullen resentment. It is a book born out of pain, and fostered by a tremendous hostility to the commonplace.

One feels that, in a certain sense, Mr. Wolfe has written a social document. His social philosophy is implicit: the present order is sterile of beauty and dignity, division between classes is sharp and irreparable, and in the last analysis man's great enemy is himself. Nor can he find salvation through beauty; Starwick, the real aesthete of the book, is a moral degenerate. The only liberated individuals are those who have thrown over all responsibilities—the expatriates in the Paris episode—and their lives are the most purposeless of all. Mr. Wolfe does not scorn life so much as those who live it. Except for Eugene, the characters are plankton, drifting and hopelessly lost.

The book has exuberance, grandeur, and excess, and here is its central fault. Judicious pruning would in no way have destroyed its vitality, such vitality as have few books in our time. If Mr. Wolfe grows lean and hard with the seasons, he will lose nothing. For he writes with heart and mind and sinew, and nothing can destroy his power. Of Time and the River is truly a prose epic; through it shakes the struggle of man in quest of himself, and the sound of clashing by night.

Helen MacAfee. *Yale Review*, 24 (Summer 1935), vi, viii.

Mr. Wolfe's second novel raises all the questions raised by his first and settles none of them. It is perfectly clear again that he can on occasions effectively raid the reader's imagination, in a surprise attack usually with some outlying detail of his large army. Can he ever so succeed in the long campaign of attrition on an extended front to which he seems to have committed his mind? The novel is a conveniently loose term lending itself to much variation of shape and size, pace and temper. It will be as impossible to say just what a good novel is as to say just what a good human being is until the last person on earth (who will, I assume, write autobiographical fiction) has delivered the last copy. Then perhaps some visiting Martian will decide. It is easier, and safer, to say now what a good novel does. For one thing, it strikes and holds the imagination of a reasonably well intentioned reader of suitable mental age. In any novel there are pretty sure to be passages that one such reader or another will consider weedy or arid, but a skilled writer will carry him over these by main force. Mr. Wolfe has plenty of force. *Of Time and the River* shows this force, I think, as still undirected through the book as a whole.

The trouble, it seems to me, lies not so much in any weakness of selection (for there is a rich variety in the novel that is certainly an element of strength) as in a faulty conception of the best means to emphasis. One of the means Mr. Wolfe uses when he wishes to impress the importance of a theme or a situation is expansion. This is a legitimate method applied in all the longer classics of fiction. But even in the best hands it is a losing game unless it is done in dramatic terms or in terms of exceptionally keen analysis. Mr. Wolfe can infuse a long passage with great dramatic vitality—the scenes in this book with the Bascoms, for example— where the characters stand up on the page as they talk. His analyses are not, for the most part, subtle enough, I think, to deserve the space given them, especially the comment upon what I suspect to be an individual or a group when stretched by the author to cover the masses. Such comment as this— "We are so lost, so naked, so lonely in America. . . . All of us are driven on forever. We have no home"—seems strained to the breaking point of rhetoric. Expansion in purely descriptive terms quickly becomes wearisome—almost at once when devoted to inorganic subjects like the weather, as any observer of conversational ebb and flow has found. It occurs to me that a good many young writers spend too much time at their desks and not enough in learning the arts of narrative from the talk around them.

Mr. Wolfe employs two other means of expansion for emphasis—elaborate variations on a stated theme and loud reiteration of a keyword, "fury," "furious," "mad fury," and so on. These are devices taken over from music which require a very special skill for flourishing transplantation to literature. Indifferent or lavish handling will meet first resistance and finally skepticism. Thus we read here many times over the old stonemason's "powerful" hands—too many times, at length, until when we come to the lines "on their granite power and symmetry,"

"the powerful sculptured weight and symmetry of his tremendous hands" with their "stony sculptured and yet living strength," we wonder whether such things hadn't better be abandoned by literature and left to the mute form of the sculptor.

The amount of space Mr. Wolfe gives to the characters varies with their closeness to the young man who occupies the centre of the stage. So does the kind of treatment they receive. The Harvard teachers, farthest from him, are profiles, rather small; the Uncle and Aunt Bascom, who interest him more, are larger realistic sketches, the immediate family full-length portraits. It is the middle group for which, it seems to me, Mr. Wolfe has the greatest gift. Here is a disinterestedness that brings their substance forward with both a greater clarity and a greater solidity than is the case with the big figures. I am among the many who believe that although Mr. Wolfe has not yet written a very good novel he should sometime do so—and for this reason I think this overlong and unwieldly but vigorous expression of his talent should receive not only attention but careful consideration.

V. F. Calverton. "Thomas Wolfe and the Great American Novel." *Modern Monthly,* 9 (June 1935), 249-250.

Not since the days of Herman Melville, when American literature still held on to certain of the virtues, in particular the dramatic eloquences and violences, of Elizabethan prose, have we been confronted with writing, vivid, intense, powerful writing, of the type that one can find in Thomas Wolfe's new novel: *Of Time and the River*. All one has to do, which by way of experiment I have just done, is to read over the descriptions of nature and the sea in *Benito Cerino, Typee,* or *Moby Dick,* and it will become immediately apparent that Thomas Wolfe is a greater genius than Herman Melville in the art of description. Wolfe at his best is a writer of a high order, of the highest order that American literature has produced, and, like Hemingway, it is only in terms of Melville, Whitman, and Poe that he can be compared. The pathetic, senile tendency of idolizing the past because it is the past, a fallacy that most critics seldom escape, prevents too many of us from recognizing greatness when it is upon us. Thomas Wolfe is essentially a great writer whose true greatness will finally emerge, however, only if those who recognize it can help him fulfill it.

The history of American literary genius, as Van Wyck Brooks pointed out a good while ago, has been a peculiarly shortlived, sporadic affair. For generations now, it has suffered from the disease of over-rapid development which has caused its bones and tissues to mature with unnatural precocity in early years, only to stop suddenly a little later, stiffen, harden, and grow no more. That is why a literary generation in America is very often a matter of only five years. We develop and age with equal prematurity. Power comes to us with over-sweeping suddenness in youth, but it goes out of us before that youth is spent. We are a land of great promise but small fulfillment.

Not so very many years ago Frank Norris was the great promise; later it

was the young Ernest Poole; then Theodore Dreiser emerged as the new prospect, followed by Sherwood Anderson and a half score of other writers whose first or second books gave foundation for such hope. Today the great hope is Thomas Wolfe, and there is reason to believe he may succeed where all others have failed.

Neither *Look Homeward Angel* nor *Of Time and the River* is the great American novel, but within both there is a composite of materials, an earth-hugging vision of life, an emotional eloquence, an over-mastering, irrepressible power and passion which, once harnessed and disciplined, may result in the creation of such a novel— or novels. Wolfe attests to fiction, as *Of Time and the River* attests even better than *Look Homeward Angel,* a descriptive genius which not only surpasses that of Melville, but which has perhaps few equals in contemporary literature. No modern author, writing in the Anglo-Saxon tradition, has been able to make nature live, earth, sea, and sky, in the vivid, palpitant sense that Joseph Conrad has—and Thomas Wolfe stands close to Conrad in such descriptive powers.

The world through Wolfe's eyes, and as it comes upon him, is a world of dark, secret wonder, pain-ridden, passion-driven, desperate with endless doubts and fears, with the agony of brevity and death written into all things both great and small, the infinite as well as the infinitesimal. Wolfe is haunted, as have been and still are all sensitive, imaginative minds, by the tragedy of being human, the tragedy of a world destined for death, of men and women caught within its maw and ground into nothingness without even a chance to struggle or escape.

Wolfe is a romantic in the best sense of the word; not in the 19th century sense of the word when romanticism became synonymous with sentimentality, and *Weltschmerz* became a patent medicine of the emotions diluted into all kinds of cloying mixtures by the De Mussets, the Hoffmanns, and the Tiecks of the period. Wolfe's romanticism is in the tradition of Omar Khayyam, Lucretius, Shakespeare, Leopardi, and Unamuno. The one element in Wolfe's romanticism, however, which prevents it from attaining its full stature is its autobiographical limitation. While *Of Time and the River* succeeds in avoiding the subjective pathos and bathos conspicuous in the work of so many of the nineteenth century romantics, at the same time it fails to get outside of itself, outside of the personal into the plane of the impersonal, where the personal lives more as an objective than as a subjective force. Flaubert in *Madame Bovary* achieved that fusion of the objective with the subjective, the impersonal with the personal; his characters live as persons, as individuals, yet without being part of the personality or individuality of the author himself. It is toward that end that Wolfe must work if he is ultimately to make his American saga or epic, with its four more volumes, into the greatest fiction America has produced.

Two unfortunate by-products of Wolfe's exaggerated autobiographical emphasis are to be discovered, first, in his inability to tell a story as a story, and secondly, in the adjectival and adverbial exuberances of his style. Wolfe becomes so interested in his own emotions and reactions to things, people, places, skies, seas, streets, offices, dreams, that it often takes him a score of pages to extricate himself from them and get to the narrative he is trying to relate. That results from the fact that he is really more interested in his own emotions and reactions than he is in his narrative; only the severest discipline, only the most determined literary stoicism, will ever make it possible for him to get over that difficulty, for it is a difficulty that is constitutional rather than epidermal. It grows out of the fact that Wolfe is essentially more of a poet than a novelist. He is in more ways than one the prose Walt Whitman of the twentieth century, singing in storm-furious rhythms, new, fresh, and compelling, of the country and the people of America, an America reseen, refelt, and renewed in his words.

But the tradition of Whitman is not the tradition of a novelist. It leads one away from rather than towards the novel. Its power is derived not from economy, precision, or organization, which are virtues necessary to the novel, but from amplitude, inclusiveness, and multifarious accumulation. Wolfe's virtues are Whitman's virtues, but they are not virtues when they appear in a novel. The truth of that observation can be noted easily by a consideration of Wolfe's shorter pieces. The best piece of writing Wolfe has ever done, and one of the best pieces of writing in American literature, is his short story, if it can be called such, *No Door*. The story part of it is inconsequential; the poetry part of it is fundamental. The farther Wolfe gets away from the story element and the closer he gets to the poetic, the better his work becomes. But to write great fiction the story element cannot be sacrificed to the poetic; the objective factors cannot be obscured by the subjective. To fuse the two, so that neither obtrudes upon the other, neither delays the other, nor injures the other, is the task which confronts Wolfe and which he must master if he is to produce the great American novel that all other American writers have failed to create.

Inherent in that same weakness is his tendency to mar an otherwise remarkable and potentially great style by over-writing which is often of the most thoughtless order. No one in America today can write more powerfully than Wolfe at his best. He can make words do strange, magical things, caress, stir, stab, burst, and explode, but he has not yet learned to do it with that economy of phrase which is the *sine qua non* of a great style. He depends too much upon adjectives and adverbs, accumulated in torrential overflow, and too little upon verbs for his effects. The real difficulty, I believe, lies in the fact that Wolfe has so much in him, so much power and passion, so abundant, so opulent an imagination, that he just can't get it all out, just can't get enough of it on paper, and in his anxiety to do justice to what he feels and what he wants to say he says too much although in his eyes it still seems too little. The result is instead of being master of his style he is very often overmastered by it.

But these weaknesses are not weaknesses in a weak writer; they are the weaknesses of a strong writer, a powerful writer, who when he overcomes them will be stronger and more powerful still. Even with those weaknesses Thomas Wolfe is one of the finest novelists this country has produced. Without them, he may become the greatest novelist in our literature.

John Slocum. *North American Review*, 240 (June 1935), 175-77.

When Thomas Wolfe published "Look Homeward Angel" in 1929, he was hailed as the novelist of young America. Critics congratulated themselves on having discovered an author who was capable of portraying "the American Scene." Here was the long needed fury, gusto, tradition, and breadth of canvas. And not since Whitman had America been so sincerely thundered in every word of a long work.

These critics were partially right. Wolfe was a sensitive young man who had written an autobiographical novel covering the first nineteen years of his life in Asheville and later at Chapel Hill. He had completed the first part of his education, had severed his childhood family ties, and was prepared to face the world and graduate work at Harvard. We leave him with a thorough knowledge of the struggle of his sensitive nature to substantiate itself in the face of his vital, garish, and unsensitive family. In the course of his development the whole town, a great number of individuals, and beyond them the whole South, have had a perceptible influence on his personality. There are a few characters who are not easy to forget—his mother and father, his brother Ben, and a girl he momentarily loves, Laura James. But as for the American Scene, he has not covered it, because it cannot be covered. What is still better, he has not even attempted it. He has vividly portrayed the section of America with which he is familiar.

One of the most unfortunate tendencies in American criticism, which dates back even before the Local Colorists of the 'seventies and 'eighties, is the demand for national consciousness in creative writing. Pressure is put on the young artist to shout America; he is made conscious of his slightest use of a continent-wide theme, and unless he is a great artist he succumbs to geographical jingoism. Paul Engle, last summer's poet, was an example of a young writer who had become a victim of this tradition. "Of Time and the River" shows that Wolfe has not altogether escaped from the influence of the critics. In an orgiastic passage on page 155, with the aid of purple adjectives and italics, he covers the country from Maine to southern California and back again.

"It is the place of the immense and lonely earth, the place of fat ears and abundance where they grow cotton, corn, and wheat, the wine-red apples of October, and the good tobacco." This goes on for pages and pages until America becomes a gigantic hoax rather than a real and living country.

This fragment of prose fiction which takes Thomas Wolfe, or Eugene Gant, from his twentieth to his twenty-fifth year, can be called neither prose nor fiction—for the characters from Jack Cecil to Professor Baker have been changed very little from actual life, and the style often approaches rhapsodic free verse. The author shows a great mastery of conversation and an ability to delineate unforgetable characters in a few vivid strokes. Then he goes on for pages and pages to describe them further, or they drop out of the story forever.

The result is that the principal characters, with the exception of old Gant, who is a truly heroic figure, tend to become caricatures. Bascom Pentland,

Eugene's Boston uncle, starts as a Dickensonian New Englander and ends a madman. Even the middle-class people who live in Melrose grow absurd when they defend their middle-class attitude. The hordes of men and women who have had a molding influence on Wolfe's life seem in a large part disturbing and irrelevant. During his adolescence, these influences were more perceptible, and these characters were indispensable. But with his first maturity, their importance becomes less and less. Eugene is a colossal egoist and is more apt to influence than to be influenced. Thus the necessity for them is destroyed, and he often appears in the rôle of a newspaper reporter rather than of a developing personality.

These characters spring from all classes of society, from the Shanty-Irish to the very wealthy on the Hudson, or to Oxford undergraduates. They are sometimes given significance by having some strange fascination for Eugene, but what this is cannot be discovered. In the case of the Coulstons, the mysteriously disgraced Oxford family, Eugene finds himself in sympathy with the daughter. They declare their affection for one another and part; there is no explanation, only the impression of some vague external force at work.

Wolfe does much of his best writing of Eugene's childhood in retrospect. There is a fine scene of his brother Ben presenting him with his first watch, and another of Gant, the mastermason at work. Probably the greatest incident in the whole book is the death of Gant, but it is also unbearable because of its length. The scene of his helplessness during a hæmorrhage is probably one of the most moving in modern fiction, but a reader is capable of only so much strong emotion. The tension is too great, and his death, when it finally does come, instead of being a tragedy is almost a relief. But the dignity of the situation is saved by a consideration of his dead hands which are expressive of his character both in life and death.

Even in this scene his words carry too much impact; he has set the timbre too high. Instead of being vivid his words are like a confused roar. When he says, "Spring came that year like a triumph and like a prophecy . . . it sang and shifted like a moth of light before the youth, but he was sure that it would bring him a glory and fulfillment he had never known," there is not much left for him in describing a circumstance a little out of the ordinary.

Bernard De Voto has called "Of Time and the River" an example of manic depression, infantile regression, and a compulsion neurosis. This is hardly literary criticism, but there are certainly many symptoms of all of these. Eugene on his first coming to Harvard is driven to reading with a maniacal fury. Later, in Dijon, when he has left his weak friend Starwick, he writes with the same impetus for fourteen to twenty hours a day. People never talk in quiet voices, they shout, howl, or cackle at the slightest happening, and the steak at Durgin Park is described with the same finality as his dead father's hands.

But Wolfe cannot be dismissed a psychological freak. In many isolated passages he shows his ability to be of a high order. When he has finished this novel of his life, for it appears from the title page that there are many volumes forthcoming, he may have objectified his experience to the extent of being able to create many inter-related characters, which will be the better for having been founded on so many sensitively absorbed personalities.

With the widening of his experience his view of America will become less self-conscious, and if he shows the same common sense that he used in fleeing to Europe from lionization this last March, there is no reason why he cannot go farther toward expressing Romantic America than any novelist living today.

Unsigned. *Wisconsin Library Bulletin,* 31 (June 1935), 78.

Eugene Gant, youngest son of the family made famous in *Look Homeward, Angel,* takes leave of his mother and sister and starts off for his three years at Harvard. The experiences here, the agonized waiting to hear whether or not his first play is accepted, the years of teaching, his sojourn in England and France, all these form the background against which are thrown all the varied personalities and experiences he encountered, written in equally varied style running the entire range from utter lack of taste to heights of sheer beauty. A work of genius of a sort but not a novel to be recommended for unrestricted circulation.

Howard Mumford Jones. "Social Notes on the South." *Virginia Quarterly Review*, 31 (July 1935), 455-56.

. . .

And then there is Mr. Wolfe. "Look Homeward, Angel" ran to 626 pages; "Of Time and the River" runs to 912; and Mr. Wolfe assures us that these are but two volumes in a series of six he intends to write. Just now Mr. Wolfe is riding on top of the wave, but whether the public will be willing to follow him through the two and a half million words which this gigantic scheme implies is a debatable question. For Mr. Wolfe, with all his virtues of strength, vividness, and sympathy, is utterly lacking in a sense of structure. "Of Time and the River" might be unkindly described as a Gargantuan rhapsody interruped from time to time by scenes from a novel. These scenes are for the most part of remarkable power and insight—Mr. Wolfe surpasses most living writers in the sheer power to *see*—but they float down the vast river of his prose like infrequent and brilliantly lighted steamers. Everything in the book is swollen in dimensions. Where other writers digress for a paragraph, Mr. Wolfe digresses for whole pages at a time. The central character, Eugene Gant, is utterly overwhelmed by this verbal torrent, and though Mr. Wolfe has the power to present the subsidiary personages with complete conviction and penetrating insight, the hero does not exist. The book is, in effect, a veiled autobiography—even Mr. Wolfe's Parisian notebooks have been dumped into the stream.

The novel occupies the time from Eugene Gant's going to college to and through his trip abroad, the end portion (a complete novel in itself) being the most coherent part of the book. It is probably appropriate that the general tone should be that of youthful bitterness and tumultuous rebellion, but a thousand pages of Werther-like tumult are a little wearing; and one of the results is that all the characters are driven by a frenetic energy. The talk of the Gant family is eternally explosive and feverish, the persons whom Eugene meets in his Odyssey whirl about like tops, the railroad journeys (the hero is perpetually restless) are journeys made in a kind of sympathetic nightmare, and, however powerful the book is in detail, the effect upon the reader who has to take it at a single stride is to exacerbate his nerves. One finds himself longing for a single chapter of calm, but if one comes across such a passage, adolescent *Schwärmerei* soon shatters such peace as there is. Greatly gifted though he be, Mr. Wolfe has not yet learned repose, as Tolstoy, whom he resembles, learned repose.

. . .

John Donald Wade. "Prodigal." *Southern Review*, 1 (July 1935), 192-198.

Mr. Sinclair Lewis has pronounced Thomas Wolfe's writing so deep and spacious that it deals with the whole of life. Undeniably it is very deep and spacious; but it hardly deals with everything. Religion, for example, however vestigial it may seem to be in the contemporary world, was, as late as 1884, in Asheville, North Carolina, a force that moved weightily and in general in worthy directions. It is highly probable that in 1935 it may still be found here or there performing nobly. It is even possible that in 1984 it may in one form or another be among the dominant forces of the world. Yet, for all of Mr. Wolfe's testimony, religion might never have existed to any good purpose. Like the waiter he tells about in the café at Nice, he apparently thinks of himself (and of everybody else, in fact) as not susceptible to religious sentiment—certainly not to ecclesiastical sentiment. Now, this is all very well for a way of thinking, but it does not fit in cleanly with gusty paeans about catholicity, and about the splendor of a young man's wanting to experience everything—oh, *everything*.

The insatiate young man who is the hero of both Mr. Wolfe's novels, *Look Homeward, Angel* (1929) and *Of Time and the River* (1935), is named Eugene Gant, and he is referred to in the third person except at rare times when the disguise somehow lapses and the hero becomes quite frankly Thomas Wolfe—"I," the text has it, "did this or that"; "reaching through the darkness she touched *me*," and so on. . . .

. . . The first novel makes clear the origins of the body's parents, but news of his gestation is given on the twentieth of the 626 pages in the book, and from that time till the end—here he graduates from the State University at Pulpit Hill—Eugene dominates the story. He and his observations and experiences and sentiments are, indeed,

all that is offered. Characters drift in, manage to assert themselves for fifty pages or more, and drift out again; except by lucky chance, Eugene only endures. And he endures with the utmost intensity and turbulence, unable, unwilling—even unaware of the obligation—to believe that he is not the absolute pioneer in living. Neither he nor anybody else is ever for an instant merely so-so. Nothing is merely so-so. Life is a flame that BURNS.

The same flame BURNS in the second novel, for five years, through 912 pages. . . . People drift into his life and drift out again. There is much, much talk of them; and they are no more. Until the last page of the second book, only the very dull are not bitterly and hopelessly lost—then, on the last page occurs a miracle—an incredible, unprecedented miracle: Eugene and a young woman who is not named, see each other and fall in love—and then two young people who are quite acutely not dull, oh, not *that*, are acutely not *lost* any more, either—forever.

The two huge novels, covering the time from 1884 till 1925, are enheartening proof of a man's ability, in our time in America, to write in the grand manner with sustained strength. When Mr. Wolfe's publishers announce that in the last five years he has written two million words, they do not mean to imply that he has necessarily written by some wholly mechanical routine; they mean on the contrary—and they are thoroughly right—that he is a very remarkable person. The two novels already published are part of a series of six, which, completed (two of the others are now ready), will range in time from 1791 to 1933. The whole great collection—and this does not guarantee that it will pass into the popular consciousness immemorably—will undoubtedly constitute one of the monumental performances in the history of American literature. For whatever are the faults of this writer, he has the virtues of stupendous gusto and energy, and quite remarkable omnivorousness. So far, his work has been the record of his own passage through the world. Whether he can transfer his peculiar virtues to books in which he is not himself protagonist, is something that the performance only can indicate.

Whoever writes so much so hurriedly is bound to write something badly. The two novels now published are not impeccable. They are occasionally repetitious and verbose merely. There are rare instances of downright bad rhetoric and there is a considerable amount of trite phraseology. In spite of his ado with *umlauts,* the author lets his American prepossession with spelling lead him into some bad dialect-recording, particularly in the sections of the book that deal with Englishmen. The hero is permitted at times to describe minutely events which in the nature of the case he had observed only fleetingly and cursorily; he uses similes out of experiences which are as yet ahead of him. Sometimes he divulges a too facile knowledge of matters that are highly technical, like medical prescriptions; and sometimes, aggressively cosmopolitan, he is provincially homespun enough to say "reasonable" when he means cheap. But these strictures are against occasional lapses only. In the main, the story is conveyed with subtlety as well as vigor, with a sure implication of the author's really welling power, and a sure and welcome implication of his acquaintance with the great humane tradition of the world.

There is the memory of Greece and Rome and of the Renaissance arts floating across great sections of the writing, and the author's wide knowledge of English literature is forever there, a sort of sounding-board for all he says. There is a sweeping command of language and vocabulary, and a majesty of style. There is a large and beautiful mysticism, attained apparently by no road yet followed, and toward which no road is marked in these books—a mysticism, then, that is in a sense regrettably selfish. The memory of medieval culture is seldom if ever present; there are no sounding-boards for any except a bigoted and sterile piety. But the richness and depth of the past are more than usually well implied; and for what is offered in that line there must be grateful acknowledgment.

Many old and good tricks and a number of new ones are requisitioned for the reader's benefit; Dickens's method is plain in the scenes relating to the stout lady who set herself up as patroness of the arts at Harvard; Sir Walter Scott's in some of those involving comic relief; Sinclair Lewis's in all of those involving the dictaphone technique; and even Joyce and Gertrude Stein are from time to time suggested—faintly but with unmistakable Wolfeian accent.

The adroitness of the Lewis-like episodes is a commentary on the ease with which that artifice may be acquired—and abused. To devote nearly a sixth of a book that supposedly covers five years of time to the various conversations of a railway journey from Asheville to Baltimore evinces an evil intoxication with one's command of mimicry. But the space given to the superbly reported conversations of the "arty" (and leprous) intellectuals around Harvard University is more to the point;

the subject is fresher, and the matter treated has bearing on the central issue of Eugene Gant's development—in its stupid mincingness, its inane irrelevancy, its dead and rotten bawdiness. It has as the author hints, sad bearing upon the development and damnation of us all, and of this nation. This waspish sophistication is worse than the vulgarity of Altamont, the jaunty unconcern of Pulpit Hill, or the surly unconcern of the City College; it is more menacing, because it is more comprehensible, than the jibberish of the intellectual expatriates in France. All of this Mr. Wolfe makes clear. However much space he takes to do so, he is heartily welcome to.

The author is a young man, born thirty-five years ago, and if on many scores he behaves himself still in the fashion of one born considerably later, he is in some ways fortunate, and may be forgiven a good deal. Too often, the folly of youth is supplanted only by the drabness of age; that should mitigate some of the doubts that might arise concerning Mr. Wolfe's literary manners. But in his particular case, it might not be too sanguine to risk wishing that time, which surely rolls, would roll a shade the faster; he is hardly likely ever to prove drab; and it is not a painful thing to imagine the day when he will no longer utter persistently, with defiant relish, many of the words that still delight him. He may not much longer find the word "guts," for instance, irresistibly fascinating, may not say "whore" as often as he now finds it good to do; may, though continuing to regard himself as basically non-Christian, come to feel that the ejaculations "Jesus Christ" and "By God" are less pertinent than he once thought them in the business of demonstrating

one's self safely independent. He may conclude, even, that (mature, at last) he should try the feat of mastering his audience without resort to the hard and raw brass knucks of sex scenes. For about sex scenes there is this: in fairness to his audience, a desperately—oh, desperately—frank and earnest and fearless writer is bound to offer either more detail than Mr. Wolfe offers or quite definitely less. It is not admirable to insist upon the individual whim with volcanic eruptiveness, and to keep all of the exciting lava meanwhile safely, meticulously, within permitted channels.

Mr. Wolfe is very unhappy over the fact that nobody really knows anybody else, and he does not derive comfort from the idea that this was true formerly and will be subsequently, world without end. He says that at twenty-two he was a madman and a fool—and that everybody else at twenty-two is also. He says that to be a great writer a man must be something of an ass. He says that he wants to experience everything, to escape nothing. All of this is very romantic sounding. Yet he long ago ceased to think of Shelley as pre-eminent among the poets; he was properly exasperated, early in his book, to have his family think of him, because he wished to write, as different from the rest of them. Yet, again, he exhibits something indistinguishable from the conventional grade of moral indignation in his attitude toward the drunkenness and perversity of Starwick, and something very close to the aphorisms of Benjamin Franklin (which Babbitt loved) in his attitude toward the importance of getting his work done.

It is surely true, as Eugene Gant declares, that no form of political government will offer surcease from the invisible worm that works unremittingly on man's heart. It is conventional to say that romantic love is sovereign in this regard, and Eugene accedes to the convention; at least he seems to value romantic love as an agency of temporary relief. It is also conventional to say that priggishness is a good remedy; and there Eugene accedes too. It is also conventional to say that religion, sweetness and humility of spirit, a sense of obligation, a regard for the happiness of one's fellows, mental as well as physical—that all of these things, while not curative in this world, are none the less palliative of man's lasting wretchedness. But talk of that order, Mr. Wolfe cannot endure, and, Holy Christ, by the blood-and-bones-of-God, he will not put up with any such s.o.b. twaddling cant, be good-and-God-damned if he will, so help him Jesus! And so on . . . It is not going too far to feel that this is very distressing.

Another remedy for man's pain, older far than sulphur and molasses or than sassafras tea, is the sense of being identified with one's people, of being actually a part, as an oak is, or a cabbage, of the earth from which one derives. It is a remedy highly spoken of, and Mr. Wolfe has evidently had word of it. He discusses it a length in connection with Eugene's disquiet in Europe—his fixed impression that neither he nor any other American could be at ease there—and his belief, which may or may not have materialized, that at home, in America, he would be less tortured.

It is a safe bet that America alone did not solve Eugene's problem effectively. For that large equation is very vague, and the problem involved demanded something definite and pointed. Away from the United States, Eugene might idealize it readily, rhapsodizing over its magnitude and the big, swift trains that go roaring across it. That idealization could not have been ultimately deep. He says in fact that for getting one's work done (that is, one's very best, artistic work, the sort of work that demands the whole functioning of the artist's nature) one place is as good as another. So much for those who feel it necessary to think of home only in terms of a continent. It would be as practical to think of the continent in terms of a cottage, which, for all the fables that science has abolished distance, the continent still very positively is not.

Eugene's friend Starwick was a Middle-Western American, and although he wished himself something else, it was true, as Eugene rightly and unanswerably explained to him, that he could never be a Frenchman, nor anything indeed except what he was. Well, Eugene is a Southerner, and though the South may not be so culturally alien from America at large as America at large is from England or France, there remains surely, for one of Eugene's sensitivity to recognize (indeed he talks much about it) a disparity between Northern ways and Southern ways. Altamont is assuredly not Mobile, nor is Eugene to be confused with, say, Lucius Rhett—fancy young Lucius, aged nineteen, shrieking to his mother "Now, for God's sake, I don't want to hear what you are saying. God-damn it, can we have no peace?" Fancy that. Oh, Eugene is not Lucius (whether he is better or worse, does not matter here); Eugene for his part forswears the South belligerently—it had jolly well never given *him* anything; he exults in his determination never again to live there.

None the less, Eugene is a Catawba, mama-and-papa-saying, Presbyterian Southerner; or he is nothing. And he is very emphatically not nothing.

"*Oh, lost, lost!*" is the refrain, constantly echoed, that this man from Old Catawba, immured now in Brooklyn, N.Y., cries piteously through most that he has written. It would be an interesting thing, and worthy of much wonder, if in his case this should prove inexorable: that to live validly and with satisfying peace he should be driven to a reconciliation with his origins; should be obliged, in the vast area of his sympathies, to make room for the people who bred him.

Paul Hoffman. "The Man of the Month: Thomas Wolfe." *Atlantic Monthly,* 156 (August 1935), 6.

This is the long-awaited successor to Mr. Wolfe's *Look Homeward, Angel.* In substance it resumes the saga of Eugene Gant (Wolfe himself, of course), covering the years 1920-1925. The book opens as Eugene, now twenty, stands on the station platform in his native Altamont, about to entrain 'for the proud unknown North,' for Cambridge and Harvard, where he is to enroll as a graduate student. In the course of the narrative he returns home, sets out once more,—this time for New York,—goes later to Oxford, to Paris, and through the French countryside, to come back home in the end to 'the huge, single, and incomparable substance of America.' It teems with characters—many of them but thinly disguised in their identities; there are those whom he knew intimately, those with whom he had the barest acquaintance, and others who were nameless but remembered with his curious flair for remembrance.

It is not the 'matter' of Wolfe, however, that is above all interesting, but the 'manner' and, behind both of these, the man himself. As in his earlier book, he has in this as well alternated in his structure between purely prosaic narrative—in which nothing is omitted, neither the slightest gesture nor the most trivial inflection—and flights of intense, personal, Whitmanesque poetry. Not that the latter is in any sense formalized verse, of course, but it easily might be, were it only arranged on the page as arbitrarily as most of Whitman's. Much of it is beautiful, exquisitely beautiful—full-throated, sonorous, and vital; and much of it is inferior, hyperbolic and adolescent. And so it is an uneven book, and in its excessive length badly proportioned.

I have used the word 'adolescent.' As a matter of fact, *Of Time and the River* is an entire history of late adolescence, of those urgent pangs that are the growing pains of the spirit especially. 'A Legend of Man's Hunger in His Youth' Wolfe has called it. I said, too, that nothing is omitted, for that is Wolfe's method. But beyond and above all methods there must in any mature work of art be implications that unify the disparate atoms of thought and action and cause their ultimate coherence, implications which constitute some mature and constructive comment on the work's substance. I find too few of these in the present book; the man, his point of view and its conscious ordering of his materials, seem essentially adolescent, too. There is too much 'hunger' here and too little 'appetite.'

The device Wolfe has adopted of telling his own story in the third person,—always, I think, a difficult and dangerous one,—explains a great deal. Detachment is hard to achieve at any time, but especially so when the subject is oneself. In the latter case the temptation is to dramatize, so that what results is likely to be distortion rather than verisimilitude. This is definitely true in Wolfe's case. I do not deny his sincerity in regarding and reproducing himself as he does: doubtless he believes in the aberrant enormity that Eugene Gant often is. But, from the reader's point of view, there is something lacking in that confused and heightened figure—something that is human and universal and immediate, lost in the long transition from 'I' to 'he.'

This distortion, I feel, was considerably less in *Look Homeward, Angel*, perhaps because the unified experience of childhood and early youth attains completeness more readily than those later years which are still near and therefore closely felt and seen, adhering to the individual although not yet to each other. It may be less again in those four volumes which are still to come in Wolfe's large series and which, together with these first two, will comprise a far-spread record of American living through a century and a half. But it is not easy, either, to re-create antecedents; there is a tendency to glorify and to disparage, to multiply imaginary distinctions or through shortsightedness to neglect obvious ones. If Wolfe is successful in this further task of his, if the fact and feeling of it are those of assimilation and not the mere sudden jets of an unorganized genius,

then his achievement will place him among the foremost, not of Americans only, but of those great world figures who, like Proust, spun and wove the fine fibres of their own lives into enduring fabrics and into patterns of beauty.

Checklist of Additional Reviews

John Chamberlain. Column "Books of the Times." New York *Times*, March 8, 1935, p. L19, and March 12, 1935, p. 19.

Harry Hansen. "The First Reader." New York *World Telegram*, March 8, 1935.

Marion L. Starkey. "Along the Course of Time and the River." Boston *Evening Transcript*, March 9, 1935, p. 1.

Franklin P. Adams. Column, "The Conning Tower." New York *Herald Tribune*, March 9, 1935, p. 11.

Clifton Fadiman. "Thomas Wolfe." *New Yorker*, 11 (March 9, 1935), 79–82.

"U.S. Voice." *Time*, 25 (March 11, 1935), 77.

"Wolfe's New Book." Asheville *Times*, March 12, 1935.

"PILGRIMAGE: Gant Continues His Quest for Life's Answers." *Newsweek*, 5 (March 16, 1935), 40.

Henry Bellamann. Column, "The Literary Highway." Charlotte *Observer*, March 17, 1935.

Phillips Russell. "Books and Writers." Charlotte *Observer*, March 17, 1935.

John S. Terry. "Calls Wolfe's Novel 'Book of America' and Work of Great Genius." Charlotte *Observer*, March 17, 1935.

Malcolm Cowley. "The Forty Days of Thomas Wolfe." *New Republic*, 82 (March 20, 1935), 163-64.

Joe Sugarman. "Thomas Wolfe Hungers On." *Carolina Magazine*, April, 1935, pp. 22-24.

John Chamberlain. *Current History*, 42 (April 1935), iii.

Ann Preston Bridgers. "Thomas Wolfe Legends of Man's Hunger in His Youth." *Saturday Review of Literature*, April 6, 1935, p. 599.

Amy Loveman. "Books of the Spring." *Saturday Review of Literature*, April 6, 1935, p. 602.

"Spring Fiction." New York *Sun*, April 12, 1935.

Weimar Jones. Asheville *Citizen*, April 21, 1935, p. 6B.

Robert Penn Warren. "A Note on the Hamlet of Thomas Wolfe." *American Review*, 5 (May 1935), 191-208.

Elizabeth Wilson. *Bluets* [Asheville], 6 (May 1935), 31-32.

Seymour Kantor. *Washington Square Critic*, 1 (May 1935), 15-16.

William Howard. "Praise for Thomas Wolfe." *New Republic*. 82 (May 1, 1935), 343.

Geoffrey Stone. "In Praise of Fury." *Commonweal*, 22 (May 10, 1935), 36-37.

Evelyn Scott. "Colossal Fragment." *Scribner's*, 97 (June 1935), 2, 4.

Herschel S. Harkins. "Tom Wolfe's Book." Asheville *Citizen-Times*, June 2, 1935.

"Author of the Month." *Digest and Review*, July, 1935.

Saturday Review [London], 160 (August 17, 1935), 56.

Seán O'Faoláin. "Fiction." *Spectator*, 155 (August 23, 1935), 300.

Peter Quennell. "New Novels." *New Statesman and Nation*, 10 (August 24, 1935), 253.

Charles I. Glicksberg. "Thomas Wolfe." *Canadian Forum*, 15 (January 1936), 24-25.

Notes

FROM DEATH
TO
MORNING

by

Thomas Wolfe

Vigil strange I kept on the field one night.

CHARLES SCRIBNER'S SONS

NEW YORK

From Death to Morning

Ferner Nuhn. "Thomas Wolfe, Six-Foot-Six." New York *Herald Tribune Books,* November 17, 1935, p. 7.

. . .

The story that follows, called "Gulliver," tells how the world looks from six feet six, and what six feet six has to suffer in the way of endless and unoriginal humor from a five-foot-eight world. (How's the weather up there? . . . Ho-lee Jeez! What's de guy standin' on!" Etc.) The story does not get much further than that.

But in a wider sense almost everything Thomas Wolfe writes is the story of a six-foot-six man in a five-foot-eight world. The extra exuberance, the unsatisfied longings, the oversized reactions to change, motion, scenes, events (and ships!), the outcries of loneliness, the floods of words poured forth to convey these emotions, the piling of Mississippi on top of Niagara—all this seems to proceed from the extra ten inches of body and appetite that can't be accommodated in the ordinary world.

The fourteen stories in the present volume are for the most part further experiences of an oversized organism in a standard-sized world. Few may be called short stories in any strict sense; lyrical essays, themes with variations, moods of reminiscence, they might perhaps be called.

Thus "No Door" describes the gap between exalted loneliness and ordinary modes of existence; "Death the Proud Brother" is in praise of the great leveler, with four examples of how he touches with dignity the little men he overtakes on city streets; "The Face of the War" gives four episodes showing the sadism, hysteria, lust and crude humor of war's violation of ordinary human standards. All these and most of the other stories are oriented to the personality of the author and pitched on the plane of his heightened sensibilities.

Of particular interest, then, are the few stories which are more objective in method. One of these, "The Far and the Near," may be dismissed as a romantic "idea" for a story, and nothing more. Another, however, "In the Park," strikes a distinctive note as it pictures, about the turn of the century, a ride through Central Park in one of the first automobiles. With its well drawn characters and sympathetic evocation of the time, it has something of the genre quality of a Currier & Ives print.

Most original in conception is a story called "The Four Lost Men." Were there actually four men named Garfield, Arthur, Harrison and Hayes? With a sort of furious affirmation, the author tries to fill in the blanks of their composite and bewhiskered legend, insisting that Garfield-Arthur-Harrison-Hayes *must* actually have lived, even if they left no evidence of the fact.

Potentially the strongest story is "The Web of Earth," a long retrospective narrative, crowded with episodes, whose underlying theme seems to contrast the homemaking stability of women with the lust, violence and wandering spirit of men. But the thread is often lost in extraneous incidents and confusing details.

The advantages of an oversized view of the world are obvious in Thomas Wolfe's work: the heightened color, mood, sweep, rush which can so easily carry lesser organisms along. But there are disadvantages, too. The bulge of an excess of emotion is as flabby in the end as the slack of an insufficient one. Readers swept off their feet have a way of picking themselves up and rejecting further rides, and this would be a pity.

There is point to the remark of the weary European traveler in "Dark in the Forest" when he says to the eager young American, "Fields, hills, mountains, riffers, cities, peoples—you vish to know zem all. Vun field, vun hill, vun riffer," the man whispered, "zat is enough." Better channeled, Thomas Wolfe's undoubted powers might carve out more solidly the shapes of the "big themes" he feels so intensely but which are too often left hollow, and the praise he has been given be protected from excessive reaction.

Howard Mumford Jones. "Thomas Wolfe's Short Stories." *Saturday Review of Literature*, 13 (November 30, 1935), 13.

I think it is Chesterton who remarks there is no such thing as a Dickens novel, but only a series of segments cut off from that vast and flowing thing which is Dickens. "From Death to Morning" is a collection of fourteen segments cut off from that vast and flowing thing which is Thomas Wolfe. The fourteenth of these, "The Web of Earth," is a large fragment from the Gant saga; the others are mainly remembrances of Mr. Wolfe's life in North Carolina, New York, Europe, or wherever his spirit has carried him. I suppose the collection is best described as a group of sketches, for none of them rises into a full-bodied short story, and only one of them, "The Men of Old Catawba," sinks into the more passive condition of the essay. But as in Mr. Wolfe's novels form cracks and dissolves in the current of emotional life, so in these sketches the ordinary canons of form disintegrate.

Mr. Wolfe has not increased his resources. The characteristic combination of brooding emotion and graphic brutality, of poetry *à la* Whitman and realism *à la* Zola which we have learned to expect of him, again appears. In certain cases the being confined to shorter space (I cannot call it form) improves the unity of impression, but Mr. Wolfe is uncertain, and often wilfully violates the simplest principles of construction. "The Four Lost Men," for example, begins as a prose rhapsody about a young man in war-time, continues as a realistic transcript of the elder Gant's conversation regarding presidential elections, and concludes as a Wolfian prose-poem about life, death, war, and time. The graphic and painful "Death the Proud Brother" describes four deaths which the author has witnessed in New York, and has, in this sense, unity, but there is neither rhyme nor reason in the proportioning of space among its fifty-five pages.

Admirers of Mr. Wolfe say these things do not matter, and they are encouraged in their indiscriminate adulation by the excitement of the reviewers, who have exhausted language in praising this writer. Mr. Wolfe has power, passion, a singular fearlessness, the ability to create individual scenes of brilliant truth, a genius for lyrical prose unequalled in contemporary letters, insight into certain types of characters and problems. But Mr. Wolfe the artist has advanced scarcely a step beyond "Look Homeward, Angel." He is full of self-pity. If he is a genius, he is still an adolescent genius. His universe is utterly or mainly subjective, and the result is a transcript of experience curiously true in some particulars, curiously false in others.

Take, for example, Mr. Wolfe's heroines. No one seems to have remarked the incredibly naive formula on which they are constructed. Most of them resemble the heroine of "Dark in the Forest" in the present volume, voluptuous and beautiful. This one is "a miracle of loveliness," of "a superb and queenly height," a "lovely figure" which "seemed never to have lost the lithe slenderness of girlhood" and is yet "undulant with all the voluptuous maturity of womanhood." Mark the

clichés. When we meet this woman in Ouida or Bulwer-Lytton, we smile at this falsity. Not so Mr. Wolfe. The thought of this wonderful creature stimulates the flow of his adjectives. She has "a vague, voluptuous smile." When she speaks, it is "eagerly, earnestly, gleefully," and her laugh is "welling low, rich, sensual, and tender." There are in his endless pages only two sorts of females—the houri and the shrew.

This simple antithesis is characteristic of the universe he creates. He sees only elemental distinctions. Life is either vast, noble, brooding, and lyric, or it is sordid and mean. Men are either demigods or cowards. He is forever in extremes, and that between the extremes there is a place for rational human life he does not seem to suspect. In fact, he has no place for reason. It may be true, as Mr. Canby says, that Mr. Wolfe "has more material, more vitality, more originality, more gusto" than any two other novelists, but this vitality, this gusto swing like a pendulum from heaven to hell, from rapture to disgust. He is the most restless of writers. His characters are forever making Gargantuan journeys over the face of the world or else sulking in one place, timid, bitter, beaten, and without will. One's first contact with this powerful spirit is like an electric shock, but after a series of such shocks the mind grows fatigued, attention wanders, and one begins to suspect that if there is something Homeric in Mr. Wolfe, there is also in him the shoddy violence of Jack London.

The American novel needs what Mr. Wolfe has to bring to it—curiosity, beauty, emotional energy—and I do not in the least mean that Mr. Wolfe is not an important writer. It is, however, precisely because he has done so well that it is essential for him to do more; and if the next portions of the Gant saga simply repeat the formula he has established, Mr. Wolfe is doomed to sink into repetitiousness. The present collection has its brilliant moments, but the total effect of the book is to make one uneasy about Mr. Wolfe's future development as an artist.

Hamilton Basso. "Mountain View." *New Republic*, 86 (January 1, 1936), 232.

There is, in this book of shorter pieces by Mr. Thomas Wolfe, one story, called "Gulliver," that might well serve as an introductory preface to all his work. It is a simple story, done with a sharp sense of humor, describing how it feels to be—as Mr. Wolfe is—a very tall man. From it we get a sense of the oneness, the isolation, that Mr. Wolfe undoubtedly has. This physical uniqueness of Mr. Wolfe (and he is not, as Mr. Ernest Hemingway says, sad like Carnera) seems to have aroused the conviction that the same uniqueness extends to his emotional and intellectual adventures—or, as it seems in "Of Time and the River," so universal an experience as riding on a train. "In an extraordinary way," writes the author, "a tall man comes to know things about the world as other people do not, cannot, know them."

The stories in this book, with two or three exceptions, are all rooted in Mr. Wolfe's conviction of his own special quality, his own uniqueness. It is testimony of his unusual talent that he

manages, even in those pieces which do not quite succeed ("The Bums at Sunset," for example, and "The Men of Old Catawba"), to invest them with a character that is, unquestionably, unique. Only in the broadest sense of the word are most of them short stories. Save for pieces like "Gulliver" and, perhaps, "Only the Dead Know Brooklyn," they might easily have been introduced into Mr. Wolfe's novels. "Death the Proud Brother," for example, is easily identified as a fragment from "Of Time and the River," and "The Face of the War" and "The Web of Earth" could well have been part of "Look Homeward, Angel."

I do not mean to say, however, that Mr. Wolfe is serving left-over fare. He is continuing the description of the world as it looks from the strange and lonely mountain-top of six feet six. What he sees excites him (the ability to become excited is one of the main sources of his power) and sometimes he must pour out his excitement in hymns and chants. "From Death to Morning" gains its chief distinction from those pages of dithyrambic declamation that resemble the hymns to America and to October contained in "Of Time and the River." Rejoicing, Mr. Wolfe can make us rejoice with him.

R. P. Blackmur. "Notes on the Novel." *Southern Review*, 1 (Spring 1936), 897-99.

. . .

How to value such a work [Conrad Aiken's *King Coffin*] will remain a problem only to those who are devotees of the fine game of literary precedence. Admitting that it belongs in a special compartment, one ought to be able to take it for what it is—the imaginative exercise of a dramatic possibility based upon the conventional melodrama of modern psychology, in short a legitimate, because persuasive, *tour de force.* But as many will refuse so simple a salute, I want to make one or two further distinctions. It should be insisted that the book itself is sane and everywhere alert to the responsibilities of the rational artist, and it is only by the seductive slight of art that the reader is made to feel otherwise. The value of that sanity and the scope of that rational responsibility may be felt most obviously in connection with works which are helpless, at bottom, because without their governance: e.g., Thomas Wolfe's *From Death to Morning* and Gordon Friesen's *Flamethrowers,* both ailing overgrowths of superabundant sensibility.

Both these authors take their material from experience felt at hysterical intensity, and as their works develop, the hysteria replaces and obscures instead of mirroring and controlling the experience. The subjects of both are the stupid, the distraught, the oppressed; and Mr. Wolfe with his greater talent and better knowledge merely expresses those qualities at their own level with more lyrical fervor than Mr. Friesen can muster. Mr. Friesen is a worse, because a more barbarous, Wolfe: both are equally guilty of the heresy of expressive form: the belief, held to exaggeration, that life best expresses itself in art by duplicating its own confusion in the transferred form of the *spectator's* emotion. Write what you see, whatever it is, and say what you

feel or ought to feel, and the thing will make itself a work of art. That most writing on this rule, not wholly turgid, is autobiographical, is the first clue to its insufficience. The fundamental insufficience, however, is in the lack of sanity in the presiding form and the absence of a rational point of view. Returning, for our point, to Mr. Aiken's book: its hero, Jasper Ammen, might be as stupid, distraught, and oppressed as any creature of Mr. Wolfe or Mr. Friesen, and as a matter of fact, on his own *intellectual* level, he is. Form, we might say, is the only sanity—the only principle of balanced response—possible to art: as lyric form will make the right nonsense into poetry; and to force your material—which is to say to condense, to elaborate, to foreshorten and give perspective and direction—into your chosen form so as to express it primarily by actualizing it—that is the minimum of your rational responsibility. You may do more if you wish; your work may come to an ideal vision like Santayana's *Last Puritan* or *Gulliver's Travels;* but if you do less, you will not have written a responsible fiction; you will have expressed, not your subject, but yourself and more or less waste matter of emotion besides.

. . .

Rollene W. Saal. "Pick of the Paperbacks." *Saturday Review of Literature,* 48 (October 23, 1965), 62.

. . . The fourteen short stories in Thomas Wolfe's *From Death to Mom-*

ing (Scribners, $1.65) remind us again how compelling a writer Wolfe was, and how careless. This collection, which includes the frequently anthologized "Only the Dead Know Brooklyn," surges with the ebullience of his original if untidy prose. . . .

Checklist of Additional Reviews

Herschel Brickell. New York *Post*, December 14, 1935, p. 15.

Lewis Gannett. New York *Herald Tribune*, November 15, 1935, p. 15.

John Chamberlain. Column, "Books of the Times." New York *Times*, November 15, 1935, p. 19.

Clayton Hoagland. New York *Sun*, November 14, 1935, p. 26.

Peter Monro Jack. "The Turbulence of Mr. Wolfe." New York *Times Book Review*, November 24, 1935, p. 6.

Edith Weigle. Chicago *Daily Tribune*, December 14, 1935, p. 16.

Paul Hoffman. *Atlantic Monthly*, 157 (April 1936), 9.

James Ball, S.J. *Best Sellers*, 17 (March 15, 1958), 431–432.

J. B. Clark. "This Wolfe Dish Tasty." Chicago *Herald-American*, March 30, 1958.

G. M. White. *The Psychiatric Quarterly* [Utica, New York], July, 1958.

A. Hamilton. *Books and Bookmen*, 7 (December 1965), 52.

Notes

the story
of a
NOVEL

By

Thomas Wolfe

CHARLES SCRIBNER'S SONS · NEW YORK
CHARLES SCRIBNER'S SONS · LTD · LONDON
1936

The Story of a Novel

Paula Snelling.
"Thomas Wolfe: The
Story of a Marvel."
Pseudopodia [*North
Georgia Review*], 1
(Spring 1936), 1, 8, 12.

When a new star bursts upon our world, astronomical or literary, our attention is most easily and quickly riveted upon its size, speed, nearness, brilliance. Only later do we pass on to a consideration of the elements of which it is composed and of its relationship to the rest of the universe. Then opinions are put forth tentatively and even more time must elapse before there is much permanent unanimity of judgment. During the last few years these phenomenal aspects of Thomas Wolfe's greatness have dazzled our eyes. Only now can interest shift to an analysis of his talents and what they are likely to mean to us.

Without doubt Thomas Wolfe is distinguished not only among his contemporaries but among the writers of all time in quantitative matters. I suspect that his sense receptors are unusually keen and that his glands function with exceptional vigor. There is a hint in one of his earlier articles that his above average size lowers the threshold of his consciousness to things mensurable. He has an insatiable appetite for sensory experiences, an almost pathological preoccupation with numbers; a compulsion not only to read a stupendous number of books and to write an unprecedented number of words but to gloat over the mere mass of these things. He sticks not one but ten fingers into life's pie, and pulls out not one but ten, twenty . . . forty . . . plums. He is charmed with the purple color of these plums . . . he would like to taste one but how can he pause to taste *one* when there are forty . . . eighty . . . ?

Those who desire to increase his reputation have made much of this mass mania. I do not know whether they have themselves been swept off their feet by the tide of his quantitative excesses, or have merely recognized and played upon the ease with which the corollary of his fame could be made to follow, in a country and a generation as marathon-minded as ours, upon America's most popular axiom: "A hundred thousand—anything—can't be wrong." True, Wolfe confessed in his *The Story of a Novel* to quite a bit of difficulty and despair before getting his first book ready for publication. So success was not too easy. But even here he seems much more engrossed with the depth and darkness and numerical frequency of his despondency than with the despondency itself.

Despite the fact that quality and quantity are so seldom seen together that the discriminating are at times tempted to take the presence of one as prima facie evidence of the absence of the other, Wolfe possesses both. For style, I take it, is a qualitative thing. And Wolfe has a style which is individual, distinctive, arresting, powerful. So impressive a style that one can hardly quarrel with Carl van Doren for putting him among the immortals in his recent Anthology of World Prose. But a careful analysis of this style leaves one with the impression that it is dependent upon his appetite for numbers. Certainly he has transmitted a multiplicity of sense impressions into phrases which in their cumulative effect resound musically and potently upon the reader. One is constantly amazed at his ability to pile adjective upon adjective until his tower of Babel reaches to the skies without incurring the curse of a confusion of tongues. But when one tries to disentangle his style from his compulsion to rush from one sensation to another with a pause only long enough to photograph its outer surface and count it, there emerges little that is unique and commanding. He seems never to have been engulfed by any one emotion long enough to plumb the depths of it, never to have been aware enough of the tragedy of any one individual or one situation to have his soul torn by it.

The great artist customarily has been made by first having his heart tortured and his mind stretched by observing or experiencing to its depths one and then another of life's tragedies until finally he arrives at a comprehension of mankind's universal suffering and weakness and nobility. He then reveals this to us in some new specific imaginative tale which is more pregnant than any one thing he has directly encountered because it preserves the essence of them all. Wolfe has short-circuited this specific-general-imaginative gamut with an amazing but not all-satisfying success. He sees the surface of innumerable situations simultaneously and reveals one of them directly with the two-dimensional accuracy of a camera and the zest of eager powerful young manhood, but this same eager youth impels him to rush on to the next glittering surface without realizing much more than the numerical significance of the last one.

When I had read about half of his first book I found myself saying "What a writer this man will be if the gods ever choose to grind him through those mills from which alone emerge the exceeding fine sensitiveness of the great artist and the emotional maturity which most of us are never buffeted into." But, now at the end of two more books, I am doubtful that he is grist for these mills. It might be as disastrous to run him through them as to run Peter Pan through them. For I suspect that Thomas Wolfe's style is a by-product of his naive vigor and that he himself is the spirit of vital potent young manhood personified—magnified—almost deified. That and nothing more. And that perhaps is as much as we should look for in any one individual. No one has ever wanted Peter Pan to grow beyond the realm of childhood; and no one, perhaps, should want Thomas Wolfe to mature beyond the realm of young manhood. There are few spectacles to which mankind can respond with such ubiquitous and spontaneous appreciation as that of zestful questing youth. And there is little likelihood that Thomas Wolfe will be frequently rivaled in the capacity to entrap that spirit on the written page.

But in the middle of *The Story of a Novel*, Wolfe himself seems to have begun wondering if he has been whoring after false gods. It appears that he has been taking stock and catching glimpses of other levels than those in which he has gloried and achieved. If he comes to doubt seriously the supreme value of his world of sensations he must lose some of his unconscious assurance, some of his teeming vitality, some of his potency, and with that his "style." And there is no indication as yet that he has any other supreme qualifications for comprehending and revealing the world of the mature artist. We can only wait and see.

Bernard De Voto. "Genius Is Not Enough." *Saturday Review of Literature*, 13 (April 25, 1936), 3–4, 14–15.

Some months ago *The Saturday Review* serialized Mr. Thomas Wolfe's account of the conception, gestation, and as yet uncompleted delivery of his Novel, and Scribners are now publishing the three articles as a book. It is one of the most appealing books of our time. No one who reads it can doubt Mr. Wolfe's complete dedication to his job or regard with anything but respect his attempt to describe the dark and nameless fury of the million-footed life swarming in his dark and unknown soul. So honest or so exhaustive an effort at self-analy-

sis in the interest of esthetics has seldom been made in the history of American literature, and "The Story of a Novel" is likely to have a long life as a source-book for students of literature and for psychologists as well. But also it brings into the public domain material that has been hitherto outside the privilege of criticism. Our first essay must be to examine it in relation to Mr. Wolfe's novels, to see what continuities and determinants it may reveal, and to inquire into their bearing on the art of fiction.

Let us begin with one of many aspects of Mr. Wolfe's novels that impress the reader, the frequent recurrence of material to which one must apply the adjective placental. (The birth metaphors are imposed by Mr. Wolfe himself. In "The Story of a Novel" he finds himself big with first a thunder cloud and then a river. The symbolism of waters is obviously important to him, and the title of his latest novel is to be that of the series as a whole.) A great part of "Look Homeward, Angel" was just the routine first-novel of the period, which many novelists had published and many others had suppressed, the story of a sensitive and rebellious adolescent who was headed toward the writing of novels. The rest of it was not so easily catalogued. Parts of it showed intuition, understanding, and ecstasy, and an ability to realize all three in character and scene, whose equal it would have been hard to point out anywhere in the fiction of the time. These looked like great talent, and in such passages as the lunchroom scene in the dawn that Mr. Wolfe called nacreous some fifty times, they seemed to exist on both a higher and a deeper level of realization than any of Mr. Wolfe's contemporaries had attained.

But also there were parts that looked very dubious indeed—long, whirling discharges of words, unabsorbed in the novel, unrelated to the proper business of fiction, badly if not altogether unacceptably written, raw gobs of emotion, aimless and quite meaningless jabber, claptrap, belches, grunts, and Tarzan-like screams. Their rawness, their unshaped quality, must be insisted upon; it was as if the birth of the novel had been accompanied by a lot of the material that had nourished its gestation. The material which nature and most novelists discard when its use has been served. It looked like one of two things, there was no telling which. It looked like the self-consciously literary posturing of a novelist too young and too naive to have learned his trade. Or, from another point of view, it looked like a document in psychic disintegration. And one of the most important questions in contemporary literature was: would the proportion of fiction to placenta increase or decrease in Mr. Wolfe's next book?

It decreased. If fiction of the quality of that lunchroom scene made up about one-fifth of "Look Homeward, Angel," it constituted, in "Of Time and the River," hardly more than a tenth. The placental material had enormously grown and, what was even more ominous, it now had a rationalization. It was as unshaped as before, but it had now been retroactively associated with the dark and nameless heaving of the voiceless and unknown womb of Time, and with the unknown and voiceless fury of the dark and lonely and lost America. There were still passages where Mr. Wolfe was a novelist not only better than most of his contemporaries but altogether out of their class. But they were pushed farther apart and

even diluted when they occurred by this dark substance which may have been nameless but was certainly far from voiceless.

Certain other aspects of the new book seemed revealing. For one thing, there was a shocking contempt of the medium. Some passages were not completely translated from the "I" in which they had apparently been written to the "he" of Eugene Gant. Other passages alluded to incidents which had probably appeared in an earlier draft but could not be found in the final one. Others contradictorily reported scenes which had already appeared, and at least once a passage that had seen service already was re-enlisted for a second hitch in a quite different context, apparently with no recollection that it had been used before.

Again, a state of mind that had been appropriate to the puberty of Eugene seemed inappropriate as the boy grew older, and might therefore be significant. I mean the giantism of the characters. Eugene himself, in "Of Time and the River," was clearly a borderline manic-depressive: he exhibited the classic cycle in his alternation between "fury" and "despair," and the classic accompaniment of obsessional neurosis in the compulsions he was under to read all the books in the world, see all the people in Boston, observe all the lives of the man-swarm, and list all the names and places in America. That was simple enough, but practically every other character in the book also suffered from fury and compulsions; and, what was more suggestive, they were all twenty feet tall, spoke with the voice of trumpets and the thunder, ate like Pantagruel, wept like Niobe, laughed like Falstaff, and bellowed like the bulls of Bashan. The significant thing was that we were seeing them all through Eugene's eyes. To a child all adults are giants: their voices are thunderous, their actions are portentous and grotesquely magnified, and all their exhibited emotions are seismic. It looked as if part of Eugene's condition was an infantile regression.

This apparance was reinforced by what seemed to be another stigma of infantilism: that all the experiences in "Of Time and the River" were on the same level and had the same value. When Mr. Gant died (of enough cancer to have exterminated an army corps), the reader accepted the accompanying frenzy as proper to the death of a man's father—which is one of the most important events in anyone's life. But when the same frenzy accompanied nearly everything else in the book—a ride on a railroad train, a literary tea-fight, a midnight lunch in the kitchen, a quarrel between friends, a walk at night, the rejection of a play, an automobile trip, a seduction that misfired, the discovery of Eugene's true love— one could only decide that something was dreadfully wrong. If the death of one's father comes out emotionally even with a ham-on-rye, then the art of fiction is cockeyed.

Well, "The Story of a Novel" puts an end to speculation and supplies some unexpected but very welcome light. To think of these matters as contempt of the medium, regression, and infantilism is to be too complex and subtle. The truth shows up in two much simpler facts: that Mr. Wolfe is still astonishingly immature, and that he has mastered neither the psychic material out of which a novel is made nor the technique of writing fiction. He does not seem aware of the first fact, but he acknowledges the second with a

frankness and an understanding that are the finest promise to date for his future books. How far either defect is reparable it is idle to speculate. But at least Mr. Wolfe realizes that he is, as yet, by no means a complete novelist.

The most flagrant evidence of his incompleteness is the fact that, so far, one indispensable part of the artist has existed not in Mr. Wolfe but in Maxwell Perkins. Such organizing faculty and such critical intelligence as have been applied to the book have come not from inside the artist, not from the artist's feeling for form and esthetic integrity, but from the office of Charles Scribner's Sons. For five years the artist pours out words "like burning lava from a volcano"—with little or no idea what their purpose is, which book they belong in, what the relation of part to part is, what is organic and what irrelevant, or what emphasis or coloration in the completed work of art is being served by the job at hand. Then Mr. Perkins decides these questions—from without, and by a process to which rumor applies the word "assembly." But works of art cannot be assembled like a carburetor—they must be grown like a plant, or in Mr. Wolfe's favorite simile, like an embryo. The artist writes a hundred thousand words about a train: Mr. Perkins decides that the train is worth only five thousand words. But such a decision as this is properly not within Mr. Perkins's power; it must be made by the highly conscious self-criticism of the artist in relation to the pulse of the book itself. Worse still, the artist goes on writing till Mr. Perkins tells him that the novel is finished. But the end of a novel is, properly, dictated by the internal pressure, osmosis, metabolism—what you will—of the novel itself, of which only the novelist can have a first-hand knowledge. There comes a point where the necessities of the book are satisfied, where its organic processes have reached completion. It is hard to see how awareness of that point can manifest itself at an editor's desk—and harder still to trust the integrity of a work of art in which not the artist but the publisher has determined where the true ends and the false begins.

All this is made more ominous by Mr. Wolfe's almost incredibly youthful attitude toward revision. No novel is written till it is revised—the process is organic, it is one of the processes of art. It is, furthermore, the process above all others that requires objectivity, a feeling for form, a knowledge of what the necessities of the book are, a determination that those necessities shall outweigh and dominate everything else. It is, if not the highest functioning of the artistic intelligence, at least a fundamental and culminating one. But the process appears to Mr. Wolfe not one which will free his book from falsity, irrelevance, and its private incumbrances, not one which will justify and so exalt the artist—but one that makes his spirit quiver "at the bloody execution" and his soul "recoil from the carnage of so many lovely things." But superfluous and mistaken things are lovely to only a very young writer, and the excision of them is bloody carnage only if the artist has not learned to subdue his ego in favor of his book. And the same juvenility makes him prowl "the streets of Paris like a maddened animal" because—for God's sake!—the reviewers may not like the job.

The placental passages are now explained. They consist of psychic material which the novelist has proved una-ble to shape into fiction. The failure may be due either to immature understanding or to insufficient technical skill: probably both causes operate here and cannot be separated. The principle is very simple. When Mr. Wolfe gives us his doctors, undertakers, and newspapermen talking in a lunchroom at dawn, he does his job—magnificently. There they are, and the reader revels in the dynamic presentation of human beings, and in something else as well that should have the greatest possible significance for Mr. Wolfe. For while the doctors and undertakers are chaffing one another, the reader gets that feeling of the glamour and mystery of American life which Mr. Wolfe elsewhere unsuccessfully labors to evoke in thousands of rhapsodic words. The novelist makes his point in the lives of his characters, not in tidal surges of rhetoric.

Is America lost, lonely, nameless, and unknown? Maybe, and maybe not. But if it is, the condition of the novelist's medium requires him to make it lost and lonely in the lives of his characters, not in blank verse, bombast, and apocalyptic delirium. You cannot represent America by hurling adjectives at it. Do "the rats of death and age and dark oblivion feed forever at the roots of sleep?" It sounds like a high school valedictory, but if in fact they do then the novelist is constrained to show them feeding so by means of what his characters do and say and feel in relation to one another, and not by chasing the ghosts of Whitman and Ezekiel through fifty pages of disembodied emotion. Such emotion is certainly the material that fiction works with, but until it is embodied in character and scene it is not fiction—it is only logorrhea. A poem should not mean but be, Mr. MacLeish tells us, and poetry is always proving that fundamental. In a homelier aphorism Mr. Cohan has expressed the same imperative of the drama: "Don't tell 'em, show 'em." In the art of fiction the *thing* is not only an imperative, it is a primary condition. A novel *is*—it cannot be asserted, ranted, or even detonated. A novelist represents life. When he does anything else, no matter how beautiful or furious or ecstatic the way in which he does it, he is not writing fiction. Mr. Wolfe can write fiction—has written some of the finest fiction of our day. But a great part of what he writes is not fiction at all: it is only material with which the novelist has struggled but which has defeated him. The most important question in American fiction today, probably, is whether he can win that encounter in his next book. It may be that "The October Fair" and "The Hills Beyond Pentland" will show him winning it, but one remembers the dilution from "Look Homeward, Angel" to "Of Time and the River" and is apprehensive. If he does win it, he must do so inside himself; Mr. Perkins and the assembly line at Scribners' can do nothing to help him.

That struggle has another aspect. A novelist utilizes the mechanism of fantasy for the creation of a novel, and there are three kinds of fantasy with which he works. One of them is unconscious fantasy, about which Dr. Kubie was writing in these columns something over a year ago. A novelist is wholly subject to its emphases and can do nothing whatever about them— though when Mr. Wolfe says that the center of all living is reconciliation with one's father he comes close to revealing its pattern in him. There remain two

kinds of fantasy which every novelist employs—but which every one employs in a different ratio. Call them identification and projection, call them automatic and directed, call them proliferating and objectified—the names do not matter. The novelist surrenders himself to the first kind, but dominates and directs the second kind. In the first kind he says "I am Napoleon" and examines himself to see how he feels. In the second kind, he wonders how Napoleon feels, and instead of identifying himself with him, he tries to discover Napoleon's necessities. If he is excessively endowed with the first kind of fantasy, he is likely to be a genius. But if he learns to utilize the second kind in the manifold inter-relationships of a novel he is certain to be an artist. Whatever Mr. Wolfe's future in the wider and looser interest of Literature, his future in the far more rigorous interest of fiction just about comes down to the question of whether he can increase his facility at the second kind of fantasy. People would stop idiotically calling him autobiographical, if he gave us less identification and more understanding. And we could do with a lot less genius, if we got a little more artist.

For the truth is that Mr. Wolfe is presented to us, and to himself, as a genius. There is no more dissent from that judgment in his thinking about himself than in Scribners' publicity. And, what is more, a genius of the good old-fashioned, romantic kind—possessed by a demon, driven by the gales of his own fury, helpless before the lava-flood of his own passion, selected and set apart for greatness, his lips touched by a live coal, consequently unable to exercise any control over what he does and in fact likely to be damaged or diminished by any effort at control. Chaos is everything, if you have enough of it in you to make a world. Yes, but what if you don't make a world—what if you just make a noise? There was chaos in Stephen Dedalus's soul, but he thought of that soul not as sufficient in itself but merely as a smithy wherein he might forge his novel. And listen to Mr. Thomas Mann:

> When I think of the masterpiece of the twentieth century, I have an idea of something that differs essentially and, in my opinion, with profit from the Wagnerian masterpiece—something exceptionally logical, clear, and well developed in form, something at once austere and serene, with no less intensity of will than his, but of cooler, nobler, even healthier spirituality, something that seeks its greatness not in the colossal, the baroque, and its beauty not in intoxication.

Something, in other words, with inescapable form, something which exists as the imposition of order on chaos, something that *is*, not is merely asserted.

One can only respect Mr. Wolfe for his determination to realize himself on the highest level and to be satisfied with nothing short of greatness. But, however useful genius may be in the writing of novels, it is not enough in itself—it never has been enough, in any art, and it never will be. At the very least it must be supported by an ability to impart shape to material, simple competence in the use of tools. Until Mr. Wolfe develops more craftsmanship, he will not be the important novelist he is now widely accepted as being. In order to be a great novelist he must also mature his emotions till he can see more profoundly into character than he now does, and he must learn to put a corset on his prose. Once more: his own smithy is the only possi-

ble place for these developments— they cannot occur in the office of any editor whom he will ever know.

Lauren Brown. "The Noble Savage as Novelist." *American Review*, 7 (May 1936), 221-224.

The foremost exemplars of "genius" in the literary world at the moment are Thomas Wolfe and William Saroyan. The fame of neither of them is dependent on his mastery of his chosen art, but rather on the accidents of his character, on that irreducible minimum of personality which marks off every man from his fellows. After reading Mr. Wolfe or Mr. Saroyan, one is not filled with admiration at the every-surprising feat of the great craftsman's imposing form and significance on his recalcitrant material; the most one can do is to exclaim "How like Wolfe—or Saroyan!" So, for those who practise that kind of criticism which asks not what a man has done but how well he has done it, these authors are never found wanting, for they are dedicated to the task of expressing themselves, and as long as they write, they perforce express themselves.

The Story of a Novel is the biography of Mr. Wolfe's as yet unfinished autobiography, of which two volumes, *Look Homeward, Angel* and *Of Time and the River,* have appeared. Mr. Wolfe is also the author of a book of short stories, *From Death to Morning,* which presumably consists of sections his editor discarded from his second novel. In view of this scanty output, there may seem to be something pretentious in issuing *The Story of a Novel;* but it is in fact perfectly consistent with the position Mr. Wolfe occupies, for there is no essential difference in his attitude and subject when he is writing about how he wrote his novel and when he is writing that novel. Mr. Wolfe, in common with many another modern writer, is greatly concerned with time, that is, he wishes to express the peculiar spirit of the age; and in that he has been successful. That this expression will speak eloquently to future ages is doubtful, since future ages are reluctant to read old works which add dullness and turgidity to length; his success means that the present age has found someone who personifies its ideal of the writer of genius.

Critics as fundamentally divergent as Irving Babbitt and Edmund Wilson have stressed the fact that for an understanding of modern literature one must look to its genesis in the Romantic Revival, and it is to be expected that a writer who embodies the contemporary ideal of genius will bear the familiar earmarks of romanticism. These marks Mr. Wolfe does bear; he is in the style of Berlioz and Byron, Werther and Atala, though clothed in good coarse homespun. Romantic genius is characterized by what Frederick Myers called the "subliminal uprush"; the romantic genius simply can't help it, he's made that way, and that's why his work is as it is. Certainly, no genius creates his genius, but he does create his work, and Mr. Wolfe's way of creating is to write until Scribner's editor says with "quiet finality" that his book is finished.

Eugene Gant, the hero of *Look Homeward, Angel* and *Of Time and the River,* it will be recalled, had the obsession with "Amount and Number" Mr. Wolfe confesses to. His obsession united with Mr. Wolfe's (if there is any distinction to be made) resulted in a proliferation of pointless descriptions and dialogues, apostrophes to feminine America and masculine railroad trains (it will be a Viennese holiday when the psychoanalysts begin searching for unwitting *doubles entendres* in Mr. Wolfe's books), and adolescent introspection. This means that Mr. Wolfe was trying, and is evidently still trying, to get life, not art, into his books. He has admitted as much himself, saying he could only meet his problem squarely "not with reason but with life"; and art is a product of reason. Life is ours till we die, and so Mr. Wolfe, who had taken to living with his pen, had to be informed by his publisher that his book was finished. His confession of this is surely one of the most naïve in the annals of the literature, yet is not an unexpected one, for, creating as he does, no one could suppose that Mr. Wolfe would himself wield the abhorrèd shears. Thus Mr. Wolfe's work is a sort of a segment out of a continuous stream; it is a fragment. Works whose size are as bulky a result of their striving for completeness as are Mr. Wolfe's may seem big fragments indeed; but the essence of the fragmentary is incompleteness, not size. It is only by reference to Mr. Wolfe that his novels surrender the meaning that should have been embodied in them through art; behind the massiveness of the books, stands the far more massive accretion of their author's experience: the material of the novels has, ultimately, no justification other than that it has been witnessed or undergone by Mr. Wolfe.

What, then, is the explanation of the

manner in which these books have been received? Mr. Wolfe is, as it were, an historical throwback, a contemporary example of the hearty ancestors of the tired petulant novelists who surround him. Those whom the latter have infected see in Mr. Wolfe their own disease justified by its glorious possibilities: this sound, this fury differs only in volume, not quality, from the feeble murmur in their own breasts. He is that Noble Savage from whose high estate they have fallen but have never ceased to yearn for.

Carl Van Doren. "Self-Portrait of an Artist as a Young Man." New York *Herald Tribune Books*, May 17, 1936, p. 5.

Thomas Wolfe is his own river and Maxwell Perkins is his levee. There have been floods along this river for years, when the water did not know where its banks were and poured itself in gigantic torrents over the land, unable to stop and blindly wondering where to go. A stupid engineer might have tried to dam the river. Maxwell Perkins, wise and shrewd, was satisfied to throw up levees here and there, helping the water find its direction until it settled to its proper channel and swept magnificently to sea. There is "Of Time and the River" as a joint monument to the river and the engineer.

And here is Mr. Wolfe's story of the book. More than that, it is the story of his literary beginnings, of the writing and reception of "Look Homeward, Angel," of his processes with his second novel, and of his advance toward mature self-knowledge. It would be hard to remember another portrait so exciting of an artist as a young man.

Study this little book and you will almost be present at an act of creation. Everything about Mr. Wolfe is on so large a scale that his story has the look of microphotography. What in many imaginative writers is relatively small and obscure is in him, as he projects it in his narrative, a picture as big as a wall. You cannot miss its meanings.

After his first novel his second did not come to him as a story, as a form, at all. It came as what the old critics used to call poetic rage: a restless fury demanding of him that he embody the wilderness of America in a work of art. He did not know how he was to do it, only that he must.

. . .

In a sense he hardly wrote the book himself. It poured out of him in a furious compulsion. And not in one stream, but in many streams bursting out on every side with no central design that he was aware of for a long time. Of course, there was a design whether he was aware of it or not. Somebody was writing it, not everybody, and Mr. Wolfe's own self furnished the design in spite of his seeming confusion. Art is never as blind as the artist sometimes thinks.

After four years he had one novel a million words long to be called "The October Fair" and another—how long he does not say—to be "The Hills Beyond Pentland." Even yet it was only an enormous skeleton. Mr. Perkins pointed out that the first was really in two parts, or cycles, which were fairly separate. They took this first part of the first novel and began to cut and shape it. The opening section, the journey of the train across Virginia, was then as long as an ordinary novel. Indispensable sections had not been written. But the river was inexhaustible and the levee was patient, and in time there was a novel.

Some of the materials in "The Story of a Novel" throw a brilliant light on certain technical literary problems, but as a whole it is about a passion and in the language of general experience. It is a note on a force of nature.

Checklist of Additional Reviews

Frederic I. Carpenter. "Frame of Reference." *Saturday Review of Litera-* ture, 13 (January 25, 1936), 9.

Peter Monro Jack. "Thomas Wolfe: The Author in Search of Himself." New York *Times Book Review*, May 3, 1936, p. 2.

Mildred C. Anderson. "Pious Dither About Form." *Saturday Review of Literature*, 14 (May 23, 1936), 9.

Clifton Fadiman. "The Cult of Emotion." *Nation*, 142 (May 27, 1936), 681-682.

Hamilton Basso. "Thomas Wolfe: A Portrait." *New Republic*, 87 (June 24, 1936), 199-202.

H. J. Davis. "Genius in Labour." *Canadian Forum*, 16 (July 1936), p. 29.

THOMAS C. WOLFE, NOVELIST, 37, DEAD

Wrote 'Look Homeward, Angel' in 1929 and 'Of Time and the River'

TEACHER FOR SIX YEARS

Began Literary Career With Plays, but Never Found Producer for Them

Pinchot

THOMAS C. WOLFE

BALTIMORE, Sept. 15 (P).— Thomas Wolfe, author of "Look Homeward, Angel," died today of an "acute cerebral infection." He was 37 years old.

The novelist underwent two operations at Johns Hopkins Hospital after his arrival Saturday. He fell ill of pneumonia in July but was recovering in Seattle when an infection began and spread to his kidneys and heart.

With him last night were his mother, Mrs. Julia E. Wolfe, and his brother, Fred, both of Asheville, N. C. Funeral services will be held at the First Presbyterian Church in Asheville Sunday afternoon.

Obituaries

Ernest Sutherland Bates. "Thomas Wolfe." *Modern Quarterly*, 11 (Fall 1938), 86–89.

The unexpected death of Tom Wolfe—unexpected by all save himself—has been universally recognized as carrying a special quality, a special meaning unlike other deaths. It is not merely that his death leaves American literature the poorer by the loss of all those works fermenting in his brain that will now never be written—never in any form—for though America should survive for a million years, it will not see another Tom Wolfe. Still less is it the sense of personal loss which even those who did not know him share to an extraordinary degree because of the intensity with which he embodied his personality in his writings, works written in blood not ink, so that one was always conscious of the man behind the words almost as if he were actually present or as if his spirit at least were present in some mystic form. National loss and personal loss can be borne with some degree of stoicism; we have lost and shall lose other writers, other friends; we know it beforehand and are in a measure steeled to meet the blow when it falls. The case of Tom Wolfe was different.

I think one can put the matter quite simply by saying that his death is unbelievable. One knows the physical causes of death, but they are so ridiculously inadequate to the momentousness of their effects that, while one accepts the fact for what it is, one cannot fit it into any rational scheme of things. This, true of every death, was superabundantly true in Tom Wolfe's case. His enormous vitality, the sense of physical power and endurance and tireless energy that emanated from him, gave him a timeless quality. I recall an occasion when after a night of discussion he left the others drowsing into a sleep of utter exhaustion at 6 A.M. when, like the Socrates of Plato's Symposium, he departed as fresh as the incoming dawn for new fields to conquer, and this instance could be paralleled by hundreds of others. The rivers of America sang in his writings, the men and women of America were in them, there was the surge of the ocean in much of his style. He was so massive, included so much of nature in himself, that he seemed imperishable. This it is, I think, that accounts for our special reaction. Other men, weaklings, might die, but not Tom Wolfe.

Now that the incredible has happened, it seems, for these reasons, a special assertion of the power of death, bringing out inescapably the central fact that the turmoil of nature gives birth to values that it cannot sustain. Today as we watch the death-agonies of nation after nation and mark the wanton destruction almost over-night of moral and cultural values which it took centuries of labor and sacrifice to achieve we know well that ours is an age of death, wherein the passing of Tom Wolfe is a symbol of the brevity of all that we love and admire.

Tom Wolfe feared and hated death and was fascinated by it. Out of that fear and hatred and fascination came his most poignant pages. He had an unshakable mystic belief that he would die young. The fact that in his case the belief was borne out by the event has little or no significance—many who have had the same belief have lived to a good, or a bad, old age—but the belief urged him on to cram all possible experience into the years that were his, and was probably responsible for that monstrous piling up of words wherein he sought to express to the uttermost syllable all that he had to express. Monstrous—and yet, as Jonathan Daniels asks in his fine appreciation in the *Saturday Review*, would we today wish for one word less? At any rate, it was a matter beyond Tom Wolfe's own control. "The critics seem to think," he remarked to the writer, "that my faults are deliberate. I would be glad to be more concise if I could." But he couldn't. The whole urge of his being drove him toward the utmost expansion of both life and writing before the swift-coming end.

In plunging down to the Titanism at the root of the American character, Tom Wolfe went deeper than anyone since Melville. One need only glance about at the defiant towers of New York for evidence of contemporary American

Titanism. But it was present from the beginning, however disguised in religious garb, in Calvinism's war upon nature, in the restless movement of the pioneers, in the acquisitive drive of the industrialist. Emersonian serenity was but a beautiful pastoral interlude in the passionate struggle that has been the reality of American life. Today the ideal of harmony with nature leaves us cold because we know, despite Wordsworth, that nature constantly betrays the heart that trusts in her. Even the ideal of rational harmony fails us because we know how rarely it has proved effective in human affairs. As we move forward into an ever-darkening future, we may salute George Santayana as the last of the happy Olympians—salute him and pass on into the darkness. But Tom Wolfe will still be with us in that darkness, for he knew all its horrors beforehand. "If America goes fascist," he once said, "I hope I shall not be here to see it." That wish at least has been gratified. But it hardly mattered, for he already lived in our desperate world in which we have lost faith in God and in nature and are on the point of the last and ultimate betrayal, that of losing faith in ourselves. Whatever may prove to be his hold upon the future, it was this contemporary world which Tom Wolfe expressed most deeply.

In such times of failure, it is natural that many should feel it would have been better never to have been born at all, better the peace of non-existence, than to cherish desires, hopes, and ideals doomed to frustration. To extract any such defeatism from the writings or personality of Tom Wolfe, seems to me to be false to his spirit. True, he was a creature of the night. One thinks of all the magnificent night scenes in his works, one thinks of the lonely night student, the lonely prowler of city streets, the heavy carouser from dusk to dawn still lonely in the midst of companions, one sees his brooding eyes, one remembers him as often like a smouldering coal ready to burst into flame, and then as the flame itself, a fire illumining the night. He took night into himself and mastered it as he took death into himself and mastered it; even his giant body could not hold death at bay physically, but he had conquered it again and again in his imaginative renderings of it. Although at this moment it is Tom Wolfe dead of whom we think, it is Tom Wolfe alive that counts. His greatness lay in the amount of life that he incorporated into himself and gave out and will continue to give out as long as his works are read. In all the turmoil of his thought he knew that the self-diremption [sic] of nature is only partial, that there is the enduring ocean as well as the changing tides. "Amid the fumbling march of races to extinction, the giant rhythms of the earth remained. The seasons passed in their majestic processionals, and germinal Spring returned forever on the land—new crops, new men, new harvests, and new gods." The universe, so far as we can judge today, is neither chaos nor cosmos but a mixture of both. And Tom Wolfe knew something else. In that marvelous mystical scene at the close of *Look Homeward, Angel* the spirit of the dead Ben, puffing the while on its cigarette, assures him that "There is no happy land. There is no end to hunger." Life consists in the hunger and the search, and Tom Wolfe never abandoned them.

Unsigned. Editorial, "Thomas Wolfe." New York *Herald Tribune,* September 16, 1938, p. 18.

The passing of Thomas Wolfe, dead at thirty-seven, removes from the American literary scene a figure who in many respects seemed like a character drawn from another and lustier age. Six feet six inches tall, a prodigious eater, a torrential conversationalist, an almost frenzied worker, he was also the possessor of eccentricities which were the delight and the despair of those who knew him. Sometimes, invited to a house for dinner, he would sit up all night, and far into the next day, delivering a harangue on his ideas of life and literature, and it seemed to matter little whether any one was listening to him. He had been observed to burst into violent sobbing fits; his friends suspected him of having delusions both of persecution and of grandeur. It is, inevitable now that there should be speculation as to what possible effect the brain ailment which caused his death had upon his way of life, his mannerisms and his methods of work. He was, in truth, a tortured soul. To some critics it appeared that, for all his facility with words, he never seemed to know just what he was driving at, but one thing was certain—he was driven on by some terrible propulsion which caused him to loose a veritable Niagara of phrases. He almost always overwrote. Somehow he never knew when to put on the brakes.

But at his best he was one of the most brilliant of them all, certainly among the younger writers. It is safe to say that his best novel, "Look Homeward, Angel," will be remembered for a long time, and many of his shorter pieces are remarkable. He was a shrewd observer of people, whether they were bartenders in the Red Hook section of Brooklyn, rural police in the South, or the strange fish at a literary tea in New York. He had an enormous appetite for life, and a deep sensitivity which showed alike in his writing and in the delicate lines of his face. American letters has lost a writer whose potentialities were realized in only a very small part. It is tragic that he died so soon.

Unsigned. *Nation,* 147 (September 24, 1938), 283.

Thomas Wolfe belonged to the lusty school of writing. He was a huge man physically, and his literary productions were commensurate. Where other men write by tens of thousands he poured out hundreds of thousands of words. In describing one of his books in process he told a friend with gusto, "The first hundred pages are about locomotives." And his prodigious output gave rise to tall tales. It was said that his manuscripts were delivered in trucks and that Maxwell Perkins of Scribner's had told him he must cut at least a hundred thousand words out of his latest opus. He burst upon the world in 1929 with "Look Homeward, Angel," which overwhelmed the critics and caused his native town of Asheville, North Carolina, to disown him. It was an unabashed and undisguised picture of his own family and his own home town, in which ordinary human appetites and human relations were projected on an enormous scale in unrestrained and romantic rhetoric. In this book, as in many autobiographical novels, the material itself was compelling, while the passionate energy and youth of the author—he was in his middle twenties—suggested wide potentialities. In his later books, however, his writing remained undisciplined, highly emotional, and charged with a vague romanticism. In short the promise of maturity in thought and style did not materialize, and though there exists an audience which regards him as the great American novelist, time, which he apostrophized so eloquently, has already relegated his work to that category of literary production which is memorable for its energy rather than for its art.

Unsigned. "Tom Wolfe." *New Republic,* 96 (September 28, 1938), 197–198.

He had more friends, he had fewer enemies than any other writer of our day. And there must have been thousands who had met him only once or twice, yet read the last news about him with a deep sense of personal loss. He talked well, but even more he was a creative listener, with an eagerness that flattered everybody and a bulk that made him respond like multitudes. He was so big and seemed so robust that it is amazing to hear of his death from a disease popularly connected with starveling poets. Pneumonia reopened an old scar in his lungs; the tubercular infection spread through his system, attacked the brain; and two operations at Johns Hopkins came too late to save him.

On one side of his literary self, Tom Wolfe was a dithyrambic poet, a Whitman turned inwards through reading James Joyce. He wrote prose-poetic hymns to America and the Artist in a language copied from Shakespeare—indeed, there are long passages in his first two novels that fall into iambic pentameters, like an Elizabethan tragedy. That is the side of his work most praised and most likely to perish. On the other side, he was an objective novelist with a talent for comic or tragic distortion that goes back to Dickens; that is the side which produced his great portraits, like the Gant family (excepting Eugene) and Uncle Bascom Hawke. There are some indications that this objective side of him was developing in his later work, though we can't be certain until Harpers edit and publish the million-word manuscript of the novel or group of novels he left behind him. Whatever that manuscript proves to be, Tom Wolfe is already a legend.

V. F. Calverton. *Current History,* 49 (November 1938), 47.

The death of Thomas Wolfe affected more people than the death of many greater men. This was because there was something so intensely personal about Wolfe, something so glowingly intimate, that it communicated itself to everyone who read his works. Although they had never met Tom Wolfe in person, they were sure they knew him much better than they knew most of their friends. Wolfe's work was so exclusively autobiographical, dealing with the members of his own family almost as intimately as with himself, that his readers frequently spoke of his characters by their first names and discussed their experiences not as figures in fiction, but as real people—which is precisely what they were. Wolfe's mother and father, sisters and brothers, relatives and neighbors, became the common property of all who read his books.

In other words, the reader who shared the joys and sorrows of Eugene's life never thought they were sharing the experiences of a fictional character; they knew that they were sharing the joys and sorrows of Tom Wolfe himself. It is no wonder, therefore, that when Tom Wolfe died they felt so keenly about it because not only a writer was gone but also a close friend.

The world through Wolfe's eyes, and as it came upon him, was a world of dark, secret wonder, pain-ridden, passion-driven, desperate with endless doubts and fears, with the agony of brevity and death written into all things both great and small, the infinite as well as the infinitesimal. Wolfe was haunted, as have been all sensitive, imaginative minds, by the tragedy of being human, the tragedy of a world destined for death, of men and women caught within its maw and ground into nothingness without even a chance to struggle or escape. Wolfe was a romantic in the best sense of the word; not in the 19th century sense of the word when romanticism became synonymous with sentimentality, and *Weltschmerz* became a patent medicine of the emotions diluted into all kinds of cloying mixtures by the De Mussets, the Hoffmanns, and the Tiecks of the period. Wolfe's romanticism was in the tradition of Omar Khayyam, Lucretius, Shakespeare and Unamuno.

Two unfortunate by-products of Wolfe's exclusive autobiographical emphasis were to be discovered, first, in his inability to tell a story as a story, and, secondly, in the adjectival and adverbial exuberances of his style. Wolfe became so interested in his own emotions and reactions to things, people, places, skies, seas, streets, offices, dreams, that it often took him a score of pages to extricate himself from them and get to the narrative he was trying to relate. That resulted from the fact that he was really more interested in his own emotions and reactions than he was in his narrative; only the severest discipline, only the most astringent of verbal diets, only the most determined literary stoicism, could ever have made it possible for him to get over that difficulty, for it was a difficulty that was constitutional rather than epidermal. It grew out of the fact that Wolfe was essentially more of a poet than a novelist. He was in more ways than one the prose Walt Whitman of the twentieth century, singing in storm-furious rhythms, new, fresh, and compelling, of the country and the people of America, an America reseen, refelt, and renewed in his words.

But the tradition of Whitman is not the tradition of a novelist. It leads one away from rather than towards the novel. Its power is derived not from economy, precision, or organization, which are virtues necessary to the novel, but from amplitude, inclusiveness, and multifarious accumulation. Wolfe's virtues were Whitman's virtues, but they were not virtues when they appeared in a novel. The truth of that observation could be noted easily by a consideration of Wolfe's shorter pieces. One of the best pieces of writing Wolfe has ever done was his short story—if it can be called such—*No Door.* The story part of it was inconsequential; the poetry part of it was fundamental. The farther Wolfe got away from the story element and the closer he got to the poetic, the better his work became. But to write great fiction the story element cannot be sacrificed to the poetic; the objective factors cannot be obscured by the subjective. To fuse the two, so that neither obtruded upon the other, neither delayed the other, nor injured the other, was the task which confronted Wolfe, and in all likelihood he would have accomplished it had he lived.

Inherent in that same weakness was Wolfe's tendency to mar an otherwise remarkable and potentially great style by over-writing which is often of the most thoughtless order. No one in America today can write more powerfully than Wolfe at his best. He could make words do strange, magical things, caress, stir, stab, burst, and explode, but he had not learned to do it with that economy of phrase which is the *sine qua non* of a great style. He depended too much upon adjectives and adverbs, accumulated in torrential overflow, and too little upon verbs for his effects. The real difficulty, I believe, lay in the fact that Wolfe had so much in him, so much power and passion, so abundant, so opulent an imagination, that he just couldn't get it all out, just couldn't get enough of it on paper, and in his anxiety to do justice to what he felt and what he wanted to say he said too much although in his eyes it still seemed too little. The result was that instead of being master of his style he was very often overmastered by it.

104

But these weaknesses were not weaknesses in a weak writer; they were the weaknesses of a strong writer, a powerful writer. Even with those weaknesses Thomas Wolfe was one of the finest novelists this country has produced. Without them, he might have become the greatest novelist in our literature.

Thurston Macauley. "Thomas Wolfe: A Writer's Problems." *Publisher's Weekly*, 134 (December 24, 1938), 2150-2152.

The tragic and untimely death of Thomas Wolfe, not quite 38, leaves still unsolved his major problems, the age-old problems of a brilliant creative artist trying desperately to find his way in a world that can help him but little.

It is not my intention here to explore the full extent of that great loss to the literature of this country, indeed of all the world. No one can say what he might have done or how far yet he would have gone: he can be judged only by the millions of words already published and yet to be published that he left behind. But the lessons to be drawn from his experience are ones that should be studied with care by everyone having anything to do with writing.

Wolfe's first novel sold some 10,000 copies in one season and renewed its life later in a *Modern Library* edition. His second, the mammoth 912-page "Of Time and the River," published in 1935, sold 45,000 in about the same period, although the book was higher priced and boom times had given way to depression. In spite of the huge bulk

of his work and whatever certain critics reiterated about his lack of form and discipline, at least people in increasing numbers were reading him.

When the 350,000-word 'script of "Look Homeward, Angel" was kicking around from publisher to publisher, one reader reported it "an autobiographical novel with flashes of talent." Wolfe's "discoverer," of course, was Maxwell Perkins of Scribner's who was unquestionably the greatest individual influence in his writing life. The debt was fully acknowledged in that generous dedication to "Of Time and the River" and again in "The Story of a Novel," Wolfe's candid literary confessions and credo. (Like Somerset Maugham's "The Summing Up," it is a "must" book for all concerned with the making of books.) Perkins it was who helped to direct the mighty torrent that raged with such fury within him and poured out, as Wolfe put it, "life burning lava from a volcano," into publishable form.

Although Perkins is Wolfe's literary executor, lately, since Wolfe changed publishers, another editor, Edward C. Aswell of Harper's, is now wrestling with the mass of writing Wolfe turned over to him last spring before he went west and caught his fatal illness. No decision has yet been made about the posthumous Wolfe book or books, although Aswell says that some part of those million words will be published next year. The title is not chosen, either: Wolfe left six possible ones.

What is known is that Wolfe's last writing, on which he had worked for over three years, was in a new direction away from the ambitious program he previously set himself. "Look Homeward, Angel" and "Of Time and the River" were to have been only a part of a great sextology covering 150 years of American life, as a publisher's note in the latter book announced.

The new work Wolfe spoke of as a "legend" that would be a digest of the sum total of his experience, but as far as possible in one book instead of six. Eugene Gant, Wolfe's autobiographical protagonist in the first two novels, is no longer the central character. Wolfe further described the work to his publishers: "It seems to be a kind of American 'Gulliver's Travels'; in its essence it is one of those books about the adventures of the average man—by which I mean the naturally innocent man, every mother's son of us, through the world."

Few books in recent years could have been awaited more eagerly by public and book world alike than is Wolfe's posthumous work. Certainly its publication will be an event of first importance in contemporary literature. And just as Wolfe's reading public increased with his second novel, so will it assuredly be larger still for his posthumous work. Already his death has had an appreciable effect on sales of his books.

It might not be out of place to suggest that another excellent and moving Wolfe book, already in shape for the press and public, may be found in the short novel published in *The New Republic* last year in three installments: "I Have a Thing to Tell You." An indictment of Nazi Germany, it is not only of extremely timely interest but contains some of the best as well as the most straightforward and direct writing Wolfe ever produced. And it cost him a lot to write it, too, because he had won for himself in Germany a reputation as great if not greater than in his own land and furthermore he had always felt a deep love for Germany, its culture and its people.

From the experience of his first novel—banned from libraries in his home town (Asheville) and even denounced from its pulpits—he had already known what it was to have an irate body of people turn against him. An instance of the things that enraged them: old Gant, the lusty stonecutter (drawn from his father), sold a marble angel for the grave of a notorious townswoman. Although it was pure fiction, people "recognized" the character as they did others in the book. The local paper even sent a photographer to the cemetery: "He took a picture of the first damned angel he came to," Wolfe said, "and it was over the grave of a perfectly good Methodist lady!" Naturally the Methodist lady's family registered an indignant protest.

One of the problems that confronted Wolfe, as it does all writers, is this: how far can you go in setting down the life about you as you see it? Wolfe answered it very well for himself in his preface to the *Modern Library* edition of "Look Homeward, Angel": ". . . it seems to him that all serious work in fiction is autobiographical . . . If the writer has used the clay of life to make his book, he has only used what all men must, what none can keep from using. Fiction is not fact, but fiction is fact selected and understood, fiction is fact arranged and charged with purpose." Somerset Maugham also advances similar arguments for using the "clay of life" in writing.

Wolfe's short life was almost all struggle, not so much the usual one for economic independence, but other sorts: first with his family and school fellows to whom he was different (as he was) and "queer"; years futilely spent trying to write plays before finding in the novel his proper medium of expression; then that long and incessant struggle which went on to the very last of controlling the flood-tide of his work.

Another was the struggle of a six and a half foot Gulliver to live in a world of five foot eight Lilliputians. He wrote tellingly of this in "Gulliver" in the "From Death to Morning" collection of his shorter pieces: he was "for ever a stranger, and alone." That sense of loneliness, of always being lost, is one of the most poignant constantly recurring notes in his books. Whether out of choice or necessity, Wolfe led for the most part a solitary life, writing furiously always, from the time he taught English at Washington Square College until a Guggenheim fellowship and then half of a *Scribner's Magazine* short novel prize for his "Portrait of Bascom Hawke" (later incorporated in "Of Time and the River") enabled him to give himself up entirely to his writing. (It was only in later years that the "slick" magazines became sufficiently interested in him to buy his stories.)

Realizing that Wolfe was an exception to most contemporary writers, who generally lead lives as normal as any business men, nevertheless in the case of so great a talent—genius, even—the tragedy of his too early death seems one that might, perhaps, have been avoided. And yet who could cope with a writer like Wolfe—who, indeed but the man himself? But should a man write with such fire and fury that he burns himself out before reaching 38? Or, if it were possible some way to hold that fury in check, would the writing, wrought so powerfully out of life, suffer in consequence? These are questions that are difficult to answer

but they should be asked all the same and, for the sake of others, an attempt made to answer them. I am sure both Perkins and Aswell did their utmost for Wolfe, and the kind and sympathetic Elizabeth Nowell, his agent, did too.

The immediate cause of Wolfe's death was pneumonia, which opened an old healed-up tuberculosis scar in his lungs. Wolfe had had that dread disease at some time past without being aware of it, perhaps thinking it only a bad cold at the time. But the pneumonia revived it and it entered the blood stream, being carried to his brain.

In this connection, a *New York Herald Tribune* editorial after his death said: "It is inevitable now that there should be speculation as to what possible effect the brain ailment which caused his death had upon his way of life, his mannerisms and his methods of work. He was, in truth, a tortured soul." Aswell answered this but for those who may have missed his reply I would like to quote what Dr. Walter E. Dandy, the distinguished brain surgeon who performed the two operations upon Wolfe, wrote Aswell: "His (Wolfe's) intracranial condition, of course, had nothing whatever to do with his mentality; this was a very acute condition, the onset of which in the brain was only of a month's duration."

It can never be known just when Wolfe had had tuberculosis, whether as a child—even then he lived quite irregularly—in Asheville (where many suffering from it go for treatment), as a too eager student trying to devour all the world's knowledge in a single gulp, or as a writer working frantically in the "bitter briefness of his day": ". . . a terrible doubt began to creep into my mind that I might not live long enough to get it out of me."

Wolfe's chief difficulty was in finding himself. When he said with that extreme modesty that is so characteristic of him that he was not a professional or even a skilled writer and that he didn't yet know how to write a story or a novel, he was simply stating the facts. He had to learn by the trial and error method. And even his methods were as unique as he was himself. He never planned a book like other writers by outlining it in advance: he afterwards fitted together in sequential order what he had written so copiously. But that does not mean that everything he wrote was not important, charged as it was with the significance that he gave to life in the strange crucible of his richly creative mind. Unfinished and cut short though it may be, few would say—even his severest critics— that his work will not live.

Unsigned. "A Young Man of Promise." *Theatre Arts Monthly,* 23 (February 1939), 150.

Thomas Wolfe was a member of the Carolina Playmakers' first playwriting group at Chapel Hill, 1918–20, and one of their leading actors. "A lanky, wild-eyed, six-and-a-half-foot-tall mountain lad striding across the Chapel Hill campus" is the way Frederick Koch describes him in the autumn issue of *The Carolina Play-Book.* Wolfe was, he says, "an outstanding figure and easily the most popular man on the campus." His first play, *The Return of Buck Gavin,* was included in the second series of Carolina Folk Plays in 1924. Another play of that period, *The Third Night,* interesting historically only, is printed in the current *Play-Book,* with a scene from the production in which Wolfe figures as a leading player. In the foreword to *Buck Gavin* Wolfe wrote a note which suggests his later approach to events around him: "It is a fallacy of the young writer to picture the dramatic as unusual and remote. . . . The dramatic is not unusual. It is happening daily in our lives." Wolfe did not stop his search for the technique of playwriting when he left Chapel Hill. He went from there to the 47 Workshop, where a one-act play and his first full-length play, *Welcome to our City,* were produced. But when he tried to find an open door to the professional theatre, the struggle was too long and too hard. "For two years," he wrote to Professor Koch, "I have worked and traveled alone, ordering the events of my life as courageously and honestly as I could. . . . In that time the honey flies who found me lacking in the promise of instant victory have turned away and forgotten me. But a few people have never forgotten; they have given unbounded loyalty to a mad fellow who made loneliness his mistress. . . ." And almost his last words on the theatre were in *Of Time and the River,* where the mother speaks to Eugene, saying, "Pshaw, boy, your life's not ended just because you find out that you weren't cut out to be a playwriter."

Lou Myrtis Vining. "Thomas Wolfe—In Memoriam." *Writer's Digest*, 19 (July 1939), 47-50.

"America deserves the best life a man can have." Thomas Wolfe was speaking. I remember him standing in the doorway, tall as the sky. I remember thinking, as did the other members of the Colorado Writers' Conference, *Greatness is in our midst.*

Maxwell Perkins, past editor of *Scribners,* called him the literary discovery of the age, and backed his statement with handsome advance royalties. *The Atlantic Monthly* columnized him once as *"The Man of the Hour,"* and Sinclair Lewis bluntly stated, "If Wolfe keeps up the promise of his first book, he has a chance to be the greatest American writer of all time." Gertrude Stein, on the other side of the critics, blinked her grey eyelashes and dotted him into syllables; he was this and that—a charming young man, certainly—but not solid at the bottom. Once I heard a shoe clerk say quite simply, "He knows exactly how I feel about a train!"

Who was Thomas Wolfe? What did he do? What did he propose to do?

As a member of the Rocky Mountain Writers' Colony in the summer of 1935, I was given an assignment to interview Wolfe by an important Southern magazine; for just then, we Southerners, were very proud of Thomas Wolfe.

If you have seen him, or heard him speak, you agree with me, I know, that no matter where or what he might have written, this workman would always have been a little better than his material.

The first time I saw Wolfe he walked, alone and unannounced, into a poetry session at the Conference. A buzz went 'round the room. All heads turned. Wolfe stood there, his eyes searching for a chair. He stood there; a mountain of a man measuring six feet six. His hands looked too big—his feet were too big. We stopped listening to the renowned English poet and gazed, curiosity stricken children that we were, and then fell silent. Time, of which Wolfe so loved to write, had for a moment stood still.

I heard Wolfe talk many times after this. I saw him perform in a skit at a beef steak fry atop Boulder's Flagstaff; he was the big bad Wolfe ready to devour the three little pigs. I took notes on his first published lecture in America—he talked as he looked, there was no ballyhoo, egotism, or conceit about this man who said, "Nothing is Trivial."

It does not matter whether or not you have read "Look Homeward, Angel"; or "Of Time and the River." It does not matter whether you ever read them. But, if you wish to write, and would write well, you must garner to yourself a thought of the dream—the word-age—the will power—that was Wolfe.

Wolfe believed, as he would have you believe, that everything that happened to him, or to anyone else in this world, is of vast importance. The conversation with your cook as she left this morning; the new sprig of lavender flower on the garden bush—ships, furniture, trains, automobiles, plows—the way October is, and the proudness of Death. We talk today of causes. Writers fight for causes and make them fashionable. If Wolfe held out a brief for any cause, the cause is eternal and bears the name of truth.

Humility marked Wolfe's words as he outlined for me the plan of his future material. Speaking of five books at a time—books peopled with from 2,000 to 2,500 characters—Wolfe spoke enthusiastically, "I shall depict three time movements: present and far moving time; past time, to include the tremendous weight of memory, the sum of the movements of the characters' lives; and time fixed and everlasting, the time of rivers, the time of the sea and earth."

. . .

Remembering the old copy book maxim that a writer must be a reader, I asked a little timidly, "What do you read?"

"I used to have a voracious hunger for reading. I read everything. Now that I'm writing, I return to a few; the Bible, Shakespear, poetry—great big fat books of poetry—" then, shyly—"Everyone would be a poet if he could. Let's see; what do I read?"

"I read *The Oxford Book of English Verse;* all of the anthologies of poetry; certain poems of Blake and Wordsworth hundreds and hundreds of times. I read *Ecclesiastes,* which is the best single piece of writing I've ever read. I read Burton's *Anatomy of Melancholy,* which contains the everlasting source of life. You cannot crack it open at any place that it is not there for you. I read the *World Almanac,* because it's beautifully hard and certain, and I read the world series batting records and clip the scores."

"And writing?" I questioned, "What about writing?"

"We write, not from memory, but from the weather of our life. We become writers because we want to write so damn bad. We write, and get life back, because we cannot bear to lose it! But when you write you have to get down into the sawdust and sweat like a man. Form is my greatest problem. I've resolved not to be frightened by it. It is restricting tightening." Wolfe knocked the ashes from his cigarette.

I arose. We had said so much. This was good-bye. He went on, I'll be in Manhattan this winter—not Brooklyn—and after I get these things out of my mind, I'm going to write a book about the night—"

About—the—night—

Now Wolfe is gone. I do not strive to write his epitaph. I am not even a personal friend. I am just another writer who happened for a brief distance to pass the same way. But I do not believe that any person who dreams of writing—who dares to try—should forget Wolfe's words, "America deserves the best life a man can have. America is a basis for a great hope. America is immortal in its power and beauty."

Checklist of Additional Obituaries

Editorial, "Thomas Wolfe." New York *Times,* September 16, 1938, p. 22.

"Unpredictable Imagination." *Time,* 32 (September 26, 1938), 66.

Jonathan Daniels. "Thomas Wolfe." *Saturday Review of Literature,* 18 (September 24, 1938), 8.

Peter Monro Jack. "Remembering Thomas Wolfe." New York *Times Book Review,* October 2, 1938, pp. 2, 28.

Notes

Thomas Wolfe

THE WEB

AND

THE ROCK

Harper & Brothers · Publishers

New York and London

1939

The Web and the Rock

May Cameron. "Thomas Wolfe's Superb Farewell." New York *Post*, June 22, 1939.

If ever a novel was thoroughly and mercilessly autobiographical, it is Thomas Wolfe's "The Web and the Rock" published today. Indeed, it is more than autobiographical; for it not only tells of the author's own life, with swagger and shame, with satire, naivete, braggadocio, wisdom, and sometimes almost immeasurable power, but it is also prophetically autobiographical (if such is possible) in that again and again it reveals intimations of its author's own doom and death.

. . .

That was George Webber's story, as it was Tom Wolfe's: in both there was too much blood, too much appetite, too much life, too much curiosity, and too much courage in sniffing at the world, to sting it, trying to gulp it whole, trying to pick it up bodily and make it to listen to the pieces inside—and too much uncompromising devotion to the self-imposed, impossible task of splitting it apart with bare fists in order to gaze upon its inner heart. And too much doubt whether, if one succeeded in cleaving inward to the core, he would find anything but draff and husks.

Indeed, it seems to me that Tom Wolfe was a man whose limitless curiosity and tremendous vitality compelled him to profess exuberant belief in life; equipped as he was, no other course of thought seemed possible to him; yet, through it all, doubt gnawed at him.

He wanted to be God, and he couldn't. . . .

Yet, so vast is the reservoir of his memory that—as far as I know—there is no duplication of incident in the new work, distilled with its predecessors out of millions of words. And the current hero, George Webber, attains a certain identity of his own although his parent-blood is always that which coursed with such hard passage through Wolfe's arteries.

Future scholars, grubbing for Ph.D.'s through a great man's remains, will find academic, mild joy in tracing characters through "Look Homeward, Angel," "Of Time and the River," and the new novel. Suffice it for a daily reviewer to say that "The Web and The Rock" abounds with veined and muscled people, as real and pungent as sweat; with anecdote and incident humorous, melancholy, and tragic, and with passages of prose as fine as any written in English in three hundred years.

Wolfe was crammed to the throat

113

with the Elizabethans, great and small. And in that great age, both great and small wrote sheer drivel as well as monumental stuff. Something of the same might be said of Wolfe. He wrote page upon page that the rankest beginner would blush to put on paper, but he wrote page on page that perhaps no writer in English since the seventeenth century has equaled or can hope to equal.

I suspect that the major interest in "The Web and The Rock" is to be found in its latter half, which tells of George Webber's love affair with Esther, a Jewish woman of wealth and charm who worked like a fury at her job of stage-designing—and of keeping Webber happy, or at least quiescent.

This whole episode is tender and gay, often broadly humorous, amorous, lecherous, ribald and truly sweet.

. . .

Wolfe himself was always hungry. Even when he had the means to command the world's finest chefs, he remained an unsated trencherman. So, in "The Web and The Rock," as in the other novels, there are pages of fine eating.

There is more humor in this, I think, than in Wolfe's other books, although some of it, in Webber's college years, leans pretty heavily on Sinclair Lewis' treatment of the YMCA-secretary type in "Arrowsmith." . . .

Just as Wolfe could not fit himself to the world, nor his books to publishers' dimensions, a reviewer can scarcely hope to give adequate treatment to "The Web and The Rock"—that is, not in a newspaper column, or a page either, for that matter. Run, do not walk, to your nearest bookstore.

Webber somewhere, in effect, tells Esther: There will never be another like me again. Let that be Tom Wolfe's epitaph, and his books his monument.

Harry Hansen. "Thomas Wolfe's Posthumous Work, *The Web and the Rock,* Recalls His *Of Time and the River."* New York *World-Telegram,* June 22, 1939.

When Thomas Wolfe died unexpectedly, on September 15, 1938, aged 37, he left the wise ones completely in the air. No one was able to say whether he would live as a major writer or as a phenomenon. No one knew whether he had turned the fashion from the bare, stripped story-telling or had merely released a flood of words and impressions with the sheer exuberance of youth. His career was still in the making.

Just before he died there was talk that he had at last submitted to the necessary renunciation demanded by the discipline of perfection. But almost immediately he broke with the one editor who had helped him most, because, it was said, he wouldn't take advice. And then, ironically, the greatest obstacle to an orderly presentation of his prose vanished with his death.

The first bite out of his legacy is *The Web and the Rock,* published today by Harper, a book so easy to lift that few will suspect that 300,000 words are packed into its 700 highly legible pages. Edward C. Aswell has been the editor, and parts of it have been appearing in magazines, including The Birthday, The Quarrel, The Child by Tiger and a rhapsodic eulogy of New York. It is the first of two books; the sequel will be called *You Can't Go Home Again.*

The Web and the Rock purports to describe the youth and young manhood of George Webber of Old Catawba, S.C., who comes to New York City, struggles to write and is drawn toward and repelled by various men and women. In essence it is of a piece with *Of Time and the River* rather than of *Look Homeward, Angel.*

This adventure "of apprenticeship and discovery" Wolfe intended to give a universal aspect. "I hope that the protagonist will illustrate in his own experience every one of us," says he, and he thinks he has invented characters. But George Webber is representative only if we assume that all young men are able to recognize, define and express that emotional upsurge that comes to a man who is volcanic in action. The exuberance of expression, the flood of visual and sensual images touched off by the slightest experience; the tumultuous flow of fantasy; the tempests of joy and anger—these are characteristic of but one writer, and identification of the reader with the character is possible only at intervals. There is but one man with such an explosive reaction to the sights, sounds, smells, visual and sensational experience of adolescence, and that is Thomas Wolfe.

Just as he was too big for his clothes, too unrestrained for a humdrum routine, so Thomas Wolfe was not amenable to writing fashions and taboos. In an age of stripped prose, sentences cut like diamonds, Wolfe could start an episode thus:

"Out of the nameless and unfathomed weavings of billion-footed life, out of the dark abyss of time and duty, blind chance had brought these two together on a ship, and their first meeting had been upon the timeless and immortal seas that beat forever at the shores of the old earth."

What is it—music? Yes, and it is also Southern oratory, reminiscent of Henry W. Grady. And when the author describes a man in love: "He was the Lord of Life, the master of the earth; he was the city's conqueror; he was the only man alive who ever had been 25 years old, the only man who ever loved or ever had a lovely woman come to meet him, and it was morning in October . . .", that and the talk of "golden moments' wine there in the goblet of his life" are almost Meredithian, save Meredith was more obviously ironical. But when he speaks of the ocean liner as "a proud, swift cat," when he writes that "the evil splinter of a shameful memory passed like a poisoned arrow through his brain," he does what many modern writers fail to do—he pricks the reader's mind into active co-operation, makes it work, and hence enjoy itself.

His George Webber travels to New York on a train—one of those train rides that always exhilarated Wolfe—and the arrival is dramatic. Here it is:

There was a grinding screech of brakes, a slight jolt and, for a moment, utter silence.

At this moment there was a terrific explosion.

It was New York.

And then, in retrospect, the implications of that arrival overwhelm him. He sees the young man at the gates of the citadel of his imagined world: "It is built up to the cloud-capped pinnacles of a boy's imagining; it is written like a golden legend in the heart of youth with a plume plucked out of an angel's wing; it lives and flames there in his heart and spirit with all the timeless faery of the magic land."

There has been nothing like that since Joseph Conrad wrote *Youth* and *Heart of Darkness*.

It is true Wolfe has invented new characters, but they are mere splinters off George Webber. And Webber's adventure is grasping "the whole passionate enigma of life." It is his years of confusion, of lyricism so buoyant that he could argue that freight cars were beautiful. It presupposes his attempt to overcome his turmoil to "a single integrity of purpose and design." That is symbolic in his violent break with Esther, the theatrical designer, who loved him, and in his comment on the School for Utility Cultures (is that N.Y.U.?), where he worked. But the book is singularly like Wolfe. In it we sample the rich sensuousness of living, but its direction eludes us. It is a book to be read aloud for its very music; it turns the literary tradition into the rhythms of swing. But the sum of its experiences never approaches the synthesis we find in Jean Christophe. It is a gustatory experience, and that suggests its limitations. For though we devote three-quarters of our lives to the satisfaction of our appetites, it is the other fourth that lives in the memory.

Paul Fisher. "Wolfe's Last Look Homeward." Kansas City *Star,* June 24, 1939, p. 14.

Nine months ago, when Thomas Wolfe died, no American who knew what he had achieved and planned could have helped realizing that we had lost a giant. For the quality of greatness was there. Wolfe had produced two huge, powerful, often inchoate novels, and he had compiled a volume of shorter Wolfe his publishers tolerantly called short stories. They were not short stories. They were the briefer rhapsodies, the shorter litanies, of a man who cast everything he touched in his own physical world of 6 feet 6, where the heart was too big for the bitter anecdote, the mind too fecund for the spare phrase.

Wolfe was 38 years old when he died of a cerebral infection induced by pneumonia. By the standards of this continent, for whose people he had sung his mighty hymns, he had known a good life. He had succeeded by an agonizing compulsion in harnessing the torrential river of memory and observation into a channel of narration. To be sure, there was no economy there such as his contemporaries, Dos Passos, Steinbeck and Hemingway, had shaped for themselves. But Wolfe had done what he sought to do, to recreate, sing, dedicate and analyze minutely through the medium of the novel the hungers, legends, beauty, hope, joy and grief we feel in this wide, turbulent and occasionally tainted nation of ours.

His moods, his tendencies toward giantism, the undisciplined sweep of his prose, irritated many men, but none of them denied that great sections of his work were the work of genius. They felt that both "Look Homeward, Angel," and "Of Time and the River," fine as those novels were, merely constituted a work in preparation. They pleaded with him to train himself, to submit to closer editing.

There seemed to be a likelihood, superficially, that Wolfe might take the advice of his critics. After "Of Time and the River" was issued in 1935, he appeared now in them in the columns of the New Yorker, the New Republic and other publications whose space limitations forbid prolixity. Meantime, he was working twelve to eighteen hours daily on a panel of novels. At his death, two of them had been completed. The first is this volume, "The Web and the Rock."

It is Wolfe again, the Wolfe of the first two novels. Certainly, the long passages in his earlier work that Bernard DeVoto called "placental" material is less evident. There is more compression here, but the tide of Wolfe in stride is evident on every page. Yet this is the most disappointing book Wolfe wrote.

For even if one remembers Wolfe was sealed ineradicably to his own pace, to the orbit he explored meticulously through Eugene Gant and his family in "Look Homeward, Angel" and "Of Time and the River," there was the hope that once he finished that great panel, he would shift his scrutiny to another terrain, to another people. He has not. Indeed, the Eugene Gant who was the protagonist of the first two novels and the George Webber who is the protagonist of "The Web and the Rock" and the novel that remains to be published are the same man. What Wolfe fails

to give here are the superb portraits he drew of the Gant and Pentland families—Uncle Bascom Pentland, Ma Gant, Starwick and a dozen others.

In his note, Wolfe says:

". . . This novel, then marks not only a turning away from the books I have written in the past, but a genuine spiritual and artistic change. It is the most objective novel I have written. . . ."

How has he turned away? Gant came from old Catawba (North Carolina). So does Webber. On his mother's side, the family of Eugene Grant long had lived there. So has Webber's maternal forbears, the Joyners. Gant's father was a man who had wandered out of Pennsylvania, a stonemason, a savage drinker, a lover of life. Webber's father came from Pennsylvania, and in old Catawba he built himself a brick and stone yard. . . .

Briefly, those are a few of the parallels. The story of Webber's love for Esther consumes the last half of "The Web and the Rock." In "Of Time and the River" Wolfe touched only briefly on the love affair of Gant; the remainder is devoted to the legend of youth and its hungers. This is that story, too, but it is fainter, less sure, and twice told.

Could it be that Wolfe, as DeVoto maintained, suffered from an artistic incompleteness? For Gant was Wolfe; Webber differs from him only in the fact that he is 5 feet 10 inches and has a simian face, for everything else he saw was precisely as Gant saw it, and therefore as Wolfe had seen the world in his early manhood. From the standpoint of artistry, Wolfe's first novel was his best—"Of Time and the River" had more power, but as Wolfe's critics said, it lacks its predecessor's evenness. With his two first books and that fine short story, "Gulliver" (which

117

is not a short story at all, but an essay), Wolfe was a front-rank man. So much was expected from him and he accomplished so much. But in "The Web and the Rock" he has repeated himself, whether tragically we may tell when his final novel is published next fall.

R. E. M. "Wolfe Adds Fresh Fuel To His Fire: Posthumous Novel Continues Story of Search for Understanding." Buffalo *Evening News,* June 24, 1939, p.

Thomas Wolfe has been dubbed genius too often, both before and after his untimely death, to permit debate on that point now.

Even so, it is to be supposed that many tasters and critics of books will attempt to alter or justify their opinions, now that this, the first of two posthumous novels has been published.

There seems to be no need of that. The Wolfe of "The Web and the Rock" is not different from the Wolfe of "Of Time and the River" or of "Look Homeward Angel," and if you will permit us to say so, we still think he's great. And that's not an attempt at sly slang, either.

The point we like to stress about Wolfe is his frankness. Some will be calling it immaturity or, perhaps, a groping. He thought it was groping, and his foreword to this novel would seem to indicate that he believed that he had finally found something firm to which to tie his creative genius.

In that, it is possible to argue that he was mistaken. There is little sign of creation here. Rather, it is a further effort to examine his own soul—his own experience and his own longings in terms of something eternal.

Well, we doubt if he ever would have achieved his aim. He was full of the desire for life, he wanted to taste all there was in the metaphorical cup, he was in a fair way to have done so. But at best, he would have been a good reporter, both of thought and scene— not a creator. If that were needed to fasten the claim of genius to him, he would have fallen short.

A hurried search of a none-too-infallible memory brings to mind several of Wolfe's type. Men they were whose experience matched in time and place many of those which Wolfe has recorded. They were vocal over a friendly glass or in front of a blazing fire, but dumb in front of a typewriter or with pen in hand.

What we have to be thankful for in Wolfe is that he allowed his thoughts to tumble forth in written form— something for the record. And if that record is not a true picture of the weltschmerz of an age, a guess has been missed. Read Wolfe and find yourself in page after page. Read Wolfe and be informed of some of the absurd profundities of the contemporary mind. Read Wolfe and think. That, I believe, is the best to be gained from "The Web and The Rock."

The story itself is a familiar one—the early days in North Carolina, the adventure into New York and abroad. The hero is a man with a book to write. It is safe to assume that there is much of Wolfe in Monk Webber. And it is just a little less safe to note the similarity of character and event in part of this story and an earlier one by Alene Bernstein—"The Journey Down." There is something there to make one wonder.

George Stevens. "Always Looking Homeward." *Saturday Review of Literature,* 20 (June 24, 1939), 5-6.

. . .

So, in a brief foreword, Thomas Wolfe explained his approach to his third and penultimate novel—a novel that has the best and the worst of Wolfe in it. Actually "The Web and the Rock" contains two distinct novels: a first half that closely parallels the material of "Look Homeward, Angel," and a second half that is a sequel to the events recorded in "Of Time and the River." A sequel to all intents and purposes, but with Eugene Gant replaced by a new hero named George Webber. The change is principally in name; there are a few alterations in detail of background and in physical appearance; but even in ancestry George Webber's experience overlaps Eugene's, and the further the novel progresses the less distinction there is between the two. George, like Eugene, is the child of a run-down puritanical family in the state of Old Catawba; and also like Eugene, he is beset by the problem of the young man in search of a father. The web and the rock of the title are shifting symbolical images: the web of experience, of environment and ancestry in which George constantly fears to drown (the mixed metaphor is

Wolfe's); the rock of the lost father, which gives his life significance. The first half of the book is George Webber's recollection of those things past which Eugene Gant forgot; the second half is the love story of Eugene, told in George's name.

If "The Web and the Rock" had been published as two novels, it would be possible to say that the first half was Wolfe's best novel, the second half his most disappointing. This is surprising, because in general the first half is repetition of what he had done before, and the second is an excursion into a new field: a passionate and tempestuous love story, into which is woven the narrative of George Webber's development as a writer and the publication of his first novel. It is the first half, also, in which Wolfe more nearly succeeded in his attempt to gain objectivity, because it is here that the character and growth of George Webber is most in the background; many of the scenes do not involve him as a direct participant. But that is all that can be said for the objectivity of "The Web and the Rock." The significance of even the earlier events is in their emotional impact on George Webber, who stands for the author as completely as Eugene Gant ever did, and through whose consciousness Wolfe projected some of his most inspired lyrical and invocational passages. The second half, the love story, is utterly subjective throughout.

The whole question of objectivity, in any event, is a red herring. "The Web and the Rock" is Wolfe exactly as we have known him since "Look Homeward, Angel" was published in 1929; it represents no positive development of his ability; what it does, at its best, is to reveal his gifts in all their power and intensity. The first half is

119

dominated by Wolfe's brooding observation of the dark corners of life, the fringes of human nature. It can flash through unforgettably in an anecdote—like that of Rance Joyner, great-uncle of George, a simple-minded mountaineer with the supernatural property of "appearing" at times of disaster; or like that of the Joyner brothers sitting for three days over the corpse of their father, discussing the Egyptian method of embalming; or like that of Aunt Mag and the idiot orphans whom she made her peons. It can magnificently sustain a long episode, as in the chapter about the butcher and his wife who brutalized their own children; as in "The Child and the Tiger," the story of a Negro gone berserk, who held a lynching party at bay until his bullets ran out; best of all, perhaps, in a meditation of George's, "Three O'Clock," about the boys whom he feared and hated—"the dwellers in accursed streets," "the vultures of the world," "made of a vile, base, incalculably evil stuff." Scene after scene, in spite of the resemblance to "Look Homeward, Angel," is breath-taking; Wolfe has illuminated a section of experience which no other novelist but Dostoievsky and Joyce have explored more searchingly; if "Look Homeward, Angel" and "Of Time and the River" were unknown, the first two hundred pages of "The Web and the Rock" would be enough to insure Wolfe's reputation.

These are followed by a section more conventional, but still good Wolfe, on George's life at the University of North Carolina and his early career in New York; and here Wolfe introduces one of his first-rate caricatures in the obese, androgynous esthete, Jerry Alsop. Unlike what has preceded, however, this part does suffer in being too repetitive of Wolfe's earlier novels; and some of it—the arrival of the youth in the big city, "trying to find himself," the recreation of the intellectual atmosphere of the metropolis in the early twenties—has a sort of local staleness about it which even Wolfe's most efflorescent verbiage cannot disguise.

If "The Web and the Rock" repeats in George's name the experiences of Eugene in "Look Homeward, Angel," it proceeds to skip "Of Time and the River" entirely. Half a page, in italics, tells us that George went to Europe. . . . Then, on the return trip, he meets and falls awkwardly in love with a woman considerably older than himself, Esther Jack, a successful designer for the theater.

The story of their love affair traces, through enormous length, the progress of a passion that turns into hysterical jealousy, of a relationship that begins in happiness and proceeds—partly because Esther refuses to marry George, partly because he projects his literary discouragements on her—to a series of violent quarrels and recriminations. At the outset the character and the past life of Esther are presented with all the power of Wolfe's imagination to make you see; the initial ecstasy of George carries conviction. But conviction is gradually lost in the violence of his increasingly egocentric torment; and the outlines of Esther (who, incidentally, takes over the web symbol) disintegrates in the subjective cyclone. The candid sensationalism of the love story may increase the popularity of Wolfe among the uncritical, and make new readers for him to whom he has heretofore been only a literary name. But although he probably sweat blood over it, although he set it all down with the honesty of that incredible memory for every detail, it is not on the level with the earlier sections. The passionate experience of Esther is never psychologically resolved in George; and from the crescendo of shrillness in which it is written one may guess that the material was not psychologically resolved in Wolfe; he could not detach himself from it as he could from the memories of childhood. Here too is the story of George's first literary venture, the novel which took so long to find a publisher; and this part of the book contains some elephantine satire on literary life in the twenties, a chapter of sarcastic extravaganza on the publishing firm of "Wright and Rawng" that is embarrassingly bad, and several rehashes of stale gossip from literary parties of fifteen years ago.

After three hundred pages in which the relationship of Esther and George becomes a protracted *Walpurgisnacht,* George goes to Germany to recover, and the book comes to a muted conclusion—but not before George has got into a brawl in Munich and had his head bashed in—in a series of lonely introspections. These resolve none of his problems, but only lead him to the conclusion, "You can't go home again"—which is the last sentence of this novel and the title of Wolfe's last novel, yet to be published.

"The Web and the Rock" contains and magnifies all Wolfe's faults and all his virtues. Where it is good, the actual writing is alive with excitement and power. The chapters on the Joyners are magnificent, the chapters presenting George's early observations and meditations are genius. Both in the lyrical evocation of distilled experience and in the perfection with which Wolfe's ear caught the speech of others,

from the mincing young esthete to the earthy talk of the mountain people, Wolfe has written passage after passage that you want to read aloud, to memorize; no novelist since Conrad has more verbal effectiveness. And mingled into these passages there are sentences and paragraphs of overwriting, of self-consciousness, of tastelessness. When George's friend, Nebraska Crane, hits a boy on the arm with a baseball bat, we get the following selection of dialogue, which sounds like the Rover Boys. . . . And the Wolfe clichés. "Million-footed life" on page 91 is multiplied in a passage of pure bombast on page 346:

Out of the nameless and unfathomed weavings of billion-footed life. . . .

But ultimately it makes no difference. In spite of everything, Wolfe was a genius. "Genius is not enough," said Bernard DeVoto in the most acute analysis of Wolfe's weaknesses that any one has written; but DeVoto takes the craft of fiction too seriously; fiction is notorious for the fact that an author whose stuff is good can get away with anything. And genius is really more important, as long as we have more good craftsmen than geniuses. Wolfe at his best is incomparable; when he is bad he has the virtue of being not meretricious, not mediocre, but just plain terrible. Good and bad, he keeps you reading by the force of that personality which diffused itself first into Eugene Gant and then into George Webber, so inextricably that one cannot read of George's introspective torments without a sensation of personal painfulness which includes the author who died last year at thirty-eight. He was a writer of magnificent fragments, imperfectly joined together. His defects were the defects of his qualities, inseparable from them, impossible for the most skillful editing to eliminate. To ask for perfection, for organization, in a novel by Thomas Wolfe is to ask for a book by another novelist—and, we cannot help feeling, a less exciting novelist.

Mary-Carter Roberts. "Writer and Hero Merge In 'Discovery of Life.'" Washington *Sunday Star*, June 25, 1939, p. F-4.

. . .

It is a work of volcanic disorder. At its outset it seems to have been planned to follow the incredibly hackneyed theme of the revolt of a small town youth against his famously narrow, famously puritanical environment. It shows us the hero as a boy misunderstood and humiliated by a pack of dreary maternal relatives, and yearning secretly after a carefree pagan kind of joyousness which he associates with his father—the town sinner No. 1. It also shows him to us in revolt against the simpering tradition of his little freshwater college, attempting there to convince his fellows that Dostoevski is as good a novelist as Dickens, making a foolish issue of it and getting himself ostracized for his trouble. And it goes still further with this desperately well-worn pattern by taking the youth finally to New York and plunging him neck and crop into the jazz age culture, where he sets about making a writer of himself down in Greenwich Village and falls in love. None of this, to be sure, would seem to allow of enough originality to be rated disorderly; it is a series of custom-made literary conventions unblemished by the slightest taint of creativeness. But this is only a very small part of the novel. It is only the story of the hero. That youth, it should be said, has a rival performer beside him in the book, and that is no other than the author, Mr. Thomas Wolfe.

For Mr. Wolfe takes the stage himself much oftener than the young man about whom he is ostensibly writing a book. And it is in these appearances of his own that he has given his work the life which it possesses. The final effect is as of a pallid and perfunctory play presented in a number of scenes, after every one of which a violent picturesque knave of a scene shifter curvets out upon the uncurtained stage and whoops and shouts to the audience as he goes about his labors, using such vitality and uproar that the memory of the colorless characters of the drama is hopelessly disturbed. The scene shifter would be Mr. Wolfe, the actor his hero, and there simply is not room for both of them in this book. Indeed, one may well wonder if there has ever been room for any character in Mr. Wolfe's work except himself. But the wonder reaches an acute stage in this present so-called novel.

. . .

It has been said that genius is chiefly energy. That would seem to explain Thomas Wolfe, for the man was beyond question a genius. He seemed to possess little discrimination, his taste was often dubious, his capacity for overwriting was incredible. The present work, indeed, is not so much a series of purple patches laid on as a whole purple composition through which a story dodges its harried way. But the energy is there. It lifts whole passages into the realm of literature and gives the book, absurd as it often is, a chaotic splendor. It does so by main force, to be sure. But it does it just the same.

Ray Warwick. Atlanta *Journal,* June 25, 1939, Magazine Section, p. 10.

When death took Thomas Wolfe last year it ended the greatest promise in American fiction since Herman Melville. In "Look Homeward, Angel" and "Of Time and the River" Wolfe caught for the first time all the complexity, rich humor and wild vitality of modern America and created immortal characters in the gargantuan Gants.

So doubts arise when we read Wolfe's foreword in which he says that "The Web and the Rock" marks "a turning away from the books I have written in the past." But when we get inside, and read, we find it is the same old Wolfe after all. The Gants are missing, but the protagonist, George Webber, with a different name and body, is really Eugene Gant again, and his home town, Libya Hill, is what Wolfe called "Altamont" before.

Like Wolfe's other books, "The Web and the Rock" is a vast, wordy, rushing panorama of American scenes and people. . . . This, briefly, is what it is about; but those who know Wolfe know there is much more. He cannot tell a story, it is true, cannot build up progressively to a conclusive climax. What he gives us is a dithyrambic prose poem

almost epic in its scope and power, and worthy at its best of being ranked with "Leaves of Grass." What he gives us is the feel, taste, smell, the very heartbeat of American life as no other modern writer has done. Maybe that should be enough.

There is much excellent writing in this book. It must be patiently mined out of a mass of exposition at times; but it is well worth the effort. Perhaps the best are the sections about George Webber's boyhood in Libya Hill and the sort of stream-of-consciousness remembering of the early life of Esther, the woman he loves. In these there is sensitive beauty and vigor combined.

. . .

Unsigned. "A Novel By Thomas Wolfe." Baltimore *Sun,* June 25, 1939, p. 8, Section 1.

This book is issued as the first of two novels that Thomas Wolfe completed a few months before his death last September; but it is perfectly obvious that it is really the first volume of a single novel, for it breaks off in mid-career. It is the story of *George Webber,* a sensitive and brilliant young man, drawn by the irresistible lure of Manhattan (the Rock) and there finding out slowly and painfully what life on the Web means. Fame and fortune elude George, but love he finds; and his is certainly one of the most astounding love stories ever presented in American fiction.

The book is huge, shaggy, inchoate, and to this extent is like the rest of Wolfe's work. It is punctuated by those explosions of brilliance, those sudden discharges of a million rockets all at once that have stupefied critics ever since Wolfe began to write; but there is something else in it. The first quarter of the book is the old Wolfe of "Look Homeward, Angel," in which he describes again the life of a North Carolina boy. But thereafter another man emerges, a harder, sharper, more acrid Wolfe, less attractive than the earlier one, but possibly more important. In a prefatory note he remarks that "satiric exaggeration belongs to the nature of life, and particularly American life," and when Thomas Wolfe goes in for satiric exaggeration he makes a very thorough job of it. There is internal evidence that prudent editors have not spared the blue pencil, but at that "The Web and the Rock" contains some of the most envenomed pages in American literature. There are portraits of certain prominent figures in the literary world, wearing the thinnest of disguises, that are masterpieces of malevolent perfection; and there are comments on the inhabitants of New York that make Mr. William Faulkner's most mordant efforts resemble panegyrics in comparison.

That the book is powerful goes without saying, but it is impossible to pass any definite judgment upon it as it stands. It is incomplete. The struggle of the artist in conflict with his environment—or, rather, in conflict with himself, incessantly torn by the power within him—is presented with prodigious force; but the book ends at a lull in the conflict. It is indubitably a good book. It may be the first half of a great one, but that depends upon what is to come.

August Derleth. "Book of the Week." Mazomanie (Wisconsin) *Sickle,* June 29, 1939.

Unquestionably the novel of the summer, if not indeed the year, is "The Web and the Rock," one of the two posthumous books left by the late Thomas Wolfe. . . . "The Web and the Rock" is the first of these; out today, it is undoubtedly destined to have a best-seller status within a fortnight of publication; everyone in the literate world will want to read it, and it will command the best critical attention because its author was recognized as one of the few American literary geniuses to emerge in recent years. For that reason, if for no other, "The Web and the Rock" deserves careful reading and careful judgment.

As will all his previous books, Wolfe's new novel is weighty, overwritten, passionately intense, beautifully lyrical, dramatic, moving, awkward, overlong, but above all, significant and important, standing head and shoulders above many better written novels by virtue of its very intensity, the brilliance of its good writing overshadowing its padded portions. This is one of the books of which Wolfe wrote not long before his death that it would be more objective than his earlier work. So it is; "The Web and the Rock" is more objective, but at the same time it is no less passionately intense than the Eugene Gant series, and the conclusion is inevitable that, objective though it purports to be, once again Wolfe drew here upon his own life for the story of George Webber, even as he did for the story of Eugene Gant. If Gant was meant to be Wolfe, then Webber is Wolfe's alter ego. Here in this emotional story is a Gant-like writer, who, typically an American boy, dreams of going to New York to find love and fame and fortune. To New York ultimately he goes; there he is impressed, burned, disillusioned, with all the dramatic fire that Wolfe can muster; he undergoes few simple emotions—rather, he experiences simple emotions which are translated into the epitome of complexity in Wolfe's feverish emotional creation.

It is as impossible to evaluate Wolfe at this time, as it is to evaluate Frost; but that one should think of both at the same time is significant enough in itself. That Wolfe remains today, despite his untimely death last September, one of the giants of contemporary American letters, is self evident; how much material he left to be published is not yet publicly known. Harpers have already announced that a second novel, "You Can't Go Home Again," will follow "The Web and the Rock" next year; there is doubtless even more material than this second novel awaiting publication. "The Web and the Rock" does indeed rank with Wolfe's "best and truest" work, as Harpers blurb. Everything he has done is reminiscent of everything else he has written, whether it is the remarkably beautiful first novel, "Look Homeward, Angel," or whether it is his "Story of a Novel." His style, often unduly heavy, often almost neurotically emotional and intense, is unique; his books are for the most part sprawling, undisciplined creations, he has overwritten almost every novel he has done; and yet, despite all these things, his greatness rose above flaws which in most other novel-ists would have served to damn them unequivocally. I would myself prefer to have on my shelves the work of Thomas Wolfe: "Look Homeward, Angel," "Of Time and the River," "The Story of a Novel," "From Death to Morning," and "The Web and the Rock": to the complete works of any one of Wolfe's contemporaries.

No literate American will want to miss "The Web and the Rock." It will be a long time before another genius with the stature of Wolfe emerges upon the American literary scene; for the time being, his new work continues to appear in magazines and books.

Henry Seidel Canby. *Book-of-the-Month Club News,* July 1939. ("Other Books Recommended This Month.")

This posthumous novel is the first half of a continuous story which will, unfortunately, conclude the versatile self-analysis and brilliant impressionism of one of the most remarkable talents of our time. As a story, it goes back to the early years from which *Look Homeward Angel* was drawn; but it is a different story, differently told. In a series of episodes—passages from youth they might be called—Wolfe gives us North Carolina, his extraordinary family, the death of a bad Negro, small-boy drama—all in a web of experiences. It is hard to exaggerate the force, the beauty, and the intense interest of these episodes. No man writing now has excelled them. I am describing the first and by far the better half of this long novel. This part seems to have been written separately, and is an artistic whole, which escapes from the formless excesses of Wolfe's earlier novels, and carries a youth from the country to his first maturity in New York with mounting interest and a restrained emotion which surely mark Wolfe as one of the really important novelists in the American tradition. The last half of the book deals with an actual affair with a brilliantly artistic married woman, who introduces the young hero to intellectual and artistic New York, as well as to love. This affair doubles and turns upon itself, rises to climaxes of great emotional intensity, and sinks to squabbles which come close to the absurd. It has much of the repetitiveness and unrestrained confession of Wolfe's earlier novels, faults entirely absent from the first part of this novel. And the scenes and characters of the New York literary world, many of them easily recognizable, have the same quality of too literal description which fascinated many of Wolfe's readers but which, to others, seemed to escape from imagination into mere reporting. Yet this part of the novel is brilliant too, and suffers only by comparison with the more excellent and more self-contained story of his first youth. It is to be hoped that when all this posthumous writing is printed, the publishers will make new divisions which will reveal, not obscure, the organism of Thomas Wolfe's achievement.

Unsigned. *Booklist,* 35 (July 1, 1939), 365.

Obviously autobiographical, the novel is an unselective outpouring of the author's own emotional reactions. As fiction it is the story of George Webber from boyhood days in a southern town to life as a writer in New York. There his search for meaning in life remained unsatisfied and anguish in a love affair led to European travel. In spite of the author's inability to discard extraneous material and an obsession with his own feelings, his genius and exceptional power in writing are evident. Limited in appeal; not for conservatives, but readers of Wolfe will want it. This is the first half of a manuscript completed before the novelist's death; the other half will be published under the title, *You Can't Go Home Again.*

Joseph Henry Jackson. "The Last Work of Thomas Wolfe, Significant Artist of His Time." San Francisco *Chronicle,* July 5, 1939, p. 13.

Of the wonderful and terrible city that is New York Mr. Wolfe writes "It is the most homeless home in all the world. It is the gigantic tenement of Here Comes Everybody. It is strange, cruel, tender, beautiful. . . ."

It is this New York, to which his young hero comes looking for he knows not what, that is one of Wolfe's major interests in this novel. With its successor, now in his publisher's hands, the book represents the last of Wolfe's work. By it and its second part, as well as by his writing of the last decade, Thomas Wolfe will eventually be judged.

The first question then is whether "The Web and the Rock" represents an advance, anything new, perhaps any development in the talent of the man who was certainly one of the important half-dozen among contemporary American writers.

The easy thing to say is that the book merely follows the conventional Wolfe pattern; that it is "Look Homeward Angel" and/or "Of Time and the River" all over again. There is enough plausibility to that argument to let it by, too. Wolfe's latest protagonist, his newest young-man-against-the-world, is like enough to Eugene Gant, for example, to lend color to the suggestion that Wolfe had only one young man to write about—the young man who was himself. It is true, too, that what Wolfe has to say about George Webber, his youthful conditioning in his North Carolina town, his endeavor to discover himself, to make his young manhood count against the terrors of the great city, does not add a great deal to what he has said before on much the same theme. All this is so, just as many another stricture in respect of Wolfe is still valid. He always had trouble in combing out his prose; he is as impatient here as ever with small niceties of construction and detail. He is, so to say, precisely as Wolfian as he was with his first page of writing.

But—well, you can say all these things, and be right about them, too, yet they simply don't matter. Because the powerful driving force that was Thomas Wolfe makes them all of no account. Wolfe's ability to brew that peculiar, heady, emotional mixture of prose and poetry in which he excells is the only thing that makes any difference. You are swept up into his book and along with it so strongly that nothing else comes into your mind.

This time, the chief interest of the book—after George Webber's youthful impressions are made clear and the city's impact on him is shown—lies in his love affair with a woman older than himself. The woman, as you can't help seeing, is woman-plus-city. In George's emotional reactions the two are inextricably mingled, part and parcel of each other. She is also all women; that is to say, in Wolfe's mind she seems to have been that. Unfortunately, Wolfe does not appear to have thought this phase of his book quite through, with the result that the section of the story dealing with this affair is confused, less convincing than most of his writing. As a matter of fact, the reader can't be altogether sure that Wolfe himself felt this portion of the book as strongly, let alone as clearly, as he felt the rest of it.

Nevertheless, it is not of so much significance that Wolfe is less good here than he is there. What is important is his unique ability to write his own kind of rushing, overwhelming, passionate prose. Call it a species of psychological gigantism if you like, it is still true that his genius for flooding his readers with swirling, roaring page after page, for wrenching the reader from his emotional and intellectual moorings completely—that genius is sufficient reason for reading every word of Wolfe.

The speculation as to what he might have done if he had lived is futile now. What remains is the inescapable truth that Wolfe, controlled artist or no, is yet as significant an artist as the period has produced. Perhaps "The Web and the Rock" is just another novel about a young man and his conflicts with life. But it's written as no other novel on the theme has ever been written, and no one who is interested in the development of American fiction can afford to leave it unread.

Louis Kronenberger. "Thomas Wolfe, Autobiographer." *Nation,* 149 (July 15, 1939), 75–76.

There has been no American first novel since the war which promised so greatly as "Look Homeward, Angel." To be sure, it was a large, sprawling record cut down from an incredibly longer and more sprawling one. With all the vitality of a born writer behind it, it showed nothing of the discipline of a born artist. It lacked perspective; it lacked proportion; the emotions it struck were too often homesick and adolescent. But nobody reading it could fail to perceive its spendthrift power, or fail to recognize the vigor with which the Gant family was brought to life, or close the book without being aware that no such rhetoric, no such energy and rush of language, had been visited upon any other young man of our time.

"Look Homeward, Angel" was an autobiographical novel, the usual beginning for a young man who wrote hotly and expressively from within. Not at once did the reader grasp that this particular young man must be always an autobiographer, because his equipment—his tortured romantic egoism,

his megalomaniac memory, his grandiose assimilation of life in terms of purely personal encounter—outlawed any other approach to literature. But this worship of selfhood was confirmed by Wolfe's second novel, the even more unrestrained "Of Time and the River." Clearly the world about him existed no farther than his eye could see; and it was a world that lacked order, objective truth, social meaning. Only what he could sink his teeth in, or fling his body upon, or whirl about in his memory, was real; and even these were things he must write about with the same vehemence and ardor that he lived them.

"The Web and the Rock" is again autobiography, full of the same raptures and incontinences, and pondering again those poetic truisms about time and love and death which are as close as Wolfe could come to thinking, and as much philosophy as the egocentric adolescent ever needs. True, Eugene Gant is here called George Webber, and grows up in some other North Carolina community, and salutes the great city with new apostrophes, and embarks with a woman older and mellower than himself on a stormy love affair. Few love affairs in fiction have been more minutely reported. Few, I should think, have been more self-consciously lived through. Scarcely any, while exposing so much, have analyzed so little. The whole business, with Wolfe, becomes a piece of violent self-dramatization.

Wolfe's real weakness was not that he dramatized his life, but that the writer dramatized it even more than the man. The man suffered; the writer merely exulted in the suffering. The man doubted and was afraid; the writer chose to celebrate himself on the grand scale. The result was not entirely hollow or cheaply operatic, but much of it might fairly be called Wagnerian. Wolfe would, to begin with, have acknowledged Wagner's dictum that all art is a way of remembering one's childhood. He had, too, Wagner's grandiosities: used *leitmotivs*, operated in tetralogies, succumbed to that mystical, mindless *Nachtkultur* which pervades "Tristan" and the "Ring." He had the Wagnerian tumidity and opulence, the love of size, the delight in effect; but though in Wagner too there are emptiness and show, Wagner knew how to work in large forms, and what Wagner created in the end—whatever we may think of it intellectually—was indeed a cosmos. Wolfe never created anything, even in disorder. He remembered, he recaptured, he elaborated on things known, and with himself for substructure threw up a great shapeless edifice. Even his prose is not really created; it is only superbly improvised. His best writing is doubtless magnificent, but even his best writing is not solid; and there is hardly one paragraph in all he wrote that is not self-indulgent. His worst prose (and there is a great deal of it) is unspeakable.

The whole body of Wolfe's work, marvelous as fragments of it are, betrays the amateur and the adolescent. One regrets the want of cerebration, the addled values, in much of Hemingway; but as a *writer*, Hemingway is altogether professional, always knows exactly what he is doing. Wolfe knew nothing of the sort, and would never have known. It was not for him to curb his excesses by learning his trade. What he was, what he achieved, resulted from a heady, untamable personality—with the bit in his mouth, he would have turned dumb. Real passion he did not have, for he was too ungovernable to

be truly intense. His energies, like his perceptions and his attachments, were adolescent. For home and the home country and the family life he had outgrown, Wolfe was insistently nostalgic. City life and the great world fascinated him to the end, I should guess, because they had fascinated him when he was growing up. "A man spends his youth dreaming out," says a mountain character in a Lola Ridge play, "and the rest of his life dreaming back." Of no one is that truer than of Wolfe.

He never acquired, of course, any values—either intellectual or moral—that were worth consideration. He had enough experience of life, and enough sensibility, to recognize what was narrow, parochial, absurd in the life he quitted; he was so carried away by romanticism that in moments of recoil he could perceive its shams, and look with some suspicion on the individualist codes it produced. But of man's place in the hard, downright living world he knew little, for to a writer so inward-looking the world and himself were one. The great arcana—time and death and fate—fascinated him; but even these, from his incorrigible habit of words, he ended by exploiting and vulgarizing.

Wolfe belonged to the high-pitched, unreal 1920's; their injunction to live fully, to seize all experience, perfectly fitted his need. When he died, young as he was, he had lived too long. For the soberer life that came after the 20's, when the accent fell not on the individual but on society, was something Wolfe could not understand. The fruits that one after another he thirstily sucked in gave him their flavor but no nourishment. One can glibly lament the awful sense of waste about his career;

yet one knows, really, that it could not have been otherwise—that his talents were wasteful by nature, that his energies were so wonderful just because they were so unharnessed. One more book of Wolfe's will be published next year. Meanwhile, what remain are the symphonic fragments of language; the tortured soul seen through the angry tumults; the brightly unrolling memory; and the vast wonder of a boy.

Harry Sylvester. "Thomas Wolfe's Posthumous Book." *Commonweal*, 30 (July 21, 1939), 321-22.

It is not unduly cynical to say that Thomas Wolfe died at exactly the right time in his life for his perpetuation as a genius. Wolfe wrote only one book that approached greatness. That book was his first, "Look Homeward, Angel," and all his work since has been a thin, watered-down repetition of the rich sensuality of that work.

For those who have not read "Look Homeward, Angel" there remains a definite experience in store. No richer novel has ever, perhaps, been written. Its values are not intellectual, and where they are spiritual, they are amorphous or esoteric, but as a purely sensual experience, as an example of the impact of sheer words and physical experience upon a reader, it has few equals.

Where that book was rich, Wolfe's succeeding novels have been merely wordy. I think the reason is that Wolfe never really grew to any extent. From this current novel and its predecessor, which was slightly better, one can only get the impression of a great oaf stumbling around the earth, trying to kid, first himself, then the public that he was on a constant journey of miraculous discovery.

The George Webber of this book is the Eugene Gant of the others, who is, of course, Wolfe, himself. It is not so much that he is mad—although he would have liked to think he was as mad as, say Keats—as that he is childish, uncontrolled and without guts. The publishers have made a great fuss about what they call "the most lifelike love story anybody ever wrote" and the "only" love story Wolfe ever wrote. This is not so. There is a very poignant love story in "Look Homeward, Angel," one of the best portrayals of young, lyrical love that has ever been written. That the "love" story in "The Web and the Rock" is nothing more than a cheap little adultery with an arty phoney old enough to be the boy's mother is perhaps more of a comment on the publisher's idea of love than on Wolfe's.

Many writers "fail to recognize a problem in art." Virtually no one writing English today can describe physical action exactly and well, with the exception of Kenneth Roberts and Ernest Hemingway. Wolfe is no better than most in this respect. But there are great holes in the book which serve as evidence that he often recognized a problem other than that of physical action, but simply did not try to solve it. He ignores the family relationship of the adulteress, who has a husband and a daughter, neither of whom speak a single word or enter into a single scene of a book 695 pages long. He makes no attempt to account for the relationship between the boy and the older woman, other than to let us know that the woman was a good cook, despite her wealth. To Wolfe, perhaps, that was enough reason to enter into such a liaison.

Like the curate's egg, however, parts of the book are excellent. A good part of the first 300 pages are worth reading, particularly the story of the negro gone berserk in the southern mountain town on a winter night. Curiously, the best parts of the book have to do with George Webber only as spectator. Apparently, if Wolfe had ever been able to get out of himself for more than a couple of pages at a time, he might have gone some place after "Look Homeward, Angel." Well, there's no use messing around with this any more. "The Web and the Rock" as a whole isn't worth reading. But if you haven't read "Look Homeward, Angel," get yourself a copy. Modern Library puts it out as one of its "giants."

Charles Angoff. "A Promise and a Legend." *North American Review,* 248 (Autumn 1939), 198-201.

Up to page 297 this first of Mr. Wolfe's posthumous works retells some of the story of *Look Homeward, Angel* in terms of George Webber, alias Eugene Gant. The remaining 400 pages concern George's four-year love affair with a married woman, Mrs. Esther Jack, about twenty years his senior. In a prefatory note Mr. Wolfe said: "This novel . . . marks not only a turning away from the books I have written in the past, but a genuine spiritual and artistic change. It is the most objective novel that I have written. . . . I have sought, through free creation, a release of my inventive powers."

Mr. Wolfe decieved himself. According to the available evidence he underwent no basic change whatever, much less, indeed, than any other American novelist taken with the same seriousness. He neither progressed nor retrogressed. After fifteen years of writing he remained almost exactly where he started from: a perennial adolescent emotionally and intellectually, extremely shaky in his feeling for words and even more so in the matter of form, and generally lacking in the ability to create character. Further, despite his Gargantuan physical appetites and verbosity, and despite his constant references to cosmic affairs, he achieved his few successes only on small canvases. The large portrayal of large people and situations escaped his grasp.

His three novels must be described as collections of brief, impressionistic pieces, and his short stories, when they make any sense at all, as little more than puffed-up, ill-digested incidents. *Look Homeward, Angel* contains good sketches of his brother Benjy, his sister Helen, and his father and mother, but the work as a whole arouses interest in the potentialities of the author rather than in the product. *Of Time and the River* must be put down as a jumble of punctuation marks, municipal catalogues, and geographical gazettes. It has the bigness of a runaway tumor, not that of a large concept beautifully executed.

In *The Web and the Rock* a few things stand out: George's youthful dreams of an afternoon, his first impressions of New York City, and Esther's letter to him on the boat. Though not of the first magnitude, these have fine feeling and fair writing. But the bulk of the volume falls short on almost all counts. The 400-page love affair begins as an ordinary pick-up on board ship and thereafter progresses to its commonplace ending without a trace of fresh insight. Neither George nor Esther ever comes to life. They make love, wrangle, and make up, and all the time she cooks wonderful meals for him, while he complains about the cosmos, but why the older woman held on to him, young enough to be her son, what attracted them to each other in the late afternoon and in the usually horrendous hours between supper and bed-time—these things Mr. Wolfe did not make clear.

He had the honesty to show up George as an amateur genius, but he did not have the artistry to explain the relationship which, by its very premises, must have contained a world of pity, beauty, and horror. Few situations hold more loveliness and pain than that of a woman, young or old, balancing her life on the smile of a man, and when the woman is nearly twice the man's age, even the angels count her tears and pray to God to be merciful to her. Mr. Wolfe was so engrossed in his own loneliness that he seldom noticed the lost looks in the faces of others, being particularly blind to woman's reddening eyes. This blindness kept him from reaching true size.

Some reviewers have remarked upon the satirical gifts displayed in *The Web and the Rock*, pointing out the onslaughts upon the publishing business (as exemplified by the firm of Rawng and Wright) and upon literary critics (as exemplified by Mr. Seamus Malone). To one reader these chapters belong to Mr. Wolfe's least successful efforts. They do not satirize their objects; they burlesque them. The truth about publishers and literary critics is so astounding that if put down simply, with proper selectivity, it would make hilarious and memorable reading. But Mr. Wolfe, with hardly any sense for the sneer between the lines, let loose with all the might of his torrential verbosity—and the result boomeranged, making him look like a teller of tall tales rather than a skillful writer.

Look Homeward, Angel stirred people because it displayed a largesse of feeling very rare in American writers, most of whom worry themselves with small pangs and smaller yearnings. The book had faults aplenty—bad writing, no organization, some cheapness—but the massiveness of emotion tended to keep them in the background. Intelligent readers hoped that he would learn to write, develop a sense of form, and find a direction for his inner turbulence. Mr. Wolfe failed them in every subsequent book, and in the end began to tire them. A man jabbering interminably at the top of his voice that the world hurts him, soon or late becomes a bore. One therefore fears that if Mr. Wolfe lives at all, it will be as a huge promise unrealized—and as a legend because of his personal traits, some of them lovable, some grotesque, and all extraordinary. How much promise and legend count for in the long run can be determined by a glance at the footnotes in any good literary history.

Paula Snelling. *North Georgia Review,* 4 (Autumn 1939), p. 31-32.

America has had so few literary geniuses that the passing of one at the age of 38 would on the face of it seem a major catastrophe. Yet one wonders, on this first anniversary of Thomas Wolfe's death, if it was a greater tragedy than his survival would have been. For, though it is dangerous to put much credence in a prediction of an artist's future books made from the blueprints of his accomplished writings, there is strong reason to believe that Wolfe's brief decade of productivity coincided almost perfectly with the zenith arc of his potentialities. And that his fate, in a few years, might have become that of Jim Randolph (a minor character in *The Web and the Rock*, who could play superbly only one role in life, and that one by its nature predestined to be brief; yet whose ego could flourish only when the spotlights played upon it).

Thomas Wolfe said that *The Web and the Rock* "marks not only a turning away from the books I have written in the past, but a genuine spiritual and artistic change. It is the most objective novel that I have written." The reader cannot echo the pronouncement. For 270 pages George Webber struggles manfully, and with intermittent success, to attain an identity of his own. Thereafter he accepts the personality of Eugene Gant with only occasional misgivings. By page 405 all pretenses have ceased. (Which, of course, is not to pass judgment, or even to speculate, on whether or not the events which befell George Webber are identical with those Thomas Wolfe experienced; but merely to state that the reactions of Webber to them are consonant with those Wolfe—alias Gant—would have had under similar circumstances.) Here, as heretofore, one sees the universe as it appears to a marvelously talented young man who, at least at the unconscious level of his being, has

never assumed other than that he is the center of it. Its gyrations are important only as they produce reactions in him. Which is all right. For this is a stage through which we all go, and it is good, both as we pass through it and as we look back upon it, to have it pictured thus splendidly and in more vivid colors and on a more gigantic canvas than it is granted the ordinary mortal to live it. But it is a stage at which one cannot with impunity remain overlong. Yet even the love affair in *The Web and the Rock* (the first Wolfe has given us) and the emotional maelstroms and the disintegration which it precipitates, are important in the author's and in the hero's eyes only as they intensify George's feelings. That is, even here the universe remains a circle revolving about the original ego, and does not shift into the more mature orbit of an ellipse whose curve is determined by two foci. And the book perhaps symbolizes, in the career of the author, what the love affair overtly precipitates in the life of the protagonist: the peril which overtakes a human being whose libido becomes too strongly rooted in any one stage of the individual's development.

But what Wolfe has done (and he has incarnated in the written word, with a completeness and a satisfyingness seldom duplicated in literature, the spirit and the flesh of eager, questing, potent young manhood) he has done so well that it is deservedly a classic. Everybody in America who reads should enjoy the spectacle of one of Wolfe's books. But since the others which have yet appeared are in their better parts and in their essence replicas of the first, there is little need to read them all.

There remains one book by Wolfe

yet to be published. Should it reveal mature talents of a scale comparable to the youthful ones heretofore displayed by the artist, then Wolfe's death would have to be written down as an incalculable loss to American letters. But pending the appearance of this last book (to be called *You Can't Go Home Again*) one speculates that Providence would have been no less unkind to him or to his readers had it permitted Wolfe his remaining three decades. For it would not have been meet, either artistically or practically, for him to have continued indefinitely in the sector where he had already accomplished so brilliantly; yet, so far, the degree to which he has deviated from the initial realm of his success has been marked by greater loss than gain. The simple facts seem to be that, though Wolfe's talents were in excess of the requirements for any artist, his maturity of outlook and of comprehension had not kept pace with his chronological years; and that he was not equipped with that emotional stamina requisite for surviving and assimilating, had he been subjected to them, the unremitting buffetings by which life acquaints our Dostoievskys with her broader and deeper truths.

CHECKLIST OF ADDITIONAL REVIEWS

Ralston Matheny. "Posthumous Novel by Wolfe is Great, Terrifying Work." Knoxville *Times,* June 16, 1939.

Arthur Rhodes. Column, "New Books in Review." Brooklyn *Eagle,* June 22, 1939.

Allen W. Porterfield. "The Book Of the Day." New York *Sun,* June 22, 1939.

Charles Poore. Column, "Books of the Times." New York *Times,* June 22, 1939, p. 21.

Boston *Herald,* June 24, 1939.

Fanny Butcher. "A Posthumous Novel Upholds Wolfe's Genius." Chicago *Tribune,* June 24, 1939.

Clifton Fadiman. "The Web and the Rock." *New Yorker,* 15 (June 24, 1939), 69-70.

O.C.D. "Tom Wolfe's Posthumous Novel Ranks With His Earlier Works." *Asheville-Citizen,* June 25, 1939.

John Selby. "Tom Wolfe's Last Book." *The Charlotte News,* June 25, 1939.

Legette Blythe. "Two Schools Will Clash Over Wolfe's New Novel." *The Charlotte Observer,* June 25, 1939.

Caro Green Russell. "Posthumous Novel." *The Durham Herald-Sun,* June 25, 1939.

Fritz Raley Simmons. "Thomas Wolfe's Novel Reveals Marked Advance in His Writing." Greensboro (N.C.) *Daily News,* June 25, 1939, p. 4D.

M. E. Fretwell. "One Man's Discovery of Life." Jacksonville, Fla. *Sunday Times-Union,* June 25, 1939.

Milwaukee *Journal,* June 25, 1939.

Alfred Kazin. "Thomas Wolfe's Significance as a Writer." New York *Herald Tribune Books,* June 25, 1939, pp. 1-2.

J. Donald Adams. "A New Novel by Thomas Wolfe." New York *Times Book Review,* June 25, 1939, p. 1.

Burton Rascoe. "Of Time and Thomas Wolfe." *Newsweek,* 13 (June 26, 1939), 36.

"Bitter Mystery." *Time,* 33 (June 26, 1939), 81.

Olive B. James. "The Web and The Rock." *The Delphian Quarterly,* 22 (July 1939), 53-54.

Howard Mumford Jones. "Prometheus in Love." Boston *Transcript,* July 1, 1939, p. 1.

Paul Jordan-Smith. Los Angeles *Times,* July 2, 1939.

R. J. Conklin. "Thomas Wolfe's Quest of Life." Springfield *Republican,* July 2, 1939, 7E.

Alicia Patterson. "Thomas Wolfe Was A Flood Of Glittering Literature." Washington, D.C. *Times-Herald,* July 9, 1939.

Malcolm Cowley. "Thomas Wolfe's Legacy." *New Republic,* 99 (July 19, 1939), 311-12.

Theodore Spencer. "The Web and The Rock." *Atlantic Monthly,* 164 (August 1939), n.p.

John Chamberlain. *Harper's,* 179 (August 1939), n.p.

"America at Night." Chicago *Midwest Daily Record,* August 17, 1939.

"Art and Fact." *Saturday Review,* August 26, 1939.

Pratt Institute Free Library Quarterly *Booklist,* Autumn, 1939, p. 29.

Wilbur L. Schramm. "Careers at Crossroads." *Virginia Quarterly Review,* Autumn, 1939.

Bernard DeVoto. "American Novels, 1939." *Atlantic Monthly,* 165 (January 1940), 69-71.

"Whitmanesque Rhapsody." *London Times Literary Supplement,* No. 2348, February 1, 1947, p. 61.

Thomas Wolfe

YOU CAN'T GO HOME AGAIN

Harper & Brothers · Publishers
New York and London

You Can't Go Home Again

Claude Simpson.
Southwest Review, 26
(Autumn 1940),
132-135.

Thomas Wolfe's new novel is the second of two books which he completed just before his death in 1938. *The Web and the Rock,* published last year, failed to add to the reputation Wolfe had achieved through his earlier work, largely because the book professed a new objectivity which is scarcely present in its pages.

You Can't Go Home Again is structurally a sequel to *The Web and the Rock.* It carries on the story of George Webber from the acceptance of his first novel to the break with his editor seven or eight years later. As is usual in Wolfe's works, the story is Wolfe's own story, so thinly veiled that the disguise is an almost embarrassing failure. Young Webber's first novel, *Home to Our Mountains,* receives a good press, but because of its frankness enrages the author's Southern home town. He goes on to a second novel, working desperately in a lonely Brooklyn cellar, roaming the wilds of lower New York when he cannot sleep at night, and finally retreating to Europe for change of scene and new perspective. After returning to America, he requires a season to reduce his bulky, formless manuscript to a publishable state (and here Wolfe paints a warm portrait of the editor—actually Maxwell Perkins of Scribner's—who patiently performed on Wolfe's own manuscripts all the major surgery without which they would never have reached the printed page). Following still another trip to Europe, and notably to Nazi Germany, Webber returns convinced that it is artistically harmful for him to continue dependent on his editor, and he makes the break.

This, in brief, is the story of Wolfe's last book. In many respects it traverses old ground. His brief but illuminating essay, *The Story of a Novel* (1936), sets forth in a fraction of the space almost everything of importance contained in the first five hundred pages of *You Can't Go Home Again.* To be sure, nothing that is strictly dramatic appears in *The Story of a Novel,* but there we do find a revelation of the author's method and moods, and above all a hint of his maturing attitude toward the external world of sensation and experience. And that is what is most important in the novel.

137

You Can't Go Home Again would have to be set down as a disappointment if it merely clothed *The Story of a Novel* with the loose folds of fiction. Actually, however, in it Wolfe goes beyond his position of 1936. The seemingly ill-advised preface to *The Web and the Rock,* if applied to the entire sweep of the two novels, is not so wide of the mark. For before he finishes, Wolfe has achieved a sort of perspective; by inference, at least, there is a fresh source of unity within the two volumes. It is not the figure of the protagonist, nor is it the misty, symbolic idea of youth's quest for the "far and lost." Rather, it is the gradual development of a deep sympathy for the nameless "disinherited of life" who have fallen prey to the ruthlessness abroad in every land. The title of the novel is Wolfe's way of saying that whatever the solution for the ills of the world, mankind cannot retreat into the safety of the past, it cannot go "back home to the escapes of Time and Memory." Wolfe believes that within limits humanity can and will progress, although his editor, a "hopeful fatalist," disagrees with him. The eloquence of Wolfe's message extends specifically to America, which since the Civil War has "turned into something ugly—and vicious—and corroded at the heart of its power with easy wealth and graft and special privilege." Freedom and individual integrity, he says, have become mere slogans, and corruption has bred serious intellectual dishonesty. This indictment is a commonplace; but Wolfe feels that the collapse of 1929 may represent the end of the old order, the beginning of something which he hopes will be finer, although he is not clear on this point. "Through it all there was one certainty, though no one saw it yet.

America was still America, and whatever new thing came of it would be American." This Whitmanesque enthusiasm is accompanied by no bill of particulars, and one may regret, if only for the record, that Wolfe's poetry is more effective than his party line.

One of the most successful sections of the book is "I Have a Thing to Tell You," published serially in *The New Republic* in 1937 and only slightly revised here. The lean and economical prose of these German chapters is not, unfortunately, duplicated in "The Party at Jack's," a tedious and flatulent expansion of the overlong first version which appeared in the final number of the old *Scribner's,* in May, 1939.

Most of the shortcomings of the well-known Wolfe manner are present in *You Can't Go Home Again*—the same startling but genuine evidences of naiveté, the same tendency to overwrite, the sophomoric rhetorical flights and threadbare melodramatic effects. But here, too, is the frequent fine sense of phrase, and the power of intense experience nakedly set down. Here too are some unforgettable portraits that are more than caricature. That of the famous red-headed American novelist (obviously Sinclair Lewis) careening through England is amusing; and the picture of the evil old man who has built a fortune on perpetual interest payments from small loans to Negroes is as true as it is bitter.

The Wolfe of *You Can't Go Home Again* is not a new Wolfe, though it is a more mature Wolfe. None of his novels is as finished as even the most tentative youthful production of Henry James; yet their power has, as with Melville, made a place for work which refused to follow the conventional rules of fiction. In the last analysis, it is probably erroneous to think of Wolfe as a novelist. Like *Moby Dick,* his books may be called novels only for want of a more precise term. But the marvelous evocative power of his best writing has made him a significant figure; and though his final place may be somewhat below that of Melville, his like Melville's is a type of wayward genius that too infrequently has brightened our horizon.

Fanny Butcher. "Thomas Wolfe Attains Heights of True Genius." Chicago *Tribune,* September 18, 1940, p. 12.

When Thomas Wolfe died on Sept. 15, 1938, he left a gargantuan manuscript. The first half of it, "The Web and the Rock," published in June of last year, ended with the phrase: "You Can't Go Home Again." The second half, published today with that title, ends with one of the most touching and beautiful epitaphs any man ever wrote, a haunting and prophetic paragraph, deeply moving to the readers who in these long, intense, honest pages have come to know their autobiographical hero with compelling intimacy.

Among the last words that Thomas Wolfe wrote before he died are the closing paragraphs to this posthumous novel, "Before I go," he wrote, "I have just one more thing to tell you:

"Something has spoken to me in the night, burning the tapers of the waning year; something has spoken in the night, and told me I shall die, I know not where. Saying:

" 'To lose the earth you know, for greater knowing; to lose the life you have, for greater life; to leave the friends you loved, for greater loving; to find a land more kind than home, more large than earth—' "

"You Can't Go Home Again" is an authentic work of art, so obviously the travail of genius that to try to do more than state the fact would be to minimize both the book and the readers which it will draw to it. Really great art has the quality of greatness plainly marked upon it. A great book vivifies its readers as inevitably as a flaming match ignites dead wood. Such a book is "You Can't Go Home Again," and thousands of readers who will never be able to tell you why it is great will know that they have met greatness within its covers.

Like "The Web and the Rock," it is apparently without form, a series of impacts upon the life and mind and emotions of George Webber, but it has the form of life itself, and its hero grows in this last volume into an adult, spiritually and emotionally, before the reader's eyes. He comes to see life not philosophically, but clearly. He sees into, not thru, people. He is a discoverer of fact but no mere accepter, even of his own discoveries.

And yet, of all the books which Thomas Wolfe has written, "You Can't Go Home Again" is the easiest to read, the simplest, the most certain of popularity, as it is the most brilliant. Real people whom countless readers will recognize have been here immortalized, among them a great editor and a great novelist, who may be remembered more sympathetically by Thomas Wolfe's scalpel-like words than by their own good works.

"You Can't Go Home Again" is no book to hurry thru. It has no "story."

139

Its 743 pages are filled with an infinitude of details, each line of which has been set down, and must also be read, with contemplative deliberation.

Charles A. Wagner. New York *Mirror,* September 18, 1940.

The last book by Thomas Wolfe is published this morning, and that is a lot of news for American literature and the American way of life.

Thousands of readers will come to this novel YOU CAN'T GO HOME AGAIN for its scenes and portraits of "moddun life," as the delightful Daisy Purvis puts it, for the development out of the modernity that ends in chaos which George Webber, the young writer protagonist of the book so richly endures.

Other thousands will want to delve and soar and sing in the wide, sonorous and tragic music of the Thomas Wolfe's prose. Still others will be drawn by the sheer morbid curiosity of a young genius's final words. And they will all be right. For this book will feed them all a surfeit beyond anything they have read for years, yes, even beyond "The Grapes of Wrath," and that still sounds like heresy.

But that is the way of genius, when it strikes. The people that parade through George Webber's mind and heart here, Daisy and Randy, his close friend, the magical and enigmatic Mrs. Jack, the bucolic alcoholic Tim Wagner, Nebraska Cane, the Cherokee ball player, his editor, Fox Edwards, and all the rest are caught in a web of circumstance which is a web laden with the very seas of civilization's own

flooding and decline.

And the prophetic close of the book, the last pages we shall have of Thomas Wolfe, the poet, ring with a poet's true vision:

I believe that we are lost here in America, but I believe we shall be found. . . .

Stephen Vincent Benét. "Thomas Wolfe's Torrent of Recollection." *Saturday Review of Literature,* 22 (September 21, 1940), 5.

This posthumous novel continues and concludes the story of George Webber—the story of Thomas Wolfe—the story of seeking and finding that is at the back of all the work which Wolfe was allowed to do. They were always saying—the well-informed and the critical—that, if he could stand off from himself, be more objective, tame, and order the extravagances of his power—well, well, then he might become the really great novelist, the conscious artist, all that sort of thing.

It was good advice for nine writers out of ten, but his power was not that sort of power. In this book, as in its predecessor, "The Web and the Rock," it is shown that he came to know himself, his strength and his weaknesses, much more clearly and objectively than was supposed. But that knowledge did not make any difference. He had to write as he wrote. He had to draw upon the giant web, the torrent of recollection, the all-feeling explorativeness, for everything in American earth, draw upon it and pour it forth again with shouts and cries, a river of sights, sounds, smells, tastes, feelings, memories, a river deafening the ears and stunning the eyes but not to be forgotten while Mississippi ran. "The forgotten moments and unnumbered hours came back to me with all the enormous cargo of my memory, together with lost voices in the mountains long ago, the voices of the kinsmen dead and never seen, and the houses they had built and died in, and the rutted roads they trod upon and every unrecorded moment."

That is how the work was done. He lacked taste at times, he was often verbose and rhetorical. He was fond of certain rubber stamps of dialect and never got over them. He was so prodigal of talent that he could and did write a thousand passages as good as the one I have quoted above. He was so little self-critical that, when his ear and his genius deserted him momentarily, he could write such appalling English as "Aristocrats of ancient lineage who had always held to a tradition of stiff-necked exclusiveness could be seen chatting familiarly with the plebeian parvenus of the new rich." He committed the errors of a giant—a small man can write bad prose but it takes a Dickens to assassinate Little Nell. And, when all is said and done, he will stand with Melville.

"You Can't Go Home Again" is the story of a man's pilgrimage, with its successive returns that meet with defeat, its successive reachings out for something that, even when grasped, eludes the hand. George Webber returns to Esther Jack and for a time they resume their old relation. But love is not enough—the two lives are too disparate—and the relation ends. He re-turns to Libya Hill and the deep roots of his childhood—and finds it in the frenzy of the boom, a city of lost men. He returns to the Germany he loved—and must say farewell to it—it is being delivered over to something old and evil. His first book brings him a brief celebrity and the hatred of his own people of Libya Hill—his second book brings him fame—and he sees through Lloyd McHarg the huge, restless disillusion that comes with fame. You can't go home again—not even to the tried friend, Foxhall Edwards. So stated, the book sounds like a study in disillusion. And is nothing of the sort.

It is written with all Wolfe's furious energy, with his devouring zest for all sorts of different human beings, with his amazing gift for sucking the very last drop of juice out of a character or a scene. It contains some telling, and some very heavy-handed, satire on literary life in New York. It well be read for that and people will babble over the various names. And none of that part is going to matter, in time, except for Piggy Logan's circus at the Jacks's where Wolfe has caught a genuine horror and a genuine scorn. The party itself, the sudden eruption of Piggy Logan's senseless young friends and the effect of the monstrous little circus of wire dolls on those who watch it— these are beautifully done. The first that follows is both well done and badly done—very few people could have done it at all and yet it does not quite come off. A good deal of the rest of the satire is a dropping of five-hundred-pound bombs to demolish gnats. The lion-hunters described in the chapter of that name shouldn't, somehow, have mattered as much as they did to George Webber.

They don't, in the end—in the real

141

plan and mass of the book. For, though there are extraneous chapters—though "You Can't Go Home Again" contains some of Wolfe's worst writing as well as much of his best—there is a clear, though winding path through the great forest of words and incidents and memories. There is a line, and a mature line. George Webber does grow up, not merely by fiat. There are such brilliant single incidents as that of Mr. Katamoto and that of the fantastic, believable meeting with Lloyd McHarg. But, more than that, though many things on the way were vanity, George Webber's pilgrimage was not vanity, and we do not feel that it was. The book ends neither in doubt nor in disillusion. It ends, in the remarkable last chapter, with a cry of faith.

> I believe that we are lost here in America but I believe we shall be found. . . .

The prose mounts to its moving end, with its strange premonition of death.

> To lose the earth you know, for greater knowing; to lose the life you have, for greater life; to leave the friends you loved, for greater loving; to find a land more kind than home, more large than earth—

These are great words, greatly spoken. To our loss, they come from the dead; but they speak to the living, and now. Out of passionate belief and faith they speak, and will keep on speaking, through the years, though the great tree is down and the wide and turbulent river sunk back into the ground.

Paul Jordan-Smith. Los Angeles *Times*, September 22, 1940.

Thomas Wolfe's novel, "You Can't Go Home Again," carries onward the story of George Webber, begun in "The Web and the Rock." But it also carries on "Of Time and the River." After all, Wolfe had but one story, his own, and the title of it is "Look Homeward Angel." So be it; and, for one, I am glad it is so. For I never tire of "Look Homeward Angel" and am only too happy to read of the continued spiritual adventures and raptures of that embodiment of zest, gusto, pain and ecstasy born of old Catawba.

Other men have exceeded him in niceties of design, in the economies and harmonies of structure. Plans were too small for this American Gargantua. But he has what the others lacked—a sense of the glory of life and its fullness; a vision the mountains could not hem; an extravagant dexterity with magic-laden words. It never satisfied him to nibble at the earth; he would swallow the cosmos at a gulp and shout for more. He didn't labor with words; they leaped out of their hiding places and ran singing 'round the world for him. What he lacked in discipline the gods supplied in genius. The grave is too small for Thomas Wolfe.

If his other novels were autobiographical, this is even more so. It is a writer's testament. George Webber tells what it was to have been a writer out of Catawba; tells how his own writing made him an exile. But he also speaks of the life problem of the writer in this terror-stricken age. What of the artist in a world where the beast is vocal?

"And it is for Now, and for us the living, that we must speak, and speak the truth, as much of it as we can see and know. With the courage of the truth within us, we shall meet the enemy as they come to us, and they shall be ours. And if, once having conquered them, new enemies approach, we shall meet them from that point, from there proceed. In the affirmation, the continuance of that unceasing war, is man's religion and his living faith."

"You Can't Go Home Again" may not shout as lustily as Wolfe's earlier novels (this is novel plus letters) but it tells the story we have waited for; it is more explicitly revealing of its creator and of his relation to his world.

Milton Rugoff. "Violently, Desperately, Hungeringly Alive." New York *Herald Tribune Books*, September 22, 1940, p. 5.

It is a strange experience now, two years after the fire of Thomas Wolfe's frantic creative energy has grown cold, to feel it flaming up as if it were more violently, desperately, hungeringly alive than ever. For "You Can't Go Home Again" is the work of a writer at last confident that his "development" must be only a supreme intensification of what he has always been. Thus this book is more self-searching than any of his others and yet more world-conscious; more realistic and yet more idealistic; more

emotional and yet more thoughtful; as overwritten as any yet more filled with all the power and magic of his manner. At those who felt he must exhaust himself as a theme he laughs, saying that a writer's self is only as limited as his own genius for exploring that self, knowing that he had such a recall of all he had ever experienced and such a power to recreate (this is as far removed from mere memory as architecture is from bricklaying) as few writers had ever had.

Thus "You Can't Go Home Again" is another of the many autobiographies Wolfe could believe he might have lived. It completes the story, begun in "The Web and the Rock," of George Webber, who was brought up in a poor Southern home, came North, aspired to literary greatness and fell in love with Esther Jack, famous stage designer. Torn by doubt, Webber had run off to Europe to escape from losing his personality in his all-consuming love for Esther, who is married, much older than he, and Jewish. "You Can't Go Home Again" carries Webber's life from 1929 to 1937—to the eve, that is, of Wolfe's death—and inevitably into the social problems of our immediate time.

Returning, Webber finds that his attachment to Esther is not yet over. What finally drives him to complete the break is a visit to his home town, and, later, a magnificent party in the Jacks' Park Avenue home. This is America on the brink of the crash, and what he finds in his home town is an hysterical landboom, inflation both financial and spiritual, feverish exultation on the surface, and, underneath, rottenness and fear. What he finds at the Park Avenue party is a flittering life of luxury and ease, won in a ruthless scramble and riddled by decadence of every sort. After the crash he came to feel that his home-town frenzy and the New York party were both part of the culmination of a materialism that had become a devastating disease. But the evil, according to Wolfe, is not so much the social system fostered by the winners as just widespread greed.

But only a reader familiar with Wolfe can appreciate how dryly this restates what he says with all that furious fullness of which he was capable, with torrents of sensory detail, with outbursts of lamentation and jubilation that are sometimes rhapsodies of genius, the high music of high emotions, and sometimes merely wild waves that dash themselves to empty foam on deafened ears. As unqualifiedly effective as ever, however, are the characters that throng these pages—from Nebraska Crane, the famous baseball player facing the end of his career, to Rumford Bland, the blind old lawyer who jeered obscenely at his own and the town's moral decay; and, of the Park Avenue group, from Mr. Jack, type of all rich men who have ever luxuriated in their wealth, to Amy Carleton, jaded, notorious thrill-seeker, epitomizing the life-sickness of this whole class. One of the most remarkable scenes in Wolfe is the abrupt end of the party when a fire breaks out and all the extraordinary tenants of that giant apartment house, from tycoons to whores, are thrown together in the central courtyard. It is an extravaganza, grotesque and satiric, pointing up the thin line which divides secure power from chaos, doubly symbolic in that the only ones who suffer in the end are two elevator men who die, like slaves, in their cages.

The second half of the book deals with Webber's novels, his fame and finally his approach to an answer to the problems which hound him. The publication of his first novel (counterpart of "Look Homeward, Angel") taught him some unpleasant truths: from the rage of hometowners whom he had painted with naively fierce candor he learned that Americans fear the facts about their lives; from hypocrites and "lion-hunters" he learned of the strings attached to fame. But it was through his writing that he met two who influenced him profoundly—Foxhall Edwards, publisher's editor, and Lloyd McHarg, international prize-winning American novelist. That these two are identifiable is less important than that they are striking character studies. The former, seemingly eccentric and cold, but to Webber a sensitive, courageous and serenely wise man, became to the young writer a father-confessor. McHarg, on the other hand, was a human volcano whose life was a continuous cycle of superhuman activity, complete collapse and swift recovery. While on a European jaunt he descends on Webber, and the flabbergasted young man is subjected to the nightmarish ordeal of being protégé to an internationally famous writer travelling across England in a state ranging from wild activity to absolute coma. But McHarg in moments of serenity becomes another and impressive kind of human being, talking with such piercing and engaging good sense and such bristling integrity as to justify the younger man's admiration. It is an astonishing episode.

Finally, in 1936, just before the publication of his second novel, Webber goes to Germany, to him dearest of all foreign lands. Treated as the greatest foreign writer there, he sees it at first as the same wonderful and haunting land it had always seemed. Then slowly (much, much too slowly from any point of view!) he awakens to the ghastly truth. By the time he left he had seen the whole abomination of what had happened to that great race. It was that, reinforcing a sense of a not unsimilar sickness spreading through America, that crystallized his credo. Where a man like Edwards accepted the vices of civilizations with a deep fatalism, Webber cried out that all his experience had at last taught him that no man's personal life could be good in a civilization sick and without honor. Europe was perhaps beyond hope but America still had a chance if it would see and speak the truth about those false traditions of selfishness and blind grabbing which it had so long accepted. Wolfe's challenge is levelled nobly and with passion, but in the end it remains vaguely lofty, personal, Shelleyan in its failure to suggest implements, to analyze its enemies, to take into account the social structure already present. The air here is too rare and thin.

The weaknesses of "You Can't Go Home Again," as of all Wolfe's books, are, so to speak, functions of its virtues. On the one hand its power and on the other its excesses both stem from his unexampled exuberance, his floodlike richness, his epic intentions. In all this he is in the tradition of "Leaves of Grass" and "Moby Dick"; his books, like these, reflect an expansiveness, an extravagance, an emotional giantism which has been called American. And, as in those earlier works, when passages in his books fail, they are above all inflated, rhetorical and intolerably redundant.

In the same way the piled-up details and hammering repetitions with which he draws characters give them at once a fierce truth and yet an excess bordering on caricature. Thus McHarg is alternately the livest and the deadest man on earth; each Dutchman or Jew seems the essence of all Dutchness or all Jewry; and a George Webber contains any number of superlatives. Sometimes it is hard to decide where intensity ends and satire begins.

But, finally, whatever the weaknesses in this book, there is in it more than ever that range which made Wolfe seem the most variously gifted American novelist of our time. There is a sensuous richness that offers to embrace all experience, an emotional fullness that is overwhelming; there is a passionate interest in human character, a boundless gift for the voice, faces, essences of all manner of men; there is a realism capable of all ugliness and darkness; there is the transforming alchemy of a poet's vision, of a deep-pulsed, rapturous prose; and there is above all a personality able to make itself seem as fraught with aspiration and despair, with goodness and vileness, with ecstasies and agonies as any that ever unburdened itself in a book.

B. L. B. "Last Is One of Wolfe's Best." Richmond *Times-Dispatch*, September 22, 1940.

When Thomas Wolfe published in 1929 his first novel, "Look Homeward, Angel," its wild, impassioned, voluminous poetry caused many critics and not a few readers to see him as a strong new voice in American literature—the often tormented voice of the little people and of the writer himself. There were even those who went so far as to proclaim that here was a new genius, sprung full-grown upon the scene.

There were those, too—especially in his home town of Libya Hill, Old Catawba (Asheville, N.C.), who, seeing themselves or believing they saw themselves pictured in the book in unpleasing light, proceeded to heap upon Wolfe all the venom and abuse they had within them. They believed the man was writing deliberately filthy and wanton stories—and besides, the line between them and reality was too thin.

Both schools of thought were strengthened considerably five years later when Wolfe's second novel, "Of Time and the River," saw the light of the bookstalls. His style was still voluminous and undisciplined; he seemed to write down everything he saw and felt, and never to edit out any of it. It was still formless, but it showed an amazing command of the English language; it was written with beauty and passion and complete conviction, and even those who criticized it seemed to believe that when the young writer had grown and matured and got the autobiographical out of his system, he might very well turn out to be a man of considerable literary stature.

After publishing two short books—a collection of stories and an account of his creative methods—Wolfe then proceeded to a new enterprise in which he put down everything he had learned from life. His tortured soul and his long struggle to reach the bracket he wanted to reach still needed an outlet before he could really get on with a writing career. . . .

To sum up a writer like Wolfe is difficult, his writings being so close to the present day and the contradictions in his work so many. At times he writes like a man inspired; at others he is pitifully mediocre. If he had been able to relax, to take life and himself less seriously, he might have been a greater author; on the other hand, his conviction and his truth of vision might have suffered thereby.

To this reviewer it is obvious, however, from this new book that he was just at the threshold of real writing, that he had just completed his apprenticeship. At a time when so much that is worthless is being written and published, it is only too regretable that one of his unquestioned talent should be lost to American writing.

William B. King. "Wolfe Bit Off More Than He Could Chew." Columbia, S.C., *State*, September 22, 1940, p. 8-A.

In "You Can't Go Home Again" Thomas Wolfe, the now-dead genius from North Carolina, tried to write a book as big as life, but he failed. He failed, however, only where life itself fails. He failed, because like life he wanted to cover all things. He failed because into one book he wanted to put all the joys, the sorrows, the searchings, the despairs and the final self-discovery of a mentally turbulent individual. A lifetime itself is hardly enough to thread through the morass of doubt and hopelessness to a credo and an answer to human existence. To

146

try to compress the same struggle between the covers of a book, even when the book runs to 743 pages, is to leave the reader gasping in a confusion of detail.

Though one says he failed in the task he set for himself, it cannot be denied that Thomas Wolfe has come nearer to success than most writers who dreamed of giving such a message to the world. One almost wishes that he had not set such a mighty task for himself, that he had been satisfied with a simpler goal. When one reads the soul searching descriptions of interacting mind and place, when one follows the bitter etched lines of caustic delineation, and when one reacts to the pure poetry that shines through his prose at frequent intervals, one knows that from Thomas Wolfe's pen has come some of the most worthwhile writing of our generation and that his voice is not one that shall soon die, despite the fact that his work is ended.

. . .

For those who have followed Wolfe from the shocked surprise of almost all eastern North Carolina when his first novel was published in 1929 until he was finally acclaimed in his hometown as the genius that he really was, this latest and last book—called by his publishers his "maturest work"—is a must item on the fall reading list. For those who have yet to discover the North Carolinian who wrote mountainous manuscripts and took all of life and the whole body of truth for his domain, now is the time to give him the attention he deserves as one of the South's greatest modern writers.

Hamilton Basso. "Thomas Wolfe: A Summing Up." *New Republic,* 103 (September 23, 1940), 422–423.

This is the last novel that will carry Thomas Wolfe's name on its title page. The first thing to be said is that his publishers do no great service to his reputation by presenting it as a finished product of his mature talent. "By 1936," they tell us, "Wolfe had completed what he looked upon as his period of apprenticeship, and was ready to embark upon a vast new enterprise—a novel or a series of novels (he did not yet know which) into which he wanted to pack everything he had learned about life. Through several years he labored strenuously at it, and as the manuscript took shape it grew into two novels, both of which were finished and turned over to his publishers in May, 1938." This statement is not altogether correct. It is best to let Wolfe himself tell what happened—what he hoped to do and how he hoped to do it. In July, 1937, he wrote to me:

> I brought most of the manuscript of the last five or six years down with me; millions of words of it, and I hope to write several hundred thousand more this summer. Eventually I hope it will begin to take shape, like another monster of the deep, and I will have another tremendous book. I believe I learn a little something about writing all the time; but I am not so sure that I will be worried so much this time by apprehensions over size and length. The very nature of a book like this is that everything can go into it. To tell such a story is to try to loot the whole treasury of human experience. . . . So I

have come back here to "set a spell and think things over"—freer, I hope, from the degrading egotisms all men know in youth; here to strike out, I hope to God, a living word. To do out of the substance of my own life, my single spirit, a better and truer work than I have ever done.

The three years from 1935 to 1938 were a period during which we saw much of each other—in New York and in the mountains of North Carolina. Occasionally he would give me a batch of manuscript to read. I know, then, that in the "millions of words" Wolfe talks about, substantial portions of this novel, and the one that preceded it, were included. Most of the section called "The Locusts Have No King," for instance, stands—as far as memory can judge—just as it stood in 1936. Another section, "I Have a Thing to Tell You," was pared to the bone and published in these pages about the same time. And the part of the book revolving about the famous novelist Lloyd McHarg—or a sizable portion of it—was also in manuscript before 1937. It is not accurate, consequently, to say that Wolfe's last two books marked a "new enterprise" or that they were finished before he died. As for the critics, those who found no "advancement" in "The Web and the Rock," will likewise probably find no advancement here. But let them hold their horses! Let them remember that this book not only contains the last writing Wolfe did—the section called "The House That Jack Built," for example, which was written in the spring and summer of 1937, just about a year before he died—but also many pages that were written as early as 1934. This is one time when no generalizations are permissible.

Wolfe disliked the critics as much as any creative writer. The charge that he wrote autobiographical novels particularly annoyed him. This is worth mentioning only because the critics were partially responsible for the rebirth of Eugene Gant as George Webber: and this in an interesting way.

Wolfe's anger with the critics frequently took the form of torrential outbursts in which he argued that all good fiction is basically autobiographical. It also kept cropping up in his letters. In one of them, partially devoted to a statement of his belief that most writers were surveyors rather than explorers, he wrote:

In another way as well, our love of neat definitions in convenient forms, our fear of essential exploration, may be the natural response of people who have to house themselves, wall themselves, give their lives some precise and formal definition. . . . Anyway, all of these things have seemed to me to be worth thinking of, and I know that we still have to fight to do our work the way we want to do it—not only against the accepted varieties of surveyordom, that is book publishers, most of the critics, popular magazines, etc.—but against even deadlier and more barren forms; deadlier because they set up as friends of exploration when they are really betrayers and enemies; I mean little magazinedom, hound and horners, young precious boys, esthetic Marxians and all the rest of it.

Nevertheless, the charges leveled at him—"autobiographical novels," "lack of objectivity," etc.,—were still a source of annoyance. The neat definitions buzzed in his mind like mosquitoes. Then, about this time, he changed publishers—taking along with him several crates of manuscript; "millions of words." A large part of this manuscript, as has been said, went into these last two novels—but the hero of the manuscript was the same hero as that of "Look Homeward, Angel" and "Of Time and the River." His name was Eugene Gant.

When he changed publishers, Wolfe found himself faced with this major problem: How to use his unpublished parts of Eugene Gant's life in a new novel or group of novels. The hero's name, of course, had to be changed. The demands of publishing called for that. More than a mere rechristening, however, was required. The life of George Webber had to be brought to the point where his early years would flow naturally into the later years of Eugene Gant. And, in writing about Webber, Wolfe believed that he could prove that he could create a non-autobiographical character—and also prove that it was within his power to write "objectively."

The whole unhappy effort was doomed from the start. If only for credibility's sake, the new hero had to be a man exactly like Eugene Gant. How else could the books have any pattern: any meaning whatsoever? This, then, is why the early pages of "The Web and the Rock" read like a loose rewriting of "Look Homeward, Angel." How could it be otherwise? Webber had to be grafted on to Gant. A trunk had to be provided for the branches and foliage already at hand. Wolfe unquestionably believed what he wrote in the preface to "The Web and the Rock"—that it was the most objective novel he had ever written. It was. But only to the extent that he was obliged to re-examine and rework some of his basic material. Gant became Webber but Gant remained. And Gant, of course, was Thomas Wolfe.

With the publication of this novel it is possible to discern the general outlines of the job Wolfe set for himself.

His plan was to write a vast cycle of novels through which the life of Eugene Gant was to run as a kind of bloodstream. They were to go back to the Civil War (somewhere among his unpublished manuscripts there must be a long short story called "Chickamauga") and would project into the future as far as Eugene Gant, in the person of Thomas Wolfe, managed to live. Speculation as to how far he would have been able to carry out this plan, and how successfully, is purposeless. It would be equally purposeless for me to try to weigh this particular book. Even if I had not already disqualified myself, I would be reluctant to say more than I used to say after reading one of his manuscripts. "When it's fine it's fine. You know what you're after better than anyone else." I still feel the same way—that he was after something, that it was something most important to be after, and that, considering the number of times he gets hold of it, the flaws in his writing do not particularly matter. I soon learned that he would never be a terse writer because he was not the least bit interested in becoming one. So what of it? It also became obvious that he would never bring the tremendous engine of his creative ability under full control and that he would be forever loose and sprawling and sometimes windy enough to blow your hat off. So what of that? The fact remains that when he gets hold, when he digs through to what he is after, he is magnificent in a way few American writers ever have been—making his detractors seem puny and feeble by comparison. This book is full of such magnificence.

The last word I had from Wolfe was a postcard mailed from Yellowstone Park about two months before he died.

It was a picture of Old Faithful and on the back he had scrawled in pencil: "Portrait of the author at the two-million-word point." It seems to me that the geyser is a pretty good picture of him. It looks vaguely like the way he used to look walking down First Avenue about two o'clock on a blowy morning and, like it, he gushed boiling and furious from his American earth. The landscape is lonelier without him.

Joseph Henry Jackson. "Thomas Wolfe's Last Book Proves He Was a Genius." San Francisco *Chronicle,* September 25, 1940, p. 17.

"The trouble with Thomas Wolfe . . .!" Those words have set off more literary arguments, perhaps, than any other five—at least in the years since "Look Homeward Angel" first burst upon fiction-wise America.

The debate has not grown any less vigorous since Wolfe's untimely death. For that matter, this new novel, his last, will simply give the argufiers another jumping-off place. Those who make a great to-do about Wolfe's enormous energy will point to "You Can't Go Home Again" as one more example of his torrential way with words, his tremendous zest. Those who like to point to his frequent bad writing will have no trouble finding samples enough here. Those who insist that he needed to learn to control his rushing flood of words will be able to prove their point in this new book, just as they have in every book Wolfe has writen.

When they've all said their say, though, it will simmer down to this: Thomas Wolfe, in spite of his faults, was a genius. It is a safe statement to make, even though it is usually better practice to wait a generation or so before coming out quite so flatly about any writer.

. . .

Briefly stated, these are the things that happen to George Webber in "You Can't Go Home Again." But, as is always the case with Wolfe, the mere incident of the book is the least of it. Like Webber, Thomas Wolfe learned about living the hard way, and like Webber he put what he was learning—as he learned it—into books.

And here, almost for the first time, Wolfe comes out with a clear statement of belief in a better tomorrow. America, as he has looked at it, is lost. But he believes also that America will find itself again. America has lost itself in petty preoccupation, in selfishness, in greed, in callowness. Read, for example, Wolfe's little scene in which Piggy Logan and his celebrated circus of wire dolls entertain Esther Jack's guests at a party. It's one of the bits in which Wolfe is wholly successful in satirizing the social half-wittedness that used to pass for amusement in certain groups. But America will find itself. . . .

If you would like to understand Thomas Wolfe better than you ever understood him before, read this final chapter in which he puts his credo into words for everyone. Perhaps you will be less troubled by his faults as a novelist after you have read them.

John Gibbons.
" 'Lycidas Is Dead.' "
Boston *Transcript,*
September 28, 1940.

Like one of the gods of his Carolina mountains, Thomas Wolfe turned prophet in "You Can't Go Home Again," the second and last of the posthumously published novels of the author of "Look Homeward, Angel." "And there came a vision," used a dozen times in the 743 pages, is the key. Sometimes the vision is of the past, the lost, Wolfe past and from it come more of those wonderful scenes, of breakfasts, landscapes, cities, oceans, rivers, that are written poetically in unmatched language and grandeur.

Sometimes the vision is of the moment, of the flood tides of emotion in America and Europe, of morning, noon and night in New York City, of black Sunday afternoon in Brooklyn, of a winter of work in London and a month of travel in Germany. But finally, and more significantly in this novel than in any of his other three, Wolfe is looking ahead, and what he sees he calls tragic but redeemed.

Tragic is again one of his favorite words. The light of the end of the day, the light of morning on the towers of New York are tragic. The faces are tragic, so are the times. Wherever this mood reaches its climax there is an explosion, for in "You Can't Go Home Again" there are explosions on almost every page. They are in brief encounters, in accidents, in the brawls along the Brooklyn streets, in the subways, where Wolfe found the drifters wrapped in newspapers, sleeping on the steps and the cold stone, in the sullen menace of the doorman, Henry, as he tries to organize the elevator operators.

These explosions are essential to Wolfe's vision of the future. They are isolated at first, as he charts them in his notebooks and ledgers. They become more frequent as he finds in them the dramatization of George Webber's adventures. They crackle like the burning of a dynamite fuse as he comes to the conclusion of the story in the incident of the Jew taken off the coach at the Belgian border as they are leaving Germany, in the clash of ideas and characters of his friends Else and Franz, and in the two days with McHarg, the distinguished American author who stops off to see him in London. In prose now they are what the boy Eugene felt in "Look Homeward, Angel." And because they are written here, rather than experienced, this fourth novel lacks the surge of the first.

Reason has subdued instinct, and confidence replaced fear. The pace is leisurely, for Wolfe. The writing is smoother than before, and clearer. Wolfe, at 36, had examined love and fame and, in a letter to his former editor, a letter that fills the last 45 pages of the novel, has found them not enough. He wants more of logic and less of emotion. As he succeeds the novel becomes less a burning story of adventure in strange places and more of a growing philosophy. And as a philosopher, even as a logician, Wolfe adds nothing to the knowledge of the times.

Where Wolfe stood it is difficult to say, because he wasn't certain himself. He wanted to see the truth and write nothing but the truth, but he was candid enough to admit that the truth is pretty much a phantom, even in these enlightened times when it's commonly known that any of a million parlor radicals will slip it to you for a cup of tea.

Wolfe might have come close to some kind of truth had he lived for another four novels. If he had I don't know that any of us who still thrill to the beauty of "Look Homeward, Angel" would have cared. We wanted more of the mountains and the skies, the morning and the evening, the spring and fall of Wolfe's world, the boy's, then the young man's adventures. We cared for the Gants, W. O., Eliza, Ben and Eugene, for the long trips, for the magic bounty and warm madness of the young author. We grieve, with the grieving wind of the Angel, for the lost.

Louis B. Salomon. "Look Homeward." *Nation*, 151 (September 28, 1940), 278.

My feeling about any novel by Thomas Wolfe is that even if it were not good I'd like it. I'd like it for its ebullient, electric vitality, its obvious sincerity, the glowing, almost incandescent poetry of its style, the sense which it gives, however confusedly, of a meaning, a unified current, recognized in the seemingly helter-skelter maze of human life. These qualities light up "You Can't Go Home Again" for me, just as they illuminated "Look Homeward, Angel," "Of Time and the River," "The Web and the Rock," and many shorter pieces; but there is no denying that Wolfe's methods, his themes, and to a large extent his materi-

al remained the same throughout his work, with the result that his inspiration suffered a gradual diminution of intensity.

That George Webber = Eugene Gant = Tom Wolfe is an equation almost too obvious to mention, in spite of the fact that George is described in "The Web and the Rock" and "You Can't Go Home Again" as short and stocky, while Wolfe was a mountain of a man and Eugene Gant was supposed to be long and rangy. When an author bestows his own personality on a hero and surrounds him with the author's own acquaintances under the transparent disguise of altered names, it makes little difference that he knocks five or six inches off his stature. If you have read "How to Write a Novel," Wolfe's account of the composing and publishing of "Look Homeward, Angel," you will find the first half of this last book virtually a retelling of that bit of autobiography. The rest of the story deals with his love affair with "Esther" and its conclusion, with the stock-market crash, and with his travels in Nazi Germany, several chapters of the latter part of the book having, if my memory does not fail me, already appeared as short stories in magazines.

His two principal themes are, as always, man's essential loneliness and the mystic movement of time, like a river that seems ever the same but is constantly shifting. You can't go home again, simply because "home" isn't there; both it and you have changed, and your romanticized memory-picture of it bears no more resemblance to the sordid reality than a surrealist painting does to an unretouched photograph.

But even themes so universally applicable as these can be overworked, and the pregnant symbolism, the driving power that made "Look Homeward, Angel" stand out above the common herd of novels like a mountain dawn, has given way to a sprawling looseness of structure that becomes more and more noticeable as the book progresses. There are diversions into long essay passages bound to the narrative by only the most tenuous threads. Nor can this be attributed altogether to the fact that the work is posthumous, not subject to final revision, since the same tendency had already manifested itself all too plainly in "Of Time and the River."

The very nature of these conventional complaints against Wolfe's art, however, makes them a sort of compliment, a grudging admission that he had something too vitally alive to be judged entirely according to the criteria of form—in short, he irritates us more, because he had the magic power and did not use it precisely as we should have liked, than does the run-of-the-mill writer who obviously was not born with the divine fire. Wolfe belongs to the tribe of Whitman, Emerson, Carlyle—especially the last. Like Carlyle, he was emotionally disturbed by the stupidity and selfishness of the world, without having any specific formula to offer as a remedy; he had a passion for work and a transcendental scorn for the shackles of form; even his style, with its purple splendor, its heavy leaning on apostrophe and impersonation, its ironic ranting against mediocrity, echoes that "stormy sophist with his mouth of thunder" who preached Cassandra-like warnings to the Victorians. Chapter 29, The Hollow Men, with its bitter allegory about Standard Concentrated Blots, sounds like an excerpt from "Past and Present."

And I feel about Wolfe very much as I feel about Carlyle: though I disagree with a great many things he says, I don't know anyone who can say them more splendidly.

J. Donald Adams. Column, "Speaking of Books." New York *Times Book Review,* September 29, 1940, p. 2.

Disagreement over Thomas Wolfe's stature as a writer was strong while he lived; it continues after his death, and it will, no doubt, be a matter of controversy for some time to come. The publication of the last novel upon which he worked, "You Can't Go Home Again," has once more fanned the blaze. It is already evident that widely differing readings of the book are going to be made.

To the writer of this column "You Can't Go Home Again" is proof that Wolfe was coming to terms with himself both as a man and a writer—that he had, before his death, found himself. He could, it seems to me, see himself more objectively, and was able, in retrospect, to place himself outside his experience to a degree which had been difficult or even impossible for him before. He had grasped the need for transmuting the stuff of his own experience into terms that would be valid for men and women everywhere. And, to some extent, he succeeded in doing that in this book; had he lived, I believe he would have gone further along that road.

Mr. Clifton Fadiman, on the other hand, writing in *The New Yorker,* finds that Wolfe remained "uncrystallized, and, I think, uncrystallizable." Both he and Mr. Ralph Thompson, writing in the daily *Times*, prefer to use the word talent rather than genius in writing of Wolfe. But genius, it seems to me, is the word. Not simply because of the torrential flow and force of Wolfe's work, though that is often an indicator, but because he was capable, even when his writing was most undisciplined, of brief flashes of illumination, of words that dropped straight as a plummet into deep and essential truth. It is these flashes of illumination, throwing a sudden and piercing light on human relationships, which talent never achieves, which only the first-rate novelist can summon.

It is true that there are still in "You Can't Go Home Again" large undigested chunks of autobiography. But in Wolfe's writing about the Nineteen Twenties in this book there is evident, I think, an assimilation of what he saw and lived through during that period. Mr. Hemingway, in his introduction to "The Great Crusade," would have us believe that "the greatest novels are all made up." But are they? Certainly not "War and Peace," and that, in the estimation of most critics, is the greatest novel in any language. I do not mean to include "You Can't Go Home Again" in that company; it is not a great novel, but it has the elements of greatness in it.

Henry Seidel Canby. *Book-of-the-Month Club News*, October 1940, p. 6.

This is the most shapely of all Tom Wolfe's sections of the one long novel which was his lifework. And, in spite of many repetitions of idea and personality from earlier portions, it contains, I think, some of his very best work. The hero now, who is, of course, Tom Wolfe himself, is a successful author, learning that a little fame gets one only to the beginning of wisdom. Alas, he has described, in his novel, his home town only too truly, although he thinks he has not copied his friends and acquaintances, but rather interpreted and expanded them. Yet all they see is scandal and exposure. He had gone home before to find them boiling in the perverted and materialistic passion of a great boom. When that bursts, the truth of his studies of the failure of his fellow Americans to live any real and valuable life of their own is only too manifest. He can't go home again, not because he is threatened by those who accuse him of exposing them, but because he sees that you never can go back in life—you must grow out of yourself before that self decays. And so this novel about a novelist takes its hero to Germany, where he is completely happy until the subtle poison of futility and defeat produces the less subtle but more dangerous romantic poison of Nazism, the poison of hate and self-inflation, which destroys the individualist's soul. From then on the story is more and more a psychoanalysis of American life, to find *its* poisons and its hopes. There is a fire in a great apartment house which provides one of Wolfe's most dramatic scenes. There is an English episode in which an obvious Sinclair Lewis is involved in a study, that should become classic, of eccentric genius committed to fame. The best mimic in America, next to Lewis himself, is Wolfe. And there is always Tom Wolfe, a seeker like the Americans of the 40's, a visionary with an intense feeling for absolute realism, a poet in prose. "I believe that we are lost here in America, but I believe we shall be found." That is his theme, and no one will finish this extraordinary flow of incident and personality—all of it the biography of a restless man with an insatiable curiosity exhausting itself upon human nature—without a new insight into his own country. And without, let me add, having the sense of a full and completed story. Like Whitman, like Melville, both true predecessors, Wolfe seems to break, and sometimes does break, all the rules of literature. Yet he remains a tide-mark in American literature—and is unique.

Adeline T. Davidson.
Library Journal, 65
(October 1, 1940), 809.

Thomas Wolfe, brilliant young American novelist, finished *You Can't Go Home Again* just before his death in 1938. Like his early novels this one is undoubtedly autobiographical. It is a continuation of *The Web and the Rock* and shows George Webber, a struggling young author, still in his search for an understanding of life in the America of the last ten years. It is a rich vital

novel of tremendous length, marking to my mind, an advance in Thomas Wolfe's power as a novelist.

Libraries that bought Wolfe's earlier work will certainly want to buy this one.

Unsigned. *Booklist,* 37
(October 1, 1940), 37.

George Webber's search for truth is continued in this sequel to *The Web and the Rock.* It is still obviously the torrential recollections of the author's own life during and after the boom of 1929. George is less volcanic than in the former book, for he has gained some control and has discovered what he wants out of life. He is again in New York and returns to the woman he loves but finds that he must give her up if he is to write. He works incessantly on a new book in Brooklyn and in England; later he observes in Germany the hidden terrors of nazism. Excellent characterizations; the book shows the same evidences of genius as are found in his other works. Frank, amoral treatment.

Harry Sylvester.
Commonweal, 33
(October 25, 1940),
29-30.

Thomas Wolfe's last novel ranks immediately after his first one, "Look Homeward, Angel," and well ahead of the two that come between the first and last. There are unmistakable signs in this book of Wolfe's growing up. To be sure, the prose is still attenuated, although not nearly so much as in "Of Time and the River" and "The Web and the Rock"; but there is a capacity for thought here and even some thinking, however misty and amorphous it may often be.

Wolfe shows in this book a social awareness which the earlier ones largely lacked. He caricatures the rich and the pompous and rails at the leftist intelligentsia with a fine scorn. Indeed, a large share of the book is just straight commentary and criticism on his times and their people. This hardly makes for a novel, but it is all interesting and often accurate and penetrating.

Although Wolfe was the absolute master of a fine, flowing, rhythmical (though hardly subtle) prose, he had many flaws, and some of them were rather serious in a writer of his supposed dimension. There are very few who can describe physical action well—only Hemingway, Kenneth Roberts and George Weller come to mind—and Wolfe was not one of them. He could describe well a continued and sustained relationship, but as he grew older he seemed to lose the ability to describe the breaks that occur in people's lives. He tells what happened before and after George Webber's (Thomas Wolfe's) breaks with his Jewish mistress in New York, with his publisher, with his German mistress in Berlin, but he never accurately tells the reasons therefore, and he never describes the moment of severance, the apex of the situation. He never even tries to here, avoiding these situations that call for a high degree of subtle skill in a writer, as so many of the bright young writers today—Farrell, Halper, Prokosch, even Morley Callaghan— avoid or fake writing of physical action;

because it is a difficult thing to do and they are not sure that they can do it.

Unlike his last two books, though, this one is distinctly readable, as much for the added light it throws on his perhaps great first book as for anything else. His genius is drawn thin in this book as in all his others but the first. That first, we think, is all that will last, if anything of his does. There was a freshness on it, a great morning of the senses. It lacked intellectual values and it is not too much to say that if we lived in a world that also lacked those values, "Look Homeward, Angel" would be that world's greatest book. Not living—thank God—in such a world, it still remains a powerful and even an awesome phenomenon. The first reading of it is shocking as the discovery of a world with new colors, new sights and heightened sensations would be shocking. He asked, as I remember it, that if one fine person were found, "will not dead faith revive, will we not see God again, as once in morning on the mountain?"

Apparently he found that person— even though it may have been only the editor of a publishing house, a lowly office indeed. . . .

Lillian Walker. "Lost Modern Who Found Himself." Nashville *Banner,* October 30, 1940, Section X, p. 6.

Someone needs to remind me to "remember my place" as I write this review. Else I'm liable to go burbling into an ode on the intimations of the immortality of Thomas Wolfe's writings.

As book reviewers so often say nowadays the American novel is 'in the middle of a very great trend of historical fiction and regional stories. Dozens of them are appearing almost daily and the American historical background grows lush and glamorous, and a section in the United States which has not been "insulted" by some book or other must feel like a forlorn little wallflower who hasn't any "it."

Thomas Wolfe is one writer who was not caught in the historical-regional book maze. In contrast he writes a contemporary (1929–1936) story which encompassed people everywhere in the cities of the civilized world.

. . .

Wolfe still uses twenty adjectives when two would do for any other writer, yet the way they are put together one can hear the very inflections of his words. Even the cadence of his paragraphs has imagery when read aloud. Quotations from the book could certainly adorn the public speeches of less creative but oratorical persons. A certain political candidate who is making Grade B on his radio speeches could well turn to page 741 of "You Can't Go Home Again" and start quoting thus: ". . . I believe that we are lost here in America, but I believe we shall be found. . . ."

Too many times we have said and let it go at that, "You either like Thomas Wolfe or you don't and that's all there is to it." "You Can't Go Home Again" is broad enough for everyone of us to find himself and his neighbor on its pages. . . .

Kimball Flaccus. *Catholic World,* 152 (November 1940), 243–44.

This novel is the fourth and last to come from the mighty pen of Thomas Wolfe. When his first novel was published in 1929, Wolfe, like Whitman, was greeted "on the threshold of a great career." But captious critics, fearing that perhaps they had overpraised the work of this wide-eyed stripling from the southern hills, lay in wait for his second novel, *Of Time and the River,* and tore it to shreds when it appeared. Wolfe, who had stormed the literary heights with *Look Homeward, Angel,* was on the one hand abused by the academicians for doing violence to what they considered the novel form, and on the other hand was made the butt of red, pink, and mauve aesthetes.

As Keats knew to his sorrow, there is no more dangerous enemy to the creative spirit than flippancy. The poet, infinitely more sensitive than other men, more trusting, more spiritually awake, must, by the very nature of his being, "keep his guard down." He is easy prey, sure prey, for the base and cruel thrust of satire. Smart-alec criticism killed Keats, and went a long way toward killing Thomas Wolfe. The tragedy of Wolfe is that during his lifetime he was judged by the standards of conventional fiction; only after his untimely death is he beginning to be recognized as the great poet he undoubtedly was.

. . .

Burton Rascoe. "Wolfe, Farrell and Hemingway." *American Mercury,* 51 (December 1940), 493–494.

Ernest Hemingway, in his latest novel, *For Whom the Bell Tolls,* again demonstrates that he is the most infantile-minded writer of great talent in our time. There was a period when I thought that the late Thomas Wolfe would oust Hemingway in the race for that honor and that James T. Farrell would be the runner-up. But Wolfe grew out of his pubescence in his thirty-fifth year, and Farrell ceased being altogether a child after he had completed the second volume of his Studs Lonigan trilogy, which is to say, when he was about thirty years old.

Wolfe achieved maturity just before he died. He left a posthumous manuscript entitled *You Can't Go Home Again.* It showed that long before Tom Wolfe died he had begun to see and feel and think like a grown-up man and not like an exuberant but depressed, angered and inhibited adolescent, at once arrogant toward and afraid of the world and its people, as he had shown himself to be in his magnificent but almost childishly crude and faulty novels, *Look Homeward, Angel* and *Of Time and the River.*

In *You Can't Go Home Again,* Wolfe is no longer the voluminously and repetitiously articulate Pantagruel of Asheville, North Carolina, ex-instructor in English at New York University, who aspired to write, instead of teaching, English, pouring out millions of une-dited and even uncorrelated words about the people and the scenes he had known, and displaying on nearly every page the peculiar terror of his heart—sometimes by arrogantly glorifying this terror which was of his own gigantic size; and yet, again, pathetically resenting his abnormal heft and stature.

Forgetting his gigantism, sometimes, Wolfe would turn on the faucet of the immense reservoir of his memory; there would come bucketfuls of impressions—homely street and domestic scenes, caricatures, personal slights, personal victories, portraits of communities, of individuals, depictions of feuds, hates, loves, ambitions, jealousies, achievements, vanities and defeats. Some of these were superb, beautiful; all reflected boundless energy. Some were the mere talkativeness of a nervously tortured man, of a man who had read too much and aspired too much, a man who wished to get away from a reality and from memories of a reality which were hateful to him, a man who was eager to feel and to experience but who was harassed by a tick in the mind which prevented him from feeling at all, except in the chill recording of his writer's brain—not the heart; a man who had energy, thirst, appetite, curiosity, but who did not, until he was in his thirties, begin to deduce the simplest truths about life which any tobacco auctioneer, tobacco farmer, or Negro roustabout in the Asheville market knows with only a few years of adult experience. In the manuscript Thomas Wolfe left to be published after his death, he had become adult enough to draw some age-old truths about life—truths as old and as valid as the mightiest of those in all great literature, from the Old Testament to Mark Twain—and to express these truths with humility, clarity, force, beauty and originality

. . .

Desmond Powell. "Wolfe's Farewells." *Accent*, 1 (Winter 1941), 114–118.

You Can't Go Home Again proves that you can go home—proves indeed that if you are an artist like Thomas Wolfe it is the only place you can go. In this book Wolfe bids farewell to many things: to his youth and the madness of his youth; to love, which is not enough; to fame, which is enough only so long as it is not won. He bids farewell to the friends of his adolescence, who have grown away from him; to the literary acquaintances of his young manhood, whose language has lost all meaning; to the greatest man he ever knew, his editor, whom he feels he must leave for reasons he does not define. He bids farewell to England, that tight little isle whose riddle he never solved, the riddle of how such a people could ever produce such a literature. He bids farewell to Germany, land of sorcery and dark enchantment, which so long laid its spell on his soul. And he bids farewell to Old Catawba, to his family, to the memories and images that flooded his first two books. He ends with a haunting passage in which he seems to say goodbye to life itself.

Most of this must be taken as symbolic of the giving up of an attitude that the artist feels he has outgrown. The last farewell, however, reads like a genuine premonition, one of those nudges which the distressed body (Wolfe was a sick man long before he contracted pneumonia in Seattle) gives the spirit, saying, "My friend, all is not well with us." At times, too, it seems as if Wolfe were bidding goodbye not only to the literary approach of his former books but to the literary material as well. There is a note of finality in the way he takes leave of many of his people; it is as if he were saying, "I have done all I can with you; I shall not deal with such as you again." It is quite true that Wolfe had done some things enough. For example, he had carried his analysis of the English about as far as it could go; he had exhausted the possibilities of conversation of the "Who, dat guy? No, duh udduh guy," type among the manciphers of the city pavement; he had said all he had to say about literary esthetes and producers of slim volumes of verse. He may even have used up the device of the train journey; at any rate he never again equalled his first treatment of it in *Of Time and the River*. The formula he had used twice, that of the small town boy leaving home, plunging into the city, struggling for fame, fleeing to Europe and returning again, had probably served its turn. There was ample reason, therefore, why Wolfe should feel that the time for a fresh start was at hand, and such a start he virtually promises us at the conclusion of this book.

Thomas Wolfe was a genius. He usually wrote well, even when he wrote too much. It would have been possible for him to forsake much of the stuff of which his first four books were made and still produce novels that, for energy and variety, would be the envy of his fellow craftsmen. But whether such books, presumably written more objectively and out of the experience of his maturity rather than of his youth, would have evidenced the sweep and power of his first volumes is open to grave doubt. Wolfe once said in conversation that the experience of youth has a clarity and completeness that more recent experience generally lacks, and that one of the perils that beset the writer is the danger of using up this material too soon. If Wolfe *had* used it up it is hard to see what he could have put in its place, for on the evidence before us it seems certain that Wolfe was at his best when writing about his Carolina past.

You Can't Go Home Again illustrates this contention very well. One has only to compare the first two sections of the book to make the point clear. "The Native's Return," which deals with people and events in Libya Hill, has an ease and strength which the New York episode called "The World that Jack Built" largely lacks. One reviewer has called the party at the Jacks a "momentous incident." Momentous or not, it is a very dull party, which is in no way saved from failure by the literary arson Wolfe commits at the end. Wolfe puts more interest in a Libya Hill realtor than in all the plausible but boring society women, bankers, and theatrical people who crowd the Jack apartment; more truth in Nebraska Crane than in Piggy Logan or Mr. Hirsch. It is hard to see why the Jacks were brought into this book at all. Mrs. Jack's affair with George Webber was fictionally finished in *The Web and the Rock*. Nothing is gained by having it peter out here like a wet firecracker. It would have been better had Wolfe left it out altogether and devoted the pages thus gained to Elsa, who is dismissed rather cavalierly at the end of

the book. One suspects that these affairs are presented as they actually happened, and that Wolfe was not yet objective enough to give them a new proportion dictated by fictional necessity.

Wolfe's other books bear out the contention that the farther he got from his Carolina past, the less vivid his characters became. Many pages of *Of Time and the River* are devoted to Starwick; we are told over and over again that here is the most fascinating creature that ever lived. Actually Wolfe presents a wavering and distasteful fellow whom no one would particularly want to know. Beside Ben Gant, who is etched in gold, Starwick is a blur. Beside Old Man Gant, who is hewn from solid rock, Starwick is a will-of-the-wisp that the reader never grasps. Old Man Gant may be a monster, as some have implied. But what a monster! What a complete, full-bodied, solid, enduring monster! How you can see him, touch him, smell him, know him! Even at the moment of his death he bestrides his narrow world like a colossus. There is no equal to him in Wolfe's later work.

One must admit that the chapter on Lloyd McHarg, in *You Can't Go Home Again,* might be quoted to disprove that statement. McHarg is a remarkable creation; unlike Foxhall Edwards, he is wholly satisfying whether the reader knows his original or not. I do not think him as important as Ben, or Eliza, or Old Man Gant; but he is an achievement of which any writer might be proud. What impresses me most about him, however, is that he, the most successful of all the characters in the book, is the only one who resembles Old Gant. And the fact leads to the further recognition of the fact that whenever Wolfe creates a memorable charater out of material other than that of his youth, that character is likely to bear a family resemblance to Gant. Think of Seamus Malone, of loyal Abe Jones, of the Rhodes Scholar Fried, all of whom possess some of the intensity, the wildness, the gift for vituperation of the old man. Think of Monk Webber himself, who in his passion and madness is Gant's own son. Wolfe spoke true when he said that his life was a search for a father; and he found his image in strange places.

It is significant that Wolfe does not say goodbye to one body of material. That is the story of an author writing a book, which he told three times in *The Web and the Rock, The Story of a Novel,* and *You Can't Go Home Again.* This would continue to be his own story as long as he lived, and out of the stuff of his own experience his novels had to be made; to this material he could not say goodbye. No doubt writers would continue to be interested in the account of his struggle with the problem of finding a language for his thought, but it is a fair question how long this struggle would continue to interest the general reader. I believe that Wolfe was greatest when writing of his youth, because the world in which he moved as a youth was not only a more vivid but a more varied world than the one he moved in as a man. *Look Homeward, Angel* is the tale of a small town, its pages swarming with sharply defined men and women: merchants, artisans, teachers; policemen, saloonkeepers, prostitutes; doctors, lawyers, housewives. We have here a picture of America, of all the elements that draw sustenance from its earth. *You Can't Go Home Again* is a tale of two continents; with such

terrain full dealing is impossible. Because he had cast his lot in with theirs, Wolfe chose as his characters writers and men connected with the business of writing: Hauser, McHarg, Edwards, Stoat, Lewald, and Reade. He takes it for granted that these people will have the same validity as the people of Altamont. As a consequence of this acceptance of literary men as literary material he devotes to the flaying of an unimportant maker of puppet plays the chapter he might have given to an old Civil War veteran of Brooklyn; he forgoes telling us about a beautiful woman in order to tell us about a German literary agent; he wastes words satirizing literary fads which his readers, if they ever heard of them, have long since forgotten. All is not loss: "The Hollow Men" is one of his finest flights of imagination; but it gets into the book because it is conceived as passing through the mind of Foxhall Edwards. These literary figures may be good of their kind, but their kind cannot have the wide appeal of the Gants and their neighbors.

It may be this concern with literary matters that is responsible for the greater restraint in style which is perceptible in this book. There are fewer unwieldy sentences in this book than in its predecessors. And there are fewer rhapsodic outbursts. When Wolfe deviated from incident and character in *Of Time and the River,* he deviated into poetry, or at least into soaring rhetoric. He still does so here, but such passages are fewer, shorter, and quieter. They are replaced by a more thoughtful treatment of the things George Webber sees in the world about him. Whether one considers this a gain will depend on one's attitude toward Wolfe's purple passages.

161

I know the general objections that can be raised to writing of this kind, and I appreciate Somerset Maugham's satire of it in *Of Human Bondage*. I know too the specific objections that have been raised to the emotional outbursts of Eugene Gant: the too lengthy catalogues; the tendency, as Wolfe himself expressed it, "rarely to use less than twenty-one adjectives where four would do"; the return to the same themes in almost the same words more times than even the plea of *leitmotiv* can excuse. The first objection is just if the catalogues are no more than catalogues; but Wolfe's have sometimes the effect of incantations. The second objection strikes closer, but it does not quite hit the mark, for it applies less often to the rhapsodic than to the matter-of-fact passages. If one examines the dirge for October which opens the Telemachus chapter in *Of Time and the River*, he must agree that here is no uncurbed outpouring of a talent uncritical of itself; these repetitions are calculated, these adjectives are chosen for their cumulative effect. And they are chosen well. The third objection is valid insofar as it applies to the design of the novel as a whole. Wolfe admitted that he never found a pattern that satisfied him. Can we say that his indulgence in flights of poetic prose hindered his finding that pattern?

Someone once said that *The Return of the Native* was a Greek tragedy in prose, and this not very penetrating remark has been repeated ever since. When talking about the form of the novel we are usually misled by analogies of this kind. *Look Homeward, Angel,* despite Wolfe's rather contemptuous dismissal of it in *The Story of a Novel,* has a discernible structure. It is not the rigorous design of a canon or a sonnet; the pattern cannot be illustrated by a geometric figure like one of those puerile triangles we meet in textbooks on the classical drama. If one must have an analogy, he may say it is like a tree, with many leaves and branches all of which attach to the main stem. There may be rust on the leaves and fungi on the trunk, but everything somehow belongs to the tree. *Of Time and the River* does not have even so loose a design as this. The death of Eugene's father brings a great story to an end, and there is nothing of like fictional magnitude to take its place. I do not think, therefore, that one can accuse the prose poems of getting in the way of the form. In a large portion of *Of Time and the River* Wolfe simply did not have a story that hung together as did the story of the Gants. When they disappear from the plot, he is left with Eugene's journey through a strange world and his emotional reactions to what he meets there. He becomes prolix and diffuse, but in the course of telling us of these reactions he gives us some of the most glowing prose that has been written in America.

To say that this prose is uncontrolled because it is violent is an error; to say that this is the violence of impotence is one of the first critical errors of our time. The emotions of youth are violent, the acts of youth are uncontrolled, the unsatisfied desires of youth lead to beatings of the breast and feelings of futility. Thomas Wolfe knew all these things and wrote them from his heart. The point is, he wrote them well. He expressed what he wanted to express. The impression that these heightened passages leave is one of power. It is well to remember, too, that the majority of them are not turbulent. Besides the roarings of Old Man Gant, the ravings of Monk Webber, and the goat cries of young Eugene, there are the solemn chants on death and sleep, the nostalgic memories of lost days, the mighty panoramas of America, the dark meditations on time. Some disservice is done these passages by making them into anthologies. They belong in their context, from which they differ less in kind than in degree. They are the peaks of Wolfe's rhetoric, and one feels no such astonishment in meeting them as, say, he may feel in meeting the rhapsodic chapters in *The Grapes of Wrath.*

The virtues and defects of Wolfe's work result from the fact that he approached the novel as a poet, and moreover as a personal romantic poet. This may be the wrong attack for the novel. Mr. Thurber stated the objections to it when he admonished Wolfe for not laboring "over an idea until he cuts it down from 6700 sprawling words to the three paragraphs which will express it perfectly; that is, bring it within the definition of Art." Wolfe was probably more conscious of what he was trying to do than this would imply. The question is, could the thing he was trying to do in his long prose poems be done better by condensation? I doubt it; his attack resulted in some unique effects that no careful search for the *mot juste* could have achieved. It is clear, however, that Wolfe had taken criticism like this to heart, and there is evidence in *You Can't Go Home Again* that he was becoming more careful and more mature. This does not mean that he was becoming a better writer. Pope was more careful than Shelley, and Coventry Patmore was more mature than Byron.

Checklist of Additional Reviews

Lewis Gannett. "Books and Things." Boston *Evening Transcript,* September 18, 1940.

Lewis Gannett. Untitled. New York *Herald Tribune.* September 18, 1940, p. 27.

William McFee. "William McFee Analyzes Thomas Wolfe as a Novelist." New York *Sun,* September 18, 1940.

Ralph Thompson. Column, "Books of the Times." New York *Times,* September 18, 1940, p. 21.

Harry Hansen. "The First Reader." New York *World-Telegram,* September 18, 1940.

New York *Cue,* September 21, 1940.

Clifton Fadiman. "Journal's End." *New Yorker,* 16 (September 21, 1940), 62-64.

O. C. D. "Wolfe's Last Novel Is Autobiographical." *Asheville-Citizen,* September 22, 1940.

Marion Hargrove. Charlotte *News,* September 22, 1940.

J. Donald Adams. "Thomas Wolfe's Last Novel." New York *Times Book Review,* September 22, 1940, p. 1.

Ralph Thompson. Column, "Books of the Times." New York *Times,* September 23, 1940, p. L15.

"Thomas Wolfe, Part Two." *Newsweek,* 16 (September 23, 1940), 46.

"Burning, Burning, Burning." *Time,* 36 (September 23, 1940), 78, 80.

Sterling North. "Thomas Wolfe's Last Testament." Chicago *Daily News,* September 25, 1940.

San Francisco *News,* September 28, 1940.

Isabel Paterson. *Mademoiselle,* October, 1940.

Dayton Kohler. *Southern Literary Messenger*, 2 (October 1940), 562-563.

Millar Ward. "Thomas Wolfe's Last Novel Cause of Death." Asheville *Advertiser*, October 4, 1940.

Charleston *News & Courier*, October 6, 1940.

Claude Simpson. "In Last Novel Thomas Wolfe Found His Relation to World." Dallas *News*, October 6, 1940.

Ray Warwick. Atlanta *Journal*, October 13, 1940, p. 10, Magazine Section.

August Derleth. Column, "Book of the Week." *East Side News* (Madison, Wis.), October 17, 1940.

J. Donald Adams. "Wolfe's Last Novel Hailed By Critic As Finest of His Works." *Asheville-Citizen*, October 20, 1940.

Henry Hart. "You Can't Go Home Again." *New Masses*, 37, (October 22, 1940), 25-26.

Open Shelf, (October-November 1940).

Carlos Baker. "A credo from the dead to the living." *Nassau Lit* (November 1940).

Birmingham *News*, November 10, 1940.

Joseph Sagmaster. "The Posthumous Wolfe." *Kenyon Review*, (Winter 1940), 116.

Gloria Caplan. "You Can't Go Home Again." *Bluets*, (January 1941).

Thomas Wolfe

THE HILLS
BEYOND

With a Note on Thomas Wolfe
by Edward C. Aswell

Harper & Brothers · Publishers
New York and London

The Hills Beyond

Clayton Hoagland. "Wolfe Dividend." New York *Sun*, October 15, 1941.

Those innumerable readers who feel strongly about the work of Thomas Wolfe are in for a surprise, whether they like or dislike his books. In this collection are seven short stories, a one-act play, two fine essays and a 50,000-word novel which gives the book its title, and which reveals a new Wolfe. There is also a 13,000-word essay by Edward C. Aswell of Harper's that is the most illuminating piece this reviewer has yet read about Thomas Wolfe.

. . .

A lusty clan, those Joyners. They will walk in your mind as creatures of authentic history, not as characters born and nurtured in a novelist's brain. Something of this magic was in old Bascom Pentland, Boston uncle of Eugene Gant in "Of Time and the River." Here, finally, is a book of them, men and women infused with vitality by the pen of a master humorist whose style became lithe while he himself, approaching forty, fattened on beer and rich food. He must have died knowing in his heart he had written better than ever, as he had always hoped he would.

This short novel may come to be known as his most mature work. It is satire of the first rank, distinguished by a sinewy prose unlike that of the Wolfe of old—a perfect medium for the anecdotes, comment and ribaldry that fills the ten chapters. "Beyond the Hills" is as American as corn likker.

Frank Brookhouser. "Tom Wolfe: A Requiem For a Giant."Philadelphia *Inquirer*, October 15, 1941.

Thomas Wolfe wrote his own best epitaph when he was 22. In a letter to his mother, he said: "I want to know life and understand it and interpret it without fear or favor . . . I will go to the end of the earth to find it, to understand it. I will know this country when I am through as I know the palm of my hand, and I will put it on paper and make it true and beautiful."

The letter, previously unpublished, is included in a long essay on Wolfe—the man, his credo, his methods—by Edward C. Aswell, his last editor, which concludes this final collection of work by the man who captured the pulse, the feeling, the sights, the sounds, the movement, and the life of the people of America as few other writers in the Nation's history had, before his death three years ago at the age of 37. The collection presents a Wolfe of many periods, many moods, and—surprisingly—of numerous styles.

The pieces were chosen from the stack of manuscripts left behind at his death. Side by side with the poignant "The Lost Boy," the story of his brother, are the satiric essay, "On Leprechauns," the biting and comic "Portrait of a Literary Critic," a one-scene play on "Gentlemen of the Press," a revealing essay on loneliness, and other sketches and stories.

But what will be read most eagerly is the longest piece, "The Hills Beyond," the novel which he had started early in his career and which he was rewriting and filling out at the end. That he was trying to strip the excess overflow from his work—and was succeeding—is plainly evident. But there is an element of sadness in the simplicity of the sentence structure. For the work, although it naturally has distinction, lacks the power and lyrical intensity that were always inherent in his writing. Twelve chapters are published. He was only getting started, and it is sensible to presume they would have developed into at least two novels.

Fortunately, they were not necessary for a final appraisal of the lonely man's work. With Sherwood Anderson, whose momentum brought to fruition the naturalistic school and, thus to its peak, our literature, he stands pre-eminent in the last 30 years—one of the few literary giants the Nation has produced.

W. A. S. Dollard. "The Vision of Thomas Wolfe." New York *Herald Tribune Books,* October 19, 1941, p. 6.

Thomas Wolfe was a great writer, who, contrary to the fairly widespread notion that he was a facile writer, slaved at revising his books. Before he ever set to paper the torrent of words he commanded, he "rehearsed" his writing over and over again to himself. Often his friends heard him tell a lusty tale or an amusing anecdote (and he told them well), which they later recognized as the bare outline of a passage in his books. Mr. Aswell, who edits the volume, remarks that in the more than a million words Wolfe left in manuscript, there were many versions of the same story.

Many of the pieces in this book of stories and essays might be considered revisions that Wolfe would have been willing to show to a critical audience, but still work that would take further rewriting. "The Lion at Morning" and "The Hills Beyond," parts of an incomplete novel, must be appraised from another point of view. They are proof that Thomas Wolfe had not shot his bolt.

With the exception of "Gentlemen of the Press," a weak, almost hackneyed theme of familiar types in a newspaper office in a Southern town, the stories here collected have qualities of Thomas Wolfe's early writing: miraculously vivid sense impressions, sharp and full characterization, poignancy, wit, Elizabethan invective, humor and musical prose. The faithful who first recognized Wolfe's talent will welcome the publication of any of his work that has some of these merits.

The best of the stories is "Chickamauga," published in 1937 in "The Yale Review." Wolfe got the tale from a great-uncle who survived the Civil War, and set it down deliberately in the repetitive phrases of the old man, but he changed the emphasis from descriptions of battles to a study of adolescent bewilderment and frustration. . . .

. . . "Chickamauga" is complete as a story, which is not generally true of Wolfe's stories. He usually thought of them as parts of longer works.

"Portrait of a Literary Critic" is a satire on Dr. Hugo Twelvetrees Turner's critical instability, and his shifts from denunciation of these wicked, "dull" moderns to a crusading position in their favor when they became virtuous by legal fiat. It is gentler and less effective than the satire in "Return of the Prodigal," an account, in two parts, of Eugene Gant's homecoming to the town he had described so unmercifully. . . .

"A Kinsman of His Blood" would require much reworking to become a successful picture of the physical and mental disintegration of an unloved son. On the other hand the first of the four sections of "The Lost Boy" is Wolfe at his best in analyzing the hurt a sensitive child suffers in a world of insensitive adults.

The essay "Leprechauns" has several excellent observations on writing and the American public: "People who live in luxury, on assured incomes, have very stern and Spartan notions about getting soft." They believe that young American writers should "get a few good kicks in the face" so that they may become great. The satire on visiting foreign writers who live in luxury here, however, misses fire.

In "God's Lonely Man" are some of the most moving and tragic sentences that Wolfe wrote. He chants a hymn of the loneliness of all men. Through love Jesus offered men a solution. But, he mourns, men like Jesus who preached love, remain unable to use the means.

That essay was a revision of an early essay. Though it represents important facts about his life and work, it does not—nor do any of the other essays—embody the important revelation of this book. We get that from "The Hills Beyond" and "The Lion at Morning." Wolfe was more interested in America and her numberless characters than he was in continuing self-portraiture. He did not live to make the scores of books about his country that his amazing energy and genius planned. But these two unfinished pieces are ample proof that he had begun to do that work.

. . .

The ten chapters of "The Hills Beyond" reveal much more. John Webber, father of George, would have been a principal character. But only one. The others were the Joyners; two had been Wolfe's ancestors; Zack and the other sons of Old Bill he invented. Southern folklore gave him clews for many of the Rabelaisian anecdotes. All the children Wolfe created imaginatively.

. . . If the book had been completed it might have been the great realistic Southern picture of Reconstruction Days. The South might have resented such a book, as Wolfe's town did the picture he gave of it. Even when he used his gift for satire most tellingly,

169

however, Wolfe never wished to annihilate. He said harsh things about every section of the country. But he loved America and he tried to sing her "unuttered song."

Marvin Sargent. "Literary Genius." Oakland *Tribune,* October 19, 1941.

He wrote standing up, using the top of a refrigerator for a table. He was well over six feet tall. His home town got mad at him when he wrote it up in his first novel, but a few years later the only ones mad were those he had left out. He wrote so many million words that at his early death there was a pile of manuscripts chin-high from the floor—enough to yield three posthumous novels with much left over for some lucky library. He was one of America's few contemporary literary geniuses. His name was Thomas Wolfe or Eugene Gant or George Webber.

Although he has been dead three years, Wolfe has not yet been evaluated as an author because his work was not completed. With the publication of "The Hills Beyond," the "Boy Wonder" of American literature rests his .case.

In a revealing essay on Wolfe appended to this collection, his last editor, Edward C. Aswell, clarifies one troublesome point. Tom Wolfe first dazzled the reading public in the frankly autogenous character of Eugene Gant. It was puzzling, therefore, to find that he had assumed a second pseudonym in George Webber, hero in his posthumous writings.

According to Aswell, this alias served several purposes: It enabled Wolfe to spare his family further publicity; it made it possible for him to tell several childhood incidents he had forgotten to include in the history of Eugene Gant, and it marked symbolically a change in Wolfe, himself, to greater objectivity. Once it is clear that Eugene Gant and George Webber are identical, says Aswell not too convincingly, it can be seen that the author's work is not as formless as critics have said. "The Hills Beyond" fits into the puzzle smoothly, making the works describe an autobiographical circle.

Aswell, probably the editor in "You Can't Go Home Again," may have been too close to Wolfe to evaluate the change he mentions. He scorns the "academic" criticism of formlessness so often applied to Wolfe's writings, but the author, himself, seems to have been feeling after conventional form in his later writings. The beautiful stories "Lost Boy" and "Return of the Prodigal" in this volume are oversimplified by topical divisions which proclaim that they have organization. Wolfe's last work of all, the novelette, "The Hills Beyond," creaks with a conscious effort at orderly factual progression which—except in the last beautiful chapter—makes it like the writings of a stranger.

Certainly the cramped quarters of conventional literary forms were a china shop to the big Southerner. This is shown again by the play, "Gentlemen of the Press" included in this collection. Wolfe bungles his attempt to fit into the demanding one-act play form, producing a humorless melodrama which he would probably have been ashamed to see in print. It was certainly no service to his memory to publish it.

Often compared with Whitman and Melville, Wolfe was in his early writing like each of them in his spontaneous, unconventional approach to form. In this phase, when he was good, he was great; when he was bad, he was horrid. But most of the time he was great. His much-heralded change to objectivity meant only a stiffening of style, an access of literary self-consciousness, as in his last, prosy novelette.

Admirers of Thomas Wolfe will want to add this volume to their shelves because, in the lyric stories of "The Lost Boy" and "The Lost Day," it will remind them of the lost artist who, youthfully lavish of adjectives and unaware of rules, wrote his heart out in the intensity of "Look Homeward Angel."

J. Donald Adams. "Thomas Wolfe's Last Book." New York *Times Book Review*, October 26, 1941, p. 1.

Three years have passed since Thomas Wolfe's death, and this is the third book which has been culled from the mountain of manuscript he left behind him. It is also, we are told, to be the last, although material remains for as many more. In the judgment of the editor with whom he last worked, Edward Aswell, and of his literary executor, Maxwell Perkins, who was also his first literary midwife, there is no reason good enough to justify publication of that remainder. Much of it is early work which Wolfe would wish to revise if he were still living; some of it material which he worked over in another form;

some of it purely experimental. These facts are set forth in the interesting note which Mr. Aswell appends to the present volume, and in which more light is cast on Wolfe's methods and aims as a writer.

"The Hills Beyond" amply justifies its publication as the last work we are to have from the man who was the most promising American writer of his generation. It contains some of his best, and certainly his most mature, work. The unfinished novel from which the book takes its title would, I think, have surpassed in creative power those other four on which his reputation must rest. Besides this, "The Hills Beyond" includes one of the finest of Wolfe's shorter pieces, "The Lost Boy," and an exceedingly well done tale of the Civil War which he had from the lips of a great-uncle ("Chickamauga"). There is also a pair of pieces, one imaginary, the other factual, on the theme of his return to Asheville seven years after the publication of "Look Homeward, Angel." These, too, are excellent, each in its kind. Of the remaining miscellaneous items, the best is a brief but suggestive and revealing essay on the theme of loneliness.

The unfinished novel, Mr. Aswell informs us, was the work with which Wolfe was chiefly occupied during the year before his death. It is, therefore, in view of the unusual manner in which Wolfe's work was published (each book being a sort of mosaic of old and new material) of exceptional interest. "The Hills Beyond" was set down by a man who felt that he was through, in his own words, "with lyrical and identifiable personal autobiography." Except for one chapter, which had magazine publication in 1936, it was written and rewritten during the months immediately preceding his death. Wolfe thought he had reached this point in "The Web and the Rock," the first of the posthumous books. I do not believe that he had. But sections of the next book, "You Can't Go Home Again," were more objective than anything previous, and with "The Hills Beyond" the goal he had set himself was definitely in sight.

In this book—how great a pity that he did not live to finish it!—he aimed to tell the story of his forebears. He found that most of what he knew that was actual about them he had already used in earlier books, and most of the people who appear in "The Hills Beyond" are not patterned after real members of the "Gant" and "Pentland" families. But they are, or would have become, full-bodied creations. Old William ("Bear") Joyner, who came into the mountains with a Revolutionary land grant in one hand and a rifle in the other, was hewn from the family tree, but the sons and grandsons who carry on the story were not. Zachariah, that fine figure of a homespun politician; Rufus, the acquisitive; Theodore, the histrionic professional Confederate warrior; Robert, the upright judge—these and others are creatures of Wolfe's making, and they are well done.

But that is not what, to my mind, is most important about this last book of Thomas Wolfe. Who would cast out from his writing those vital portraits of his own father and mother, or the tender and searing memory of his older brother which is captured in "The Lost Boy"? Whether they were real or imagined, Wolfe could make his people live. We require that of any novelist worth his salt. But Tom Wolfe had more than that to give. There was that marvelous sensory equipment of his, that vibrant sensitivity, evident from the first. He had the power of evocation as only the best writers have—the magic touch that gives wings to a reader's thought. A page of his best prose is worth a shelf full of laborious fact-finding in the name of fiction. These were qualities that came out of his emotional wealth; his mind, for nearly all his life, did not keep pace with them. But Wolfe was growing—growing fast, when death overtook him. The integration that he needed was under way. He was finding himself in relation to life, in relation to his world.

The indications of this growth in "The Hills Beyond" are plentiful. One of them is the increasing number of passages in which he does not simply feel, but thinks. There is stuff for reflection in what he writes about the American attitude toward lawyers and the law—so different from that of any other people on earth.

We made the lawyers our medicine men, and the law itself, as practiced by ambitious men, was made a means to an end—the end being that of business itself—personal advantage and private profit before all else, in politics or elsewhere. The social function of the law became obscured.

Read what he writes of the role of the county court house in our rural communities and its meaning in the whole fabric of American life:

> The county court house was, in short, America—the wilderness America, the sprawling, huge chaotic, criminal America. . . .

I think that if Thomas Wolfe had lived he would have gotten more of what has made us the people we are into his fiction than any novelist we

172

have had, for his understanding of his country and his people was approaching the depth of his love for them. It was a love no less intense than Whitman's. It flames at the core of all he wrote.

He died at 37. And he was, I am now convinced, only on the threshold of the achievement for which he was fitted. There is talk, here and there, of a Wolfe "cult." That is foolish talk. There was, too, one remembers, a Whitman cult. Thomas Wolfe was born for greatness, and he reached no small measure of it before he left us. Much time may pass before we see his like again.

Rowena W. Tobias. "Wolfe's Last Work Collected." Charleston (South Carolina) *News and Courier*, November 2, 1941, p. 2, III.

Thomas Wolfe probably has stirred up more controversy in high-sounding phrases than any writer of his time. During the last three years it has often been difficult to remember that he is dead, for in this time half of his published work has appeared—two major books that complete the Gant-Webber cycle, and this book of stories, essays, and a fragment of a novel that gives the volume its title, "The Hills Beyond."

. . . Before distance and tragedy lend nostalgic enchantment, now is the time to examine the repeated statement of Wolfe's editors that, before his death, he was fitting his writing into the form and discipline that his four published novels lack.

The main support of that contention must be the ten chapters of "The Hills Beyond" which this book includes, "the manuscript which he had been writing and rewriting just before he died." What there is of it nestles within the novel form more closely than anything else he ever wrote—for he and his editors have good reason for saying that he really produced one huge book, that he was a writer rather than a novelist. He has been called an "eavesdropper on life", but although that is an apt and partly true phrase it does not do justice to the quality of his work.

Wolfe was primarily a man with an amazing and at times overpowering ability to recall and set down every nuance of every sight, smell, sound or emotion that had ever touched him. His "eavesdropping" went through a sea change in his own emotional sensitivity. The fault of Wolfe as an artist, the flaw that will bar him from the ranks of truly great writers, was his lack of selectivity. Everything was poured out on the same level, a part of a vast gigantic flood that inundated his readers.

But to return to "The Hills Beyond." It is no part of that Wolfe tidal wave. In contrast, it is almost the skeleton of a book, bare and wholly unenriched in long passages, sprinkled with polemical tirades that are fascinating to read but arid and ill-at-ease in a fictional setting. It is, of course, unfinished and there is great danger in judging any man by a fragment of what he proposed to do. But what is here is not the core of a great creative work. It is creative only in the sense that Wolfe drew its characters from his own imagination rather than from his own

173

past or that of his ancestors. And it proves, to me at least, that Wolfe was an autobiographical writer (an unhandy tag that often flays the critic worse than the writer, but there seems to be no other term for it). In other words, Wolfe wrote at times too fully but always richly and stirringly and compellingly about what he, through himself or those close to him, had experienced. When that was done, he had no more to say. When he died, although he may not have known it, his work was done, completed in the story of Eugene Gant-George Webber-Thomas Wolfe.

. . .

John Tebbel. "The Long Dream of Thomas Wolfe." *American Mercury,* 53 (December 1941), 752-754.

Those of us who knew and loved Thomas Wolfe only through the books he wrote have been able to understand him solely by instinct. We have had little illumination from the friends who watched his work and worked with him. Consequently, the long "note" by Edward C. Aswell at the end of *The Hills Beyond* is really more important than the tag-ends of Wolfe manuscript which comprise the book itself because Aswell, who was Tom's last editor, answers many of the questions which Wolfe left hanging when he died in September 1938.

It is now clear that the gangling North Carolina boy studying at Harvard in 1922 had already envisioned as a whole the vast saga which he was to work

at continuously in his too-brief lifetime. This "book," as he always called it, was a complete entity in his mind before he began to write it. The mechanical fact that it ultimately appeared as four long novels, a tale of more than four thousand printed pages, was immaterial to him. He knew what he wanted to write and worked hard at it.

Wolfe, says Aswell, wrote whatever part of the saga it moved him on any particular day to undertake. He wrote scenes several different ways. He rewrote until he had pinned down what he knew was true and right, which dispels the popular illusion that Wolfe poured out millions of words without revision. And he saved everthing he wrote, dumping it into two big packing cases. To put a Wolfe book together was a process of removing from these cases the sections of his work which would form the novel at hand, and then joining the sections. Amazingly, Aswell reports, these varied pieces, sometimes written years apart, went together like a jigsaw puzzle.

This explains the unevenness of his work; it explains why *The Web and the Rock* falls into two distinct halves, each in a different style. For Wolfe strove earnestly until he died to write even better than he did. At the end, he had achieved a true creativeness lacking in his earlier work; he had refined his style; he had found himself and was ready to do the greater things he most certainly would have done.

The stories in *The Hills Beyond,* extracted from the waist-high pile of manuscript Wolfe left behind him, are excellent illustrations for Aswell's valuable critical commentary. "The Lost Boy," first story in the book, is a fine piece which deals, on four separate levels, with the death of Tom's brother Grover in St. Louis, an incident touched briefly in *Look Homeward, Angel.* "Chickamauga" is a first-person Civil War reminiscence by one of Eugene Gant's Pentland relatives, hitherto unintroduced, and it is, as Aswell says, one of the best stories Wolfe ever wrote.

There are other essays and stories of unequal merit in the book, including the magnificent essay on loneliness called "God's Lonely Man" which was published in THE AMERICAN MERCURY under another title. The name piece comprises the major part of the book and perhaps the best part because it indicates the kind of thing Wolfe would have been able to produce had he lived. Written near the end of his life, it is a story told with a comparative economy of words, an objective simplicity which is quite remote from his earlier lyricism. Some readers, of whom I am one, will prefer Wolfe as poet, but it is undeniable that this final style of his has a solid drive to it which displays unsuspected objective power. Furthermore, as Aswell says, it is a work of pure imagination. It answers forever those critics who claim that Wolfe would have nothing to say once he had finished with himself and his family.

Aswell frequently compares Wolfe to James Joyce but it is possible to find an even closer resemblance to Marcel Proust. Wolfe had Proust's virtually unlimited capacity for observation and the "feel" of things, and a similar tremendous power of recall. But he had something else that Proust partly lacked: a feeling of brotherhood with the people he wrote about which gives to his books a fine-textured humanity.

Thomas Wolfe despised the critical minds who hail every new writer as an equal of Tolstoi, Balzac, or any one of the established immortals. He expounds this idea with an acid sharpness in "Portrait of a Literary Critic," which also first appeared in THE AMERICAN MERCURY. Nevertheless, on the basis of his lifetime's work, now complete in this present volume, I think it is no exaggeration to say that Wolfe will certainly be recorded as one of the great American writers and may well occupy a prominent place in the history of world literature. He possessed the realism of the realists, the poetry of the poets and his genius encompassed the individual talents of all his gifted contemporaries. He stands above these lesser writers as the blue hills rise timeless and lonely over his native city.

E. M. F. "Here We Go Again." *Trend,* 1 (January 1942), 20-21.

By this time it should be evident that Thomas Wolfe can no longer be referred to as "a promising author," as a writer "struggling to reach a form;" but this is just what does happen every time a new Wolfe book appears. With the publication of what we are told is to be the last of the posthumous selections from the huge manuscript Wolfe left (*The Hills Beyond*), it is clear that the entire body of his work must be considered as an accomplished artistic fact: the form is achieved, whether good or bad. And yet it must not be forgotten that Wolfe was, and still is, one of the most vitally alive novelists of our times—a fact which has produced appalling critical misconceptions about his work, rather than a wholehearted delight in an organic art.

So it has come upon us, like a plague of Japanese beetles, that Thomas Wolfe has had his name bandied about as a subjective, autobiographical, but, of course, talented young man. As a strange and rather late concession to horse sense, this final volume has been praised as the most objective of all the novels. Had it been completed, we are informed, it may well have been Wolfe's masterpiece; certainly it marks the way to a new and greater production in that unfinished future. This conclusion, I trust, is valid; if it is not, it is a good thing Wolfe died young—for an artist is as good as dead if he has stopped making progress. The speculation is futile, however, and the analysis which produced it is worse: it is misinterpretation. Like all Wolfe criticism, it is based upon the notion that the books are guilty of subjectivism—that they are autobiographical, and lack true artistic form.

But all art is subjective: it must come from an amalgam of the artist's experience, an amalgam which is cut and shaped and monkeyed with until the artist has squeezed a lot of disparate incidents and characters into the form he desires. The only subjective (as versus objective) element that can be discussed in art is the technique. That is, some writers hide the precise, exact situations that they have experienced and from which they make their artistic synthesis by juxtaposing characters and incidents and locales kaleidoscopically, so that the original is unrecognizable; this, obviously, is the objective technique, for the story is told in terms of an object outside the artist himself as a person (never, of course, as artist). Wolfe did not use this technique; he did not disguise the elements of his experience beyond recognition, and therefore his novels are told in terms of himself as a subject. Indeed, he did not even bother to find new situations and new characters each time he wrote a book. It might be said of him that he wrote but one story, composed of several novels and a number of short stories.

It would be incorrect, however, to say that he wrote only one novel, broken up into several volumes—such a novel as that of Proust, for instance—for Wolfe progresses from one book to another in only two instances (from *Look Homeward Angel* to *Of Time and the River,* and from *The Web and the Rock* to *You Can't Go Home Again*); his story is repeated, retold in a different way. Also, the characters change, again except in the above progressions: the shift from Eugene Gant to George Webber is not only nominal, it is a fundamental shift in outlook and understanding.

With some such view of Wolfe's work as a total organism it is possible to arrive at a definite idea of his form. The collection of sketches and short stories in the volume under consideration aids us no little here by showing how many different aspects the single story took: the story of the Gant-Pentland-Webber-Joyner families as Wolfe heard it in his youth, or as he was part of it during his lifetime. Many complex incidents from 1830 to 1937 are woven into the total story, but make up individual and self-sustaining literary works by themselves. Actually, this amounts, in the long run, to a disregard for story qua story tantamount to that of the Elizabethan dramatists. Wolfe knew that any *good* story would do for his work; the one he used was the one he knew best, and he never bothered to seek for another one.

What becomes important, then, is outside any strict plot analysis, or any discussion of the plot as autobiographical or concocted. The importance is in Wolfe's relationships of growth, beliefs, attitudes of individuals; in his pervading concepts of loneliness, speed, and travel (spacial and spiritual); in the vital significance of time. These things are shown in different ways, with new emphases, and from different viewpoints in all Wolfe's work—they emerge from, and become part of, the basic structure of the unit story. The form of the novels is in the disciplined play of these elements against each other, and within the single plot. Certainly this is, in conception, as fine and well-mannered a form as any sensible reader could desire.

To what extent Wolfe succeeds or fails within the scope of such an analysis of his form and purpose is a problem deserving the attention of critics in the future, a problem which, in its study, will make for some intelligent understanding of one of the important novelists of this century.

For the present, it is of some value to note that *The Hills Beyond,* both title-piece and collected stories and essays, is an excellent source-book for any study and revaluation that may be attempted. The book contains, it is true, some specimens of Wolfe's work that make one wonder if the editor had his senses about him when he decided to include them, and if the publisher had read them when he jacket-blurbed "Some of Wolfe's best fiction." Indeed, the whole book has more interest for the student of Wolfe's technique and artistic growth than for the lay novel reader. It performs, I think, a fine public service, and a good artistic and scholarly function; it is not to be con-

strued, however, as comparable with the four preceding novels.

W. G. Key. "Last Work of a Genius." Atlanta *Constitution,* March 15, 1942, p. 6.

Three years have passed since the day when Thomas Wolfe walked into the hills beyond, leaving behind a mountain of manuscript that yielded three books; books that are peculiarly those of a man destined to die as the wheat of his genius ripens. There is much in Wolfe's life that recalls that of another genius, Donn Byrne, his life, too, snuffed soon after he had found himself.

"The Hills Beyond," his publishers say, is the last of his works and the manuscript that remains will probably go eventually to some college library. Taken from the manuscript he left have been "The Web and the Rock," and "You Can't Go Home Again," the first published in 1939 and the second in 1940.

This last volume probably will be generally described as a collection of short stories. Yet it is not. The title piece is a story running 10 chapters; some of the others are biographical studies of all that is finest in Wolfe, while still others are bitter and brilliant satire. Many of the chapters of this book could just as well have been a part of others he has written.

Checklist of Additional Reviews

Sterling North. "Thomas Wolfe (Heaven Forbid) Might Have Penned Historical Novels." Chicago *Daily News*, October 15, 1941.

Fanny Butcher. Chicago *Tribune*, October 15, 1941.

Ralph Thompson. Column "Books of the Times." New York *Times*, October 15, 1941, p. 19.

Harry Hansen. New York *World Telegram*, October 15, 1941.

Clifton Fadiman. "More Posthumous Wolfe." *New Yorker*, 17 (October 18, 1941), 93.

Boston *Daily Globe*, October 19, 1941.

Ft. Worth *Star-Telegram*, October 19, 1941.

Frances Stover. "New Riches Out of Treasure of Thomas Wolfe." Milwaukee *Journal*, October 19, 1941.

Washington *Star*, October 19, 1941.

"Last Words." *Time*, 38 (October 20, 1941), 108.

Paul Fisher. Kansas City *Star*, October 25, 1941.

Howard Mumford Jones. *Saturday Review*, 24 (October 25, 1941), 7-8.

Rosamond Milner. "A Mixed Ration." Louisville *Courier-Journal*, November 2, 1941.

Malcolm Cowley. "Wolfe and the Lost People." *New Republic*, 105 (November 3, 1941), 592-594.

Sister Mariella, O.S.B. *Commonweal*, 35 (November 14, 1941), 97.

San Francisco *Chronicle*, November 16, 1941.

Angelica Canfield. *Book-of-the-Month Club*, November 19, 1941.

R. E. Danielson. *Atlantic Monthly*, 168 (December 1941), n.p.

Ray Warwick. Atlanta *Journal*, December 14, 1941, Magazine Section, p. 10.

Louis Nicholas. Philadelphia *Record*, December 28, 1941.

Book Review Digest, February, 1942.

Cresset (Menasha, Wis.), March, 1942.

Notes

Thomas Wolfe's
LETTERS TO HIS MOTHER
Julia Elizabeth Wolfe

———————

EDITED WITH AN INTRODUCTION

BY

JOHN SKALLY TERRY

Department of English
Washington Square College
New York University

NEW YORK

CHARLES SCRIBNER'S SONS

1943

Thomas Wolfe's Letters to His Mother

W. T. Scott. "Thomas Wolfe as He Revealed Himself in Letters to Mother." Providence *Journal*, May—, 1943, p. 4.

. . .

No man's letters to his mother add up to his complete biography, but Wolfe's to the woman he immortalised as Eliza Gant are, as you might expect, far fuller than most. He both adored and resented his family. There were times when his mother seemed to him to represent all the small town respectability and narrowness he would flee from and disavow; times when he set her apart from it in his mind. She was practical, constantly turning a good penny with her real estate ventures and her rooming house. Tom was in every Asheville sense impractical, he used his family's money for his education and was sometimes in his letters very young about it. . . .

He was tortured enough, sensitive enough, self-dramatizing enough to soar or seethe at the slightest encouragement or fancied disregard; had just enough of Asheville in him to want to shine—to show Asheville a thing or two. He wanted none of it—except to wring its confession of his greatness; none of it—except all of it for his material and his books.

. . .

There is too much repetitiousness of mood and of small stuff in these letters to make them constantly interesting; but much of them is interesting, even exciting, and all of them tell a great deal about Wolfe growing from a gawky, bookish boy to a giant of a man. They are charming at times—fulsome with life-and-death philosophy, then "P.S. Yes, I want the shirts". . . .

His mother is now 83, still running a rooming house—with her great hands and her appraising glance. . . .

This book is one more picture of the way her strange son saw her, and also of the way he saw himself. Amidst all the darknesses and turbulences one has, nonetheless, "a feeling of victory."

Unsigned. "Thomas Wolfe's Mother Compiles Book of Letters." Dallas *Times Herald*, May 2, 1943.

The untimely death of Thomas Wolfe at 37 cut short the career of one of America's greatest novelists of all time.

Idol of millions of American readers for a decade, the real Thomas Wolfe has been a more or less obscure personality. The intimate details of his life and character are revealed in three large suitcases of his letters, from the third grade at elementary school to just before his death, written to his mother.

· · ·

Throughout Wolfe displays a tremendous zest for living and working and an amazing vitality. He wrote with great rapidity, scorning the typewriter for the pencil or pen. He plunged whole-heartedly into his work and frequently kept going for long sessions that were ended only by hunger or sheer exhaustion.

· · ·

Mr. Terry, with the aid of Julia Wolfe, is at present preparing a biography of the novelist.

Thomas Wolfe usually is either greatly admired or thoroughly detested by the literary world. For those millions who form the first group, the letters will be a treasured possession.

John T. Frederick. "Thomas Wolfe's Letters." Chicago *Sun Book Week*, May 9, 1943, p. 4.

This book will hold interest and value for American readers a century from now, two centuries from now. It is a rare and exciting experience to be able to say that with confidence of a newly-published book. I can say it of "Thomas Wolfe's Letters to His Mother." No writer of our time seems to me more certain to be read by future generations than Thomas Wolfe; and these letters, which throw indispensable light on his life and work and are true expressions of the man, will live, with "Look Homeward, Angel" and "You Can't Go Home Again."

The one subject about which Wolfe wrote most frequently to his mother is money. His mother's money took him to Harvard for graduate study, after his father had paid the bills for his four years at the University of North Carolina. His mother's money supported him in the months that followed Harvard, when with Prof. Baker's encouragement—following Wolfe's brilliant performance in the famous "47 Workshop" course—he was trying to place his plays on Broadway. We owe to her in this direct way much of Wolfe's opportunity for development and self-discovery.

There is some indication in the letters that Julia Wolfe was more interested in the investments she was making in Florida real estate in those years of the early 20's than she was in the investments she was making in the genius of her son. But there is no evidence that she was more disturbed than most parents would have been about his failure to solve his own financial problems or to settle down to a job. Probably he suffered less from lack of money than he thought he did; and what would have sufficed for another was painfully inadequate for Tom Wolfe. He regarded an 8-pound steak as an appropriate meal for three people, and—when his mother had to supplement his salary after he began teaching at New York University—declared that "no one lives on $150 a month in New York."

Nor did Mrs. Wolfe seriously resent, apparently, her son's portrayal of herself and other members of the family in his books. She cannot have been so self-deceived or inconsistent as Wolfe himself was on this point. Repeatedly he declared that his work was purely fictional, and he fiercely denounced his Asheville critics for identifying characters in "Look Homeward, Angel" with real people. Yet he wrote of his father, "He is headed straight, not for one of my plays, but a series."

Wolfe's consciousness of himself as artist, his faith in himself and knowledge of his great powers, is the second theme most frequently and strikingly expressed in his letters to his mother. Just out of college—and trying to explain his refusal of a safe job in his home town—he declared that he meant to express himself "to the last ounce." Out of the struggle and discouragement of the attempt both to write and to teach, in 1924, comes the sudden avowal: "I shall be great—if I do not die too soon—and you will be known as my mother. I say that seriously—I believe it. There is no one like me, and I shall conquer."

With Wolfe's faith in his art and himself went faith in America, and at the same time a vigorous resentment of what was unworthy and destructive in American life, and a sense of his own prophetic calling to rebuke and denounce this smug materialism. "What I shall try to get into their dusty little pint-measure minds," he wrote in 1923, "is that a full belly, a good automobile, paved streets, and so on, do not make them one whit better or finer."

With the sense of his powers came also the sense of their wasting; with his awareness of himself as artist, the artist's keen awareness of time. Few artists make time their friend, and Wolfe was not one of them. To him time was always the arch-enemy. "There is a footprint in the dark, a bell strikes twelve, and the flying year has gone. My life is like water which has passed the mill. It turns no wheel."

He reckoned his years: "I should have 15 or 20 big books by the time I am 55 or 60 (if I last that long). This should be enough for me to have my say." "Live a little now," he adjured his mother. But as the years of his great production pass, the note of tiredness, of the need of rest, comes into his own letters with ominously increasing frequency: "I am terribly tired. . . . I am planning to get some real rest. . . . I am exhausted."

Finally, in the last long letter in the book, written on May 7, 1938, he told his mother: "I am going to get some rest. . . . As I have got at least a year of very hard work before me, it is pretty important that I get it now." A few weeks later the 78-year-old mother came to Chicago to meet her son, dying at 37.

Tremaine McDowell. "A Gargantuan Primer to Novels of Thomas Wolfe." Chicago *Sunday Tribune*, May 9, 1943, p. 15.

"Mama," wrote Thomas Wolfe at the age of 22, "in the name of God, guard Papa's letters to me with your life. There has never been anybody like Papa. I mean to say that, all in all, he is the most unique human being I have ever known." Thus young Wolfe, these letters reveal, hoarded his memories of early years in Asheville and of his family, who were to sit for the portraits of the Gants and their kindred in his novels.

At the same time Wolfe was developing a passionate interest in himself. "I am changing so rapidly," he wrote at 18, "that I find myself an evergrowing object of interest. Sounds egotistical, doesn't it?" At 22: "I am inevitable. I sincerely believe that the only thing that can stop me now is insanity, disease or death." And a few days later, in terms which Rousseau himself might well have used: "No one in this country is writing plays like mine. Good or bad, they're my own. . . . I am in full bud and this thing inside me is growing beyond control."

Why Thomas Wolfe turned from drama to the novel is one of the many questions which this necessarily fragmentary record of his life does not answer. Clearly exemplified, however, are such traits as his magnificent optimism in financial matters, which led him to expect three dollars to do the work of one and vice versa; his equally magnificent inability to understand why his novels seemed libelous to his relatives in Asheville, the town to which for many years he quite understandably could not bring himself to return; and his tremendous devotion to that shrewd and determined woman, his mother.

Not only family but friends emerge from these pages. George Pierce Baker of 47 Workshop at Harvard, who encouraged Wolfe, according to the letter, to devote his life to the drama, but "never told me by what means I could live." Maxwell E. Perkins of Scribners, who sweat blood over the revisions of Wolfe's immense manuscripts. Mr. Terry himself, editor of these letters and actually a good friend of Wolfe, even tho [sic] Tom wrote to Mama in a moment of anger: "I think the greatest disappointment . . . has been the conduct of John Terry."

All told, this volume is a gargantuan primer to Thomas Wolfe. A primer, because Wolfe here sets himself down in simple terms, with few of the mannerisms which individualized his novels. A primer also, because only his most evident characteristics are fully recorded. And, for a primer, gargantuan, because Mr. Terry has chosen to print every surviving word which Wolfe wrote to his mother, including telegrams . . . scribblings on post cards . . . repetitious passages in which the son forgets that he has already told mother all this, and a mass of trivia, significant only to a reverent biographer. Having faithfully placed these letters on public record, Mr. Terry will be left free, one hopes, to winnow out all the chaff from his forthcoming biography of Wolfe, and to offer nothing except sound grain.

John Selby. "Wolfe's Letters Reveal A Background of Genius." New Orleans *Times-Picayune*, May 9, 1943, p. 9, Section II.

It is without doubt sacrilege, but it is true that I was much more affected by "Thomas Wolfe's Letters to His Mother" than by anything else Wolfe ever wrote. The volume begins with a note about grammar school grades, and ends with a postcard from Vancouver, and a postscript by Julia Elizabeth Wolfe, his mother. In between, there is the record of a young man's ripening, and of the departments of his life in which he did not ripen.

Altogether, it is not a pretty record. Wolfe was too much the typical stage genius to be all-winning, although he had at every period of his life the ability to convince people of his worth, and to get things from them. What is affecting is his complete belief in his own genius, and the ways in which he worked to justify the belief. It is a little silly to find him moaning because a light teaching schedule at New York university interfered with his "creative powers," when you think of the conditions under which dozens of greater writers have done their job. But Wolfe did keep working, in spite of all his talk, and that is the important thing.

The letters back to Asheville begin (for practical purposes) in Chapel Hill, N.C., and it is a shame that there are not more from that village, since anybody who has talked with "Proff" Koch of the Playmakers, or any one of half a dozen other men, cannot doubt that the boy made an impression on the village and the University of North Carolina. But the fury of letter-writing did not really descend until Wolfe was in Harvard.

Then New York, then Europe, then the Wolfe that most interested persons know best—the determined writer scribbling on scarred tables, refrigerators, whatnot. Wolfe thought he was a playwright, and he turned out to be a novelist. He took money year after year from his mother, and did not hesitate to take favors of all sorts from acquaintances as well as friends. He was sure he was a genius, and repeatedly says so. His letters explain him fully—his lack of discipline, his rushing, tumbling style, his pitiful egotism, his headstrong manner, even his genius.

Harry Lee. Atlanta *Journal*, May 23, 1943, p. 17 (Magazine).

Those who found in Thomas Wolfe a great spirit of the somewhat frantic interlude between two world wars will discover through this book that gathers together his letters to his mother a different view of the raw and naked loneliness of his genius. It is the same Tom Wolfe who speaks, though his material here is the events of his everyday living. The passion, the hunger, the lost seeking are the same. And since the fabric of his living and his writing were inextricably interwoven for him, the people, too, are the same, Eliza, Ben, Foxhall Morton Edwards, wearing here for the first time the names by which Wolfe knew them in actuality.

Such a collection of personal writing

never intended for public view, is interesting for a number of reasons. The letters reveal for one thing that peculiar adaptive process by which a man aware of his own talent nevertheless learns that he must deal with the world on its terms in many things. The letters home asking for money, the recurrent apologizing for the expense to which he puts his family, the assurances that he will try to do better, the accounting for small expenditures, reveal complete sacrifice of any thought that his talent gave him right to an easiness of living that did not belong to any other man. The references to writing, the mention of the constant fatigue, the long hours, the intense struggle to state fully, indicate, too, the nature of the privilege which he desired to exercise at whatever cost.

But there is another revelation perhaps more interesting than these. The reader becomes aware of the transfiguring nature of the love which Wolfe bore life. A comparison between the picture of the people whom he knew, and with whom he lived in actuality, with the characters of fiction that appeared in his novels reflects upon the man responsible for the transmutation. As they appear in his books they are immeasurably greater for his touch. The greed, the fixed opinions of ignorance, the egotism of mediocrity, are not subtracted, but seen as insignificant. The base elements are fired by a magnificent faith in the essential importance of something beneath and beyond them. But the faith was Wolfe's.

. . .

Lillian Walker. "Unposed Self-Portrait of Wolfe." Nashville *Banner*, May 26, 1943, p. 14.

For years Thomas Wolfe's mother has been one of the most talked of women in literary America. Lorgnetted ladies and Oedipused gentlemen would say, "Thomas Wolfe is a great writer all right, but I don't see how he could write that way about his own mother." What they mean, dear reader, in case you have not read any of Thomas Wolfe's novels is that the character, Eliza Gant, the mother in "Look Homeward, Angel" is so real and convincing that people immediately jump to the conclusion that she could be no other than the author's own mother.

Countless gossiping and embryonic legends mushroomed up (the poison kind) concerning Wolfe and a sort of Paul Gauguinesque relation to his family and his native Asheville, N.C. Wolfe himself quashed much of this popular, superficial conclusion-jumping with the publication of his "Story of a Novel." This essay explains the sources of a writer's material and the subsequent process of the writer's creative imagination upon the material to make it into a story. Like the chemical processes upon wood and air to make rayon, or lithium and hydrogen into helium.

After all, people are burning with curiosity about Thomas Wolfe and they fall into a sort of, "Ah, did you once see Shelley plain" attitude upon meeting someone who knew this great writer when he was living. (I should have said

Browning with curiosity instead of burning.) These letters to his mother are a perfect self-portrait of Thomas Wolfe. Unposed and not written with any thought of being exhibited to the public eye, they are as valuable [an] insight to the man as are the self-portraits of Rembrandt or Reubens. They form one of the most revealing documents published in many years.

. . .

Thomas Wolfe often apologizes for not putting more time and effort into writing his mother, explaining all his writing energy went into "little patterns of words on paper." In spite of his effort at economy, the writing instinct gets the better of him once he gets pen in hand. He lets himself go in describing his travels and opinions of the peoples in the lands of England, France, Germany and Italy. In these passages his driving, pulsating style swings into the rhythm familiar to his readers. There is the impetus of the singer with every phrase—the vibrato of the violinist on every word. Besides people and places he tells of his own progress at writing—especially during the years of the Harvard play-writing class—and of almost but not quite getting a play produced. Which of course now ripens the time for one of them to have a posthumous production on Broadway.

The lawsuits with the erratic literary agent, the misunderstandings about his book, his love of people and zest for living could all be fashioned into a marvelous new play. When one thinks of the numerous biographies bound to appear as his genius is more and more recognized, there are prospects for a sort of "Thomas Wolfe business"—comparable to the "Shakespeare's in-dustry" or "Browningiana." One other thing the letters do: The maligned Eliza or overtones of Mrs. Wolfe whichever way you take it are forever vindicated. Like the verse by Alline Kilmer wherein Queen Elizabeth is redeemed for her bloody deeds—because she gave Shakespeare gold, Thomas Wolfe frequently wrote for, received and thanked his mother for hundreds of dollars for his education, travels and freedom in which to write—for many years beyond the free, white and twenty-one maturity state.

. . .

Thomas Sugrue. "Thomas Wolfe Looks Homeward." *Saturday Review,* 26 (May 29, 1943), 17.

These letters will make your heart ache; yet they tell a tale which is not new, which has a hackneyed plot, and which, in this instance, had a fairly happy ending. It is the old story of a creative imagination born into the brain of an apparently average child in a middle-class family. When the creative imagination began to express itself, truculent misunderstanding rose to bar the path. From then on it was Thomas Wolfe against the world, with only his mother standing firmly by.

It is typical of America, where everyone has to make his own way and be proud as Lucifer about accepting help from anyone, that many people feel that Wolfe should not have taken money from his mother for his education at Harvard, and at odd times thereafter.

This attitude also reflects a misunderstanding of the relationship between mother and son. Tom was the last and therefore the favorite child. He was not weaned until he was three and a half years old. He was petted and adored by the older children. His mother early recognized his gigantic ambitions, and was his ally in the attempt to achieve them. The money she sent him never took the bread from her mouth. She could afford to go to Florida every winter, and to dabble in real estate. Her preoccupation with poverty rose from a naturally frugal nature and the chronic "poor mouth" which seems to afflict the whole South as a result of the Civil War. Wolfe was constantly and sincerely apologetic about the money he received from home; he obviously didn't waste it; and he obviously didn't get any too much. As soon as he made a little himself he offfered it to his mother and his family. In the end he gave them, through his achievements, more than they could possibly have given him, ever.

Wolfe's central problem was that which confronts every man in a material world who finds himself with an artistic talent. Should he sacrifice those early, vigorous years, when he could be accomplishing so much in a trade or profession, to the development of an ability which in the end might turn out to be mediocre—or, what is even worse, be so great that it could not earn him a living? Wolfe was convinced that the sacrifice was worthwhile, but he lived in the agonizing consciousness that no one else did, and that even his mother was sticking by him more through love than conviction. Yet love, he found, was better than conviction, for when Professor Baker, of Harvard, insisted that the boy stay away from

teaching and devote himself to writing, he was lofty and silent about how the six-foot seven-inch body was to be fed during the period between effort and success. Mrs. Wolfe never talked platitudes. She sent the money.

The letters are an excellent record of Wolfe's discovery, development, and expression of his talent. It is amazing that he did all of his fiction writing in so brief a period of years—ten in all. Had he chosen to earn his living primarily, and write when he could, it would have taken him at least twenty years to produce the same amount of work. Since he was to die at thirty-eight it is better that he chose to crowd himself. If he had to depend somewhat on family, friends, and acquaintances during that time, it was to no more an extent than do dipsomaniacs, paranoids, hypochondriacs, and black sheep in general. These give nothing in return. Wolfe gave the friendship of a rich personality, and an opportunity— as it turned out—to be partially responsible for some fine writing.

The Thomas Wolfe who emerges from these letters is a man frantically concerned with the urge to write, consumed with the fire of literary creation, eager for "a hundred hands" to set down all he sees, thinks, and feels. He loves people, but, being an artist, he has to learn to live by himself, nourishing solitude because in its soil alone can his talent grow and express itself. So he turns back on his memories of gregariousness, to his childhood, to his family, to his home town of Asheville, North Carolina. No artist, however skilled, is as good an observer as a child, and to his childhood Wolfe went for the material he needed. The letters express his preoccupation with his early years, and with the consciousness that they were slipping away from him in time. He hates time, he fights it constantly, aware that it is carrying him back to the black womb of death from which he so shortly emerged.

. . .

Later, when "Look Homeward, Angel" had appeared, he settled to his task with some hope, but as words poured from him by the hundred thousand he began to tire, and realized that even his great strength was unequal to the task he had set for himself.

. . .

. . . Mrs. Wolfe is like her son in many ways, and the traits which she gave to him in positive form have, it seems, remained with her in a negative, reflective way. It is no wonder that the two were devoted to each other, and that these letters were written with such affection and preserved with such devotion.

R. M. Kain. "Thomas Wolfe Unbosoms Himself to Mother." Louisville *Courier Journal,* May 30, 1943, p. 9, Section 3.

For the last fifteen years the public has been absorbed by the legend of Thomas Wolfe. In his voluminous manuscripts, printed in over four thousand pages, it has read with interest and sympathy his epic of the young American artist.

In reading these informal letters to his mother one feels more intimately,

if less intensely, the emotional richness of the man. One follows his quest for fame, suffers with him the anxieties and disappointments of his carreer, feels the amazing vitality, ambition, and enthusiasm which were his.

Here, too, are the germs of Wolfe's major themes—his sense of the web of the past, his physical feeling for time, his contempt for American commercialism, his mystical response to the spirit of America. The reader feels himself on the very threshold of the creative process as he sees these themes unfold in the author's imagination.

To the student of Wolfe the most valuable feature of this collection will be the light it throws upon the mother-son relationship. For the Eliza Gant whom Wolfe excoriated for her parsimony and lack of spiritual depth in "Look Homeward, Angel," is none other than the recipient of these letters, the author's mother. The restraint with which the writer confides his dreams of literary creation to an uncomprehending admirer, the pathetic pleas for understanding, the half-veiled contempt of his wishes for her business success—these form an interesting sidelight on Wolfe's character.

As the author finds himself his letters become increasingly impersonal. Consequently the most revealing of the letters are those written before the publication of his first book, 1929.

The volume is attractively presented by an intimate friend of the author. The introduction gives revealing character sketches of Wolfe and his mother, together with a valuable transcript of the mother's colloquial style of reminiscence. Those who recall Wolfe's novelette, "The Web of Earth," will note the success with which the author reproduces the character and mental outlook of the mother. And, incidentally, it is probably not accidental that the one work of fiction which the author discusses freely with his mother is this sketch, where she plays such a key role.

Henry Miller. "Mother and Son." *Nation,* 156 (June 5, 1943), 811.

The letters of a genius are always interesting even when they are dull, and these letters of Wolfe, like his books, are dull. Every other letter seems to be about money and how it gets that way. And when finally money does begin to flow his way, then come the lawsuits. Poor Wolfe discovers that even a halfwit has the right, in a democracy, to sue you, bleed you, though he hasn't a leg to stand on. In the course of a short life Wolfe seems to have discovered many things which the ordinary schoolboy knows instinctively. One of the most amusing statements is the one concerning Professor Baker of Harvard. "I think he's bitterly disappointed because I began teaching, but he never told me by what means I could live." Aye, there's the rub. And there is something pathetic about the inability of editors and publishers, in a land that worships money, power, fame, and success, to keep alive a man of genius whose needs are few. To receive $250 for something like 30,000 words is the sort of encouragement which makes a writer wonder if he wouldn't be better off digging ditches or robbing banks.

There is also something amusing and pathetic about the valiant and, to my mind, misguided efforts of the good Max Perkins to whip the amorphous volume of Wolfe's writings into some acceptable form. The only book of Wolfe's I could ever finish was the little volume called "The Story of a Novel." I was violently moved by this account and convinced, moreover, that a crime had been committed against Wolfe by the very man who tried to help him. It is quite possible, to be sure, that without editorial assistance Wolfe might never have brought any of his books to a conclusion. But would that have mattered? Just as his mother tried to keep him a child, so his publishers tried to keep him readable. A child who is weaned at the age of three and a half is never weaned; a boy who is kept in curls until he is a young man never becomes a young man; a giant who sleeps with his mother until it is time to find a mate never finds a mate. And a young genius who begins like a Niagara can never be made into an acceptable wooden novelist such as publishers are constantly looking for. Left to his own resources, encouraged to do as he pleased, Thomas Wolfe might have committed suicide at an early age, leaving to posterity a grandiose unfinished opus which would have been the pride of American letters.

The saddest thing about Wolfe is the feeling he gives of being alone in the world. And though he was always tied to his mother by the umbilical cord, he gives the impression frequently that he had been abandoned even by her. In trying to tell her what his first novel is about, he writes: "It says that we are born alone—all of us who ever lived or will live—that we live alone, and die alone, and that we are strangers to one another, and never come to know one another." Quite naturally this feeling was accompanied by a mania to devour the world; it was the only means left him to connect with the world. Instead of incorporating the world, however, he dies of glut. In this he reminds one of Balzac. The pattern of his life is that of the treadmill. He becomes a victim of work. No death, no phoenix rising from the ashes. Just a huge machine waging a hopeless battle with time.

His malady was gigantism, in all its manifestations. His tentacles spread everywhere, but they never light upon the golden shears which will liberate him and give him atonement. He is a river with a blind mouth, a moving panorama which erases itself with every turn of the bend. He will remember everything from the day he was born, and record it with the exactitude of a physicist, but though he labor like a fiend he will never succeed in laying the cornerstone of the temple he longs to inhabit. He remains the infant Gargantua, stumbling through the world nursery and scattering débris everywhere. An utterly humorless prodigy to boot. Alone, misshapen, misunderstood. A misfit. A giant for whom a toothache assumes the proportions of a tragedy: something to write home about, something to wrest a tear from that monument to real estate who could have been a writer too—if she had had the training.

His admirers are right in regarding him as a genuine American. He had all their faults and all their virtues. "I could never be anything but American if I tried," he writes. Yet again and again he expresses his disgust with "the huge, loud, noisy madhouse" that America is. And then, like all genuine Americans, he can add: "We have it in us to be a really great people, I think, whenever we find what is sometimes called a soul." In this utterance we have an intimation of the real tragedy which confronts every great American artist. For, until that soul emerges, how are we ever going to stop killing off our creative spirits? What place is there for a poet in a garden where automobile parts are at a premium? With Wolfe's death we are left with at most two or three writers of unmistakable genius. The others are the successful writers whom the mothers worship.

Ernest Kirschten. "Letters of Thomas Wolfe: A Portrait of His Mother." St. Louis *Post Dispatch,* June 8, 1943, p. 2B (Part II).

Thomas Wolfe put the purple patch on that fertile period of American writing which began with the end of the last war, but he also produced one of the finest of all American novels in "Look Homeward, Angel." Those who have read it, and the other long novels which followed it, may well feel that what there is to know about Thomas Wolfe they know.

Perhaps they are right, but they had better dip into the letters which he was always writing to his mother, a woman with much of the same gusto that he displayed, if only on the theory that there can never—well, hardly ever—be too much of a good thing.

The Mrs. Wolfe who is indirectly reflected in these letters—and very directly presented in the fine introduction by her son's friend, John S. Terry—is a wonderful character. She had the same faith in her son that he had in himself, and her confidence enabled him to justify his own.

. . .

But there are wonderfully full years recorded between those two brief little messages, wide-ranging, fruitful years. There was the teaching which he did not like, but there were also good understanding friends like Aline Bernstein. And there was always writing.

The letters—and all the postcards and the birthday messages, the requests for bits of family lore which escaped his colossal memory—they are all very natural, all a little hasty, a little incomplete. It would be hard to pick out a single one and say that here is something profound, something original, something wonderful. But out of the sum total of them comes a new light on a great writer.

Charles Lee Snyder. "Thomas Wolfe." *Yale Review*, 33 (Winter 1944), 373–374.

Thomas Wolfe wrote novels of uncommon power; hence these letters of his are documents of uncommon interest. No writer of genius, one is tempted to say, has ever left a more intimate and eloquent account of his hopes and fears, toils and aspirations, than these letters contain. The book, too, is enriched by a charming introduction by John Terry. Mr. Terry, who is now writing the life of his old friend, gives a vivid portrait of Wolfe in his New York days, and also a vivid portrait of Wolfe's mother. Into this part of the book he has fitted also some interesting

reminiscences by the mother—parts of a longer story recorded on the dictaphone.

. . .

Six feet, seven inches tall, "earthy, sensuous," he could eat enough for two men, drink (beer) enough for three men, and laugh with the gusto of half a dozen. But fundamentally Wolfe was as serious as a Fundamentalist elder. An illness in his twentieth year, which for a time he feared might prove fatal, had burned into his consciousness the fact that time is fleeting, and filled him with determination to express himself to the last ounce. "His plans and dreams," says Mr. Terry, "were actually those of a superman." He was passionately determined to encompass all living experience in a series of great novels.

As a child, Wolfe was precocious; as a boy in Asheville he seems to have been the very counterpart of his Eugene Gant of Altamont. At the University of North Carolina, under Koch, Greenlaw, and Horace Williams, he found a sort of intellectual Arcadia, and blossomed out into a sort of literary phenomenon. During his years at Harvard, under Professor George P. Baker, he showed great promise of becoming a dramatist, and almost succeeded in selling a play for New York production. In his twenty-fourth year, being obliged to earn his living, he accepted a teaching job at New York University, and two years later began "Look Homeward, Angel." An extraordinary first novel, it brought him financial support, and a goodly measure of fame, before he was thirty. His second novel, "Of Time and the River," fulfilled the promise of his first, and before his untimely death, at thiry-seven, he had already achieved for himself a permanent place in American literature. His life offers an attractive subject for a classic biography, and one hopes that Mr. Terry will do it full and signal justice.

Checklist of Additional Reviews

Lorine Pruette. "Self Portrait of a Giant Artist." New York *Herald Tribune Weekly Book Review*, May 2, 1943, p. 4.

Thomas Lyle Collins. "Letters Tom Wolfe Sent Home." New York *Times Book Review*, May 2, 1943, p. 6.

Emanuel Slotnick. "Tom Wolfe's Letters Home." Springfield *Republican*, May 2, 1943, p. E7.

Lewis Gannett. "Books and Things." New York *Herald Tribune*, May 3, 1943.

Clayton Hoagland. New York *Sun*, May 3, 1943.

John Chamberlain. New York *Times*, May 8, 1943, p. 13.

New Yorker, May 8, 1943.

R. E. M. "The Private Life of Thomas Wolfe." Atlanta *Constitution*, May 9, 1943, p. 5D.

Katherine de M. Hoskins. "Way Of The Artist." Washington *Post*, May 9, 1943, p. 5L.

"Of Time and Thomas Wolfe." *Newsweek*, May 10, 1943, p. 80.

"Mother and Son." *Time*, 41 (May 10, 1943), 100, 102.

Kansas City *Star*, May 15, 1943.

Cuthbert Wright. *Commonweal*, 38 (May 21, 1943), 127-128.

A Stone, A Leaf, A Door

POEMS

BY THOMAS WOLFE

Selected and Arranged in Verse by

JOHN S. BARNES

With a Foreword by
LOUIS UNTERMEYER

New York

CHARLES SCRIBNER'S SONS

A Stone, a Leaf, a Door: Poems by Thomas Wolfe

William Rose Benét. *Book-of-the-Month Club News,* September 1945, p. 19.

The late Thomas Wolfe was a major writer. When a major writer dies, the executors usually gather up the New Testamentary twelve baskets of the fragments left from the nutriment he has provided for his nation and the world. Much of Thomas Wolfe's prose was poetry, or rhetoric. He had in him the rhythm of life itself. He was first of all a poet. He was impatient of form, and had he written always in free verse, I suppose he would have been a new kind of Whitman. He could never have stood the restrictions of rhyme and metre. Here, in unrhymed cadence, in slow rhythm and rapid, in brooding and meditation, in sorrow and anger, is some of the poetry he left behind. All the lines are not good, much of the poetry is not great; but it is assuredly poetry, because it is living rhythm and conveys Man's eternal dream. The phraseology is not always memorable. There is repetition, there are discords not intended, sour notes, stumblings. But there is also a great deal of poetry, explicit or implicit, in these rolling lines. I shall remember certain things in the verses a long time: the locomotive, the bird songs at dawn, the poems on Brooklyn and New York and America, the American who is lonely in Europe and in England. Here is a burning phrase concerning spring, here are clear vignettes of the South, the sounds of ships in harbor, the epic of rivers, words of men and women overheard, carrying the horror and the pathos of Man. I think that this book is worthy to stand beside Thomas Wolfe's prose, and should interest all who have been amazed by that young Samson among American writers, who burst every bond of discipline, yet whose sheer native genius prevailed mightily—as Christopher Marlowe's mighty line prevailed in the time of the Elizabethans, though he was assuredly no Shakespeare.

E. C. Kiessling. "Turning Prose of Thomas Wolfe Into Fine Poetry." Milwaukee *Journal,* September 16, 1945, p. V, 3.

This is perhaps the first time in literary history that parts of an author's work originally published in prose are offered to the public a second time in the form of poetry. Sgt. J. S. Barnes, in going through the seven long novels of Thomas Wolfe, was struck by the number of lyrical passages they contained. Choosing a representative number, he turned them into poems merely by respacing their lines. The results, presented in this volume—to quote Louis Untermeyer—"restore Wolfe to the company from which he fearfully excluded himself and to which he rightfully belongs."

Thomas Wolfe was not of course the first author who was essentially a poet but elected to write in prose. Many of the famous stylists of previous centuries used a language that lay in the borderland between prose and verse. Their sonorous paragraphs can be transformed into staves of exquisite poetry as easily as Wolfe's. It is these authors, incidentally, that Wolfe resembles most in theme as well as in manner.

His magnificent outpouring entitled "Death, Loneliness and Sleep" is reminiscent—and not unworthy—of Sir Thomas Browne's "Urn Burial" or the final chapter of Ecclesiates or Browning's noble apostrophes to death. . . .

Wolfe's soliloquy on the four ages of man, "This Is Man," is as melancholy as that of Jacques' on man's supposed seven ages. . . .

Most of the poems reflect Wolfe's romantic, tempestuous soul—his double strain of doubt and affirmation of world weariness and zest for living. Only two or three of them are realistic character portraits, only one, "Plum Tree," is a nature lyric. Yet few books of verse in recent years can match these poems of Thomas Wolfe in range and power.

Paul Jordan-Smith. Los Angeles *Times,* September 30, 1945, Part III, p. 4.

Most of Thomas Wolfe's readers felt that he was a poet, but it remained for John S. Barnes to arrange some of his finest passages in verse form and thus prove to the eye what the ear knew. His selection bears the title "A Stone, a Leaf, a Door," and the volume holds a foreword by Louis Untermeyer. Untermeyer anticipates the objection that some may make, calling this a typographical trick; but, he writes: "the rearrangement is neither arbitrary nor whimsical; it is implicit in Wolfe's language, logical in the rise and fall of the sentences, in the ebb and flow which reflect the tidal emotions. In no prose and only in a small body of verse has there been expressed a greater sense of American life: its range and richness, its vast pride and intemperate gusto." To which we give a hearty "amen!"

Alfred Kreymborg. "Thomas Wolfe, Poet." *Saturday Review of Literature*, 28 (November 3, 1945), 32.

The experiment made by John S. Barnes in going over the novels of Thomas Wolfe for the purpose of selecting and arranging passages in cadenced verse is one that could not have been made with the average American novelist. The success of Sergeant Barnes in his field raises the question: Who are some of the other authors of fiction whose writings are inherently poetic? One thinks immediately of Hawthorne and Melville, of Sherwood Anderson, and in our day of Hemingway and Katherine Anne Porter. Each of these masters of the art of literature has revealed a deeply personal nature whose intensity of expression ranges life on a lyrical or dramatic scale and whose particular ritual found its form in poetic prose.

It is possible to read and enjoy "A Stone, A Leaf, A Door" as a book of poems and to disregard the novels from which they were drawn. Here, from beginning to end, one is confronted by an impassioned youth imprisoned in flesh and spirit seeking escape from personal exile and ranging from the womb to the grave in a rhapsodic state of despair and exultation. The book is a theme with variations, and the theme is the author himself seizing on natural images to symbolize his embattled existence and destiny. At times he sounds like one of the Hebrew mystics:

Which of us has known his brother?
Which of us has looked into his father's heart?

Which of us has not remained forever prison-pent?
Which of us is not forever a stranger and alone?

And he seeks "the great forgotten language,"

The lost lane-end into heaven,
A stone, a leaf, an unfound door.

While the book is primarily concerned with time and eternity and there is hardly any reference to specific events, the above lines are prophetic of the dilemmas of mankind in a second post-war world. The loneliness of Wolfe in a state of perpetual auto-intoxication belongs to an age when individualism and isolation were paramount. In a sense, the poet inherited the mood of the first post-war world which gave rise to Gertrude Stein's "lost generation." And yet, in reaching out from an inner to an outer self, or to a personal universe, he was never guilty of the petty disdain and cynicism of most of his fellows. His vision of an age in decline was larger and more heroic than theirs and reminds one of Ecclesiastes in the lines:

The laurel, the lizard and the stone
Will come no more.
The women weeping at the gate are gone,
And will not come again.
And pain and pride and death will pass,
And will not come again.

The poems are generally composed in broad running lines which remind us of Whitman as well, and of Hart Crane and his belief in rivers, bridges, and the sea. And Wolfe, in the midst of his tumult and rhapsodic vein, was capable of carving an image in the manner of the supposedly out-dated Imagists:

And who shall say—
Whatever disenchantment follows—

That we can ever forget magic,
Or that we can ever betray,
On this leaden earth,
The apple-tree, the singing,
And the gold?

In one of his many unrhymed odes, Thomas Wolfe, after arraigning mankind for its bestiality and destructiveness, concludes that "it is impossible to scorn this creature."

For out of his strong belief in life,
This puny man made love.

The poet shares with Whitman, Crane, and Stephen Vincent Benét a faith in America in the face of every evil our land or its misleaders have committed. Wolfe died in his fortieth year and remained youthful and visionary to the end. But there are mature as well as youthful questions in "Where Are We to Seek?," a remarkably pregnant poem for which not alone America, but the family of nations in consultation, must find the earliest answer.

The years flow by like water,
And one day it is spring again.
Shall we ever ride out of the gates of the
East again,
As we did once at morning,
And seek again, as we did then,
New lands, the promise of the war,
And glory, joy, and triumph.
And a shining city?

O youth, still wounded,
Living, feeling with a woe unutterable,
Still grieving with a grief intolerable,
Still thirsting with a thirst unquench-
able—
Where are we to seek?

For the wild tempest breaks above us,
The wild fury beats about us,
The wild hunger feeds upon us—
And we are houseless, doorless, unas-
suaged,
And driven on forever;
And our brains are mad,
Our hearts are wild and wordless,
And we cannot speak.

John Holmes. "Awareness of Life, Love and Cruelty." Boston *Herald,* November 26, 1945, p. 12

Thomas Wolfe is to the present younger generation what Hemingway was 15 years ago, but Hemingway could never be presented as a poet. Wolfe was a latter-day Whitman, full of gusto, energy, and the love of all life. It was inevitable that much of his writing should beat itself into the rhythms of poetry. Wolfe had the feelings of a poet, and in fact had always wanted to be a poet. His newest critical editor, Sgt. John S. Barnes, has shown by his excellent selection and arrangement, in this book, that Wolfe never let the poet in him die, but gave him voice and space in many dimensions and at many times in all his novels.

The passages Mr. Barnes has chosen exhibit his own sensitivity for mood and scene, for image and rhythm, at the same time that they reveal the deep, the powerful, the troubled feelings out of which Wolfe's writings came. We find here the whole range of awareness of life, "ecstasy and disillusion, love and cruelty, and the wanderings and passions of the human spirit," as Louis Untermeyer says in his brief introduction.

Louis Untermeyer. "New Books in Review." *Yale Review,* 35 (Winter 1946), 337-38.

. . .

Having written the introduction to Thomas Wolfe's "A Stone, A Leaf, A Door," the present reviewer disqualifies himself from reappraising it. It can be stated, however, that the rearrangement of prose lines into roughly rhythmical ones—an arrangement that is both daring and logical—imposes a new order and a clean [sic] pattern upon Wolfe's long plunging paragraphs. There are superficial resemblances to Whitman and Melville, and some of the more hortatory passages recall the Old Testament, but the vision as well as the vigor of these meditations and rhapsodies comes through with fresh strength. Such pages prove that Wolfe was what he always desired to be but, because of his medium, feared he never could become: a resolute and representative poet.

. . .

Checklist of Additional Reviews

Sterling North. New York *Post,* September 20, 1945.

———. *Book Week,* September 23, 1945, p. 2.

Margaret Shafer. Nashville *Tennessean,* Sunday, September 23, 1945, p. 7C.

Susan Quinn. Column "Off the Bookshelves." Richmond *Times-Dispatch,* September 23, 1945, p. D5.

Atlanta *Journal,* September 30, 1945.

Robert Hillyer. "Prose-Poems from Thomas Wolfe." New York *Times Book Review,* September 30, 1945, pp. 7, 22.

Time, (October 1, 1945).

Hartford *Courant,* October 21, 1945, Magazine, p. 12.

"Thomas Wolfe's Prose as Poetry." Philadelphia *Inquirer,* December 2, 1945.

St. Louis *Globe Democrat,* December 9, 1945.

Horace Gregory. "Did Thomas Wolfe Pen Poetry or Prose?" New York *Herald Tribune Weekly Book Reviews,* January 13, 1946, p. 5.

MANNERHOUSE

A Play

in a Prologue and Three Acts

by

Thomas Wolfe

NEW YORK

HARPER & BROTHERS PUBLISHERS

1948

Mannerhouse

Guy Savino. "Flowering Talent." Newark *News,* November 11, 1948.

Thomas Wolfe wrote the first act of "Mannerhouse" when he was 19. A year later he wrote to his mother that George Pierce Baker, the great Harvard drama teacher, was "especially anxious" for him to finish the play, which was "the play of the decayed Southern aristocracy; it has never been adequately dealt with."

. . .

And so, Eugene, the young protagonist of the story, who, in his creator's 19th year would have walked firmly away from the decaying house instead, because the author has turned a weary 25, returns and seeks tragically to identify himself again with the era that has passed.

Besides shedding a bit more light on the tempestuous changes through which Thomas Wolfe's philosophy passed, "Mannerhouse" is interesting from other points of view. It is not great drama. It is not even successful writing. But it is a fascinating picture of a major American talent beginning to show the first compelling traces of its ultimate flowering.

John Mebane. "Buds of Wolfe's Genius Found in 'Mannerhouse.'" Atlanta *Journal,* November 28, 1948, p. 16D.

The first love of Thomas Wolfe—and he was a man of many loves and was tormented by them all—was the theater. . . .

"Mannerhouse" is one of the three plays Tom Wolfe wrote—plays for which in his youth he tried to find a producer, and failed. It probably was written in 1926, three years before the publication of "Look Homeward, Angel" thrust him almost ruthlessly, a bewildered and groping young man, before a nation of astonished critics. The play was first produced this fall by New Stages in New York City.

In this play, a prologue and three acts, one encounters those same influences which shaped the later work of one of the most creative and tireless minds of this generation. Here, too, one finds the legend that he encounters in all the later work of Wolfe—that of man's loneliness in his youth.

. . .

One finds in "Mannerhouse" evidences of immaturity. But one finds here also the buds which were later to flower into the genius of Thomas Wolfe. One finds Wolfe's thesis that though evil exists, it can be battled and beaten down. In spite of its faults, there is much in this play that is moving and stimulating. No admirer of the vast talent of Thomas Wolfe would want to miss reading it.

Anna C. Hunter. Savannah *News,* November 29, 1948, p. 24.

Appearance of a work by Thomas Wolfe unpublished during his lifetime is an event in literary annals and though the play, *Mannerhouse* has been produced in New York, the publication in book form of this drama in a prologue and three acts will be welcomed by a wide audience.

The sheer beauty of Wolfe's prose would be enough to gratify the discriminating, but as is usual with this great American writer there are tremendous currents surging through the play, which though written probably in 1926 throws a searching light on Wolfe's philosophy. The drama deals with the South and its war period, yet the content of the book, as eloquent as it is on the South's tragic era, goes beyond a period or even a people. It is an epic of man and his search for an abiding faith, it is humanity against humanity in its eternal conflict of values.

The theme deals with a Southern home and a way of life and develops a contrast between fixed values and enduring ones impregnable against the march of time. There is little action yet enormous tension. The prologue sets a majestic rhythm, picturing the movement to and fro of black slaves and strikes the note of combined fierceness and gentleness echoed throughout. Here is being built the house, a symbol of many things—of security of man's hope and faith, even perhaps of the South itself. Here is the traditional gentlemen of Manner House, the embodiment of the ruling class, a man whose head is "carried fiercely and swiftly and beautifully above his straight body . . . there is nothing which is not carried gauntly and magnificently."

In the final act, almost an epilogue, the man is dying and the house which was to have been indestructible, being dismantled. Only valiance is left. Eugene, the son, unlike his father, has no world of set values. He is more aged than his father with his sardonic humor covering a great tenderness, his soul racked by love for his father and his inheritance on the one hand and his awareness of the greater issues at stake on the other. He is at once bound and alienated by a wisdom which transcends values as his generation knows them.

The prose is sheer poetry the theme mounting in anguish like a great psalm. Here is Wolfe in his youth, yet there is much that is redolent of his later years.

The stage directions are little gems in themselves, beautifully and scrupulously set forth. The very drop of the water from the roof of the house as decay sets in is vastly impressive.

There is a universality in the theme of the drama which is peculiarly adaptable to events as they are in the world today, the issues, though placed in the

South being dealt with on a general scale.

Harold Clurman. "Wolfe Looks Homeward in His Only Play." New York *Star*, December 5, 1948.

When I first heard that in 1926, when he was 26 years old, Thomas Wolfe had written a play which someone planned to produce on Broadway this season, the theater blood in me began to boil with excitement. When I read the play in manuscript the usual managerial doubts assailed me: Tom Wolfe was not a playwright—the play's chief interest would be philological—it had little chance of success.

Reading the published play has altered my perspective. There is nothing in the play that I cannot find fault with; yet I discover myself strongly attracted to it. It is not a "good play," it is not a work of special literary significance, but it is unmistakably Tom Wolfe—and that is enough to make me regard it with affection, and even to regret that we have no theater where some dear damn fool might try to grapple with it. For make no mistake about it: this adolescent, confused, awkward, sometimes even absurd essay in dramatic writing is many times more alive and more provocative than two or three current Broadway successes I could name.

Tom Wolfe was no "professional": he wrote from passion. There are few playwrights today of whom this may be said. Wolfe moreover was impassioned about vital matters. His work aspires toward a universality of thought and a fullness of statement that is characteristic of the great dramatic poets who are forever bent on the interpretation and making of myths. Wolfe used his subjective experience and his environment as the material from which he helped to wrench great chunks of meaning. That he often failed—because for one thing he was hardly mature—only partly diminishes the validity of his work. He mined for essential ore, and, crude though many of his findings were, they contained much precious metal.

Wolfe believed his play *Mannerhouse* to be a defense of ancient Southern valiance. His hero fights for the men of the South even though his reason rejects their cause. Actually, the play proves Wolfe a rebel unwilling to be made captive by them. Thus, *Mannerhouse* reveals a fascinating psychological duality: the young poet (Wolfe) ready to break with his basic attachment to the soil that nourished him and the faith that once sustained him, feels the need to pay tortured tribute to them before embarking on his new course—the course which led to the novels he was to write shortly after.

Mannerhouse is full of echoes, from Shakespeare, the Greek dramatists and the Bible to the rhetoric of ante-bellum Southern statesmen. With this is a young and poignant eloquence that is entirely personal and altogether endearing. There are lines of dialogue in the play which merely grope, others that sound with remembered splendor, but now and again a phrase flashes with true fire or sings with the purity of great feeling.

. . .

203

Bill Bedell. "Tom Wolfe's Drama: Filling A Gap in the Over-All Picture." Houston *Post,* December 12, 1948, p. 28, Section 6.

"I tell you now that there can be no victory. There is only valiance. . . .

"We are forever beaten; we are proud, and we are forever cast down; we are forever broken by His strength, and at last we always die."

And:

"We are loyal to the destiny of ruin and death; that is the secret thing that all men know, that I have seen in all men's eyes. In that is our brotherhood. When the manner goes, then we are naked—"

In those four score words, Thomas Wolfe gave his message to the world, a message that he later expanded with endless variations into trunksful of manuscript, that inspired some of the most soaring prose-poetry extant, but which he never basically changed.

. . .

The play is not important because it says anything new but because it fills out a gap in the over-all picture of Wolfe, because it shows that long before the peak of his writing he knew what he had to say and was already struggling for a way to say it, and because it shows a tragic literary lack was already shadowing his life.

. . .

Wolfe admitted even then that for Wolfe no medium that man had em-ployed in the past would do. From then on he battled murderously with himself to achieve a form of writing adequate to his incredible imagination and his sea-bottom to mountain-top range of emotions.

He wrote the four novels, climaxed by "You Can't Go Home Again." In the last he came nearest to his goal of order, but it was not his foremost. The first, "Look Homeward, Angel," was his most disorderly and his best.

In his last he showed signs of mellowing, of believing that good was good and truth was truth, and that "divine falsehood" was the real myth. But so long as he lived the words he wrote in "Mannerhouse" in 1925 or 1926, the 80 words that open this review, remained gospel to him. And no formal pattern could contain his writing.

Novels, Wolfe called his works, but they are not novels. They are biography, with overtones of poetry, fiction, essays and pure sermonizing, a grand amalgamation of all living.

A play Wolfe called "Mannerhouse," but it is not a play. It is the chrysalis of his novels, containing in unfinished stage many of the ideas he developed later, and as such it will be a godsend to Wolfe students.

. . .

But it is not only a Civil war play. It is Thomas Wolfe's look at all war, at all love, at all men. General Ramsay could have worn a toga or a suit of mail or an Eisenhower jacket and his words would have been just as timeless and timely.

It is, however, Thomas Wolfe, and the confines of the dramatic form were too tight for him. But the seeds of later greatness are there. . . .

204

Before a word of Act 1 Wolfe has already created a picture that only Wolfe could create, that no stage could equal.

In Act 1, Eugene speaks to a cadet: "Go back to your dance, Cadet. There will be gray dawns, hereafter. Tonight you are young, and you can never die."

Later he refined these words.

Remember Laura James and Eugene Gant during their tryst in "Look Homeward, Angel":

"Their world was a singing voice again: they were young and they could never die. This would endure."

In the play the sardonic words of a sick soldier-to-be. In the novel one of the loveliest love scenes in American literature. But still sardonic.

Eugene to Margaret:

"Go away, go away, my ghost."

But in "Look Homeward, Angel," a complete about face, though still as unhappy as the first: the helpless, haunting, eternal cry:

"O lost, and by the wind grieved, ghost, come back again."

The same thoughts, some of the same words, and the same Eugene as the novels. Though "Mannerhouse" is advertised as non-biographical, the Eugene Ramsay of the play is Thomas Wolfe just as the Eugene Gant of the novels is Thomas Wolfe. Wolfe had simply not acquired the nerve or the egotism to be his own hero and instead was using his youthful dreams of what he might have been.

But this reviewer, who is proud to be one of Wolfe's deepest admirers, must not evade the true tragedy in this make-believe tragedy. That is the tragedy of Wolfe himself.

"Mannerhouse" is indisputably Shakespearean in spots. Wolfe doubtless unconsciously copied mannerisms and even words. Remember, he was hunting a road, and it is human to follow landmarks. . . .

In this comparison to Shakespeare, a comparison that has been used before, may rest the damning tragedy of Thomas Wolfe.

Shakespeare had discipline. Thomas Wolfe had none.

Had he possessed discipline, Wolfe might some day have ranked with Shakespeare among the mightiest writers of all time.

Dayton Kohler. "A Southern House And Its Downfall." Louisville *Courier-Journal*, December 12, 1948, p. 16, Section 3.

"Mannerhouse," Thomas Wolfe's full-length and unproduced play, has been the subject of so much literary gossip that it is certain to be widely read. It is, among other things, the work attributed to Eugene Gant and described with considerable detail in "Of Time and the River." Aside from its interest as an association item, however, the play can add little to Wolfe's literary reputation or personal legend. The truth of the matter is that Wolfe's imagination was, except for short flights, lyric rather than dramatic, and his play shows his inability to sustain the passage-work of action and dialogue the theater demands. The Wolfe rhetoric and the youthful agony are here, but their effect is curiously static without Wolfe himself to stand at the reader's elbow in the combined role of property man and chorus, as he did in his novels in those long passages of poetry and rhetoric which were the expression of his tremendous but private sensibility.

What he attempted in "Mannerhouse" was dramatic treatment of a Southern myth. The house of the Ramsays stands for a culture, a social order, built according to the old plan and the old values. Its disintegration begins with the Civil War; its degradation is shown by a new proprietorship of the materialistic but ambitious poor white; its collapse is symbolized when the black servant, descendant of the slaves who built the house, pulls down the sagging structure upon fallen aristocrat and grasping exploiter alike. But Wolfe's play lacks the deeper realism, personal bitterness, or social significance of William Faulkner's treatment of the same theme in his stories of the Sartorises and the Snopeses. "Mannerhouse" is a young man's literary effort owing more to sentimentality and a reading of other playwrights than to the realities of Southern life.

Frank Brookhouser. "Echo of Thomas Wolfe." Philadelphia *Inquirer*, December 19, 1948.

This is a play Thomas Wolfe wrote when he was a young man, and those who admire his work will want to read it even though it is not a very good play.

Among the unpublished manuscripts Wolfe left behind, *Mannerhouse*, the publishers say, was probably written in 1926, three years before publication of *Look Homeward, Angel*, that first novel which startled a nation with its sweep and power and eloquence.

When Mannerhouse was written, Wolfe described it in a letter as "an expression of my secret life, of my own dark faith. . . . If you would know what that faith is, distilled, my play tries to express my passionate belief in all myth, in the necessity of defending and living not for truth—but for divine falsehood."

Actually, however, the course charted by Wolfe is probably more accurately indicated in a line spoken by Eugene, one of the characters in the play:

". . . the youth of the world, under my leadership, will band together for freedom, truth, beauty, art and love, and will wage merciless war on hypocrisy, custom and tradition: for they have been tricked."

The time of *Mannerhouse* is the Civil War, the scene is a large estate in Georgia. The theme is the impact of war on one old Southern family and the collapse of a way of living.

. . .

Mannerhouse is also to some extent a tract against the emptiness and futility of war, a theme particularly popular at the time when Wolfe wrote the play. The preachment is voiced by the wild, bitter and cynical Eugene who, much like a later Eugene in Wolfe's novels, likes to shock his family and friends.

Full of sound and symbol, the tragic play has moments which are impressive.

But the truth of the matter is that the play was not Wolfe's forte. It was too confining, it cramped him, it didn't give him enough space to let himself go. Only the novel allowed Wolfe the majestic sweep and eloquence in which his greatness lay.

Elinor Hughes. "Wolfe Play Dwarfs Work of Moderns." Boston *Traveler,* December 29, 1948.

The sur[g]ing, enormous talent of the late Thomas Wolfe finds striking expression in this play, "Mannerhouse," which, for all the problems it might present, still deserves a production on our stage, for it is a work of power, eloquence and vivid imagination. Between the building 200 years ago, of a great Southern mansion and its destruction after the Civil War, the playwright paints a memorable picture of the decline and fall of a civilization built on a series of heroic conceptions of man's place in the world and doomed because its foundation was the institution of slavery.

Wolfe's prologue is stunning, and his epilogue, reminiscent of the destruction of the temple by the blind Samson, is something to read about, though it mightn't be too easy to present. "Mannerhouse," in short, tends to dwarf most modern plays as its author did his contemporaries.

Morse Allen. "Romantic 'Closet Dramas.'" Hartford *Courant,* February 20, 1949.

Closet dramas—plays written to be read rather than acted—have always been attractive to young romantic writers who possess emotions, ideals and fine language but have not yet found an effective literary form in which to present them. Drama seems to offer a solution for their problem. Its definiteness and concreteness appears to furnish a crucible which will contain their molten ore, an armature which will support the beautiful curves in which they mold their clay. But again and again drama, when used as a short-cut, has proved misleading. Shelley and Henry James, to cite only two examples, discovered in the hard way that the dramatic form is a Procrustean bed on which undramatic material is mutilated, not supported.

Thomas Wolfe and Kerr Rainsford have here written what amount to closet dramas, and neither are successful. Wolfe, indeed, never found the ideal medium in which to express himself; he was a poet and a novelist, unable to discipline himself sufficiently to write either real poetry or a real novel. He might have succeeded with Whitman's form but writing lyrics would have been as impossible as putting dolphins into goldfish bowls.

The drama demands condensation and orderly unity; like an explosive shell it must have a definite trajectory; Wolfe's genius was more like a minefield. In "Mannerhouse" he begins with a prologue dated two centuries ago, treats the beginning and the result of the Civil War, and ends with the destruction of both the Old and New South in a slam-bang catastrophe patterned after Samson's grand finale at Gaza.

A "Eugene" is, as usual with Wolfe, the distraught hero. There are effective scenes and moving passages, but they are like Leacock's Lord Ronald when he "flung himself from the room, flung himself upon his horse and rode madly off in all directions." Wolfe's ideas tend to cancel themselves out, as when in the bombastic major, he satirizes old age, but then has Eugene deliver a bitter attack on youth, concluding, "Major, there is only one thing that exceeds the stupidity of young men: that is the stupidity of old men."

. . .

Checklist of Additional Reviews

Robert W. Minton. "Thomas Wolfe Play is Revived." New York *Sun*, November 24, 1948.

Houston *Press*, November 26, 1948.

"Play By Wolfe." Cleveland *Press*, November 30, 1948.

New Yorker, December 4, 1948.

Marion Townend. Column, "Odds and Book Ends." Charlotte *Observer*, December 5, 1948.

Fanny Butcher. "Thomas Wolfe's Controversial War Drama." Chicago *Sunday Tribune*, December 5, 1948.

Thomas Quinn Curtiss. New York *Times Book Review*, December 19, 1948, p. 9.

Book Review Digest, January, 1949.

Jay Smith. "Wolfe as a Dramatist." St. Louis *Post Dispatch*, January 8, 1949.

John Woodburn. "Wolfe's Hamlet." *New Republic*, 120 (January 17, 1949), 24-25.

Walter Prichard Eaton. "A Play by Thomas Wolfe." New York *Herald Tribune Books*, January 20, 1949, p. 20.

Greensboro *News*, February 1, 1949.

George White Graice. *Theatre Arts*, 33 (March 1949), 8.

V. E. "Early Wolfe Play Shows Origins." New Orleans *Times Picayune*, April, 1949.

Yale Daily News, May 6, 1949.

W. P. Cumming. *North Carolina Historical Review*, 26 (July 1949), 368-69.

Notes

THE LETTERS OF
THOMAS
WOLFE

Collected and Edited,
with an Introduction and
Explanatory Text, by

ELIZABETH NOWELL

New York

CHARLES SCRIBNER'S SONS

The Letters of Thomas Wolfe

Unsigned. *Booklist*, 53 (October 1, 1956), 70.

Unmailed letters found in Wolfe's files as well as letters actually sent are included as equally revealing of Wolfe's character and work. The collection is an unusually fine autobiographical study of creative genius since Wolfe wrote freely and at length of the subject with which he was most absorbed—his own writings. Omitted from this collection are Wolfe's letters to his mother, published elsewhere, those to Aline Bernstein, replies to fan mail, and routine business correspondence.

Maxwell Geismar. "Faithfully Yours, Thomas Wolfe." New York *Times Book Review*, October 7, 1956, pp. 1, 34.

What American literature at the mid-century lacks and needs is a vital center—though I do not mean conformity. The glittering virtuoso talents of the Nineteen Twenties—the Hemingways, Fitzgeralds and Faulkners—derived from and were preceded by a solid core of earlier native realists all the way from William Dean Howells to Theodore Dreiser. And Thomas Wolfe himself, for all his romantic egoism, his verbal frenzies and exacerbated emotions, belonged precisely to the central and solid middle-ground of American fiction. The first value of the present collection of Wolfe's letters will be to dispel the myths and legends which sprang up around his large-size frame and talent, and to clarify his true literary position.

There are other values in this collection; like the author of the letters, it is massive, varied, illuminating and entertaining in turn; and somehow Elizabeth Nowell has managed to keep out much of what was often ponderous and repetitious in Wolfe's work. The book is described as a form of autobiography, but, as with most Wolfean autobiography, it is also a form of fiction. It might almost be called the last of Wolfe's novels, since he often used these letters—many of which he never sent to his ostensible correspondents—as a kind of preliminary sketchbook for his ideas, scenes, portraits, and what his later editor called Wolfe's "dithyrambs."

Thus the central focus of the present book is on certain very sharply defined areas of American life and society, quite as much as it is on the rebellious and provincial artist-hero. If the forward movement in Wolfe's life was to attain freedom and originality for himself and his writing, the backward and binding tie—in what he called the web of memory—was with his own early origins and environment. Unlike the expatriate generation of the post-war period, Wolfe never disdained and never looked down upon—though he might often rant about—his homely provincial ties. He continued to write to his family, to his childhood and college friends, throughout his life. He was horrified, indeed, after the publication of "Look Homeward, Angel" in 1929, when Asheville, N.C., nearly repudiated *him!* His realism was devouring and ruthless, and almost unconscious. He could never understand why his relatives, friends and acquaintances protested—and sometimes brought libel suits—at having been "caricatured."

Since Wolfe's letters to his mother—perhaps the least engaging aspect of his personality—have already been published in a separate volume, the present collection moves almost directly into the Harvard years, when Wolfe had set out to be a playwright and received his first literary defeat. (Very likely the lingering prejudice with which he always viewed New York theatrical and literary society stemmed from this first wound.) Meanwhile his mother kept reminding him of the "wasted money" that was being spent on his education—and here, after his break with the great Professor Baker of the Drama Workshop, began the first of a famous series of Wolfe's farewell letters.

This pattern of idolization, disenchantment and rejection was to continue through Wolfe's mature emotional life. He was never one to let a friendship pass in sorrow and silence. He moved on to New York University—later to become the "School for Utility Culture"—where his first novel, the "Angel" itself, was taken by Maxwell Perkins of Scribner's, and where he had found in Aline Bernstein (the Mrs. Jack of the later novels) the central love affair of his life. These were the years of the fame and glory which the young artist had craved beyond all else; how bright they were, and how brief! For Wolfe was already obsessed by a series of future novels he had planned: gigantic and impossible projects which brought him to the brink of desperation. And then came the break-up with Mrs. Bernstein herself, in "the black spring of love."

The more personal letters of this relationship are not included in the present volume; but certainly Wolfe's inner despair contributed to the difficulties which surrounded his second novel. "Of Time and the River" took six years of turmoil, which later Wolfe himself brilliantly described in "The Story of a Novel." He was always poor; his family had been wiped out in the depression; and during most of this period he lived in and prowled through the Brooklyn slums. When he did not have troubles, one might add, he appeared to invent them. There was the anonymous and dreadful young man of these letters who became the "agent" for Wolfe's manuscripts, and then threatened (in another of the tragi-comic lawsuits which marked Wolfe's meteoric career) to publish obscene sections from them.

The European trips were almost

Wolfe's only moments of relaxation and pleasure, though he managed to get involved in a nightmarish brawl at the Munich Oktoberfest. He had always been drawn to Germany, where he had been lionized in the middle Thirties; it was another wrench to his spirit, as well as to his vanity and pocketbook, when he realized the nature of the Nazi terror. And meanwhile his deep relationship with Maxwell Perkins—who had surely been a kind of foster-father as well as editor and friend to him—was drawing to a close. The letters to Perkins form a central strand in this volume: the dissolution of the friendship is even more complex, tortuous, harried, distraught and unhappy than anything which has gone before. And more eloquent.

I have hardly had time to mention here the scores of letters which Wolfe wrote to such constant friends as Olin Dows, James Boyd, John Hall Wheelock, Henry Volkening, A. S. Frere, Jonathan Daniels, Alfred Dashiell and many others. Nor have I had space to mention the famous interchange with Scott Fitzgerald—a dialogue between two generations in which Wolfe established his claim to speak for the writing of the Nineteen Thirties. That he did; and that he does over and over again in the present book, and excellently.

During the writing of his last two novels—"The Web and the Rock" and "You Can't Go Home Again"—Wolfe almost felt that he had lost everything. He doubted even his physical vitality, his fading looks. His paranoid visions assailed him constantly. This was the black side of grief and melancholia in the poet of the American dream; just as there is a very similar darkness in the inner thought, say, of Melville or Whitman. And what Wolfe had gained during these years of lonely and tormented struggle was the experience and the perspective, the central view of life, which put his novels in the main stream of our literature. Like his illustrious literary ancestors of the nineteenth and twentieth centuries, he had an insatiable appetite for life and a fixed purpose to tell the truth about it. The letters bring this all back to us, and how we could use it again today!

Geoffrey Hellman. "Literary Estate." New Yorker, 32 (February 9, 1957), 24-26.

The recent flurry of excitement over Thomas Wolfe—the publication of seven hundred of his letters by Scribner's and a long article about him in *Life*—goaded us into a research project we'd had in mind since last summer, when we read in *Publishers' Weekly* that his estate had an income of close to ninety thousand dollars in 1955. Our idea was to find out more about this property—one of the few purely literary estates going, with no stocks, no bonds, just prose—and this we've now done, thanks to several pleasant and instructive hours spent in the company of Mr. Edward C. Aswell, who, as its administrator, has run it since 1947.

"Wolfe died in 1938," Mr. Aswell said when we called on him in his office at Doubleday & Co., where he is an editor. "You wouldn't expect him to have made a will, but he did make one. He had Melville Cane, of the firm of Ernst, Cane & Berner, which specializes in copyrights, draw one up in 1937.

As Mr. Cane told it to me, Wolfe, whom he had represented in some legal controversies, ran into him at the Mont D'Or Restaurant one night, said 'I'd like to make a will,' and a few evenings later, over a dinner at Cherio's, outlined the terms. At the time the will was made, Wolfe had broken with Scribner's as his publishers, and consequently with Maxwell E. Perkins as his editor—in fact, he was about to come to Harper's, where I became his editor—but he was still a friend of Max's, and named him sole executor of his estate. His will left his mother ten thousand dollars in trust and divided the residuary estate equally among his two brothers, Frank C. and Fred W., and his two sisters, Effie W. Gambrell and Mabel W. Wheaton. Well, he didn't leave ten thousand dollars—only a little more than eight, the remains of a ten-thousand-dollar advance we'd given him for the 'The Web and the Rock,' which, like 'You Can't Go Home Again' and 'The Hills Beyond,' was published posthumously. So the residuary estate consisted entirely of his published and unpublished writings. Max Perkins died in June, 1947. I'd been active during the intervening years in preparing posthumous Wolfe material for publication, and his beneficiaries appealed to the Surrogates' Court to have me appointed 'administrator under the will.' An executor is succeeded by an administrator under the will. The Surrogate appointed me the following month, so I have run my accounting on a July-to-July fiscal-year basis. Here it is."

Mr. Aswell handed us a sheaf of papers and gave us a desk, a pad, and a pencil, and while he busied himself with Doubleday matters, we proceeded to analyze the papers every which way.

Our conclusion is that a purely literary estate is a whole lot more exciting than the ordinary stock-and-bond estate, because it fluctuates so wildly. The beneficiaries (in the case of the Wolfe estate, three legatees survive; the income from the fourth share, owing to two deaths, is now divided among six Wolfe nieces and nephews, the husband of a deceased niece, and two grandnephews) don't know where they are from fiscal year to fiscal year. For example, in the nine July-to-Julys during which Mr. Aswell has been at the helm, starting with 1947–48 and running through 1955–56, receipts have come to $36,951.34, $10,195.84, $7,196.73, $5,886.97, $6,992.74, $6,286.83, $8,525.26, $86,805.04, and $14,227.12. The reasons for these fluctuations involve nothing as hum-drum as Standard Oil of New Jersey, which, in any case, was never like this. In 1947–48, the thirty-six-thousand-dollar year, the estate got $24,450 from Liberty Films, Inc., for the movie rights to "Look Homeward, Angel;" $3,939.59 in Harper royalties and reprint fees; and $5,246.75 in Scribner royalties. In 1948–49, the Scribner income was down ($3,993.66), and so was the Harper income ($3,644.41), but there was a five-hundred-dollar advance for the German dramatic rights to "Mannerhouse," a play that Wolfe wrote while taking the late George Pierce Baker's Forty-seven Workshop course at Harvard in 1922 and 1923. "Mannerhouse," which Harper's published posthumously and which has been produced in this country only by the Forty-seven Workshop and the Yale Dramatic Association, has been touring West Germany for several years and is still going strong there. It has also been broadcast, in an abridged form, in Denmark and Sweden. It brought the estate $1,239.02 in German royalties in 1954—55 and $5,385.54 in 1955-56, or more than a third of the total take ($14,227.12) in the latter fiscal year. The big item in 1954-55 was $75,000, paid by Gregory-Goldman Enterprises for the movie rights to whichever one of three Wolfe novels—"The Web and the Rock," "Of Time and the River," and "You Can't Go Home Again"—the Enterprises might wish to film. The administrator gets a commission of two per cent on the total receipts—an arrangement that struck us as modest.

Mr. Aswell took us to lunch, and over a Martini at the Laurent Restaurant he informed us that the estate's lawyers are still Ernst, Cane & Berner; that Charles Laughton, the initiator of the Gregory-Goldman proposal, is an admirer of Wolfe's; that—even apart from movie money—the estate's income had in every year of his administration been higher than Wolfe's average annual earnings during his lifetime; and that "Mannerhouse" deals with a rich Southern family that lost its money during the Civil War and saw its property taken over by some lower-class folk.

"I think its theme—the dispossession of formerly powerful people and their replacement by those they regard as inferior—strikes a responsive chord in the Germans of today," he said. "Wolfe wrote another play while at Harvard— 'Welcome to Our City,' a study of anti-Negro prejudice—and that is still unpublished."

. . .

". . . Practically everything has been published except that second play, 'Welcome to Our City'; some of his letters; some unfinished manuscripts; and his notebooks, which I hope to publish someday. His novels have been printed in ten languages. The Japanese are after them now. I'm perfectly agreeable to this, but there's a financial problem."

Mr. Aswell said he was confident that this could be licked, and we asked him what he thought of Standard Oil of New Jersey.

Louis D. Rubin, Jr. *American Literature,* 29 (March 1957), 106–107.

The Letters of Thomas Wolfe comprise 778 pages of smallish-sized type. They are not the collected letters, but a selection, made by Elizabeth Nowell, once his literary agent. Not included are a number written to Aline Bernstein, the Esther Jack of the novels. Mrs. Bernstein before her recent death permitted use of some of the letters, but those of a more intimate nature were withheld, and will presumably be published later. Wolfe's letters to his mother have already been published, in a separate volume.

For the student with biographical inclinations, Wolfe's letters are invaluable. Again and again they reveal the actual genesis of incidents later transformed into fiction in the novels. The question which has puzzled some critics, Wolfe's literary relationship with Maxwell Perkins, is exhaustively revealed in a series of letters to his first editor which should forever end speculations as to Perkins's role and responsibility in the creation of Wolfe's fiction. It was a close relationship, and Perkins did a great deal of cutting, arranging, and plotting. Commentators who have claimed he was only a kind of fatherly mentor, who made occasional general suggestions, are wrong.

The letters afford detailed evidence, too, of Wolfe's literary influences, as well as the absence of them. Those who have felt that his interest in the time relationship was drawn in large part from Proust will find that, though Wolfe occasionally mentioned Proust, he obviously had no idea of what the French novelist was trying to do with time and memory. On the other hand, readers who have seen affinities with Tolstoy will learn that Wolfe was strongly attracted to *War and Peace*, that he read it several times.

The letters naturally throw much light on the autobiographical nature of Wolfe's work. Among other matters, they destroy the legend, advanced by Edward Aswell, that the character Nebraska Crane in *The Web and the Rock* and *You Can't Go Home Again* was purely fictional, and that Wolfe made him up out of whole cloth, without the usual "real life" counterpart. In a letter to the baseball writer, Arthur Mann, Wolfe declares in so many words that Crane is modeled after a childhood friend, who played professional baseball but never reached the big leagues.

But the chief value of these letters lies in what they have to show us about the literary process. They constitute the best possible rejoinder to those who would attribute Wolfe's importance to his "great soul" and his "Gargantuan appetites" and so forth. The experience recounted in these letters to friends is neither quantitatively nor qualitatively remarkable. It is what Wolfe was able to do with it in a literary way that makes his best fiction so memorable. To compare the incidents in these letters with the characters and events of the novels and stories is to see a consummate craftsman at work.

In one remarkable letter to Aline Bernstein, Wolfe discusses her volume of stories, *Three Blue Suits*, in which he appears as Eugene Lyons. "You always thought that you were the worker and that I had the inspiration without your capacity for work," he tells her. "Wouldn't it be funny if just the opposite were true?" Then he tells her what he means: ". . . I think you could have done better if you had worked harder. By work in an artist's life, I do not mean eight hours a day or fourteen hours a day, or all the different things you get accomplished, but I mean an integrity of purpose, a spiritual intensity, and a final expenditure of energy that most people in the world have no conception of."

Those who label Wolfe a "literary amateur" fail to consider the kind of conscious craftsmanship discussed above. When Wolfe is at his best (and he is not always so) he possessed that kind of integrity, energy, intensity of perception. It was not luck or raw memory that produced a W. O. Gant, an Eliza, an Esther Jack; it was painstaking artistry, and these letters prove it.

So perceptive a literary artist was Wolfe that the chief character of his novels, Thomas Wolfe, is sufficiently interesting for us to want to read almost everything we can about him. These letters are part of that characterization.

Unsigned. *Yale Review,* 46 (March 1957), pp. xviii, xx.

It will take at least a generation of critical counterrevolution to subdue the current disparagement of Thomas Wolfe, or his fiction, or its role in American literary history. When the inevitable reassessment occurs, however, this collection of his correspondence will surely be a major instrument in judicious appraisal. Taken as a unit these letters are an impressive document. They should reassure Wolfe's supporters and, if they will read them, should send his detractors back to the fiction itself for a second look.

The collection is a monumental one—approximately seven hundred letters in all—and, as might be expected from so prodigal a vitality, it includes very few of the meaningless notes or trivial fragments with which many such collections have to be basted. It has been assembled by Elizabeth Nowell, who knew Wolfe both as an employee of his first publisher and, later, as his literary agent from 1934 until his death in 1938.

Miss Nowell culled the correspondence from the Wolfe papers at Harvard and North Carolina, from the Scribner files, and from relatives, friends, and a number of literary correspondents. The collection is rich in virtually every period of Wolfe's life, but it is particularly abundant, happily, during such provocative and hitherto elusive episodes as his association with George Baker and the final mature years when he was trying to recast his talent. Many of the letters are unmailed or rough drafts. The general reader and the specialist are both in Miss Nowell's debt. "For the first time in my life," Wolfe writes in one of the long letters he never sent, "I resent being talked about by acquaintances." This collection ought to stimulate new talk about Wolfe of the kind to which his achievement entitles him.

Milton Hindus. "An American Writer." *Commentary,* 22 (December 1958), 585–588.

Characteristically, this book of Wolfe's letters is a behemoth. Wolfe was one of those writers—and there were better ones than he who did the same thing (e.g. Rabelais and Whitman)—who never used one word where three might serve just as well. He emphatically did not believe in the virtue of concentration and vigorously defended his own position against Scott Fitzgerald's friendly recommendation to him of the attractions of "the novel of selected incidents." Wolfe replied to Fitzgerald (in a letter printed here but already available to us in *The Crack-Up*): "You say that the great writer like Flaubert has consciously left out the stuff that Bill or Joe will come along presently and put in. Well, don't forget, Scott, that a great writer is not only a leaver-outer but also a putter-inner, and that Shakespeare and Cervantes and Dostoievsky were great putter-inners— greater putter-inners in fact, than taker-outers—and they will be remembered for what they put in—remembered, I venture to say, as long as

Monsieur Flaubert will be remembered for what he left out."

Wolfe was perfectly right, though not perhaps as regards his own work—which was what Fitzgerald was talking about. The final result alone counts. We may become impatient with a wordy writer, but if he manages to transmute quantity into power, we are not going to complain. With Wolfe, unfortunately, it wasn't always so. He gives the impression sometimes of a man being buffeted by a high wind and unable to distinguish the wind from inspiration. That is not, I confess, how he appeared to me when I was an undergraduate and he was, together with Romain Rolland, one of my favorite writers. But the years have not been kind to either Wolfe or Rolland. There are certain books which go to pieces for us without our ever rereading them. Our experiences and reflections confirm the insights of certain artists, so that they gain with the passing of time, while ruthlessly breaking down others which once appeared valid.

Wolfe was born in 1900 and died about two months short of his thirty-eighth birthday. For a writer who was so prolific and so much in the public eye, he made curiously little money. In a letter to Charles Scribner III, written not long before his death, he says that the $3,000 that he had to spend in settling a libel suit represented 10 per cent of the earnings of his whole literary career. Since Wolfe had begun to earn money in 1929 with *Look Homeward, Angel,* that would work out to something between $3,000 and $4,000 a year, which, even considering that these were depression years, is pathetically little. Wolfe never worked for Hollywood, though tempted, and when his novel *Of Time and the River* became

a success in 1935 he began worrying and wrote his editor: "How unreasonable and contradictory our natures are! It would be fantastic and comical to know that I had written a 'best seller,' it would be wonderful to get the money that would come from it, and yet I would be troubled by it too—to know I had written a best-seller, was a best-seller kind of writer: I would worry then to know what was wrong with my book, whether you and I had done something to cheapen it and make it popular." He needn't have worried on this score, because he could not help being himself at all times. One of his early critics perceived "a dangerous facility" in Wolfe's work, and we know what he meant by this: that Wolfe could turn it on or off like a tap of water. But this facility never became the kind of adroitness which could serve purposes alien to his own feelings. Except on one or two occasions, he never broke into the big-circulation magazines. Had he gone to Hollywood he would have done even worse than Fitzgerald did there, for Fitzgerald (to his ultimate loss) was gifted with a cleverness and detachment that Wolfe never had.

Elizabeth Nowell, who introduces this correspondence, succeeds in outlining the shape of Wolfe's abortive career as a man of letters very distinctly. The three most important relationships of Wolfe's adult life were with George Pierce Baker, the director of Harvard's famous 47 Dramatic Workshop, with Maxwell Perkins, his editor at Scribner's, and with Aline Bernstein. Through Baker he tried to become a playwright but failed to secure production by any but small amateur groups. Under Perkin's intelligent and sensitive handling, the importance of which he

218

himself acknowledged in the dedication of his second book, Wolfe very nearly became a popular novelist. But he eventually broke with Baker and even with Perkins, who had become a kind of father-surrogate to him, not so much because he found fault with them, but—as he himself recognized—because of his strong drive toward a condition of loneliness. This, indeed, is the central theme of his work: the book that became his first novel was originally supposed to be called "Alone, Alone" and the epigraph was to be the well-known stanza from Coleridge's *Ancient Mariner* that begins with those words.

With Aline Bernstein, who has long been known to have played a very important role in Wolfe's life (and with whom, incidentally, only a fraction of the correspondence that exists has been published in this book), he broke too; in his disillusioned view of her, she was simply "a middle-aged Jewish woman old enough to be my mother." This, in context, is meant to be more descriptive than malicious. But Wolfe never lost sight of her Jewishness. After their break, when she published a book of stories in which he was portrayed, he wrote her: "In all your stories you show the remarkably sharp, accurate and cynical observation of your race." This, too, in context, is not an entirely hostile observation. Wolfe's treatment of Jewish characters in his novels brought an accusation of anti-Semitism upon him. But in his letters he defends himself several times against this imputation. To one correspondent he insists that he has been misunderstood and that he regards anti-Semitism as a "hostile and ugly feeling which, I am sure, we both abhor." To another correspondent, who had been a student of his at New York University, he writes that the charge of anti-Semitism is "absolutely groundless." These protestations ring true, though his own emotions on this point, as on so many others in his life, were probably not entirely clear to him. At one time in the 30's, there was a rumor (without any clear basis in fact) that Wolfe himself was partly Jewish, and this disturbed him very much. It should perhaps be added, to round out the record, that he took an unequivocal stand against the Nazis (after being wined and flattered by them during a visit to Germany) in a piece which appeared in the *New Republic.* It was proposed to translate this into Yiddish, but Wolfe hesitated to grant permission since, he said, he had not intended to make propaganda.

Wolfe's letters confirm certain notions one has always had concerning his literary affinities and origins. He is probably the most distinguished descendant in the line of Whitman—more distinguished than Sandburg, who is a literal-minded imitator of the master's manner, or even than Hart Crane. And it is understandable, too, that his admiration of the Bible should be expressed even more ecstatically than Whitman's. In 1930 he writes Perkins: "I am all alone and sometimes I doubt: do you think I'll ever amount to anything? I read Shakespeare, Racine, the English Poets, and the Bible. . . ."

Wolfe's work (and these letters) betray a more immediate parentage in Joyce and Proust. What might have been guessed from his *Story of a Novel* can be pinned down decisively here. It is from Proust that he took his emphasis on sensory impressions as a way of resurrecting the dead past; from Joyce came some of the verbalism (without the control) as well as the idea

219

that every man was on a journey in search of a lost father.

The "insatiable bookishness" that Wolfe speaks of in one of his early letters is a source of both strength and weakness. He read, he admits in another of his letters, "not analytically but voraciously," and compares his habits in this respect to those of Coleridge. His Gargantuan appetite found no better food than print. He was born to devour libraries in the manner of Johnson or Gibbon, though odd little mistakes in the references to books seem to show that he could not always keep from being swamped by what he read. That he was not sufficiently critical he admitted, but even this admission does not prepare us for his coupling of the names of Wassermann and Mann—some sort of pun there perhaps!

I must say that these letters have changed my opinion of Wolfe somewhat; he now appears to me as something better than an epigone of Whitman. I am not sure if in the canon of his own work this may not prove to be his strongest and most sympathetic volume. Certainly, I was moved by his character as it comes through here. He was a very hard worker, and scrupulous in his effort to give back to the world more than he took from it. I kept thinking afterward of Keats's friend, the painter Benjamin Robert Haydon, who relied for his lasting fame on vast historical canvases which are mostly forgotten but who lives on in the autobiography which was a mere by-product, a shaving of his major effort. Wolfe did not intend these letters as an apologia, and yet they serve to justify his life.

Like three of the great English Romantics of the early 19th century— Keats, Shelley, Byron—and like two other Romantics of our own time—Hart Crane and Dylan Thomas—Wolfe died before his fortieth year. What he might have become had he lived longer we can never know, but what he was, now that the ballyhoo has died down a little, becomes increasingly plain. Keats, shortly before his death, asserted that it was his destiny to be "among the English poets." A generation later, he was elevated by Matthew Arnold not only "among the English poets" but to a position "with Shakespeare." Wolfe will never achieve such glory, but it is safe to say, fifty-six years after his birth, that he will be remembered among the American writers of our time.

Checklist of Additional Reviews

Ralph Thompson. *Book of the Month Club News,* October 1956, p. 8.

Edmund Fuller. *Episcopal Church News* [Richmond], 122 (October 1956), 3.

Earle F. Walbridge. *Library Journal,* 81 (October 1, 1956), 2555.

Horace Reynolds. "Wolfe's Autobiography in Letters." *Christian Science Monitor,* October 4, 1956, p. 11.

Orville Prescott. Column, "Books of the Times." New York *Times,* October 5, 1956, p. 23.

Irving Howe. "Thomas Wolfe's Genius and Anguish in His Letters." New York *Herald Tribune Book Review,* October 7, 1956, pp. 1, 8.

"In Flooding Words." *Newsweek,* 48 (October 8, 1956), 92-94.

"Letters from Leviathan." *Time,* 68 (October 8, 1956), 113-114.

Oscar Cargill. "The Letters of Thomas

Wolfe." *Saturday Review*, 39 (October 13, 1956), 13-14.

Milton Hindus. Chicago *Sunday Tribune*, October 14, 1956, p. 2.

New Yorker, 32 (October 20, 1956), 198.

R. C. Butz. San Francisco *Chronicle*, October 21, 1956, p. 19.

C. Fecher. *Books On Trial*, 15 (November 1956), 124.

Gerald S. Sloyan. *America*, 96 (November 3, 1956), 132-33.

Thomas F. Curley. "Novelist of the Normal." *Commonweal*, 65 (November 23, 1956), 209-211.

Nolan Miller. "Joyce and Wolfe." *Antioch Review*, 16 (December 1956), 511-517.

"Honorable Mention: The Letters of Thomas Wolfe." *Publishers' Weekly*, 171 (January 14, 1957), 20-21.

Charles I. Glicksberg. "The Letters of Thomas Wolfe." *Prairie Schooner*, 31 (Summer 1957), 102, 157-161.

College English, 19 (November 1957), 88.

George M. Reeves, Jr. "A Note on the Life and Letters of Thomas Wolfe." *South Atlantic Quarterly*, 57 (Spring 1958), 216-221.

"The Colossus of Asheville." *London Times Literary Supplement*, September 26, 1958, p. 544.

V. S. Pritchett. "Self-Portrait of a Mastodon." *New Statesman*, 56 (September 27, 1958), 423-424.

Doris Lessing. *Manchester Guardian Weekly*, October 9, 1958, p. 11.

Pamela Hansford Johnson. "Thomas Wolfe and the Kicking Season." *Encounter*, 12 (April 1959), 77-80.

THE SHORT NOVELS OF

Thomas Wolfe

EDITED,
WITH AN INTRODUCTION
AND NOTES BY

C. HUGH HOLMAN

CHARLES SCRIBNER'S SONS New York

The Short Novels of Thomas Wolfe

Samuel Hazo. "Wolfe Still A Master." Pittsburg *Press,* April 2, 1961, p. 11, Section 4.

Those who believe that Thomas Wolfe's skill was confined only to the leviathan "books" (Wolfe's word), shaped by Maxwell Perkins from Wolfe's prodigious notebook-manuscripts, will be pleased to learn that C. Hugh Holman has attempted to right the scales.

Holman, chairman of the English Department at the University of North Carolina, has edited an attractive collection of "The Short Novels of Thomas Wolfe."

. . .

Indeed, Holman's point is essentially that Wolfe's short novels "have an integrity and a consummate craftsmanship" that "Of Time and the River" and his two posthumous books lack.

For this reason, Holman has chosen to publish these five short novels, not as they were shaped for inclusion in the longer works, but as they were published originally in "Scribner's

Magazine" and "The New Republic."

Wolfe's reputation can only be enriched by this anthology, and Holman is to be commended for seeing to its appearance and providing such excellent introductions to each of the novels.

Albert L. Abbott. "A New View of Wolfe." Detroit *News,* April 16, 1961, p. G-3.

Despite its somewhat misleading title, "The Short Novels of Thomas Wolfe" is full of rewards for readers who know the prodigious American writer only through his four sprawling major novels.

Actually, the stories in this attractively printed new collection are not "the" short novels of Wolfe, but rather a selection of five such short novels. Like other similar writings of Wolfe, all originally appeared in the 1930s as magazine articles or in book form, following the success of Wolfe's first long novel, "Look Homeward Angel."

With some changes, all but one of these five later were incorporated into Wolfe's other three major novels—"Of

Time and the River," "The Web and the Rock," and "You Can't Go Home Again." In the present collection they are restored to the form in which they first appeared, and in that form each has an impact and controlled unity that was lost when the stories were transformed into episodes of the longer novels.

. . .

Wolfe's admirers—and detractors—will find new perspective in reading these stories as integrated wholes. Strangers to Wolfe will find them an interesting introduction to his work.
. . .

Fred Shaw. "Gather Ye Cliches While Ye May." Miami *News,* April 16, 1961, p. 6B.

We agreed, my friend and I, that much of what passes for knowledge is a web of cliches, stereotypes, and easy generalizations that lull us into feeling that the chaos of human experience is as neat and orderly as a formal garden. There is nothing harder than thinking. It is much easier to press the button that releases the cliche. Repeated often enough, our stereotypes first sound good, then like the beginning of wisdom, and finally like the kind of revealed truth the men fight and die for.

The no-think system can save us the trouble of making difficult decisions in religion, politics, and all the social sciences. It is particularly useful in literary criticism; for once we have pinned an author to the wall with our critical cliches, we can talk about him forever without bothering to reexamine his work.

The next logical step will dispense with reading entirely. Someday a bold new college, impressed by the simple beauty of my plan, will offer courses in Basic Stereotypes 101, Easy Generalizations 215, and Advanced Cliches 445. The college seal should bear this inspiring motto: "Gather ye stereotypes while ye may."

With a little practice the graduate can talk about Marlowe's "mighty line," the loftiness, deliberate vagueness, and majestic sweep of Milton's blank verse, and the rational, epigrammatic felicitous couplets of Alexander Pope. Without reading a line of poetry he can say that Keats was of the earth but that Shelley reached for the stars. Reading can ever be a handicap, for reading breeds skepticism of even our own cherished opinions. And as almost everyone knows, skepticism, like thinking, leads only to migraine.

Yet someone is always tampering with our stereotypes. We work up a neat set on Thomas Wolfe, conceding him great talent, but chuckling over his lack of control. A man of passion, certainly; in Sinclair Lewis's phrase a "Gargantuan creature with great gusto for life"—but what did he know of unity, structure, form. We speak of him as "the fury-driven author of a vast saga of one man's pilgrimage on earth, a saga so formless that the term novel can be applied to its parts only with extreme caution."

Then just as we have safely catalogued him, a butterfly pinned neatly to his card, comes a book like "The Short Novels of Thomas Wolfe"—edited, with an introduction and notes by C. Hugh Holman—to mess everything up. Four of the novellas published here appeared in Scribner's Magazine, the fifth in The New Republic. Wolfe used the materials of three of them in his novels, though in changed and extended form.

The strange, the paradoxical—I am tempted to say the shocking—thing about the short novels is that they exhibit the very qualities that we have thought Tom Wolfe lacked.

Here he is the deliberate, conscious artist, the experimenter in style and structure, committed to "a thoroughly organic view of art, one in which the thing to be said dictates the form in which it is uttered." The word "sprawling"—so often applied to his novels—has no place here. Wolfe was working in limited space; the longest of the novellas, "The Web of Earth," contains fewer than 40,000 words.

Admirers of Wolfe will feel at home with the splendid energy, fine characters, and lyrical intensity of the short novels; but there is nothing to prepare them for the compression, unity, and sharp focus that they'll find here. All five novellas represent Wolfe at his best. Two of them are especially valuable because they are so unlike the rest of his work. One, "I Have a Thing to Tell You," the story of the disease that brutalized Germany and threatened to destroy the world, is direct, objective, fast moving, almost terse. The other, "The Party at Jack's," an attempt to present social criticism through the juxtaposition of a wide range of characters, is just as economical; it is in Wolfe's words "the most densely woven piece of writing" he ever attempted.

Part of the Wolfe stereotype is that he could have never published a book without the help of inspired editors.

Thus it's a blow to learn that when Max Perkins read "The Web of Earth," he told Tom that "Not one word of this should be changed."

Oh well, one thing I admire about us graduates of Stereotype U. is that we never give up. We just regroup, gather our energy, and try a few new cliches for size.

Dennis Powers. "Wolfe Collection Is a Revelation." Oakland (California) *Tribune*, April 23, 1961.

Two new biographies of Thomas Wolfe and paperback reprints of his novels have paved the way for this new collection from Scribner's.

This volume, which has a good introduction and notes by C. Hugh Holman, presents each work in its original form, for each was first written as a short novel, complete in itself. Only later were some of them incorporated into Wolfe's more expansive works.

Wolfe found the short novel an excellent form for some of his ideas, and he works in it with ease and grace. Most of us have an image of Wolfe as a huge, sensuous, brilliant man from whom beautiful combinations of words poured unceasingly. We think of him (if we think of him at all) as a disheveled genius who wrote magnificent prose but whose endless novels are marred by his immoderation and his shocking disregard for form and discipline.

This new collection reveals Wolfe as a writer of shorter fiction displaying not only a good deal of discipline and control, but also a marked respect for the needs of this particular form.

The first two selections deal, in opposite points of view, with old age. "A Portrait of Bascom Hawke," an account by a young man of some incidents in the life of his old uncle, is a superb study of relations between the young and the old. "The Web of Earth" is a beautifully and wisely composed monologue by an aged mother whose memory wanders over various moments in her long life.

"No Door" is a series of observations by a wanderer, a writer who finds himself unaccountably set apart from other men. It contains some wonderful prose, and it is, as Holman tells us, "an interpretation of one aspect of Wolfe's personal experience."

"The Short Novels of Thomas Wolfe" makes us aware of the full range of Wolfe's abilities, and thus it has much value, the kind of value not affected by the passing of dark time.

Sylvia E. Bowman. "Stories Show Wolfe at His Best." Fort Wayne News-Sentinel, April 29, 1961, p. 4.

Many fans of Thomas Wolfe will be grateful to C. Hugh Holman for rescuing from dusty magazines the novelettes which he has collected here. Professor Holman asserts that republication of these short fictional works should make it clear that Wolfe was capable of writing controlled and well-formed fiction; he was, therefore, not just the uncontrolled, exuberant writer of monumental, formless manuscripts which had to be ruthlessly cut.

This collection also indicates the multiple ways an author may use his work as he searches for a full expression of his view of reality. Although these novelettes were greatly changed when Wolfe incorporated them into his longer novels, some of these stories will have a familiar ring to Wolfe readers.

But any reader will enjoy the differing views of life of youth and of age in "A Portrait of Bascom Hawke," the web-like, dialectic narrative of "The Web of Earth" in which Wolfe's mother is obviously the narrator and in which she presents in her rambling, unconscious fashion the poignancy and richness of a life almost spent. In it, the reader meets again Mr. Gant of "Look Homeward, Angel," sensuous descriptions of food; and anecdotes which, with the voice of the people they express, make Wolfe enjoyable reading.

In "No Door," Wolfe presented—as he wrote his sister—his "own life" as he interpreted it "for the last ten or fifteen years." Using the month of October as the setting in time, the first pieces trace the loneliness, the "black, bitter, aching loneliness" which is frequently a Wolfe subject. But after tracing the loneliness of Brooklyn, of the home from which the father is now missing, of the foreigner in England, and of the "ruined, lost, or broken" Coulson family and the "no doors," the setting switches to April of 1928. In lyrical passages "a single tongueless voice" speaks about "the wisdom of labor, fury and despair, spoke to me . . . in the hour of evening, and remained with me in all madness and despair that I would know at night." The "tongueless image" spoke to his listener of patience, of belief, and of the passing of the hectic passions of a youth who would devour all the experiences of the earth. But he also spoke to him of the dignity of man, of the doors men might find, of the things which do not change.

"I Have a Thing to Tell You" is about a historically past situation, and with it Wolfe the artist consciously sacrificed popularity and welcome in Germany to relate the moving story of Nazi oppression of the Jews. Sharply, un-emotionally narrated, the novelette makes the reader as uncomfortable about man's inhumanity to man as were the travelers on the train who saw the Jew arrested. But in "The Party at Jack's" American society is reminded that the little man may mean very little; and, as the scenically developed tale unfolds, one realizes the need for unity of mankind—and the lack of it.

In these novelettes which record the differing attitudes of youth and age and which also trace Wolfe's search and development, Wolfe is at his best—and he is a Wolfe who reminds that the strange, dark beauty of life is everyone's web and that everyone must seek his own doors.

William J. Lynch. *Best Sellers,* 21 (May 15, 1961), 83-84.

The present position of Thomas Wolfe in American letters is rather definite by now, though how he will rank to future generations is something else again. Certainly his full length novels are impressive, but at his worst, his naturally lyrical gifts become forced, his Whitmanesque romanticism far-fetched and his sense of compression, nonexistent. He struggles to embrace all reality within two covers and, too often, he resents the very presence of the binding.

Happily, in C. Hugh Holman's edition of *The Short Novels of Thomas Wolfe,* we see a Wolfe forced to observe verbal economy and compression for the sake of magazine publication (four novels published by *Scribner's,* the other by the *New Republic*), and the results, with one exception, are amazingly good.

The first selection, *A Portrait of Bascom Hawke,* is the best. It is a remarkable character study of a miserly, agnostic New England ex-minister, uncle to the narrator of the story. Bascom is an eccentric, probably slightly mad Bostonian who spends his post-ministerial days as a landlord of low-rental homes ("Widower's houses," as Shaw would say), and whose less fanatic youth had included moments of love and happiness. We see, in flashback, the gradual unbalancing of a man who, bit by bit, lost his grip on life and reality to become a tragic-comic figure, symbolic of the strange and grotesquely beautiful thing which, for the author, is old age. It is a magnificent portrait of physical, emotional and spiritual sterility, and ends in a characteristically lyrical outburst on the narrator's part on the virtues of grasping love and youth while they are yet available and very close to one's heart.

The second short novel, *The Web of Earth,* is a dramatic monologue of reminiscence rendered by a woman in old age, whose character was suggested by Wolfe's own mother. It is evidently (and admittedly) based on the final Molly Bloom soliloquy in *Ulysses* and the author felt it at least Joyce's equal.

I really believe . . . although this is a

terribly boastful thing to say, that I knew this old woman better than Joyce knew that woman at the end of *Ulysses,* and furthermore that my old woman is a grander, richer, and more tremendous figure than his was.

Maybe. But Joyce's ingenious stream-of-consciousness technique lends more credibility to the wayward wanderings of his wayward heroine, than does the often anecdotal straight narrative of Eliza Gant's efforts to keep her drunken stonecutter husband off the bottle, and her befriending of an escaped town murderer whose presence outside her house is sensed supernaturally by this remarkable woman. Eliza is the last of a hardy lot and we, like Wolfe, doff our hats to her and her ilk.

No Door, the third selection, best reveals the poetic gifts of Wolfe who, in one part, sings paeans of joy to the beauties of Brooklyn, then to the British Isles, as he tells of a disgraced English family with whom the American narrator lives during a period of foreign study. He makes a pathetic effort to take the daughter back to The States with him, but she refuses, preferring to stay with her family to face with dignity the stares of their neighbors. This selection is written in diary form, and the entry of "October, 1923," in which he blends his father's death with the imagery of the dying year, is beautiful beyond description, as is the final "April, 1928" entry in which hope is revived for the narrator and for all mankind in a Whitman-like affirmation of the regenerative powers of love and belief culminating in an inevitable and eternal springtime.

I Have a Thing to Tell You, the *New Republic* novella, is a Chekhovian lament for the plight of the refugee Jew in Nazi Germany, in which the narrator helplessly sees a fellow passenger whisked off a train by Nazi officials, and away from the freedom he so deserves. The social message is undeniable and praiseworthy but the propaganda ring detracts from the characterization.

The Party at Jack's is more successful. In this final selection, two elevator men burn to death in an apartment house elevator, while a group of selfish, small-souled participants in a pseudosophisticated soiré in the same building watch impassively. Only one member, Webber, realizes the petty existence of the lot, and leaves them, apparently forever. It is an effective bit of mordant contrast, reminiscent of O'Casey's magnificent scene in *Juno and the Paycock* when, in the midst of a liquid songfest in a Dublin tenement flat, the action is interrupted by the funeral procession of a young Irregular soldier whose death is an ironic contrast to the carefree conduct within.

These five novels, in summary, show their author, for the most part, at his best which, as American Literature scholars know, is very good indeed. Mr. Holman's introductions to the stories and to the book proper are perceptive and eminently just. It is a book which I am very glad to have read, which should give the average reader much pleasure, and which is certainly a mandatory purchase for every serious student of our country's contemporary literature.

Harry T. Moore. "The Best of Wolfe." St. Louis *Post-Dispatch*, May 28, 1961, p. 4B.

To one who has just reread Thomas Wolfe's four long novels, this collection of his shorter work comes as a relief. As Professor Holman suggests in his introduction to the present volume, the last three of those longer novels are painfully lacking in unity; and certainly even the first and best of them, "Look Homeward, Angel," doesn't successfully assimilate all its raw material. But in the short novel Wolfe is often amazingly successful. The form helps him to concentrate his power.

In going through the long novels again, I was often struck by the idea that much of the material would be more effective if broken off and used separately, and I recalled that some of the sections of these books had originally appeared as short novels. There was, for example, "A Portrait of Bascom Hawke," which was first printed in Scribner's magazine in 1932; three years later it was disintegrated and scattered through the long and unwieldy novel, "Of Time and the River." Now, fortunately, the original version appears, along with six others, including "No Door" and "The Web of Earth."

Robert E. Spiller. "Wolfe Is Still at the Door." *Sewanee Review,* 71 (Autumn 1963), 658–659.

If anyone could restore Thomas Wolfe to full status as an object of serious literary study, research, and criticism, Hugh Holman has performed that service to the somewhat battered giant. During the past three years he has offered to the academic profession a summary critical estimate in one of the Minnesota pamphlets, a Scribner research anthology with a selection of documents by and about Wolfe as a writer and person, and a volume of five short novels to substantiate the claim that it is in this form that Wolfe most excels as a literary artist. The result is a convincing definition of Wolfe's place in the American literary firmament—a definition which is substantiated further rather than questioned by the subsequent exhaustive study of Richard S. Kennedy. Whether he is viewed as a belated nineteenth-century romantic in the manner of Whitman or as an original modern genius who was stifled by his editors, it is easier now to get the problem of his literary fame into focus.

Mr. Holman does not contest what have by now become the commonplaces of Wolfe criticism: that his claim to fame lies in the power and passion of his vision rather than in any mastery of the novel form or technique; that his style is uneven, varying from magnificent periods to empty rhetoric; that his great promise was unfulfilled partly because his editors, Perkins, Aswell, and Nowell, did him at least as much harm as good by their efforts to restrain and channel his genius. What Mr. Holman does best is to single out and stress qualities of his art which are in the credit column: his fascination with language and his ear for vivid and accurate dialogue; his concentration on the theme of loneliness as the core of human experience rather than on such limited (and assigned) themes as the search for a father; his epic sense of America; his power of total recall combined with sharp visual imagery in his descriptive passages; his ability to understand and to bring to life a total human character; and his use of three overlaid concepts of time to gain perspective on past experience. Such gifts—whatever their compensating faults might be—ought surely to rank their possessor among the literary masters; but Mr. Holman makes no claim for his subject—he allows the facts to speak for themselves.

His own special contribution, however, is his belief that Wolfe did achieve in his short novels what he failed to achieve in his longer work: an organic form sufficiently tightly knit of theme and action to bind a single work of art into a structural and textural unit. As evidence he offers several novelettes of from sixteen to thirty thousand words each, which Wolfe wrote and occasionally published as units and then broke up and distributed through the more loosely knit pages of "the book." Of these there is no doubt that "The Web of Earth," the record of his mother's stream-of-consciousness ramblings is a masterpiece and that the other four are at least satisfactory wholes. There is also no doubt that, in this form, Wolfe stands up to the rigors of analytical criticism

far better than in his longer work. But we cannot conclude even so that in these shorter works Wolfe is a greater artist than he was in his more ambitious attempts. As Faulkner pointed out, greatness may be measured by failure as well as by success. The student who now turns to the documents as collected by Mr. Holman may further explore the evidence and make up his own mind on the larger issues. In doing so he may learn something about the varieties of literary experience and the dangers of too rigid critical formulae.

Checklist of Additional Reviews

Earle F. Walbridge. *Library Journal*, 86 (April 1, 1961), 1482.

Louis D. Rubin, Jr. Roanoke (Virginia) *Times*, April 16, 1961, p. 8B.

Marty Buskin. "Another Side of Wolfe's Literary Genius." *Newsday* (Garden City, N.Y.), April 22, 1961.

A.P. "Wolfe's Novel Collection Proves He Can Be Concise." *The Arizona Republic* (Phoenix), April 23, 1961, p. G-23.

George Popkin. "Distinctive Fiction." Providence *Sunday Journal*, April 23, 1961.

Day Thorpe. (Washington, D.C.) *Sunday Star*, April 23, 1961, p. 5B.

Walter Stewart. "Wolfe In Short Clothing." Toronto *Telegram*, April 29, 1961.

San Francisco *Sunday Chronicle*, May 14, 1961, p. 34.

Booklist, 57 (May 15, 1961), 573.

New York *Herald Tribune Lively Arts*, May 28, 1961, p. 30.

Albert Van Nostrand. Boston *Daily*

Herald, June 2, 1961, Brown Supplement, p. 24.

A. W. Phinney. "Wolfe in Less Than Epic Proportions." *Christian Science Monitor,* June 15, 1961, p. 11.

Frank Tanderjian. "Wolfe Unchanged." *The New Guard* (New York City), September, 1961, 16.

Paschal Reeves. *South Atlantic Quarterly,* 61 (Winter 1962), 115.

THE NOTEBOOKS OF
Thomas Wolfe

Edited by
RICHARD S. KENNEDY
and
PASCHAL REEVES

Volume 1

THE UNIVERSITY OF
NORTH CAROLINA PRESS
Chapel Hill

The Notebooks of Thomas Wolfe

Alice P. Hackett. "Forecasts." *Publishers' Weekly,* 196, part 3 (November 17, 1969), 76.

This is an important book, not only for the present but for years ahead. We can see a constant demand in libraries and college stores. It also makes fascinating reading for all those interested in the literary scene of the 20s and 30s and for those, whether aspiring writers or not, who want to enter into a great writer's mind. At first Thomas Wolfe kept his personal notes on stray sheets of paper, but soon he began keeping "Pocket Notebooks." He was an inveterate listmaker and bookshop visitor. He made lists of books he'd read or wanted to read, restaurants he'd been too, states he'd visited, writers he'd met, and many more. These are sidelights; the real meat of the notebooks, which are all here, lies in the notes for and thoughts about his novels, and preliminary drafts of scenes, characters and sections which were to be incorporated in finished volumes. The editors have added valuable explanatory background sections and notes as well as a long introduction. Another important feature is the detailed chronology of Wolfe's life.

Robert Kirsch. "Thomas Wolfe 'Caught Hot and Instant'." *Los Angeles Times Calendar,* February 22, 1970, p. 38.

. . .

The passage is Wolfe, last of the romantics, with much of his power and a suggestion of his weakness, an intoxication with words which led to excess and hyperbole.

Yet, surprisingly *The Notebooks of Thomas Wolfe,* edited by Richard S. Kennedy and Paschal Reeves, published for the first time (with the exception of his last notebook which was published some years ago), are on the whole free of these faults.

Notes and fragments, hastily written, in a series of 35 pocket notebooks, represented a different context of writing. His characteristic mode of composition, long periods of writing, fighting fatigue, isolated from life, ordeals of creation, kept the seemingly interminable flow constant. Here time interfered, distraction interrupted; the materials of observation and awareness were put down on paper quickly.

That the publication of these notebooks is a literary event of the first magnitude is apparent. What is unexpected is that they are not solely of interest to the scholar. The reader, even one who is not widely read in the works of Wolfe themselves, cannot fail to be interested. For here is the sensitive writer at the contacting and sensing edge of experience.

Wolfe was moved at first, while a student at Harvard studying with John Livingston Lowes (those who have read "The Road to Xanadu" will know why), to consider the idea of a notebook, keeping in mind that "unconscious cerebration" which Coleridge wrote about. But Wolfe, unsystematic and untidy, did not really start until a few years later to record random ideas and observations.

These are not diaries or journals or commonplace books. They are rather the record of thinking and feeling, a jumble of plans and projects, character sketches and outlines, meditations and opinions, first drafts of passages and letters, speculations on life and literature, notes on books read, women loved, restaurants dined in, dreams dreamt.

We see the transmutation of raw experience into fiction, some close to the verbatim account of an episode witnessed, some so remote it takes the skill of a detective to trace their roots.

Of greater consequence is the utter honesty, the confrontation with self and cosmos which most of these jottings

reveal. In 1930, he writes a single line from a popular song, "Could I reveal eggs-ac-lly what I *feel?*" That question pervades the notebooks. The answer is yes. There is no compromise here with fashion or taste, no self-censorship. His concern with sex and love, with his guilts, biases, hostilities, self-pity, obsessions, has no screen. The editors write: "Indeed, Wolfe tries to be so honest with himself that reading his notebooks is like a plunge into his psyche . . ."

Some of the lines are pregnant with meaning: "Meditation of a gentleman in the subway on the subject of death: 'Well, I don't know—he may be lucky at that.' "

. . .

Sometimes an evocation of Whitman:

. . .

Always a concern with America, with capturing its complex and epic challenge.

. . .

We see another side of Wolfe here, the critical, the faculty he is supposed to lack.

"God knows, I could be helped by criticism as much as any man alive—but how much more critical am I, who am generally supposed to be so totally lacking in the critical faculty, than my critics.—Every intelligent artist, I believe, as he grows older, wishes to profit and learn and grow through the persuasions of a wise critique—but how rare—how damnably rare—how much rarer even than the great master-works of art itself such criticism is."

And he makes the point, relevant even today, that those who criticized his language and method, left him nothing, no alternative: "Well," he writes of one lady reviewer, "having got away to a good start by taking away my adjectives, why not do a really good job and take away my nouns, pronouns, participles, verbs, adverbs, conjunctives, and parts of speech whatever— furnish me with a vocabulary of her own choosing . . . forbid me to write any more about 'myself' or any people or experience I have managed to see or know in my thirty-four years—lock me up in a cell and thrusting the approved vocabulary and a sheaf of papers in my hands, hiss venomously: 'Here damn you—Use these! And mind you write about something you know nothing at all about! We'll see if you can really write, you dog!'"

Exaggerated! Yes. But with Wolfe, exaggeration is the underscoring of his purpose. His characters are larger than men, his settings vaster, his emotions stronger, his words more emphatic, his very repetition—he knew instinctively as an artist that the disappearance of these components would result in diminishing him.

His great triumph was evocation—of a sort which enveloped the reader, surrounded him, forced him to taste, touch, smell, hear and see, awakened the sense memory deep within him. His subject was America: "My name is Wolfe. I am an American." This is his affirmation and his challenge. In this only two writers, Whitman and Melville, bear comparison with him.

Perhaps the most compelling theme in his notebooks is the Promethean effort to capture the variety, depth and complexity which is America. "Out of the billion forms of America; out of the savage violence and the dense complexity of all its swarming life; from the unique and single substance of this

land and life of ours, must we draw the power and energy of our own life, the articulation of our speech, the substance of our art."

In the end he was not big enough. He had neither the compassion and love of Whitman nor the moral mystique of Melville, nor for that matter the humor of Twain. He was trapped in his biases; his effort at the wide embrace of America fell short in the provincial prejudices with which he was bound. But this too was an authentic part of America and he was its authentic, tormented and occasionally triumphant bard.

Harry T. Moore. "Motes in the Eye of a Mountainous Man." *Saturday Review,* 53 (March 7, 1970), 23–24, 46.

"The mountains were my masters," Thomas Wolfe noted in 1924, "the unyielding mountains which were beyond the necessity of growth and change." He put that down in a hitherto unpublished travel diary on his first trip to Europe at the age of twenty-four, when publication of his first novel, *Look Homeward, Angel,* lay just five years ahead. The sentence was prophetic of all his writings, for although he struggled to achieve growth and change before his death at thirty-seven, his talent remained unyielding, and his fiction had the fixed and jagged immensity of a mountain range.

Critics have tended to deal severely with Wolfe because his novels are almost invariably autobiographical, and because he too often yielded to the enticements of a Southern-style rhetoric that became repetitious, bloated, and wearying. Yet he was always an intense observer who could vigorously record grotesqueries of human behavior, so that even if his central figure remained rather monotonously the same ("O lost!") he was often surrounded by characters who, though also not growing, stood out as vivid and engaging, often attractively comic.

The story of Wolfe and the two editors—Maxwell Perkins and Edward C. Aswell—who struggled to give some unity to his work is sufficiently well known to need no retelling here, but is must be said that the *Notebooks* add greatly to our understanding of the ordeal of those two men and of Wolfe's own ambitions and purposes. Richard S. Kennedy and Paschal Reeves, the editors of these volumes of his journals, were also under drastic pressure as they worked for five strenuous years at deciphering Wolfe's often smudged penciled scrawls in thirty-three pocket notebooks, one ledger, and a great many loose papers. But as well as for their magnifying-glass labors these editors deserve congratulations for the way they have carried out their intention to "present a kind of interior biography of Wolfe beginning with his years at Harvard, the time of his first serious literary endeavors."

At the end of their two volumes the editors include the last of Wolfe's writings (except for some letters), "A Western Journal," parts of which have been published before. About one-tenth of the available material in these notebooks is left out, such as repetitious statistics concerning cities, people, and books, grocery lists, American Express Travelers Cheque numbers, and similar matters. One necessary omission is mentioned in a beguilingly deadpan note: "At this point Wolfe sets down a list of the women with whom he has had sexual relations in the United States and the states in which they were born." For the sake of the curious it might be added that most of this material, including the above suppressed item, is at Harvard, though probably scrupulously guarded.

Despite the exclusions, a good many lists remain in the text—authors from various countries, projected characters, records of royalties—but, perhaps surprisingly, these are frequently interesting. The most absorbing passages, however, are Wolfe's instant impressions of places or people, hasty and often unpunctuated jottings. They display his gift for observation, and they come up from the page bright and living, as they might not when incorporated into his grandiloquent sentences. Many times such rough notations inform the "interior biography" and provide piquant travelogue as well, both European and American. There are also numerous fairly long "written out" sections which supply examples of Wolfe's early drafts of published and occasionally unpublished novels, stories, or sketches.

. . .

. . . The important point is that the editing of these *Notebooks* is sound in the major areas. Richard S. Kennedy in 1962 brought out *The Window of Memory,* a valuable forerunner of these new volumes, and last year the other editor, Paschal Reeves, published *Thomas Wolfe's Albatross: Race and*

Nationality in America, in which Wolfe's xenophobia frequently manifests itself. As the editors comment, because Wolfe never properly accepted the diversity of origins and beliefs among Americans, he could not in this area of the national experience "qualify as the epic spokesman because he lacked the wide embrace of a Whitman." To him, blacks were usually niggers; he wrote disparagingly of Americanized "foreign types," and he was, as these *Notebooks* consistently show, far more anti-Semitic than his apologists seem to have known. He was, it is plain, genuinely in love with Aline Bernstein, his mistress for several years; but in his journals he usually referred to her, with an evident but perhaps partly unconscious resentment, as "my Jew" or "the Jew." These volumes contain the draft of a 1934 letter to her that was cruelly anti-Semitic; apparently Wolfe had the good grace not to send it. The editors point out that Wolfe is usually assumed to have developed his anti-Semitism after a long series of quarrels with Mrs. Bernstein, but they include a diary fragment from his Harvard years that shows how deeply the anti-Jewish clichés were embedded in his consciousness.

Yet Wolfe escaped at least partly from such attitudes toward the end of his life, as his long story "I Have a Thing to Tell You" demonstrates. It also reveals his post-1936 disillusionment with Germany, previously his favorite foreign country. As readers of that novella know, it was the Nazis' vicious treatment of a Jew trying to get out of Germany that turned Wolfe against the régime. When he began to write the story he started the third paragraph with "I don't like Jews," but he cut the qualification later, for he had a thing to tell us.

You Can't Go Home Again was the title his editor gave to Wolfe's last novel, published posthumously; the phrase was one he often used. Yet in the last two years of his life he *was* in some ways going home again, and he not only explored a large part of Western America but made his first visit in eight years to his native Asheville, the Altamont and Lybia Hill of his novels. If he had lived he might have discovered for himself a new America. Certainly he was jaded, at least at that time, with Europe. When he stopped in Paris for the last time in 1936, the city he had always rejoiced in—particularly its restaurants and cafés— seemed to him a "sad and enervating town." He complained of "The eternal monotony of French life—The banal life of cafés—the people gesticulating and talking—and to what purpose?" This was quite different from his earlier lively impressions, as in the spring of 1935:

. . .

There is no such animation in the 1936 notes; Wolfe merely mentions the places where he ate and drank, obviously with little zest, and adds some censure of the American expatriates who had celebrated Paris in the 1920s and who in his view had produced nothing worthwhile.

As did many of his fellow-writers of the time, however, Wolfe soon veered somewhat to the Left, writing for liberal journals and even, in the case of a story he could have sold for a profit, presenting the piece gratis to *The New Masses.* Like so many liberal or United Front writers, he began speaking of people

237

he didn't like as Fascists, and in a 1937 entry in these *Notebooks* he amusingly listed "Potential Fascist Literary Groups and Individuals," where lo! *SR*'s name led all the rest. Wolfe had been furious at *SR*'s editor, Bernard De Voto, for his 1936 review ("Genius Is Not Enough") of Wolfe's *The Story of a Novel*, which had first appeared as a three-part serial in *SR* in 1935, the year Wolfe's second novel, *Of Time and the River*, came out. That book had, with certain qualifications, been treated favorably by the departing editor of *SR*, Henry Seidel Canby. Wolfe's agent, Elizabeth Nowell, in her 1960 biography of her author, recalled that Canby's was "the first major review to turn the tide in favor of *Of Time and the River*." But Wolfe had something of a tendency toward megalomania, which went with his mountainous image of himself; people had to be with him 100 per cent of the way or they were altogether against him. And, although Canby's name was omitted from the potential-Fascist enumeration, Wolfe's inevitable denigration of him appeared in the last posthumous collection of his fiction, *The Hills Beyond* (1941), which depicted *SR*'s founder in that rather crude pasquinade "Portrait of a Literary Critic," dated by Aswell "after 1935."

It is interesting to note that Thomas Wolfe included in his "Fascist" list not only the *New York Times Book Review* but also its editor at that time, J. Donald Adams. The *Virginia Quarterly Review* qualified, too, as did the Southern Agrarians and the literary newspaper columns of Herschel Brickell and Harry Hansen. The New York *Sun* was likewise blasted, along with the American Academy of Arts and Letters, to say nothing of the National Institute (Wolfe called it the Academy) of Arts and Letters, in which Wolfe had not long before accepted membership. After the appearance of his first book he sometimes felt hostility toward other writers or was at least uncomfortable with them, and he did not get along particularly well even with F. Scott Fitzgerald and Ernest Hemingway, though Perkins wanted all Scribner's authors to be happy together.

Yet there are signs that Wolfe was mellowing toward the end of his life. Before he left Paris for that last time in 1936, he wrote, in the fragmentary first draft of "I Have a Thing to Tell You," some words that he of course meant for all mankind. ". . . brothers, we must brothers be—or die," a curious anticipation of the famous line in the early versions of Auden's "September 1, 1939": "We must love one another or die." Perhaps, after all, Thomas Wolfe was, in a most human way, preparing to go home again.

Frederick Shroyer. "The Intimate Notebooks of Thomas Wolfe." Los Angeles *Herald-Examiner,* March 15, 1970, p. G-10.

Someone once said that the reason that young people liked Thomas Wolfe's novels was not that they wanted to write as he did but because they already were writing that way. There is much truth in this assessment of Wolfe's prose, for truly he wrote too long, was horribly afflicted with terminal adjectivitis, and was utterly incapable of rendering his ambergris into perfume. Let us face it, he only had one thing going for him: he was a literary genius who despite all of his faults stood as a Gulliver, a Titan in the midst of the America of his decades.

. . .

When Wolfe died, Harvard acquired over two tons of his books and papers. Among them were the thirty-five notebooks edited and collected in this edition. Of these journals, only one, the last, has been printed before. That they are all now available in a creatively and intelligently edited, prefaced, and ordered edition is due to the almost-Wolfian efforts of Professors Richard Kennedy and Paschal Reeves. The former began work on the notebooks in 1963 and was joined by the latter the following year. The two men spent five years preparing this edition, which presents nine-tenths of the notebooks' contents omitting only such material as train schedules, some of the more elongated statistical lists aforementioned, and grocery lists. In effect, everything is here except the kitchen sink.

The editors, with that ease of presentation which accompanies true scholarship, have created an edition of Wolfe's notebooks that will afford the general reader many, many hours of delight. It can be dipped into anywhere, though it may be rather difficult to put down. Simply, the magic of these books are that they accumulate until it becomes what is truly an "interior" autobiography of a vast, sprawling, complex and gifted man. Here is Thomas Wolfe ranging through America, visiting Hollywood, driven by his demon time and time again to Europe, and always there are trains, moving windows over America, haunted—yet magic casements opening upon the vast mysterious abyss wherein dwells America's soul.

Yes, here is Tom Wolfe in love, or more often, in lust; drunk, sober; his hate-love relationship with Aline Bernstein, his despair and his joy; a Tom Wolfe who bayed the moon and roamed the earth with hungry heart until he died of tuberculosis of the brain on September 15, 1938.

In addition to having created an exemplary study, the editors offer an excellent, most useful Chronology and an Index that works.

Unsigned. "Wolfe's Notebooks." Atlanta *Journal,* March 16, 1970, p. 16-A.

Thomas Wolfe is a handy literary target for lazy critics because in his attempt to paint a land as big as this one he overwhelmed the page with words. There are reasons to believe he would have brought the reigns in had he not died at age 37. What stands of his work has been probed every which way by critics whose common bond is repetition.

Fortunately, there appears to be a reawakening to Wolfe's virtues and that is good because at the heart he was a storyteller in the truest front-porch tradition. Helping to create this reawakening is a professor at the University of Georgia.

Paschal Reeves has written a study of Wolfe's curious attitudes toward Negroes and Jews and co-edited an important work, "The Notebooks of Thomas Wolfe."

This two-volume collection of previously unpublished Wolfe material includes the significant and revealing entries of the writer's voluminous diaries. Critics say the work adds considerably to understanding what made Wolfe tick. The notebooks picture him as a wildly sensual and driven man who made art his life and his own life art. Dr. Reeves spent a good while going over Wolfe's notebooks. It was a hard task. But the sum of it is a fine contribution to literature.

R. H. W. Dillard. "Hungry Gullivers' Itch To Tell It All." Roanoke Times, April 26, 1970, p. B-14.

Thomas Wolfe, the famous "hungry gulliver" from Asheville, North Carolina, who once inflamed American young people as Janis Joplin or Mick Jagger do today, has fallen on hard times in recent years. His major novel, "Of Time and the River," is, to my knowledge, out of print, and his last two novels, "The Web and the Rock," and "You Can't Go Home Again," we now know to be rather crudely and unfairly patched up pieces of editing, and not Wolfe's real work. His work burns in the darkness he always feared, but somehow it survives, perhaps as much because of what it strove to be as for what it really is.

Wolfe strove to put the world into a book. Like the young Gertrude Stein who believed that if she "could only go on long enough and talk and hear

and look and see and feel enough and long enough I could finally describe, really describe, every kind of human being that ever was or is or would be living," Wolfe was driven to live to the full and to hold that living, vital and fresh, in words, great torrents of words, moving like blood in the flesh, never slowing down, never excluding a living moment.

He was, of course, doomed to failure. His novels may not be as tedious as Gertrude Stein's "The Making of Americans," but they do not contain the whole world, no matter how long they are, nor how deeply and intensely they were felt and written. But what a stirring quest! To shape out of time and the river a written monument to the essence of the moving and mutable world is a quest worthy of an ancient hero, for it is truly a striving with the gods.

All of this indicates the real and exciting value of this new and excellent selection of a thousand pages from Wolfe's notebooks. For here we are able to see Wolfe's struggle to master and record his experience in the rough: lists of names, streets, books; descriptions of towns, cities, countries; records of conversations and overheard conversations; records of expenses, timetables, plans for essays and speeches, fragments of fiction. When he loses notes for a few days or fails to record them, he feels the "awful feeling of having lost something," for experience unrecorded dies into the stream of time. But he also knows that "things cannot be tallied up so easily."

"The years slide by like water," and Wolfe struggles with them. He tries to come to terms with the "dark wound of America" which he recognizes is his own; he cries out for us to "do what

240

Whitman dreamed—let us stick to each other as long as we live—and let us find out who and what and why we are!" The notebooks are, perhaps even more than the novels, a major work, if not of refined art, of the raw yearning of the spirit from which all art springs.

Borges has told us that the "composition of vast books is a laborious and impoverishing extravagance," that we should rather "pretend that these books already exist, and then . . . offer a resume, a commentary." These notebooks are resumes of dozens of books Wolfe planned and dreamed, and they are here in essence; unwritten, they nevertheless exist perhaps even more purely in the pages of these notebooks. To read these two volumes is to read a man's life work, the vast books of Wolfe's enormous dream. Perhaps here we do find out more about who and what and why we are, much more.

These notebooks are more, then, than the usual scholarly aid for the understanding of an author's work, for they extend and multiply Wolfe's work, give him a range and reality far beyond that of his published fiction. They may, because of the great fund of material in them, cause a revival of interest in Wolfe's work. But, more important to my mind, is their own intrinsic value, the opportunity they afford us of coming into direct contact with a mind trying to encompass the whole of the moving world. We are all indebted to Professors Kennedy and Reeves for their successful labors, for allowing us to share the range and fury of Wolfe's mind.

M. Thomas Inge. "Voluminous 'Jottings' Illuminate Writings." Nashville *Tennessean,* July 12, 1970, p. 6-C.

Thomas Wolfe was noted for his prodigious daily output as a writer, and he was known, as well, for his presumed inability to shape his enormous output into disciplined fictional forms without the aid of an effective editor, such as Maxwell Perkins.

Wolfe was, apparently, seldom caught without pen and pad in hand, as evidenced by the 35 pocket notebooks he intermittently carried between 1926, as he began work on *Look Homeward, Angel,* and 1938, the year of his death.

The material contained in these notebooks (at least, nine-tenths of the total) is published in these volumes for the first time, edited and annotated with the utmost scholarly care and intelligence by professors Richard S. Kennedy of Temple University and Paschal Reeves of University of Georgia.

. . .

Several notes reveal that, like Faulkner, Wolfe often played the "reputation of America authors" game, except he appeared concerned over the number of novels they had produced (one list ranks the top authors by the number published) and their respective ages ("Faulkner 38 or 39, Hemingway 38 or 39, Fitzgerald 39, Caldwell 32 or 33, Myself 34").

. . .

241

To their extensive labors as editors, professors Kennedy and Reeves have added a succinct introduction summarizing the relevance of the notebooks to understanding Wolfe's career, a chronology of his life, and a thorough index. These are valuable primary documents for the study of American literature.

Lewis P. Simpson.
South Atlantic Quarterly, 69 (Autumn 1970), 544-46.

Grounded in a meticulous scholarship and shaped by an imaginative grasp of the inner drama of Thomas Wolfe's life and work, these volumes will become the source of important studies of Wolfe's relatively brief but large career in American letters. Through the patient, skillful, and perceptive labor of Kennedy and Reeves, we have opened up a number of interesting directions we may take toward achieving a more substantial estimate of Wolfe's importance than has been made so far, even in the distinguished studies the editors themselves have already published.

One direction future Wolfe studies should unquestionably follow is strongly suggested by the *Notebooks,* so much so that it is well worth singling out for special comment. This is Wolfe's relation to the history of the literary vocation in America. Implicit in the varied entries in the *Notebooks*—in the Wolfean catalogues of drink, food, journeyings, places, and people (most of all people) and in the plans and pieces of his stories—is the struggle central to this history: the struggle of the American writer to be at the same time a literary artist and an American. The *Notebooks* contain significant indications that in this struggle Wolfe had a vision of the character of the American writer essentially different from the one envisioned by his major contemporaries Hemingway and Faulkner (and by Fitzgerald, though this may be a little more trouble to demonstrate). They identified themselves with the figure of the American writer as an exile from, and an opponent of, the modern industrial society. This society had destroyed the simple agrarian or pastoral America that was supposed to have become the redemption of the complex corruption of Western civilization. The faith in the pastoral power of America—its classic statement was made by Crèvecoeur and augmented by Jefferson—postulated the emergence of a new moral existence under the pastoral condition, as opposed to the feudal and urban conditions of Europe. The fulfillment of the pastoral dream was made a historical impossibility by the rapid emergence of the industrial age in America; ironically, it nonetheless became dominant in the myth of America. Only in the pastoral guise could the American writer find a unifying sense of his identity as literary artist and American.

Thus in the twentieth century we have the image of the American writer as hunter and fisherman in Hemingway and as farmer and countryman in Faulkner; and we have a tendency on the part of both (feeling among other things the connection between writing and publishing and the industrial processes of production and consumption) to say that they were not writers, or only incidentally writers, indeed at times to seem to hate the notion of being writers. They suggest to us that under the pastoral compulsion the American writer has been in a way like Hamlet—brooding, introspective, uncertain of his meaning or function. He has been locked in a dream of what might have been *if* America had not been conceived at the same moment when the cotton gin, the steamboat, and the railroad were invented; and he has been somehow filled with a desire for revenge on the modern world for attempting to transcend through a sophisticated technology man's natural limitations and inferior spiritual capacities.

But Wolfe was not an American Hamlet. Nothing may be more significant in his career finally than his conception of himself as an American Faust. In November, 1928, Wolfe saw a performance of *Faust* in a German theater. Afterwards he wrote: "Faust's own problem touches me more than Hamlet's—his problem is mine, it is the problem of modern life. He wants to know everything, to be a god—and he is caught in the terrible net of human incapacity." Not repudiating the Faustian compulsion in American life as many of our writers have, not really questioning it, Wolfe was pulled, the *Notebooks* show, toward a vision of America in the context of the Faustian dream. He found the technological conquest of the continent an epic drama of which the spiritual potentialities had not been realized. Instead of seeing a trainyard full of boxcars as a wasteland, he saw it as a place of spiritual promise, for in the American conquest of vast distances represented by the boxcars lay the promise of the conquest of the spiritual distances among people. Instead of seeing the American writer as

hunter or farmer, Wolfe saw him as a rider of railroads. His Faustian metaphor of the literary vocation deserves thoughtful study.

William Braswell. "An 'Interior Biography' of Thomas Wolfe." *Southern Literary Journal*, 3 (Fall 1970), 145-50.

When Thomas Wolfe was visiting New Orleans in January 1937, he recorded in a notebook in a list of people he had met there, "Willie B. Wisdom—an autograph collector, but he likes me." Fortunately for Wolfe and those interested in him, William Wisdom, a business man, was much more than a collector of autographs and a casual admirer. Early convinced of Wolfe's significance, he began his collection of Wolfe material and, after the author's death, bought the entire two-ton collection of Wolfe papers and books and deposited it in the Houghton Library at Harvard.

Two of the scholars who have made valuable use of this rich accumulation are Richard S. Kennedy, in *The Window of Memory: The Literary Career of Thomas Wolfe* (1962), and Paschal Reeves, in *Thomas Wolfe's Albatross: Race and Nationality in America* (1968). Now, after five years of painstaking labor together, Professors Kennedy and Reeves have made available, in a handsome two-volume, thousand-page edition, some of the most fascinating material in the collection: *The Notebooks of Thomas Wolfe. . . .*

The editors were confronted by a

243

number of problems, which they apparently solved satisfactorily. Except for representative samples they omitted such entries as grocery lists, train schedules, and names and addresses. They also left out repetitions of literary outlines, some of the many statistical lists (such as cities visited), many recorded conversations overheard in bars and cafes, and a few incoherent and mostly illegible passages which Wolfe wrote when deep in his cups. They estimate that they reproduced about nine-tenths of the total material in the notebooks. Their carefully done notes and commentary are very helpful to the reader. All told, they succeed admirably in carrying out their declared intention: "The idea was to provide sufficient notes and commentary and to go back far enough with Wolfe's scattered jottings so that the edition would present a kind of interior biography of Wolfe beginning with his years at Harvard, the time of his first serious literary endeavors."

An "interior biography" is likely to be as jumbled as life itself. There is a great variety of entries in the notebooks: impressions of people and scenes, literary ideas, first drafts of letters, opinions on race, religion, and politics, records of dreams, lists (of states and countries visited, of women slept with [discreetly omitted here], of restaurants dined in), and opinions on contemporary literary figures, to cite a few examples. Trivial and valuable biographical facts appear on the same page. One sees Wolfe in many moods—exuberant, depressed, good-humored, mean-spirited. One learns of his anxieties, hostilities, and obsessions, his selfishness and self-pity. One sees him facing personal crises. Loose leaf notes from his Harvard days show

him on the eve of his twenty-first birthday making a covenant with God to live a better life. On a visit with his family in Asheville in September 1928 he writes, "O God . . . the sadness and the loneliness of my life—to *what* did I belong, to *what* do I belong . . . ? . . . No more do I belong!" Passages on his relations with Aline Bernstein show not only the bliss that love brought, but also the anguish that came with the breaking away, when he blamed the loss of his creativity on her possessiveness. Since Wolfe's association with Mrs. Bernstein was so vitally important in his development as a writer, the editors provide unusually detailed commentary on it and also include a number of excerpts from the unpublished correspondence. Much in their association is painful to read about, and Wolfe at times acted shamefully, but those who would understand him will be grateful for the revealing details assembled here.

As anyone might suspect who has read *Of Time and the River,* the Faust theme runs through the notebooks. Wolfe wrote to Mrs. Bernstein after seeing a production of *Faust* in 1928, "Faust's own problem touches me more than Hamlet's—his problem is mine, it is the problem of modern life. He wants to know everything, to be a god—and he is caught in the terrible net of human incapacity." Many pages here testify to the value he placed on quantity as a means of knowing it all—long lists of plays read, the thousands of miles traveled and the cities, states, and countries visited, the scores of paintings seen in museums. He seems at times to have been obsessed by the idea that he had to examine countless old volumes in bookshops for fear he might miss one that had "a little beauty, a little wisdom" for him. Yet he could go on to cry out against this "terrible vomit of print that covers the earth" and has paralyzed him with "its stench of hopelessness." After drawing up a list of books to make a library for a young man of today, he writes, "But I am tired—the desire for it *All* comes from an evil gluttony in me—a weakness—a lack of belief." One of his most important statements on the subject was recorded in a transatlantic voyage the night before he landed in New York, December 31, 1928:

> Never has the many-ness and the muchness of things caused me such trouble as in the past six months—But never have I had so firm a conviction that our lives can live upon only a few things, that we must find them, and begin to build our fences.
> All creation is the building of a fence.
> But deeper study always, sharper senses, profounder living: *Never* an end to curiosity!
> The fruit of all this comes later—I must think. I must mix it all with myself and with America. I have caught much of it on paper. But infinitely the greater part is in the wash of my brain and blood.

Six years later he recalls a friend's saying that after forty, like a camel, he will live off his hump, and he wonders whether this is already happening to him: "Am no longer so ravenously hungry for new sights, new experiences as I was ten years ago." But he still had a great zest for new sights of America. Out West shortly before his death when he was invited to make a tour of eleven national parks and one of the great federal dams in the space of only two weeks, he gladly accepted, though he was amused by the "gigantic *unconscious* humor" of the situation— " 'making every national park' without seeing any of them. . . ." His zealous

recording of the new sights reveals his avid interest.

The notebooks provide abundant evidence of Wolfe's effort to realize the multiplicity and diversity of American life. After his first book drew praise for being in the best native tradition, he resolved to try to give full expression to American life with his own experience at the center, and to that end he recorded in the notebooks the sight and sound of the varied life about him— types of passengers on an early morning subway train, places of business on a certain street, actions of people in a national park, speech patterns of taxi drivers, policemen, college boys—details that would give the ring of reality to his fiction. His sharp perception, his sensitive ear, and his gift for description served him well. Memories of American ideals and achievements often came to him abroad when he remarked on the shortcomings of other countries in comparison with his own. When in America, he noted, he saw the worst of it; when away, he thought of the best of it. "A man belongs to his country as an arm belongs to its socket. Any permanent separation from it is an amputation."

But for all his dedication and effort, he had limitations as a writer expressing the spirit of America. While absorbing so much of his country, he also accepted uncritically prejudices and intolerance that prevented his treating sympathetically all his fellow countrymen. Proud of having sprung from the "old" Americans whose families played so important a role in shaping the nation, he had toward "new" Americans the narrow, nativistic attitude common to the homogeneous region where he grew up. His racial attitudes—he used the word *race* loosely—give an ugly slant

245

to certain passages in his notebooks as in his fiction. His attitude toward the Jews is often offensive. He generally refers to a Negro as a "nigger." Slighting references to ethnic minorities are quite common. As Wolfe sailed into New York harbor in 1928 on a ship carrying many immigrants, he commented thus on the fact that they would soon be his countrymen: "This boat too is America—this swarthy stew of Italians, Greeks, and God knows what other combinations." His difficulty in adapting to the diversity of peoples that make up our nation kept him from being the epic spokesman that he aspired to be. There is much here to back up Mr. Reeves' argument on this subject as set forth at length in *Thomas Wolfe's Albatross*. But the 1930's brought about a change in Wolfe's social consciousness as in that of the country at large: The Depression made him more sympathetic toward his suffering countrymen, and the injustice shown minorities in totalitarian nations, especially the persecution of the Jews under Hitler, made him more keenly aware of the brotherhood of all men. To use words that he wrote toward the end of his life, "brothers, we must brothers be—or die." His broader social views are clearly revealed in *You Can't Go Home Again.*

The notebooks have a special value for the reader interested in seeing the artist in his workshop. Here are ideas for stories and sketches, descriptions of characters and scenes that appear later in published works, first drafts of passages used in the novels, lists of possible titles, outlines of longer works that are not shaping up satisfactorily. Book-length narratives, it is obvious, presented special problems. The editors have also included enlightening details on the cutting of manuscripts being prepared for publication: it is interesting to have described, for instance, some of the passages left out of *Look Homeward, Angel* for one reason or another. And glimpses are given of Edward Aswell at work after Wolfe's death getting ready for the printer the mass of manuscript that Wolfe had turned over to him just before setting out for the West. Under July 14, 1930, after a quotation from Wolfe the editors note, "It continues with the material published in Chapter 17 of *The Web and the Rock* and includes the entire passage 'What Is Man?' which Edward Aswell revised and placed in *You Can't Go Home Again.*" Another editorial comment indicates how Aswell "very inappropriately" used "some of Wolfe's words about fictional aims" at the beginning of *The Web and the Rock;* and still another, on a passage about George Webber and Nebraska Crane, points out that "Aswell used most of it in *You Can't Go Home Again. . . .*" Such comments as these, together with kindred revelations and extended discussion in Mr. Kennedy's *The Window of Memory*, make one wish for a detailed account of just what editorial changes Aswell made in Wolfe's manuscript. Over a decade ago C. Hugh Holman raised the question of the need for critical editions of *The Web and the Rock* and *You Can't Go Home Again.* Students of American fiction would welcome such editions, and it is hard to think of scholars more highly qualified for such a demanding task than Professors Holman, Kennedy, and Reeves.

Bart Lanier Stafford, III. "The Notebooks of Thomas Wolfe." El Paso *Times,* October 18, 1970, p. 22, Sundial.

The two volumes of this massive work should be invaluable to the student of American literature who has had little besides intuition to guide him in the workings of the mind of the writer and the man who was Thomas Wolfe.

The notebooks are unique in that no other author ever tried to create a literature out of his own self to the extent that Wolfe did. Every word was an autobiography; every breath, every movement, every sight, sound, sensation was essential to Wolfe as a writer, and down it went in one of the notebooks for future use. The man himself was his only source of inspiration, the funnel through which ten million written words cascaded in a furious surge of animal energy. He wrote in a frenzy, drawing from notes he had previously made of scenes, characters, his family, his pick-up girl friends (53 in 75 weeks, according to one of his lists), his experiences in the south, in NYU, in the artist colony in Paris, in the beerstubes of Berlin.

Wolfe was the master cataloguer. He made lists of people he had met, meals he had eaten, streets he had walked. He catalogued the books in one bookstore, the canned goods in a supermarket, the number of miles he had traveled in a given time, the populations of the hundred largest cities in the U.S. He would write on any page of the notebook that was open; often, he would begin at either end of the notebook and work in toward the middle, much of it illegible, and all of it smudged and battered, with eloquent descriptive passages next to grocery lists and memos to pick up clothes from the tailor shop. He was thoroughly disorganized and often disoriented, a great hulking mass of inconsistent feelings, capable of vast pettiness and great acts of kindness, avowedly anti-Semitic yet loving with uncontrolled passion the set-designer Aline Bernstein; doing what he could against Franco in the Spanish Civil War, yet admiring the order and the power of Hitler's Third Reich.

We are able to see this man in his own private world of reactions and things and lists, we see the contradictions in him, and the torment, the pettiness and the greatness, the shine and the genius, and we rush back to "Look Homeward Angel" and "You Can't Go Home Again," his best books, for confirmation or refutation of our earlier evaluation of Thomas Wolfe as America's greatest author, or as a "one-book poseur."

The present Notebooks do not answer the question regarding Wolfe's stature as an author. If anything, they add fuel to the fire, giving each side additional ammunition with which to "prove" a given theory. The questions remain largely "up for grabs."

This is a monumental work of the editing done by two resourceful and dedicated editors. As such, it would grace any man's library!

Richard Walser. "A Mine of Literary Origins." *Virginia Quarterly Review*, 44 (Winter 1970), 141–44.

Among the primary documents of Thomas Wolfe long withheld from publication, the appearance of none has been more anticipated than that of his "Notebooks." As in the case of Emerson's "Journals," one would find here, it was thought, the genesis of those ideas later spun out in his literary works. Now that the meticulously edited two volumes are at hand, the expectation is not one of disappointment. Yet a comparison with the thoughtfully framed sentences of Emerson is invalid, for what we have is a jumbled record of twists and turns and impulsive jottings, constituting no diary or commonplace book or any definable genre. Since even the chronology is uncertain and there are months when no entries were made or at any rate dated, the editors made the happy decision to supplement the notebooks with miscellaneous unpublished papers. With these and with the printing of some nine-tenths of the material from the thirty-three notebooks he kept between 1920 and 1938, Wolfe's muddled log is rather complete. Principal omissions are repetitious lists of states visited or miles traveled, of telephone numbers, and, regrettably but necessarily, of women he slept with.

Clearly Wolfe's notebooks were quite important to him, and in time they constituted his quest for meaning and order, his method of research and eval-

uation. If pages here and there cannot escape pedestrian dullness or puzzling significance, a goodly percentage of the raw Wolfe is fresh and inventive. Some of the best parts are clipt Pepysian entries, like the long paragraph of details of a Sunday in London, or those times when he recounts his seemingly aimless movements, maybe in Cambridge or Norwich, and writes down data with the chance that they may someday come in handy. The statistician in Wolfe is ever busy tabulating experience. In European art museums he must record the endless titles of pictures he sees. Arriving in a city, he wants before him an orderly catalogue of the places he wishes to visit. Standing at the window of a foreign bookshop, he lists the names of the books on display. Weeks later, at some distant spot he recalls the people he has met in that place, the restaurants where he has eaten, and other minutiae of the American abroad. If such matters are in fact of slight concern, they nevertheless prove the warm and enduring adolescence of the man.

Of more autobiographical value are the rough drafts of letters he wrote to those with whom he was irritated. Most of them were either revised for mailing or never posted at all. It was his way of letting off steam. Wolfe was no mild-tempered fellow, he was no gentle F. Scott Fitzgerald, and the white heat of his vehemence demanded an escape valve. Here in the "Notebooks" are the undispatched letters to some uncomplimentary critic of his novels, to Aline Bernstein when his love affair with her had cooled, to Maxwell Perkins at the time of his break with Scribner's. On other occasions, the posted letters are merely wiser and less revealing copies of the originals, as in his first communication to Perkins about "Look Homeward, Angel." From Vienna in 1928, he confessed to Perkins: "I write too much"; then in the final copy he struck through the words and tapered off with the moderate statement that while he was able "to criticize wordiness and over-abundance in others," he was not able to criticize it in himself.

In tracing the growth from tentative notions to published work, one can here find numerous initial versions of chapters and scattered episodes. Some of them Wolfe abandoned entirely. Other fragments he eventually revised and used, like the character sketch of Henry Seidel Canby printed as "Portrait of a Literary Critic" in "The Hills Beyond." There are dozens of outlines of projected novels, including a sixteen-page plan for "Of Time and the River." Random narrative experiments are followed by bits of overheard conversation, in which Wolfe attempts to catch the intonations and rhythms of speech. A few ventures into serious poetry are surprisingly good.

For the reviewer, the temptation to quote is not to be denied. Wolfe's isolated pentametric inspirations bring to mind the love of language characteristic of a Renaissance poet: "O bitterly bitterly Boston one time more," "Moonwards the camels turn into Bythinia," "Loot a few cells of this my swarming brain," and "All winterwild, All blown is their hair." Turn the page, and Wolfe's sense of humor supports him at the opera in Munich: "I was in the fifth and last gallery, wedged on the side with frauleins kicking holes in my kidneys." At other moments he tries to analyze himself: "I am ugly, cruel, and mad . . .: if anyone loves me I torture them, curse and revile them, and try to drive them away. The best friend,

the only person who ever loved me with all her heart, I treated in this way." On a ship returning to New York from Europe, he writes: "I must mix it all with myself and with America. I have caught much of it on paper. But infinitely the greater part is in the wash of my brain and blood." And in 1935 he ponders the mystery of his native region: "There is something in the South that is twisted, dark, and full of pain, which we [Southerners] have known with our lives, and which is rooted in our souls beyond all contradiction, but of which no one has dared to write, of which no one has spoken yet."

. . .

. . . The "Notebooks" stand as a mine of literary origins, available to him who would observe the stuff of an artistic struggle. In the last year of his life, troubled yet ever optimistic about Americans, Wolfe wrote, "Let us do what Whitman dreamed—let us stick to each other as long as we live— and let us find out who and what and why we are!" The "Notebooks" remind us that Wolfe, though he died young, may yet turn out to be the most American of our writers, beyond Whitman, beyond Twain.

Gerald J. Delcambre. *Sunday Iberian* (New Iberia, La.), January 3, 1971, p. 4.

Joy of joys! In this magnificent two-volume boxed set published in beautiful fashion by the University of North Carolina Press an even more detailed look at this famous author is afforded.

This boxed set is a must for all fans of Thomas Wolfe, for here, in information taken from notebooks carried by the author since 1926, one sees him in a different light. Readers of this powerful writer will again be inspired by the words pouring forth from these notebooks, from which nine-tenths of the information was taken.

. . .

A marvelous job is what these two editors produced in these two fine books taken from the notebooks of Wolfe. The two books cover the author's life from the early days to his rise to fame as the author of powerful novels of lyrical prose.

These two books are the result of work over 35 pocket notebooks that Wolfe carried intermittently from 1926, when he was just beginning his first novel, *Look Homeward Angel*, until just before his death in 1938. Only one of them, his last notebook has been published before. A few scattered notebook entries were published by Wolfe himself as Eugene Gant's Parish notebook in *Of Time and the River*. But the preponderant bulk of the material is here published for the first time.

This box set should, indeed, find its way onto all bookshelves of American readers, and certainly on those who relish the words of this writer, long deceased but living through his powerful novels.

Checklist of Additional Reviews

Zoe Brockman. "The Very Soul of Wolfe." Gastonia [North Carolina] *Gazette,* January 29, 1970.

Louis D. Rubin, Jr. "Books: Compiling the Jottings of Thomas Wolfe." Washington *Sunday Star,* February 8, 1970, p. D-2.

Betsy Lindau. *The Pilot* [Southern Pines, North Carolina], February 18, 1970.

Walter Spearman. "The Private World of Tom Wolfe." Chapel Hill *Weekly,* February 22, 1970, p. 4.

"Much of Local Interest Packed in Wolfe's Notebooks." Asheville *Citizen-Times,* February 22, 1970, p. 10C.

Albert H. Norman. "The Cry of the Wolfe." *Newsweek,* 75 (February 23, 1970), 102–03.

Kenneth T. Reed. *American Notes and Queries,* March, 1970.

Jonathan Yardley. Greensboro [North Carolina] *Daily News,* March 1, 1970, p. E2.

Glares Backes. "Travels with Wolfe." Chicago *Tribune,* March 2, 1970.

Robert Gorham Davis. "The hero's record of the part he played in his own epic." New York *Times Book Review,* March 15, 1970, pp. 1, 48.

Maurice Duke. "Notebooks of Thomas Wolfe Give Deep Insight to His Personality." Richmond *Times-Dispatch,* March 15, 1970, p. F-5.

Tulsa *World,* March 15, 1970.

Fred C. Hobson, Jr. "Notebooks Tell Tom Wolfe Story." Winston-Salem *Journal and Sentinel,* March 22, 1970.

Van Allen Bradley. "Tom Wolfe Clearly

Seen in 'Notebooks.'" Louisville [Kentucky] *Times*, March 31, 1970.

"A Writer's Despair." *National Observer*, April 13, 1970.

Dorothy L. Parker. "He tried to inventory the world." *Christian Science Monitor*, April 16, 1970, p. 11.

Jonathan Daniels. "Thomas Wolfe— The Man Was a Mountain." Raleigh *News and Observer*, April 26, 1970.

Glen W. Naves. "Wolfe's Notebooks Rekindle His Flame." Spartanburg *Journal*, July 11, 1970.

"Desiring it all." London *Times Literary Supplement*, No. 3,572, August 14, 1970, p. 892.

B. R. McElderry, Jr. *Georgia Review*, 24 (Fall 1970), 368-71.

John E. Drewry. "UGa Professor Edits Thomas Wolfe's Papers." Athens [Georgia] *Banner-Herald*, November 5, 1970, p. 4.

Francis E. Skipp. *American Literature*, 42 (January 1971), 595-96.

INDEX OF CRITICS

DATE			